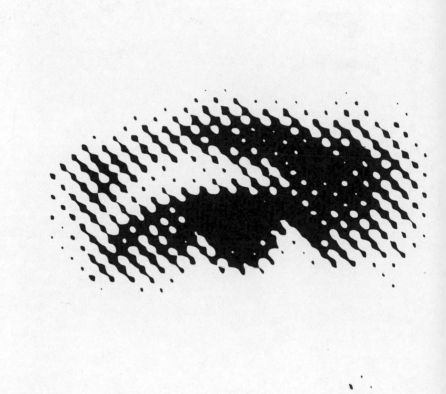

University of Nebraska Press: Lincoln & London

by Thelma S. Guild

& Harvey L. Carter

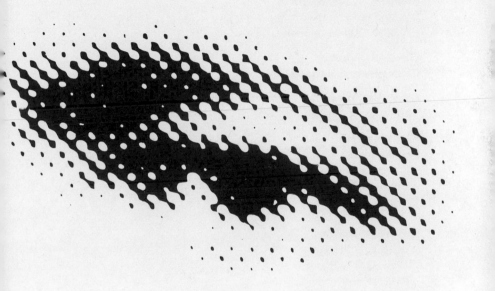

Kit Carson

A Pattern for Heroes

The paper in this book meets
the guidelines for
permanence and durability of
the Committee on
Production Guidelines for
Book Longevity of the
Council on Library Resources.

Library of Congress
Cataloging in Publication Data

Guild, Thelma S., 1911-
Kit Carson : a pattern for heroes.

Bibliography: p.
Includes index.
1. Carson, Kit, 1809-1868.
2. Pioneers – West (U.S.) –
History.   3. Scouts and
scouting – West (U.S.) –
Biography.   4. Soldiers –
West (U.S.) – Biography.
5. West (U.S.) – History.
I. Carter, Harvey Lewis, 1904-
II. Title.
F592.C33G84   1984
978'.02'0924   83-21628
ISBN 0-8032-2118-5

To Ruth, Jack, & Nancy, whose encouragement made a difference

Contents

Preface

The first biography of Kit Carson was published ten years before his death. A number of others have appeared since that time, some better than others. Why, then, another life of Carson? The answer to this question can be briefly stated.

When, in 1968 on the hundredth anniversary of his death, one of the present authors published *'Dear Old Kit': The Historical Christopher Carson, with a New Edition of the Carson Memoirs*, it was something of a landmark in Carson bibliography. This work has now been out of print for several years. No biography currently in print utilizes the contributions to Carson scholarship made in *'Dear Old Kit'*. The number and length of the footnotes in that work were a boon to Carson scholars but a formidable obstacle to those who wished to read it for information and enjoyment. A more conventional biography that embodies the reliability of *'Dear Old Kit'* in more readable form is sorely needed. Closed minds and permanent prejudices still exist, at opposite poles, concerning Carson. Between them lies a great segment of the population to whom Kit Carson is a familiar name but little else. It is this body of the reading public that the present authors have endeavored to reach, as well as those who delight in any new work on Carson.

It has been the aim of the authors to narrate the life of Kit Carson chronologically, against a descriptive background of the physical environment and an exposition of the social milieu in which he lived. Our study reveals Carson as a product of the early American frontier. All his life was lived on the extreme edge of that expanding frontier. Americans who moved west did not consider their migration a conquest of the Indians but rather settlement of unoccupied land. The old conflict between farmer and nomad was repeated, neither side capable of understanding the other. Both Indians and whites fought in defense of their homes and possessions, for the control of territory, and for life itself. Parties of both races rode out on punitive raids in retaliation for wrongs already committed. Excesses were committed by both.

In his early years, Carson was conditioned to regard Indians as a threat to his survival, but his long association with them in both war and peace brought him to a sympathetic understanding of their problems. In some respects, he was more compatible with the mode of life and the set of values practiced by Indians than with those practiced by the political and military leaders of his own people. Though he was an Indian fighter, he was not an Indian hater. No expression of hate or prejudice toward Indians is to be found in Carson's *Memoirs*. In the few instances when it appears to us that Carson went beyond what one would expect, under the circumstances, of a man of good will, we have not hesitated to point out his departure from his usual principles.

Our effort has been to present Carson as much as possible in his own words, quoting often from his memoirs. Material shown by *'Dear Old Kit'* to have been spurious has usually been excluded from the present work without comment. Since overwhelming evidence indicates that he was illiterate, however, we have thought it necessary to state this explicitly. He enjoyed having others read to him, but whatever ability he may have had in recognizing simple, familiar words was insufficient for him to carry on his business and personal affairs without depending on others to read and write for him.

We have in several instances been able to expand knowledge of Carson beyond that presented in *'Dear Old Kit'*. These instances include recollections of Carson preserved by the Utes, some knowledge of the earlier and later years of Carson's friend Dick Owens, the certainty that it was Antoine Godin, not Alexis Godey, who trapped on the Humboldt with Carson, reasons for thinking that Carson's Arapaho wife, Waanibe, may have accompanied the Humboldt trapping party, precise dates for Carson's later military assignments, a fuller and more exact account of his Fort Garland period, and a letter giving the exact date of Josefa Carson's death. When speculative statements have been necessary, we have, as a rule, given reasons for such speculation.

Our study shows Carson to have been a simple and direct man of action, conscious of his own lack of education, but possessed of a strong sense of duty and a desire to do his best. He was unspoiled by the enormous adulation he received from the public and remained characteristically modest and unassuming. His only regret was that he had been too responsive to public duty and not attentive enough to the needs of his family. However, statements by those who knew him repeat again and again how well he was loved by his family and the people among whom he lived and worked—Mexican, American, and Indian. After hearing about Carson from an uncle who knew him, Edgar L. Hewett wrote, "He fixed in my mind a pattern for heroes . . . of quiet, steel-nerved courage . . . an ideal of what a real man should be." He was and has remained one of America's most widely known and most deserving heroes.

This work does not aim to replace 'Dear Old Kit' and does not include all the references that enrich the earlier biography. Instead, its appeal will be more general. Neither its descriptive backgrounds nor facts uncovered by recent research are included in any previous biography of Carson. We hope the reader will find it an easily readable and eminently reliable book.

The staffs of libraries we consulted in preparing to write this book need to be commended for their expertise, patience, and perseverence in finding materials needed. Especially helpful and ingenious were the staffs of the A. M. Willis Library, North Texas State University, Denton; the Charles M. Tutt Library of Colorado College, Colorado Springs; and the Alderman Library of the University of Virginia, Charlottesville. We are also grateful to the staffs of the Stephen H. Hart Library, Colorado Historical Society, Denver; the University of New Mexico Library, Albuquerque; the University of Richmond Library, Richmond, Virginia; the University of Wyoming Library, Laramie; and the Virginia State Library,

Richmond. Much helpful cooperation was given by the staffs of the National Archives, Washington, D.C.; the Pioneer's Museum, Colorado Springs; and the State Archives and Records Division and the Historical Museum of New Mexico at Santa Fe.

We owe special appreciation to Jack and Genevieve Scroggs of Denton, Texas, and to Ruth Carter of Colorado Springs for their extreme kindness and encouragement, as well as guidance, and to Jack Boyer and his staff at the Kit Carson Home and Museum at Taos for ready help and encouragement; to Mary Lund Settle, Dennis Ottoson, Richard Owings and George Stewart for bringing to our attention pertinent information that adds to the authenticity and interest of the narrative; and to Nancy Sandlin for her insight, encouragement, and appreciation.

To all others who have helped or encouraged us in one way or another we also wish to express our thanks.

Kit Carson

Chapter 1

Moving West

In dictating his memoirs, Kit Carson covered the important events of his childhood in one short paragraph:

I was born on 24 Decr. 1809 in Madison County, Kentucky. My parents moved to Missouri when I was one year old. They settled in what is now Howard County. For two or three years after our arrival, we had to remain forted and it was necessary to have men stationed at the extremities of the fields for the protection of those that were laboring.[1]

At the age of fifty-six, Carson was trying to set down what seemed to interest his contemporaries, to whom the circumstances and daily events of the frontier were already familiar. It is unlikely that he surmised that these events might one day have historic importance and be as fascinating as the elements of some ancient herioc age, which indeed they were to become.

Originating in Scotland, the Carsons had been on the move for over a hundred years. In the late seventeenth century the Scots had gained the right to worship as Presbyterians but had thereby forfeited the right to hold political office. By 1700 many of them, including Alexander Carson, had moved across the sea to northern Ireland, where land was cheap, but political freedom was no greater, and there was less economic freedom. William Carson, Kit's grandfather, was born in northern Ireland, the third of four sons.

Still seeking freedom as well as land of his own, Alexander Carson sailed for America. He settled in the wilderness of Lancaster County, Pennsylvania, where a fifth son was born.[2] The small, stump-infested clearings were plowed using oxen. The livestock ran wild. Indians were generally friendly in this Quaker colony, and game was plentiful. Deer came up to the cabins, and wild turkeys roosted in nearby trees. Bears and buffalo appeared frequently near the clearings. Hunting was the main source of food.

The Quaker George Boone, whose grandson would become a prototype of the great pioneer, had also migrated to Pennsylvania. Finding the Quaker Meeting of Oley Township, Berks County, too intolerant, Squire Boone, son of old George and father of Daniel, sold out in 1750 and joined the great migration down the Shenandoah Valley. William Carson, Alexander's son, was also riding south down the Great Valley. The Boones finally settled on the Yadkin River in North Carolina. Carson rode farther and took up land in Iredell County.[3]

Many Scotch-Irish were settling in the area, among them the McDuffs, with two handsome and spirited daughters, Mollie and Eleanor. Before long William and Eleanor were wed. Lindsey, the eldest of their six children, was born August 1, 1754. Andrew, Robert, Sarah, Eleanor, and Alexander arrived at two- or three-year intervals. When Lindsey was about nineteen, his father, having become overheated from working in the fields, drank too freely of the cold water from a nearby spring and died.

About two years later, Eleanor married John Scroggs, also from Scotland by way of Ireland and Pennsylvania, and this late marriage produced one son, James. John, Jr., Jeremiah, David, and four daughters, children of John Scroggs by an earlier marriage, and Eleanor's six children found the union of the two families highly congenial. In due time John, Jr., and Sarah Carson were married, as were two other couples among the stepbrothers and stepsisters.[4]

Eleanor's three eldest sons were drawn into the American Revolution, serving under General Wade Hampton. After the war was over, Lindsey and Robert went to South Carolina. There Lindsey married Lucy Bradley, with whom he later returned to Iredell

County, where they lived until the urge to follow Daniel Boone drew them westward.[5]

Daniel Boone, born in Pennsylvania in 1734, was a grown man when Lindsey was born. At sixteen he was already an accomplished woodsman. By 1773, when he led a caravan of emigrants toward Kentucky, there were probably few who knew him who would not have followed him. This attempt at a new settlement was foiled by a devastating attack by the Shawnees. But by the time the New England colonists defied the British and precipitated the war, Boone had led a second train of settlers into Kentucky and was starting a "new colony" at Boonesborough.

Boonesborough was not finished before hostilities began. Using British arms, and with the help of a few British officers, the Shawnees fought relentlessly. Throughout a long siege by the Indians, Boone and a few steadfast settlers and their wives and daughters held Boonesborough and thereby served as a bastion guarding the western approaches to the colonies. Although the Treaty of Paris ended the war in 1782, the Indians were not a party to the agreement, and it was not until Anthony Wayne's victory at Fallen Timbers in 1794 that their organized resistance was finally broken up.

Security for the settlers lay in greater numbers, and the Transylvania Company, sponsoring the colony, publicized the cheapness and fertility of the land, the abundance of game, and the reputation of Daniel Boone. Good, cheap land was a powerful attraction. In 1793 Lindsey Carson loaded a wagon with his wife, Lucy, and their four children—William, Sarah, Andrew, and Moses—and followed where Boone had led over the uneven, rutted Wilderness Road. Soon after the arrival in Kentucky, a second daughter, Sophie, was born. Not long afterward, Lucy died.

Two years later, Lindsey married Rebecca Robinson from Greenbrier County, Virginia.[6] Six of their children were born in Kentucky: Elizabeth, Nancy, Robert, Matilda, Hamilton, and Christopher Houston. Kit came into the world the day before Christmas, 1809, making thirteen persons to share the log cabin Lindsey had built on Tate's Creek in Madison County.[7] The cabin had three rooms and a loft, a puncheon floor, a roof of hand-split shingles, doors of hand-split boards, and window holes covered with oiled paper to let in a little light and fitted with solid shutters to close against the darkness and the cold. The main room had a large stone fireplace for cooking and heating and contained most of the furniture, all of it homemade. A ladder led to the loft where most of the children slept. A small bedroom and a storeroom opened off the main room. Extra clothing hung on pegs in the corners out of the way. Antlers fastened high on the walls held the rifles. Guns were absolutely necessary for life, both for hunting and for protection.[8]

Lindsey and his sons cut logs and rafted them down the creeks and rivers to New Orleans, planted corn in the clearing, hunted and trapped, gradually carving a farm out of the wilderness. Travelers sometimes stopped at the cabin, where they were always welcome to a meal and a place to sleep.

By 1799 Daniel Boone had become hopelessly entangled in problems of land ownership in Kentucky. He had lost his own land, in part through legal red tape, in part through lawsuits. As a surveyor, he was harassed by accusations of dishonesty when land he had laid out for his clients overlapped tracts claimed by others. Heartsick and angry, he finally obtained a grant of land from Spain and settled beyond the Mississippi, just north of the Missouri.[9] Following the Louisiana Purchase and the Lewis and Clark Expedition, interest in Upper Louisiana quickened. The wayfarers who stopped at the Carson cabin had tales to tell about Old Daniel, about the good hunting and trapping, the generally friendly Indians, the cheap, fertile land. In 1811 Lindsey sold his Madison County farm and headed west.

Kit, now a year and a half old, rode in the saddle in front of his mother. Many years later he said his years in the saddle had made him slightly bowlegged, a process doubtless begun with the baby legs curling around the pommel on the long ride to Missouri. Some of the older brothers rode their own horses, but most of the children walked alongside the horses or the oxcarts, which contained the family's belongings and the children too small to keep up.

In 1810 William Carson had married Millie Boone, Daniel's grandniece, who had died giving birth to a daughter, Adaline. Leaving the baby with his sister-in-law, Cassandra Boone, William rode away with Lindsey and his family. During most of the summer and fall of 1811, the caravan crept along the road west, living mostly on the game the hunters were able to bring in, pausing long enough at noon and stopping early in the evening for the animals to graze.

Lindsey took up land in the Boonslick area,[10] but before he could settle his family upon it, the War of 1812 broke out and with it renewed danger from Indians. At the first sign of hostilities, earlier settlers had built Fort Kinkead, Fort Cooper, and Fort Hempstead. Into these were crowded the new families, each occupying one of the log cabins built against the palisades, the roofs sloping inward, the walls pierced by spy holes commanding the clearings around the forts. However, these spy holes were not always to the advantage of the settlers. One stormy night an Indian approached the cabin of Sarshall Cooper, captain of Fort Cooper, and shot him dead as he sat among his family, his youngest child on his lap.[11]

When the caravan of 1811 arrived in what soon became the Territory of Missouri, Boonslick was so far from the headquarters of the territory that it had no government at all. The people had to depend upon themselves to keep the peace, protect themselves from the Indians, amuse themselves when they had time to spare, take care of their health, and share what learning they had with their children. Joseph and Stephen Cooper, whose father had come to Missouri in 1807, gave a vivid description of this frontier life.

The open prairie was laid off as in modern cities, each block belonging to its respective party. When it required cultivation, the person it suited at the particular time cultivated the entire field irrespective of ownership, while others were hunting or standing picket on some high eminence. . . . Dissentions were . . . arbitrated. . . . We had no need for justices of the peace or courts of equity. The Indians were very friendly toward us . . . they would occasionally steal our horses and put us to some trouble to recover them, until about March, 1812, when they killed . . . Jonathan Todd and Thomas Smith . . . . mutilated their bodies and [displayed] their heads and hearts . . . on poles . . . .

There were no schools. . . . In . . . 1810 . . . Boonslick [was] 100

miles from a settlement. . . . By [1812] we had considerable settle-
ments, but found it necessary to build forts for our protection. . . .
Capt. Sarshall Cooper was . . . leader of all the forts. We had great
abundance of horses, cattle, hogs, and sheep. Had no stores. Lived
pretty plain. We raised hemp, flax, and cotton, and with the wool of
our sheep, our women manufactured clothing. . . . The men wore
buckskin pantaloons and buckskin moccasins. No man owing a
dollar, no taxes to pay, we lived happy and prosperous until 1812.[12]

In this self-sufficient society Kit Carson passed his early youth,
but his earliest memories were of the fort, of anxiety among his
elders. Alertness and vigilance were constant. Sudden tension in
the cabin, breathless listening, the abrupt departure of Lindsey and
the older boys, rifles in hand, meant Indians. Few soldiers could be
spared for the frontier. Lindsey and his older sons, serving in the
militia, were sometimes away all night.

Kit would awaken in the dawn, lying on his pallet on the floor,
the warm, pleasant smell of cooking drifting from the other end of
the room where his mother was busy at the fireplace. Rustlings
and thumpings on the planks of the loft told him that his brothers
and sisters were getting up. Soon feet came over the edge of the loft
hole, searching for the ladder, and the Carson family began to as-
semble around the fireplace.

Lindsey came home one night with two fingers of his left hand
shot away.[13] Whether Kit remembered that, or whether he heard
from the others about the awe and anger aroused by the event, the
old twisted scars were always there, a perpetual reminder of the
Indians, who had once been peaceful, even friendly neighbors.

A treaty ending the War of 1812 was signed on Kit's fifth birth-
day, December 24, 1814, but news had to cross the Atlantic by
sailing ship. When the people heard that the war was over, they
began to move to their own land, but it had been easier to arouse
the Indians to fight than it was to get them to stop. Even after a
treaty was signed with them in 1816, raids continued sporadically
for several years.

In 1820, after having been informed of a fight in which three
warriors were killed, an Osage tribal leader wrote to the white
leaders:

We are glad that you sent us a paper and a good man to tell us about your men killing three of our men. They were good men, but were killed for the bad men's faults. You say they began the quarrel; we do not know it. . . .

We want that you should send us the 5 guns, 1 bow & arrow, and 5 powder horns, that your men took from our men when they killed them. You demand the stolen horses and you shall have them. You tell us to open our eyes and to walk in the good road. Your men have killed 3 of our men, and we cannot walk in the good road, and let your men walk in the bad road.

We cannot keep our young bad men from mischief, no better than you can keep your young bad men from mischief. . . . We have hard work to govern them.

We want that you should take care of the wounded prisoner, till we go down and see you. We and you have walked in the good road—it may be that we have both missed it—if we have, we will try to find it, and both keep in it, or out of it, but we hope in it. We want to say more, but we hope this is enough, in behalf of the chief warriors and head men of the Little Osage village.

WALK IN RAIN

Principal captain of the L. O. village.

N. B.—We thank you for the tobacco you sent us—it was not enough to give us all a smoke—we want that you should send us more next time.[14]

Their participation in the War of 1812 was only one signal that the Indians were awakening to the destiny threatening them. Many on the Atlantic Coast had welcomed the first white men, shared food with them, showed them how to plant corn and tobacco. There had seemed to be plenty of room for all to hunt and to grow food, and the whites exchanged fine gifts such as the Indians had never seen before. As more and more ships came and the white families moved inland, killing and frightening the game and destroying its habitat, the Indians first watched with astonishment and dismay, then began to fight back, resisting the superior weapons of the whites by their own superior knowledge of the woods and their highly cultivated aptitude for guerilla warfare. But they were no match for the whites in the art of destruction, either of life or of pride. Increasingly, more of the Indians considered the whites cold-blooded, ruthless aggressors, fit only for destruction. As Walk In Rain implied, no chief or council of chiefs was ever able to bind the whole tribe by any agreement.

The Indians also differed basically from the whites in their concept of owning land, claiming an indefinite and often-changing area as their hunting range. Their concept of transfer of land by treaty was also uncertain. When they "sold" a large tract of land to the government for annuities, they only gradually realized that it would be resold to whites and cleared for farming, ruining their hunting.

Among white men, on the other hand, resistance to hunting preserves was older than the tale of Robin Hood. The pioneers never thought of themselves as aggressors driving the Indians from their homeland. Since the Indians did not work the land, or even build permanent homes on it, the farmers considered it to be empty, the forest waiting to be cleared, the soil to be planted. No amount of treaties by the government would stop them from moving westward and settling on any land that seemed to them to be unoccupied.[15] Indian resistance led to the bloody conflicts that characterized the American frontier, in which atrocities were committed by both sides. In the end, the whites always won because of their superior numbers and resources.

There was often curiosity and affection on both sides, but seldom complete trust. Some evidence suggests that Kit had some peaceable and friendly contact with Indian children when he was growing up in Missouri.[16] However, most of his early experiences caused him to have a typical frontier attitude toward Indians; they were different and not to be trusted.

By the time Kit was six years old, the family was living in its own cabin on its own land, going to the fort only in time of danger. Many houses were raised as the settlers left the forts. Some time before the day for building, trees would be felled, logs hewn, rafters, boards, and shingles split. Because they had lived in the forts during the war, the people had become well acquainted, and on the appointed day they came from miles around. While the men hoisted logs and timbers and drove pegs into place, the women laid out such delicacies as they had been able to prepare from their gardens of beans, corn, and greens, and the wild berries, venison, squirrel, rabbit, and bear meat of the forest and prairie. A few had managed to save cows and chickens through the forting, had obtained a little flour, and turned up with the first pies and cakes some of the settlers had seen since leaving North Carolina or Virginia. Jugs of whiskey made from corn were passed among the men and homemade elderberry or blackberry wine among the women. By the time the roof was on and the feast was over, most were having a rollicking good time, and the first note of the fiddle signaled the dance that climaxed the long day.

Occasionally a hunter would drop by a neighbor's cabin and sit a while to exchange news, but most social events were work parties: husking bees, hominy makings, and other cooperative efforts, as well as house and barn raisings. The one exception was the Fourth of July. On this great holiday there were speeches, and the Declaration of Independence was read with style and emotion. Delicacies were saved, and many hours of preparation were dedicated to the greatest feast of the year. After the feast there were play party games, running and shooting contests, fiddling and dancing, and usually some fights.[17]

The Carsons now had another baby, Mary Ann, who was four-and-a-half years younger than Kit, and who became his favorite sister and his most ardent admirer. Two more sons arrived later, Sarshall and Lindsey, Jr. The latter was born September 11, 1818, a week after his father's death.

Each move into the wilderness had increased the work of providing for the family, for each time the family was larger and Lindsey had to start over again. Now the eldest sons were out on their own. Lucy's daughters had married back in Kentucky, William had gone back, married Cassandra Boone, and brought her and Adaline to Howard County, where he bought a farm near his father.[18] He and Lindsey often swapped work, and his children grew up with their young aunts and uncles. Adaline, only a little younger than Kit, was the favorite playmate of his early childhood.

Moses and Andrew hunted and trapped along the Missouri River and its tributaries. Often in the evening they would sit talking with Lindsey and William in front of the cabin, whippoorwills singing among the low woodlands by the creek, while Rebecca and the girls kept up a smudge fire to drive away the mosquitoes. Kit, Robert, and Hamilton sat silent in the soft dusk, learning about the ways of Indians and wild animals, hearing tales of the dangers, hardships, and excitement the trappers found along the rivers toward the west. By comparison, the work they did with Lindsey—chopping down trees, grubbing out roots and stumps, planting, hoeing, and gathering corn, peas, beans, potatoes, and cradling and threshing wheat—was slow and back-breaking and, worst of all, confining and dull.

Kit had very little formal schooling. He was certainly learning, but largely from his older brother and from the wilderness. Much later he told Jessie Benton Frémont, wife of the great explorer and good friend to Kit, "I was a young boy in the school house when the cry came, 'Indians!' I jumped to my rifle and threw down my spelling book, and there it lies."[19] Whatever skill he acquired as a child at reading and writing did not stick with him in later life. He had to relearn even how to sign his own name.[20]

Lindsey lost his life working at his endless project of clearing land. One day in early September 1818, while he was working near a burning tree, a flaming limb broke away and fell on him, killing him instantly. He was sixty-four years old.

A week later, Lindsey, Jr. was born, giving Rebecca at least eight children to support. Nancy and Elizabeth were probably already married. Hampton was only six; Mary Ann, four; Sarshall, two. Matilda, at thirteen, was doubtless a great help in the house as well as in the field, but Rebecca depended most heavily upon her three eldest sons. Robert, at fifteen, was considered almost a man. With the help of Hamilton, almost eleven, and Kit, almost nine, he tried to keep the farm going.

After four years of managing her large family alone, Rebecca married Joseph Martin, a widower with several children. Rebecca's sons found it hard to take orders from a stepfather after they had kept the farm going through their own efforts, and they rebelled in various ways. Robert was old enough to go with one of the pack trains headed toward the mountains, as Kit longed to do. The story was handed down in the Boonslick area that, at thirteen, Kit became hard to manage. He lived part of the time with his brother

William on the next farm, but Adaline, his old playmate, could no longer be the companion he needed, and William lost patience with him. Eventually he became the ward of John Ryland, later a Missouri supreme court judge.[21]

When Kit was fifteen, he was apprenticed to David Workman, a saddler in Franklin. That he was learning a useful trade was no compensation for having to sit at a workbench, sawing and smoothing and gluing pieces of wood, pushing an awl through tough leather. He knew that beyond the Missouri men were using the gear he was making or mending as they rode through the tall grass, heading into the wind that blew forever from the old Spanish town of Santa Fe.

Kit disliked the work, but the situation was by no means the worst thing that could have happened to him. David Workman and his brother William were curious about the West, and during Kit's apprenticeship, Franklin was the point of departure for this distant, mysterious frontier. Many of the customers were trappers or traders, just in from the mountains or about to set out on the trail. A little encouragement from the Workmans would set them to talking about the Indians, the grizzlies, the rivers and mountains, recounting adventures and tall tales of the mountain men. These tales were the literature of Kit's youth, a large part of his education. The more he saw and heard, the more he wanted to desert his workbench and go west.

While Kit had been growing up, important events had been occurring in the West. The Spanish viceroys of Mexico had monopolized trade with all parts of the colony, but provincial governors were ambivalent about enforcing this monopoly. They wanted the goods brought by the Americans because Chihuahua, the nearest Mexican city, was far away. They also wanted the import duties they were able to impose. Even so, they sometimes simply confiscated the goods and threw the traders in prison. Sometimes they sent patrols into the mountains north of Santa Fe, looking for trappers or traders with the Indians. Some of the intruders, like Jacques d'Eglise, were murdered.[22] Some, like Baptiste LaLande, denied permission to leave because the colony needed their skills, settled down to become prosperous citizens in Taos or Santa Fe.[23] Others, like the explorer Zebulon Pike and his men, were sent down to Chihuahua, over three hundred miles inside Mexico, kept for a time under light restraint, then escorted back to the United States.[24]

Traders, lured across the plains by the profitable market, never knew what to expect. Jules de Mun, after being repeatedly ordered out of the Rockies, was finally imprisoned in Santa Fe and his good confiscated.[25] Robert McKnight, James Baird, Samuel Chambers, and six others, in addition to being stripped of their goods, were imprisoned in Chihuahua and Durango for nine years. Forced to work for his board, McKnight learned the Spanish language and the science of copper mining. Though nominally in prison, he married, settled down at Guarasimas, and fathered a daughter. Although he returned to the United States in 1822 after being freed, he went back to New Mexico, became a Mexican citizen, resumed his mining career, and died there in 1846.[26]

In 1821 Mexico won its independence, became a free republic, and, in spite of various restrictions, welcomed American trade. William Becknell of Franklin set out the same year with a pack train and four men. Following the established road along the Missouri River, he crossed that turbulent, muddy stream on the ferry at Arrow Rock, then went southwest across the prairie until he reached the Arkansas River. He followed the Arkansas toward the Rocky Mountains until he came to what he described as the left fork of the river, probably the Purgatoire, and ascended it toward the Southwest. When a spur of the Rockies blocked his path, he worried his pack horses across the boulder-strewn Raton Pass. Regaining the plain, he skirted the Sangre de Cristo Mountains on the eastern side until he reached San Miguel, then curved northwest to Santa Fe.

After spending five months in Santa Fe disposing of his goods, he returned to Missouri in January 1822. Some of his merchandise had sold for six times what he had paid for it. "My father saw them unload when they returned," an old resident reported, "and when their rawhide packages of silver dollars were dumped on the sidewalk one of the men cut the thongs and the money spilled out and clinking on the stone pavement rolled into the gutter."[27] It must have been quite a sight for frontiersmen who, living mostly by barter, seldom got their hands on a piece of silver.

After stopping just long enough to organize another expedition, Becknell took twenty-one men and three wagonloads of goods and set out again. To avoid crossing the Raton Pass and to shorten the distance, he crossed the Arkansas River a little west of its great bend (near present-day Fort Dodge, Kansas) and headed as straight as he could across the barren land toward the Cimarron River. When the Cimarron bore west, he continued on his straight route to the Canadian River, then turned more southerly to round the Sangre de Cristo Range at San Miguel as before. The new route cut the time of the journey from seventy-three to sixty-two days.

Becknell had started out to make money, but he made history as well. White men had been traveling across the deserts and plains since the days of Coronado, but there had never been a regular road. In his two journeys, Becknell established the two main routes of the Santa Fe Trail. Other traders were soon leading their caravans the way he had gone. By the time George Champlin Sibley was commissioned to survey the Trail in 1825, a clear "trace" had been worn in many places by the wagon wheels.

Accompanying Sibley on the surveying expedition were Kit's half-brother Andrew and his brother Robert as well as Andrew Broadus and William Sherley Williams, later known as "Old Bill." Williams, who had spent the years from 1805 to 1825 as a Baptist missionary among the Osage Indians, came to a momentous decision when he left his Osage wife and two daughters to help Sibley survey the trail. He remained in the Rockies and became one of the most skillful and most eccentric of the mountain men.

When Andrew and Robert returned, they had tales to add to those Kit heard in the saddler's shop and to those he had heard since early childhood from his half-brother Moses. As a member of the Missouri Fur Company with Joshua Pilcher, Moses had been up and down the Missouri River many times before Kit started to learn the saddler's trade. He knew how John Colter, sent by Manuel Lisa to open up trade with the Blackfeet, was forced to race for his life against their strongest and fleetest young men, and how he won, but only after killing the swiftest of them.[28] The chronic hostility of the Blackfeet had been aggravated in 1806 when Meriwether Lewis had stabbed one warrior and shot another to prevent the theft of the expedition's guns and horses.[29] Colter's coup, though made in self-defense, had excited them still further. No American was safe near the headwaters of the Missouri. Kit was to suffer at the hands of Blackfeet the only serious wound he ever received.

Moses was almost a part of William Ashley's famous fight with the Arikaras in 1823.[30] After spending an evening trading for horses and feasting with these Indians, Ashley and his party were attacked at dawn. Fourteen men and all the horses were killed. Eleven men were wounded. Moses served as a lieutenant in the Missouri Legion organized by Colonel Henry Leavenworth and Joshua Pilcher to punish this treachery. Because of Leavenworth's lack of experience or faulty notions of Indian psychology, this expedition was unsuccessful, but Kit learned from it what Moses had learned: that force, success, and especially courage won the Indians' respect and that weakness, hesitation, or failure invited scorn and attack; that a leader was capable of fatal mistakes; and that neither the army nor the fur companies could be relied upon to protect the trappers or to avenge their wrongs. In extreme crises or when hard pressed, each man could rely only on himself.

Moses knew the story of Hugh Glass, who, badly mauled by a grizzly bear, had been left by two companions who thought he would soon die. Recovering consciousness and finding himself abandoned, the terribly wounded man had dragged himself many miles under the burning sun, contested with wolves for the flesh of a buffalo calf the animals had killed, escaped the vengeful Arikaras, and finally confronted his faithless companions and lived, like the Ancient Mariner, to tell his tale to all who would listen.[31]

The mountain men would hardly have noted Ashley's unexpected meeting near the mouth of the Uintah River with Etienne Provost, who had brought a party of trappers up from Taos. But Provost's escape from a treacherous attack in the lodge of Bad Gocha, when the Snake chief massacred most of Provost's men to get revenge on a Hudson's Bay Company trader was a story Kit was likely to have heard, for it was long remembered and often repeated.[32]

After two years in the saddler's shop, Kit's desire to take part in the adventures of which he had heard became too strong to resist. In his own words:

> For fifteen years I remained in Missouri. During that time I remained in Howard County. I was apprenticed to David Workman . . . remained with him two years . . . . having heard so many tales of life in the Mountains of the West, I concluded to leave him. He was a good man, and I often recall the kind treatment I received. . . . But . . . if I remained with him . . . I would have to pass my life in labor that was distasteful for me, and being anxious to travel for the purpose of seeing different countries, I concluded to join the first party for the Rocky Mts.[33]

In the spring of 1825, William Workman, David's brother, joined a caravan for Santa Fe.[34] A little over a year passed before Kit mustered the audacity to follow.

Chapter 2

Across the Prairie

"In August, 1826, I had the fortune to hear of a party bound for that country to which I desired to go. I made application to join this party, and without any difficulty, I was permitted to join them."[1] Andrew Broadus, the one member of the party named by Kit, left Fort Osage, Missouri, in August 1826 with a wagon train led by Elisha Stanley and William Wolfskill and bound for Santa Fe.[2] Fort Osage was across the Missouri and about eighty miles in a straight line from Franklin, but Kit's uncanny sense of direction and position led him to the camp.

Perhaps the greatest problem he faced was leaving home. Mary Ann reported that he asked his mother and was told he could leave after he had finished his contract with Mr. Workman. Since he had made up his mind to go, he had to decide whether to defy his mother or to wait until the house was quiet and slip away in the night. He was also said to have borrowed a neighbor's mule, which he turned loose after reaching the caravan, trusting it to find its way home. Evidently he slipped quietly away.[3]

Several members of the caravan knew him as the saddler's apprentice and also as one of the younger brothers of the Carsons. Andrew Broadus had been with Andrew and Robert in the Sibley surveying crew. William Wolfskill, one of Becknell's caravan of

1822, probably knew William Carson, who had gone out with Becknell in 1821.[4] Since Kit was a good shot with a rifle as well as a skillful rider, they ignored his apprenticeship and let him go as cavvy boy to help with the extra animals, or Caballada, that every caravan took along to replace any that became sick, ran away, or were stolen.

There is no record that anyone was greatly shocked at his going. Rebecca had seen one son after another light out for the West, and none had yet fallen victim to grizzlies, Indians, starving times, thunderstorms, blizzards, or other perils of plains and mountains. Kit had often been alone in the forest or on the turbulent river. It may have been several days before Rebecca knew for sure that he had left.

Not until October 6 did David Workman run an advertisement in the *Missouri Intelligencer*, Franklin's newspaper:[5]

Notice is hereby given to all persons, THAT CHRISTOPHER CARSON, a boy about 16 years old, small of his age, but thick set; light hair, ran away from the subscriber, living in Franklin, Howard county, Missouri, to whom he had been bound to learn the saddler's trade, on or about the first of September last. He is supposed to have made his way towards the upper part of the state. All persons are notified not to harbor, support or assist said boy under the penalty of the law. One cent reward will be given to any person who will bring back the said boy.

Required by law to advertise, Workman waited a month to do so, gave a false clue concerning Kit's probable whereabouts, and offered a reward of only one cent for his return. It would seem that the master was aiding the boy in his flight. David Workman himself went out to Santa Fe in May 1827.[6]

Kit's memoirs tell us nothing about the country, conditions, or details of travel, but the Santa Fe Trail soon became so well traveled that descriptions abound.[7] Most of the preparations for the journey were probably finished by the time Kit reached the camp. The wagons were packed with the greatest care to protect and preserve the goods being taken out for trade. Heavy wagon sheets stretched across the bows, with sometimes a blanket or two between the sheets to further protect the goods below and to add a little merchandise that would escape the attention of customs officials.

The economy of the trade never had much importance for Kit, who was not by nature a trader. His care was to keep the extra stock from straying onto the prairie, where the autumn grass was sometimes as tall as a man on horseback, and to keep the animals from being run off by Indians or buffalo. In the excitement of departure, subduing their mulish independence was not easy.

After an early breakfast the captain shouted, "Catch up! Catch up!" The dawn rang with repetitions—booming with authority, piping with excitement, singing out with joy—"Catch up! Catch up! Catch up!" The wagoners hastened to harness their mules, swearing at the unruly beasts, heaving on halters, jingling the bells and the chains of the harness, slapping the leather collars upon the sleek hair of the animals' necks, yelling, "Whoa, back!" as they strained to hook the trace chains to the single trees.

At last "All's set!" rang across the prairie and was soon echoed from all directions. "Stretch out!" yelled the captain, and the drivers called, "Hep!" and cracked their whips, the mules jangled the chains anew as they strained upon the traces, hubs rumbled upon axles, and the heavy wagons lumbered into the tall grass. The owners cantered along the line of wagons, checking to see that all was in order, while Kit ranged from side to side, keeping a sharp eye on the *caballada*, urging his charges to fall into line and constantly alert to keep them there.

In about a week the caravan reached Council Grove, where they paused for a final shaping up. Here they cut extra lengths of wood and slung them under the wagons in case something broke on the way, for in this grove grew the last of the good hardwood timber. Henceforth cottonwoods and willows grew along the streams, with an occasional elm or hackberry. Sometimes the men rode unaware right up to creeks where not even a bush was growing. These treeless areas were caused, some believed, by fierce fires that raged through the tall grass almost yearly, set accidentally by lightning or by the trading caravans, or intentionally by Indians.

In 1841 Rufus B. Sage described such a fire on the Oregon Trail:

18

The wind . . . was tossing the flames toward us . . . lighting the heavens with their lurid glare, and transforming the darkness . . . into a more than noonday splendor! An "ocean of flame" far as the eye could reach—dancing with fiery wavelets in the wind, or rolling . . . shooting its glowing missiles far, far ahead . . . or towering aloft . . . then shooting whole sheets of the raging element . . . in front . . . a sublime spectacle . . . terrible in its beauty![8]

After such a fire the prairie would be blackened wasteland for a time; then the swelling earth would begin to look like a lazy green ocean as fresh grass pushed upward. The Indians set these fires to provide this prime food for buffalo and for their ponies, though they sometimes used the fire as a weapon in battle or in hunting meat.

Except in a very dry year, these fires usually occurred in late autumn or winter. In August and September the prairie grasses waved across the gentle swells, over any one of which might come charging a band of Indians, whooping and racing their ponies straight for the *caballada*. Thievery was the main mischief of the Indians, especially when travelers were well armed and alert. The painted faces and bodies, outlandish cries, and wildly skillful horsemanship struck terror among travelers, but surprisingly few deaths occurred along the trail.[9]

Loss of animals, however, could impose great danger. In 1826 a small band of twelve men encamped on the Cimarron, with only four serviceable guns among them, were visited by a party of Indians who, seeing the men uncertain and timid because of their scanty defense, first begged a horse for each warrior, then two. Finally, yelling and swinging their *lazos* over their heads, they drove off the entire *caballada* of nearly five hundred head of horses, mules, and asses, leaving the men to reach a settlement if they could.[10] If Kit heard of this disaster, it too became an important part of his education, for in his later encounters with Indians he never appeared uncertain or timid, no matter what the weakness of his position.

Drawn into a circle at night, the wagons of the caravan made a snug corral. When grazing, the animals were hobbled. The men

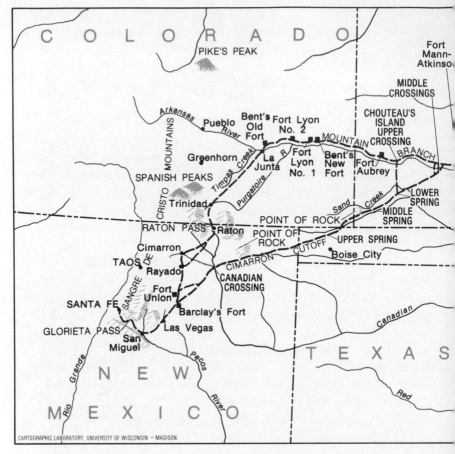

The Santa Fe Trail and Its Branches: Kit Carson traversed the whole trail (Cimarron Cutoff) from east to west in 1826 and traveled parts of it in 1827, 1842, 1843, 1847, 1851, 1865, and probably in some other years.

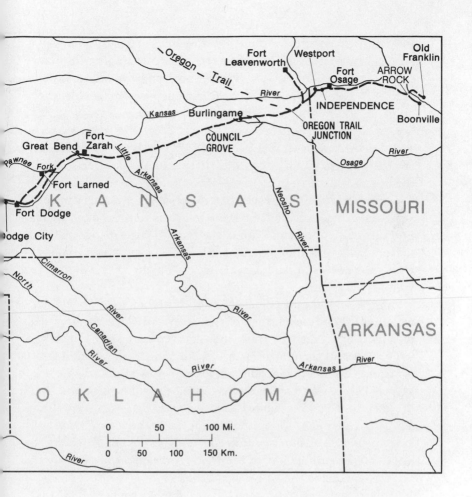

took turns at guard duty during the night. As always, there were false alarms, but no Indians attacked. The caravan ran into fierce storms, with lightning splitting the sky and exploding around them in volleys of thunder, rain beating upon their backs as they crouched in the saddles. During these terrifying displays, all the horsemen were needed to keep the *caballada* together. Wagons mired to their hubs, so that extra beasts had to be hitched to them and men had to strain at the muddy spokes of the wheels before they would budge. At other times creek banks had to be dug away to permit passage of the wagons. Startled rattlers occasionally struck at the animals, causing them to leap in terror and try to bolt into the prairie. The sun burned the men without mercy, and the fierce wind tore at their clothing, filled their eyes, noses, and ears with dust and sand, and threatened to rip the sheets from the wagons.

But travelers also had glorious moments when the first buffalos were sighted and the ecstasy of the chase seized them; mounted men raced out across the grass, inciting even those without horses to bound across the prairie after the galloping herds, shooting out of sheer excitement, without any possibility of hitting the fleeing animals. There were brilliant days when the sky was so blue and the grass so redgold as it bowed in the breeze that even the dullest felt its magnificence. Some nights the stars were so brilliant and looked so close that it seemed the crackling of sparks could be heard if, in the immensity of the prairie, the yipping of the coyotes and the howling of the wolves would cease.

Wolves were especially plentiful in buffalo country. They did not attack the stock, but their presence annoyed some of the travelers, their howls sounded threatening. The only trouble on the whole journey that Kit noted occurred because of this animosity toward wolves:

On the road . . . Andrew Broadus . . . was taking his rifle out of a wagon for the purpose of shooting a wolf and . . . it . . . was accidentally discharged, [he] receiving the contents in the right arm. He suffered greatly. . . . We had no medical man in the party. His arm began to mortify and amputation was necessary. One of the party . . . set to work and cut the flesh with a razor and the bone with an old saw. The arteries being cut, to stop the bleeding he heated a king bolt of one of the wagons and burned the affected parts, and then applied a plaster of tar taken from off the wheel of a wagon. The man became perfectly well before our arrival in New Mexico.[11]

This dramatic event occurred near the Great Bend of the Arkansas.[12] The grass had gradually dwindled in size since Council Grove. Now the caravan was reaching the country of short bunch grass, or buffalo grass, dry and dead looking during most of the year, but so nutritious that the prairie was thick with herds of buffalos. Travelers often had to exert great effort and ingenuity to divert the herds away from the *caballada,* and not always with success. In 1824 twenty or thirty animals belonging to a company of traders had stampeded with the herd. Hunters, leaping off their horses to give the *coup de grace* to a wounded buffalo, sometimes had to watch helplessly as their mounts took out after the fleeing game and disappeared with all their gear, never to be seen again.

The great herds were not always approachable, but when the hunters were able to bring in the game, the camp was a scene of gluttonous feasting, each man holding his own stick over the fire, on which fat and lean alternated, the whole dripping liquid fat upon the *bois de vache,* or dried droppings of the buffalos, adding fuel for the cooking.[13] The *boudin,* intestine containing half-digested food, both ends tied to prevent the fat from wasting, was roasting along with the rest.

When it was pronounced "good" by the hungry, impatient judges, it was taken off the hot coals, puffed up with heat and fat, the steam escaping from little punctures, and coiled on the ground or a not particularly clean saddle blanket, looking for all the world like a dead snake. The fortunate owner shouts, "Hyar's the doins, and hyar's the coon as savvys 'poor Bull' from 'fat cow', freeze into it, boys!" And all fall to with ready knives, cutting off savory pieces of this exquistely appetizing prairie production.[14]

Lewis H. Garrard, the writer of this enthusiastic appreciation of the gourmet's delight of the prairies, was a seventeen-year-old boy of good family, on a jaunt for the sake of his health twenty years

23

after Kit's journey. The same pleasure was expressed by Josiah Gregg, who first made the journey in 1831. Since the travelers generally had one meal a day, consisting often of bread and coffee, arrival among the buffalos would inevitably trigger delirious excitement and gluttony.

While crossing the buffalo country, travelers tried to save as much meat as possible. Along the sides of their wagons were strung lines on which hung thin strips of meat, drying in the sun and the ceaselessly blowing wind. When thoroughly dry, the slabs were stacked inside the wagons. Though tough as leather, this meat kept very well and fed the men on the barren stretches they could expect to endure before reaching Santa Fe.

Buffalo meat fed the travelers as they cut across the prairie past Pawnee Rock, the only thing resembling a rocky bluff for hundreds of miles in any direction. Travelers paused there to scratch their names, messages, or mottos into the granite, obliterating remnants of old marks that had withstood the wind-driven sand and sleet since before the white men came.

Buffalo herds were plentiful as the caravan crept southwestward to meet the Arkansas again, and to a lesser degree in the dryer region south of the river. A stray buffalo has been credited with saving the Becknell party in 1822. After leaving the Arkansas, this group traveled for two days without finding any water. They killed their dogs and cut off the ears of their mules, hoping to alleviate their terrible thirst with the hot blood, but this only aggravated their suffering. Desperate, they scattered in every direction to search for water, but without success. Not knowing that they were already near the Cimarron, they decided to return to the Arkansas. Some fell and were unable to rise, but a small group happened upon a buffalo that had just drunk its fill at the river. They shot the animal and drank the water from its stomach. A member of that expedition later declared that "nothing ever passed his lips which gave him such exquisite delight as his first draught of that filthy beverage."[15] That draught gave them enough strength to reach the river. After assuaging their thirst, they filled their canteens and returned to the relief of their comrades.

On this *jornada* the party of Jedediah Smith ran dry in the summer of 1831, and Smith lost his life to the Comanches when he set out to follow a buffalo path to water. His plan for finding water was successful, but as he stopped to drink, the Indians swept over a rise and fatally wounded him before he could get to his horse and rifle. He jerked his pistols from their holsters and killed two of the Indians before he fell.[16]

After leaving the Cimarron, caravans soon arrived among the tributaries of the Canadian, and the closer they came to the mountains, the more plentiful and sparkling the water became and the more numerous and recognizable the landmarks. Finally they came to San Miguel, an irregular cluster of adobe huts in the valley of the Rio Pecos. From there the road curved to the northwest through detached ridges and mesas at the southern end of the Sangre de Cristo Mountains. At last they reached a ridge from which a valley extended toward the northwest, with occasional groups of trees among corn and wheat fields, brownish yellow now in the late autumn, with here and there a square, block-like building of brown, red, or whitewashed adobe. When the buildings appeared huddled together in irregular clusters, the old hands told them they were looking at Santa Fe.

A flurry of activity began, every wagoner tying a brand new cracker to the lash of his whip, all the men washing, putting on clean clothes, wetting and combing their hair. When sufficiently well groomed, they descended into the town, the drivers flourishing their whips, the riders tightening the reins and using their spurs to display their tired mounts to the best advantage, all grinning down into the glistening black eyes of the women and boys who poured out of the doorways, exclaiming, *"Los Americanos!"*—*"Los Carros!"*—*"Otra caravana!"*[17]

Few of the men could understand Spanish, but they called out greetings and endearments and were willingly led off to be fed in the homes of these friendly and generous *señoritas*, to dance at the *fandangos* got up on the spur of the moment to celebrate their arrival, to relish to the full the joy and excitement of their welcome into this exotic and hospitable little city.

Chapter 3

Too Small, Too Young, Too Green

If Kit, at sixteen, was fascinated by the black-eyed señoritas of Santa Fe, he made no mention of it thirty years later. In fact, this sturdy mountaineer with his Scotch Presbyterian background would seem, from his memoirs, to have had almost no contact with any women at all. He refers to them only five times, twice in general statements describing fights between whites and Indians, three times more specifically: recording the fact of his marriage to Josefa Jaramillo, mentioning the kindness of Lieutenant Beale's mother when Kit was in Washington, and deploring his inability to help Mrs. White.

Some of the traders were going on to Taos, and Kit traveled with them through the hills of juniper and piñon along the western edge of the Sangre de Cristos, then along the Rio Grande through a canyon often rugged and bleak. Finally they climbed sharply away from the canyon and looked across the wide, nearly flat, roughly circular Valle de Taos. At first the plain seemed empty. As they advanced, they could distinguish the adobe villages huddled against the dark blue mountains.

Twenty years later, seventeen-year-old Lewis Garrard described his own entry into the town, coming from the opposite direction:

The first house we passed was a distillery where the "mountain dew" of New Mexico—aguardiente de Taos—is made; and such is the demand, it is imbibed before attaining a very drinkable age, by both foreigners and residents, with great avidity.

A fiercely moustached native, with broad-brimmed, glazed sombrero *and gay-colored* sarape *disposed in graceful folds on his lithe figure, and a woman in gray* reboza *enveloping her head and shoulders . . . replied gayly to one [our] "buenas le dai, Señorita."[1] . . . Reaching the suburbs of Fernandez, I recognized a* ranchero, *driving before him a mule laden with shucks.*

He exclaimed, as he doffed his hat—"Comme le va, Señors, esta buen . . . Señora [Será (?)] una fandango grandote, esta noche," his eye brightening as he spoke, "muy Señoritas bonita."[2]

Passing some low, flat roofed mud structures, . . . we met at every step gracefully moving women and sarape-enveloped men, the shuck cigarilla between the lips of many.[3]

Garrard was fortunate to be invited to stay at the home of Ceran St. Vrain, who had been captain of the caravan from Westport. Kit was equally fortunate to come to the notice of a former neighbor from Missouri:

An early Santa Fe trader, one of Taos' first distillers, Colorado's first cattleman, a founder of Fort Pueblo—all these interesting titles belong to Mathew Kinkead, but because he took into his Taos home a boy he had known in Missouri, he lost his identity in the legend of Kit Carson, and has since been famous only for his hospitality.[4]

Son of David Kinkead, who had built the Fort Kinkead that sheltered Kit as a tiny boy, Mathew was born in Madison County, Kentucky, in 1795. By 1812 the Kinkeads were living in the Boonslick area, and Mathew was old enough to serve with Lindsey and the older Carson boys in the militia defending the forts. In 1824 he and his father mortgaged a Negro girl named Jane to raise $325, and Mathew bought goods to trade on his first trip to Santa Fe. In 1825 both he and his brother John came out with the caravan, Mathew paying duties on goods worth $1,123.76. This time he rode on up to Taos, where he and William Workman made plans to start a distillery.[5]

When Kit came into the plaza with the traders, his immediate future must have looked decidedly unpromising. As at Santa Fe, people milled around, eager to see what the traders had to offer. Suddenly within the edge of his vision appeared a familiar face— Mathew Kinkead come to the plaza to see who had arrived. Kinkead could hardly do less than invite the runaway to his home.

Fernandez de Taos was the third largest town in New Mexico, with a population in 1827 of 3,606.[6] Having spent the preceding year in the area, Kinkead had acquired some information about his adopted country and some knowledge of the language.[7] In this little foreign city whose inhabitants spoke mostly Spanish, Kit discovered that he had a facility for learning languages. He rapidly acquired enough Spanish to explore the town and improved his fluency by using their own language to become better acquainted with the essentially friendly natives. Although rather modest and shy, Kit was himself basically friendly. He liked people, and they almost invariably liked him. Like many small men, he was quick to stand up for his rights, but his intelligence was quick to measure what those rights were. He was not aggressive or acquisitive, though he was gamesome enough to enjoy a "pretty fight." These traits enabled him to adjust easily to the culture of the people of the Southwest, who eventually accepted him as one of their own.

There is good reason to believe that Kinkead and Workman were busy that winter getting their distillery into operation. Workman paid duty on goods brought into Santa Fe in December 1826. This is not known to have been distillery equipment, but two pieces of evidence seem to indicate that it was: Workman later became known as a manufacturer of "Taos Lightnin'," and during the winter of 1827–28, George Yount helped take furs into a still house that "had been converted into a recepticle of smuggled goods, and an under ground passage led to the great subterranean cache."[8] Young and Workman had been trapping with a party on the Gila River. To prevent Manuel Armijo, governor of New Mexico, from confiscating the furs, as he had done with Ewing Young's

28

the preceding summer, they were brought in after dark and deposited in the cellar of the distillery—presumably that run by Workman, Kinkead, and Chambers.

The activities of Kinkead and Workman were so foreign to what Kit had hoped for and expected that he may have repaid the hospitality given him by helping reluctantly or not at all. However, if Kinkead was busy with the distillery, he may have allowed Kit to bring in the meat. Since Kit later earned his keep by cooking for Ewing Young, he may also have cooked for the two distillers.

The surrounding country, including Taos Pueblo, offered much to interest Kit. At an altitude of almost eight thousand feet, Taos Valley has cold, usually dry winters. Because the rainy season occurs during the summer, snow is seldom so deep as to hamper freedom of movement in the valley, and the dry, cold air becomes uncomfortable only when strong winds blow up the valley. In addition to having a delightful climate and being handy for trapping the mountain streams, the valley has always had a peculiar beauty and charm, the muted blue and orange colors common to New Mexico enhanced by the startling sunsets that gave name and mystery to the Sangre de Cristo Mountains.[9]

Kit fell in love with the valley and the town, but something seemed to be lacking in his relationship with his host, for he never spoke appreciatively of Kinkead's help or hospitality. When spring came, something—discouragement, homesickness, a feeling of guilt at having run away from his family and his contract—impelled him to join the party of Paul Ballio, which started to Missouri on April 7. On the Arkansas he met a caravan bound for New Mexico, very likely the May caravan carrying David Workman west. Consisting of 105 men, commanded by the veteran Ezekiel Williams, the fifty-three wagons of this caravan made an impressive sight, strung out for a mile across the plains.[10] Carson gives no clue to what happened on the Arkansas, but when the two caravans separated, he was again headed west.

In Santa Fe he found work driving a wagon to El Paso. The road rolled over ridges dotted with juniper and piñon, seeking the Rio Grande, which it followed through the village of Bernalillo, through Albuquerque, seat of the Armijos and leading city of the Rio Abajo,[11] over increasingly arid hills to the adobe village of

Socorro, where "the men appear to have no other employment than smoking and basking in the sun, wrapped in their serapes; the women in dancing and intrigue."[12] From there, avoiding the canyon carrying the Rio Grande in a deep curve to the west, the road dragged south across ninety miles of grassless, waterless desert, a dread *Jornada del Muerto.*

The El Paso of Carson's time lay south of the Rio Grande, the valley a veritable garden of plots watered by acequias flowing from the dammed-up river.[13] Away from this valley the soft earth colors of northern New Mexico gave way to reddish brown semidesert, with meager tussocks of yucca, creosote bush, sagebrush clinging as if barely held by the loose mounds of earth, the friable soil having been scooped away by the wind. The barren mountains, eroded and ragged, held no attraction for Kit. As soon as his wagon arrived in El Paso, he resigned and started back to Santa Fe.

Scarcely pausing, he want on to Taos, where Ewing Young and William Wolfskill were opening a store to outfit trappers for the mountains. Hoping to find work with a party of trappers, Kit made inquiries at the store. Offered board and lodging through the winter in return for service as a cook, he had no choice but to accept. Hanging around the store and listening to the men talk, watching as they fastened all their belongings on a pack horse or two, he could only gaze after them when they cantered off toward the north. If he ever asked to be taken along, he was turned down— still too small, too young, too green.

In the spring of 1828 he again started to Missouri, met a caravan on the Arkansas as before, and turned back to Santa Fe. His two years in New Mexico suddenly made a small opening for him, though at first the importance of the opportunity was not apparent. Philip and William Trammel, merchants in Santa Fe for the past year, were preparing a party to carry goods to Chihuahua, and they needed an interpreter.[14] At least Kit had learned to speak Spanish. His soft voice, surely a handicap in offering himself as a comrade for a band of mountain-hardened trappers, was a positive asset to him as prospective assistant to a merchant. He applied to Colonel Philip Trammel for the post of interpreter and was hired.[15]

Chihuahua, a city of eight or ten thousand, lay over five hundred miles south of Santa Fe. The country just beyond El Paso consisted of perfectly barren hills; then a huge, rolling mass of shifting sand lay across the way, without a road, the track marked by the skeletons of oxen, mules, horses—even human bones half-hidden by the sand. Farther south, a few haciendas dotted the plain; a few lakes, stagnant pools, little streams offered relief from the burning heat. But many miles of waterless desert stretched before the Trammel party as they rode farther into Mexico.

The sight of Chihuahua was all the more welcome, with its white houses, church spires, and gardens contrasting vividly with the barren plain. Built at the close of the seventeenth century, it was not so old as Santa Fe, but an aqueduct had been built to bring water to the city, and the products of its mines had been cause for a mint to be established. It boasted a cathedral, the facade adorned with statues of the twelve apostles, and an unfinished convent. Begun by the Jesuits before their expulsion from Mexico in 1767, the convent had been used by the Spaniards to imprison the patriot Hidalgo. The rumor that this revolutionary priest had successfully thrown off the Spanish yoke, together with the publication of Zebulon Pike's *Journals* relative to his captivity in Mexico, were responsible for the attempt in 1812 of Robert McKnight and his party to open trade with Mexico. Far from being successful, Hidalgo had been executed in a yard behind the convent in 1811.[16]

After his return to New Mexico, McKnight had become involved in operating the famous Santa Rita del Cobre mines among the juniper-studded hills between the Gila and the Mimbres Rivers, northwest of El Paso.[17] A man of consequence in the mining industry, McKnight happened to be in Chihuahua at the same time as Kit and Trammel. When Kit was no longer needed by the merchant, McKnight offered him work at the copper mines, and Kit accepted. Growing dissatisfied with driving a team, however, he quit after a few months.[18]

When he reached Taos in August 1829, he heard that Young was calling for volunteers to go to the aid of Charles and William Bent's wagon train under attack by Indians south of the Cimarron Crossing.[19] Young may have been surprised, even amused, to see his small, soft-spoken cook among close to a hundred men riding with him toward the Arkansas. The Indians fled at the approach of the Taoseños, but Young had a chance to see young Carson's horsemanship, adaptability, and courage. When the young man soon put himself forward as a candidate for a trapping brigade, he was accepted.

Ewing Young, who was a strong and decisive influence in Kit's life, first came to the West in 1821 with William Becknell, intending to manufacture gunpowder for the Mexican government. Failing to obtain sufficient nitre, he returned to Missouri, but in 1822 he again came out with Becknell. The party included William Wolfskill, with whom Young trapped the Pecos River southeast and east of Santa Fe and the San Juan to the northwest, bringing in $10,000 worth of furs.[20] After other trapping-trading ventures, he and Wolfskill became partners in the store in Taos.[21]

Young was by choice a businessman, not an Indian fighter or seeker of adventure, but in 1826 he had engaged in one of the most adventurous and financially least rewarding exploits of his career. With a license in the name of Joaquín Joon (the Spanish attempt to spell his name) obtained from Governor Narbona, he set out with eighteen trappers including Milton Sublette and Thomas L. (later Peg-leg) Smith. Soon his party was joined by sixteen more men, including George Yount. Near the junction of the Salt and the Gila, they met Miguel Robidoux, James Ohio Pattie, and one other man, the only survivors of an attack by the Papago Indians. Young led an attack on the Papago village, killed many warriors, burned the village, recovered much of the plunder, and buried the dismembered bodies of Robidoux's men.

Taking Robidoux and Pattie, the party trapped down the Gila to its mouth, then moved up the Colorado. When some Mojave Indians came into camp and saw many red circles leaning against the trees—beaver skins on their stretching frames—one of the chiefs claimed the beaver as his own and demanded a horse in payment. Being refused, he shot an arrow into a tree to indicate his displeasure. Young shot a bullet into the arrow. This did not discourage the Indians, who continued to harass the trappers so insistently that Young pushed on up the Colorado. Once free of the Mojaves, he began trapping, following the river far to the north.[22] He crossed the Continental Divide near Long's Peak and descended to the South Platte. Turning northwest to the Laramie River, he continued to the North Platte and ascended as far as the

Sweetwater before turning south. Reaching the Little Snake River, he followed it to the Yampa, rode upstream over a hundred fifty miles, through its beautiful valley, crossed the height of land to the Colorado, ascended the Eagle River to its source in the high Rockies, and crossed the Continental Divide to the headwaters of the Arkansas. For almost a year he had trapped and explored the streams and trails, losing five men to the Indians but none to the mountains. His pack animals carried about $20,000 worth of furs when he reached Santa Fe in June 1827.

Manuel Armijo had replaced Narbona as governor. Refusing to honor the license made out to Joaquín Joon, Armijo seized the furs Young's party brought in. Before reaching the city, Young had been warned of the change of policy and had left twenty-nine packs of beaver in the home of Cabeza de Baca. Apprised of this, Armijo sent soldiers to get them. The Mexican resisted and was killed, whereupon Armijo charged that Young, by leaving the furs with Cabeza de Baca, was responsible for the murder. Young was so outraged that, even as Armijo was questioning him, he turned his back and walked out.

While the case was pending, Armijo gave three of Young's men permission to lay the furs in the sun in the plaza to air and dust them. Milton Sublette found two bundles belonging to him, threw them on his back, and walked away. By the time the soldiers reached the house where Sublette was staying, he had left town. His fury increasing, Armijo jailed Young but released him when he denied all knowledge of Sublette's whereabouts. Finally the furs, damaged by a great rain storm, were sold for only a fraction of their original value. There is no record that Young or his men ever received any of the money they brought.[23]

Young did not tarry to worry over the matter. He was getting ready to open his store in Taos, where Kit spent the winter of 1827–28 as his cook. With this very enterprising man, Kit was ready in 1829 to take his apprenticeship as mountain man and explorer.

Chapter 4

Trapping to California

Before Kit's return from the copper mines, Young had sent a party to trap the Gila down toward the Colorado. Somewhere on the headwaters of the Gila they were waylaid by Apaches, who had become increasingly dangerous since their acquisition of horses in the late seventeenth century. After an all-day fight, Young's men had turned back, convinced that they could make no successful hunt in that area.

Young then enlisted forty men—Americans, Canadians, and Frenchmen from the Louisiana Territory—and took command himself. To avoid another fiasco like the one he had suffered two years before when Armijo had revoked his license, Young traveled north about fifty miles, as if planning to trap along the Front Range of the Rockies, then turned southwest. Kit, now nearly twenty years old, was one of the forty men riding with him.

Young was not the kind of leader to take along a poorly equipped man. Kit was riding a dependable animal, and across the saddle in front of him lay a good rifle. One or two *apishamores* protected the back of his animal.[1] Fastened to his saddle were a buffalo-skin bag containing powder and lead, a blanket, extra moccasins or dressed dearskin for making them, and anything else that he felt he could not get along without, such as tobacco, awl, needles, medicine. Over his left shoulder and under his right arm hung his powder horn and bullet pouch, in which he carried balls, flint, steel. Attached to his belt by a steel chain he wore a sheath of buffalo hide that held a large butcher knife. The steel chain also held a little buckskin case containing a whetstone. He may have carried a tomahawk in his belt or fastened to the pommel of his saddle. Somewhere about him he carried a small wooden box containing castoreum, a strong-smelling, oily substance obtained from the sexual glands of beaver and used for bait. Around his neck he wore a thong holding his tobacco sack, containing his pipe, tobacco, and flint and steel.

For comfort a trapper preferred a flannel or cotton shirt, but antelope skin would serve and usually did before the end of the season. He wore leather or woolen breeches, leggings and coat made of blanket cloth or buffalo robe, a hat or cap of wool, fur, or leather. His hose were pieces of blanket lapped around his feet under his moccasins. It can be assumed that Kit, in choosing his outfit, avoided the picturesque attire sometimes associated with mountain men. Descriptions of him always picture him as dressed in ordinary clothing.

Kit had earned the right to a feeling of exultation and pride as he rode with the trappers beyond the last settlement, turned west, climbed a long slope, and proceeded across the beautiful rolling uplands of the southeastern spur of the San Juan Mountains. After descending the steep western slope, the party rode southwest through the undulating plains of sage and wildflowers toward the distant mesas, orange and red and purple and yellow, north of the Zuni villages.

Zuni Pueblo was a way-station for travelers into the Gila country. From there the trappers struck across high valleys, probably following the Zuni River as it bore off southwest toward its junction with the Little Colorado. Young was headed for the deep, rugged canyons that carry small streams down the south slopes of the Mogollon Plateau. These form the headwaters of the Black River, which arcs to the southwest and back and picks up the White River as it curves west after tumbling down from the plateau. The Salt River, born of this union, rushes tortuously through canyons and between the rugged brown hills below the Sierra Ancha. After picking up the Verde River, it joins the Gila above the great bend to the south and the quiet meander across the desert to the Colorado.

As the band rode across the rugged terrain, every man was aware that they were in the area where the Apaches had harried their comrades, and all were constantly on the alert. Somewhere on the headwaters of the Salt River, their vigilance was rewarded.[2] Catching a glimpse of the Indians before they had a chance to examine the camp, Young directed most of his men to hide under blankets, pack saddles, or whatever was handy. Soon the slope above the camp was alive with Indians. Seeing so few men in camp, they came leaping and whooping down among the pines. Young let them come until they were right in the camp, then gave the word to fire. Seeing forty men springing up from the camp gear, guns leveled, the Indians turned and fled, but not before fifteen or twenty of them were killed. Although the Apaches had been severely punished for their former attacks, that was not the end of it. As the party trapped down the Salt and up the Verde,[3] Indians crawled into camp nearly every night, stealing a trap or two, killing a mule or a horse, harassing the trappers in any way they could.

Below the mountains the Salt and the Verde Rivers run between barren ridges, the low-water margins of the streams ragged with willows, cottonwood growing along the banks, greasewood, salt bush, mesquite, cactus, palo verde, sage, and other desert plants scattered above the banks and up the lower slopes of the ridges. Both the Verde and the Salt were good beaver streams. Men and animals fared well, with plenty of grass and water. With a constant supply of beaver, the tails of which rival buffalo in flavor and nourishment, hunting among the surrounding ridges was unnecessary.[4] When Young thought of pushing on and needed meat for the journey, the men faced their first real hardship.

At the head of the Verde, Young sent twenty-two men back to Taos to take the beaver they had caught and to buy traps and animals to replace those taken by the Indians. With eighteen men, including Carson, he prepared to cross the desert to California. The first need was food, but they found game very scarce. After three days of continuous hunting, they had killed only three deer. These they dressed carefully, making tanks of the skins and drying all the meat they could spare. Indians who came into camp told them they would find plenty of beaver in the valley beyond the desert, but they would suffer before they arrived at that place.

With the promise of beaver, they started out in high spirits, their tanks full of water, before them terrain never before, so far as they knew, explored by white men. "The first four days march was over a country sandy, burned up, and not a drop of water. We received at night a small quantity of water from the tanks. . . A guard was then placed over the tanks to prohibit anyone from making use of more than his due allowance."[5]

They were plodding northwest through a country of low, brown, deeply eroded ridges, impassable, criss-crossing ravines, areas of loose, porous soil in which the mules sank to their fetlocks, a country of dry washes, cactus, an occasional yucca or stunted creosote bush. Nothing moved but themselves and the wavering currents of heated air, and nothing but the darkness of night offered respite from the burning glare of the sun. Incredibly, in this arid waste they found water. They may have been the first white men to discover the pool, and without the pack mules they might have missed it.[6] The animals smelled the water and rushed forward with their last reserves of strength. Soon they were strung out across the desert for miles, and the men had to push their mounts to the utmost to reach the pool and preserve the water from being fouled beyond use.

They rested by the pool for two days to let the animals recover, then refilled their tanks and set out again. The country remained the same—dry, ragged, desolate, shimmering with heat. For another four days they were tortured by thirst and hunger, their eyes red-rimmed, skin caked with dust, lips cracked. When they tried to blow the dust from their nostrils, the dessicated membranes shed flecks of blood. The animals, without the daily ration the men were getting from their tanks, suffered most. On the fourth day, with indescribable joy, they arrived at the Colorado below the Grand Canyon.

About the same time they came upon a party of Mojave Indians, who traded them a mare, heavy with foal. They soon had the animal butchered, not neglecting the foal, and the meat roasting beside the fire. They began eating while the meat was almost raw and continued until they had devoured it all. For three days they camped by the great river, resting, recruiting their animals, and trading for whatever beans and corn the Indians could spare.

Leaving the Colorado, they plunged into the Mojave Desert. After three days they came to the bed of the Mojave River, and two more days brought them to water. They were on the Old Spanish Trail, developed over the years by Indians and Spanish priests, the western and eastern ends linked the year before by Jedediah Smith. Smith called the stream the "Inconstant River" because it repeatedly disappeared "into the desert, only to reappear a few miles farther on." One early traveler described it as "a long line of little rippling lakes, from two to two-and-a-half feet deep, at one time sunken among hard, flinty hills or piles of driving sand, and at others gurgling through narrow vales covered with grass and fields and forest in which live the deer, the black bear, the elk, the hare, and many a singing bird."[7] After three days through the unrelieved desert, these little oases seemed like paradise to the parched and weary travelers. After six days along this river bed, they left it and traveled west. Four more days brought them to the Mission of San Gabriel.

This mission, founded in 1771 by the famous Franciscan pioneer, Padre Junípero Serra, lay eight or ten miles east of Los Angeles in a level valley with pretty streams of running water, lofty mountains to the north timbered with pine and cedar, low, grassy mountains to the south. It was a show place among Spanish missions, with thousands of acres of rich, fertile land grazing thirty thousand head of cattle, and horses, sheep, hogs, and so forth, in proportion. Cultivated land yielded an abundance of grapes, fruit, vegetables, corn, and three or four thousand bushels of wheat annually.[8] In addition to feeding and clothing the thousand Indians who lived and worked there, the establishment earned yearly fifty-five or sixty thousand dollars from the sale of hides, tallow, soap, wine, aguardiente, wheat and corn.

The priest in charge was Padre José Bernardino Sánchez, Spanish born, well educated, hospitable, diplomatic, a perfect host who made the Americans comfortable, gave them plenty to eat and drink, avoided the embarrassing problem of their status as aliens by referring situations concerning them to Governor José María de Echeandía at San Diego, and ignored sensitive areas such as their religion, their bedraggled condition, their ignorance of the etiquette of a Spanish gentleman, and their inability to speak Spanish, the last a handicap Young and Carson did not have.

When Jedediah Smith's men stayed at the mission from November 28, 1826, to January 17, 1827, while Smith was explaining his reason for being there and obtaining permission to buy supplies and leave, they discovered that San Gabriel had both good and bad points.[9] Kit was not there long enough to become aware of the latter. Young never tarried to make explanations or to ask permission. He remained one day, traded butcher knives for beef at the rate of four knives for one animal, and when he left, Carson had the impression that San Gabriel "was a paradise on earth."[10]

One day away they came to San Fernando Mission, twenty miles north of Los Angeles, about as populous as San Gabriel but not so well administered. Finding a pass through the mountains, they rode on northwest to the San Joaquin Valley, another paradise with elk, deer, and antelope by the thousands and an abundance of grass. They found signs of trappers on the San Joaquin, followed their trail for a few days, and overtook a party of sixty men commanded by Peter Skene Ogden.

Ogden was probably the most able, active, and aggressive of the captains of the Hudson's Bay Company, which had resolved to squeeze the Americans out of the jointly exploited Oregon country. They were attempting to trap the streams between them and the Americans so bare of beaver that the mountain men would find it unprofitable to bring their traps into the area.

Ogden had learned of the good trapping along the San Joaquin and the Sacramento in conversations with Jedediah Smith, after the massacre of Smith's men on the Umpqua. Although he admitted privately that he worked against the Americans, refusing to sell needed supplies and preventing the Indians from doing so,[11] Ogden and his men seem to have been entirely amiable and cooperative with Young's party. They trapped together as far as the Pit River, one of the forks of the Sacramento.[12]

When Ogden headed up the Sacramento toward the Columbia, the Americans turned back down the Sacramento, amusing themselves by hunting game during the off-season for beaver. More serious duties soon developed, however, when a party of Indians ran away from one of the missions and took refuge with a village un-

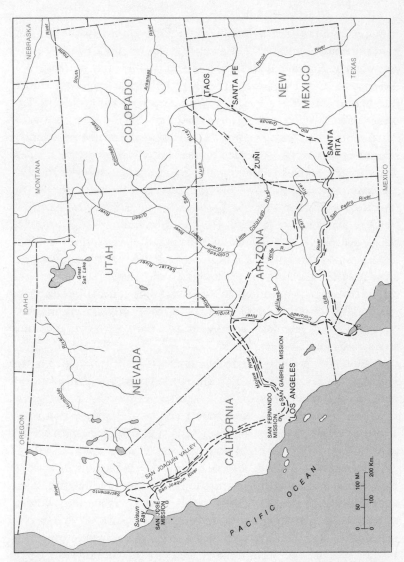

Ewing Young's Second California Expedition, 1829–31: Kit Carson's first trapping venture made him a veteran since it took him to California and back. Young relied on Carson, despite his youth, and Carson learned much from his experiences on this expedition.

friendly to the priests. The priest sent a party of fifteen Indians in pursuit, but these were defeated and had to retreat. Coming to the Americans, they asked for help, and Young sent Carson and eleven men to join them. After fighting for an entire day and losing a great number of men, the rebels fled. The attackers triumphantly entered the village and burned it to the ground.

The next day some of the rebellious Indians returned. The Americans again demanded the runaways, threatening not to leave one alive if they did not comply. The runaways were returned and handed over to the Indians the priest had sent. Young, Carson, and three others went back to the mission with them, taking the beaver they had caught. The people at the mission gave them a hearty welcome.

Carson recalled the mission as San Rafael,[13] but researchers have identified it as San José, which would have been a likely victim of this type of rebellion.[14] Established in 1797, it was next to San Gabriel in size and wealth, and it owed its prosperity to Father Narciso Durán, who had been its head since 1806. A brilliant, versatile, and energetic man, he had designed the mission's irrigation system, with a picturesque fountain in the plaza having facilities for washing and bathing. An excellent musician, he had trained an Indian orchestra that made his mission famous. He encouraged music and sedate dancing on Sunday and allowed games and bear-and-bull fights, but no heavy gambling. When the revelers became weary, he had chocolate and cigars served, but no rum or wine.

The Indians at the mission did the manual work in return for security and order, both physical and spiritual, for Father Durán sometimes baptized them by force when his exhortations proved ineffective. Possessed of a strong sense of the rightness of his cause and his opinions, he found it incomprehensible that some of them found the constraint unbearable and ran off to the mountains.

It would not have occurred to either Young or Carson that they were taking part in a controversial matter that definitely was not their concern. Slavery was legal in the United States, and in the Southwest captive Indians were regularly bought and used as servants. Both Young and Carson were from southern states where it was considered a man's duty to intercept and return runaway slaves. Helping the mission to recover the escaped Indians seemed as natural to them as it did to Father Durán.

Young had brought the furs in the hope that he could trade them for horses. At the mission, he found Don José Asero, whose trading schooner lay offshore. Don José bought the furs, Young bought the horses he needed, and the trappers returned to camp.[15] A party of Horse-eating Indians galloped up in the night, whooping and charging the horses. The next morning only fourteen horses were near the camp; the Indians had driven off sixty. Now that Young had disposed of the furs, the men could get mounts for the return journey only by recovering those stolen. Carson and eleven others saddled up and took the trail of the thieves, following over a hundred miles into the Sierra Nevada. Surprising the Indians feasting on some of the stolen animals, they killed eight of the men, took three children as prisoners, and drove all the animals back to camp except six that had been slaughtered.

The fate of the three young hostages is not given. Since it would have been considered an act of mercy to turn them over to the mission to be educated as Christians, this is probably what happened. Their destiny is not the only mystery of this period. Young had been very astute in handling his men up to this time. Dissatisfied for unknown reasons, François Turcote, Jean Vaillant, and Anastase Carier decided to go back to New Mexico and rode over to Monterey to get passports. Young followed and brought them back, but not before they had alerted Mexican officials to their unauthorized presence.[16] Thereafter they were "wanted men".

Young may not have known of Smith's difficulties with those same officials two years before, but he had himself tangled with Armijo and experienced the frustrations that could be met in dealing with Mexican bureaucracy. That he did not take the nearest way out of the country may have resulted from a false feeling of security growing out of his good relations with the mission. Having heard about the Pueblo de la Reina de los Angeles, a lively little town with some seven hundred inhabitants, the trappers would object to starting the long, dry journey across the desert without visiting it.[17]

The pueblo had been founded forty-nine years earlier by the priests of the San Gabriel Mission. Each of its forty-six inhabitants received a house and land, oxen, a cow, a horse, a burro, sheep, goats, mules, mares, and tools as well as a subsidy in supplies for five years. The village had grown into a boisterous melting pot of descendants of the original settlers, newcomers from Mexico, Indians, Kanakas from the Sandwich Islands,[18] and sailors and traders from all over the world, up from the neighboring port of San Pedro. The music, dancing, games, and bull-and-bear baits of the missions were supplemented by cock-fights, bull-fights, and dimly lighted *pulquerias*,[19] with gambling and dark-eyed, black-haired, laughing women. The priests said the inhabitants were a set of idlers who expected the work to be done by Indians, while the young men on horseback cavorted about the dusty streets and the neighboring ranchos "soliciting the women to immorality."[20] This was the most glamorous sink of iniquity on the West Coast. The trappers were a rough lot, and Young, intent upon getting them safely away, depended increasingly on Kit for the organization of the camp.

At Los Angeles, the authorities demanded their passports. Since they had none, the officers intended to arrest them but were deterred by the rough appearance of the trappers. Resorting to subterfuge, they offered the men whiskey, hoping to befuddle them enough so that they could be subdued with little difficulty. Young could not stop the men from buying the whiskey; neither would he let them be placed in prison. Picking out three men to help Carson, he sent them ahead with all the loose animals and the packs to find a suitable place to camp for the night. If Young and the rest of the men did not reach the camp by dawn, Carson was to take his small party forward as best he could. Upon arriving in New Mexico, he was to report the others dead, including Young, who refused to leave his men.

About dark Young and the others caught up. The Mexicans had succeeded in getting all drunk except Young, but found them even more frightening when drunk. When James Higgins slipped from his horse, deliberately aimed his gun at James Lawrence, and pulled the trigger, the Mexicans did not stop to see whether the fallen man was dead. Whirling their mounts, they galloped back toward Los Angeles lest they catch a wanton bullet in the back.[21]

Carson had camped to the east of San Gabriel. The next morning the party moved toward the Mojave Desert, and nine days later reached the Colorado, where they stopped to rest the animals and do some trapping. The second day, while Young and most of the men were visiting their traps, Carson and the rest were working about the camp, mending harness, clothing, moccasins, stretching hides, sharpening knives, cleaning guns. As Carson told it:

At least five hundred Indian warriors came to our camp. They pretended friendship, but . . . we mistrusted them and . . . discovered where they had their weapons concealed, and then it became apparent to us that their design was to murder the party. . . . I considered the safest way to act was not to let the Indians know of our mistrust and to act in a fearless manner. One of the Indians could speak Spanish. I directed him to state to the Indians that they must leave our camp inside of ten minutes. If one should be found after the expiration of that time, he would be shot. Before the expiration of the ten minutes, everyone had left.[22]

A traveling companion of later years reported that in addressing an ultimatum to threatening Indians, Carson's voice rang, his eyes flashed, and he grasped his rifle "with all the energy of an iron will."[23] Though not quite twenty-one at the time, Kit must have impressed the Indians on the Colorado with that passionate determination.

After trapping down the Colorado to tidewater, the men crossed the river and trapped up the opposite side to the mouth of the Gila, then up the Gila. Near the mouth of the San Pedro they saw a large herd of horses, mules, and asses. Knowing that Indians had stolen the animals and probably committed murder in doing so, the trappers

concluded to deprive them of their stock. We charged their camp. They fled, and we took possession of the animals. The same evening we heard a noise . . . like . . . distant thunder. We sprung for our arms, . . . sallied out to reconnoiter, . . . discovered a party of Indians driving some two hundred horses, charged them, firing a few shots. The Indians run, leaving us sole possessors of the horses . . . stolen . . . from Mexicans in Sonora. Having now more animals than we could take care of, we . . . chose out as many as

we required for riding and packing, . . . killed ten, dried the meat
to take with us, and left the balance loose. I presume the Indians
got them.[24]

The San Pedro rises in the mountains of Sonora and flows west
of north through the desert. It meets the Gila about a hundred
miles above its junction with the Salt River, on the headwaters of
which the men had fought the Apaches on the way west. They
were now following the main stream of the Gila into New Mexico.
When they reached a point near the copper mines, they left the
river and crossed over to the mines to find Robert McKnight. They
had no license to trap in Mexican territory, and they hoped that
McKnight would allow the furs to be stored at the mine. He had no
objections, and Young directed the men to unload the packs and
carry then into one of the deep holes left by the miners.

While the main party left for Taos, Young and Carson stayed a
few days with McKnight, then rode on to Santa Fe. After obtaining
a license to trade with Indians on the Gila, Young sent a few men
to the mines to bring in the beaver. When they returned with two
thousand pounds of fur, they were congratulated upon the fine
trade they had made in so short a time.

In April 1831, the men were paid. For the first time in his life
Carson received a considerable sum of money, which he proceeded
to use in the way that seemed most satisfactory at the time:

Each of us having several hundred dollars, we passed the time
gloriously, spending our money freely—never thinking that our
lives were risked in gaining it. Our only idea was to get rid of the
dross as soon as possible but, at the same time, have as much
pleasure and enjoyment as the country would afford. Trappers
and sailors are similar in regard to the money that they earn so
dearly, daily being in danger of losing their lives. But when the
voyage has been made [and they have] received their pay, they
think not of the hardships and danger through which they have
passed, spend all they have and are ready for another trip. In all
probability [they] have to be furnished with all that is necessary
for their outfit.[25]

Chapter 5

Rocky Mountain Men

The year Carson came over the Santa Fe Trail "for the purpose of seeing different countries," Jedediah Smith, a modern Ulysses, was pushing south and west for the same purpose. In his relentless search for beaver, Smith reached the Mexican missions and ranchos of southern California, returned across the burning wastes of the Great Basin to rendezvous with his partners, then retraced his route to Los Angeles and explored the great inner valley of California, before pushing into coastal Oregon.

Carson had reached California with Young only three years after Smith had been there, but by the time he got to the Rocky Mountains, the age of discovery in that area was largely over. French *coureurs de bois*, the first white men there, had had no interest in exploration as such. Lewis and Clark, Zebulon M. Pike, and Stephen H. Long had explored with purpose and some precision. The Astorians,[1] preoccupied with their efforts to traverse the wilderness, had been too troubled to collect much data, but William Ashley and his men, though only incidentally concerned with topography, came to know the land intimately in the practice of their trade.

In 1824 Jim Bridger canoed down the Bear River to Great Salt Lake, though Etienne Provost, trapping up from Taos, may have seen the lake before he did.[2] In April and May 1825, Ashley and six of his men embarked in bullboats about the mouth of Sandy Creek and rode the waters of Green River across the desert and through the rapids, whirlpools, and cascades of the Uintah Mountain canyons, the first white men to do so.[3] From May to July 1828, Jedediah Smith and his men pushed up the Pacific Coast, through tangled canyons, along the steep and brushy ridges, across rushing, swollen streams until all but four were massacred by the Indians on the Umpqua, at the edge of country already familiar to men of the Hudson's Bay Company.[4]

Old Bill Williams had been prowling and wandering and fighting around the West ever since the first or second decade of the century, when he was living as an Osage Indian, and his intimate knowledge of its peaks, canyons, and streams outstripped that of any other white man.[5] Joseph Reddeford Walker surpassed him in knowledge of the desert regions and the routes to California. Sent by Bonneville to California in 1833, Walker crossed the Great Basin via Mary's River, ascended the Sierra Nevada from East Walker River, discovered Yosemite Valley, and followed the Merced River to the San Joaquin. On his way back, the Indians helped him to "discover" Walker Pass, from which he reached the Great Basin and rode up the eastern edge of the mountains to the route he had followed west.[6]

Thomas Fitzpatrick was not among those climbing mountains to see what lay beyond. Already twenty-four years old when he joined Ashley in 1823, he was brave and tireless, willing to trap, trade, or haul freight to get ahead in the fur business. In 1832 he met a party of trappers working for John Gantt and Jefferson Blackwell and told them Gantt and Blackwell were insolvent.[7] The brigade leader, a man named Stevens, sold his furs to Fitzpatrick and joined him. This rumor floated by Fitzpatrick contributed much to the failure of Gantt and Blackwell two years later.[8]

Fitzpatrick accompanied the caravan of Smith, Jackson, and Sublette that left St. Louis in April 1831 for Santa Fe. It was on this trip that Smith was killed.[9] After receiving supplies for his partners of the Rocky Mountain Fur Company—Milton Sublette, Jim Bridger, Henry Fraeb, and Jean Baptiste Gervais—Fitzpatrick headed north. On the way he picked up thirty additional trappers.

Among these was Kit Carson, recently returned from California with Ewing Young and ready for action after the spree the trappers had enjoyed. However carefree Carson remembered this celebration to have been, he had had enough forethought to outfit himself before allowing the last of his pay to slip through his fingers. When he decided to leave the Rocky Mountain Fur Company, he was free to go. As he recalled his first trip into the heart of the beaver country, "In the fall of 1830 [1831] I joined the party under Fitzpatrick, for the Rocky Mountains. . . . We traveled north till we struck the Platte River and then . . . trapped to the head of the Sweetwater and then on to Green River, and then to Jackson's Hole, a fork of the Columbia River; and from there on to the head of the Salmon River."[10] Thus Carson summarized his journey into some of the most spectacular and beaver-rich areas of the Rockies, where he would first encounter the Blackfeet, and where he would spend most of the next ten years.

Arising in a high mountain valley, the North Platte makes a great curve north, skirting the Medicine Bow Mountains on their west side, the Laramie Mountains on their north, before swinging southeast to its junction with the South Platte. Somewhere along this great curve, Fitzpatrick met Henry Fraeb, out looking for the delayed supplies. Fitzpatrick turned back to St. Louis to procure goods for the next year.[11] Carson accompanied Fraeb up the Sweetwater, which heads in the Wind River Mountains but, as a gentle, rippling stream, skirts the long rolling slopes of sage and grass leading to South Pass. Beyond the pass, the men descended Big Sandy Creek, which meanders across the desert to the Green, an affluent of the Colorado. Trapping up the Green, Carson first entered the high mountains, with the Continental Divide to the east and the Hoback and Gros Ventre Rivers to the west, both flowing toward Jackson's Hole. Between this beautiful valley and the headwaters of the Salmon River lay two hundered miles of difficult terrain, including the majestic Teton Mountains.

The grassy valleys at the head of the Salmon were a favorite wintering place of the Nez Perce Indians as well as the trappers, but it had two drawbacks. Being at the verge of the buffalo country, the area did not always furnish abundant food; and the Lemhi and Bannock Passes gave the Blackfeet easy access to the region from their traditional range east of the Bitterroot Mountains.

Already late in bringing the supplies, Fraeb delayed still further while the men trapped the streams along the way. In early November the band arrived at the Big Hole, one of the sources of the Jefferson River, and Carson entered his first winter camp. Several days of riotous celebration greeted the arrival of supplies before the liquor kegs were bunged and the men settled down to get ready for winter. They bought all the dried meat the Flathead and Nez Perce Indians could spare, as well as buffalo robes. They then put up lodges for themselves opposite a pass to the Horse Prairie, a pleasant, rolling plain fifty or sixty miles in circumference, surrounded by lofty mountains. After this was done, they visited one another, exchanged good-humored stories, and feasted. The American Fur Company camp of Andrew Drips was not far away on the Salmon River, and the men visited back and forth to get supplies, exchange news, or enjoy a greater variety of companionship.

Hunting parties were constantly harassed by the Blackfeet, who sometimes descended on the camps, trying to run off the horses. On one occasion several boldly entered the camp of Warren G. Ferris, American Fur Company trader. One of them mounted a beautiful horse and rode through the camp then through the neighboring Rocky Mountain Fur Company camp, replying to challenges from the guards in the Flathead language, and coolly rode away. When the owner of the horse discovered that it was missing, he and a companion rode in pursuit. They killed one Blackfoot, but about twenty got away, taking eight stolen horses.[12] While hunting buffalo, five men from Carson's camp were killed by Blackfeet.

In April 1832 Carson started south with the Rocky Mountain Fur Company, trapped as far as Bear River, then northeast to the Green. There they met Alexander Sinclair and his party, who had left Taos shortly after Carson.[13] This Arkansas party had wintered on the Little Bear River.[14] Carson was interested to learn that Captain Gantt and his party had wintered near the Laramie and had gone to New Park to hunt.

The Laramie, gentle for a mountain stream, flows from the high ridges of the Medicine Bow Mountains. New Park, also called North Park, Park Kyack, or the Bull Pen (for the buffalo that usually roamed there), is a broad, almost flat, valley surrounded by the snow-capped peaks of the Medicine Bow Mountains and the Park Range. Here the small streams draining the snowy slopes collect into the headwaters of the North Platte River. Like the Laramie, New Park was a favorite habitat of the beaver.

Carson and three others decided to join Gantt and found him ten days later still trapping the New Park. They remained in the Park for some time, then descended the Platte, crossed the Laramie Plains between the Laramie and the Medicine Bow Mountains, trapped the tributaries of the South Platte and rode on south to the tributaries of the Arkansas. Gantt took the accumulated beaver to Taos, while the men remained on the Arkansas, trapping.

Thus Carson missed one of the most widely known fights between Indians and mountain men. The rendezvous of 1832 in Pierre's Hole was one of the largest in the history of the fur trade. As it began to break up, a group of Gros Ventre Indians met the parties of Henry Fraeb, Milton Sublette, Nathaniel Wyeth, and others as they were leaving. Antoine Godin, Fraeb's half-Indian guide, was eager to avenge the death of his father at the hands of the Gros Ventres. When the Indian chief advanced, making signs of peace, Godin and a companion rode forward, treacherously killed him, and galloped away, Godin snatching the chief's red blanket and flourishing it as a trophy.

Immediately both sides took cover and the battle was on. Those trappers still at the rendezvous came streaming up the valley. The Indians took refuge in a thicket, reinforcing their cover with blankets and whatever they could lay their hands on. The battle raged until nightfall, with many killed, among them Alexander Sinclair, and many wounded, including William Sublette. Under cover of darkness the Indians retreated into the mountains. The next day the trappers and traders packed up their supplies and furs and left.[15] This fight made the beautiful valley just across the Tetons from Jackson's Hole one of the most famous in the mountains, but it was never again used as a place of rendezvous by the trappers.

Back on the Arkansas, Gantt returned with supplies for the winter, and the men trapped industriously until the streams began to freeze. Going into winter quarters on the Arkansas, they built log cabins near the mouth of the *Fontaine qui Bouille*.[16] Plenty of buffalo were wintering nearby, kept within easy reach of the camp by deep snow. This small camp on the Arkansas lacked the excitement of the one near the Salmon, but Carson recorded that the men passed a pleasant time. Other winter quarters that he shared were recorded in more detail by companions of later times, some of whose observations follow.[17]

Since a number of the trappers had Indian wives, skin-covered lodges as well as log huts were usually huddled around the winter encampment. With hunters riding in and out of camp, children playing, dogs barking, women and men calling to one another and laughing and gossiping, the winter camp was usually a lively place. When a hunter came riding in with game slung across his horse, his Indian wife, if he had one, would take over, cut up the meat and dry what was not needed for immediate use, cure and dress the skins, and make clothing and moccasins for the family. She kept the fire going and the lodge tidy, carried wood and water, and cooked the meals. Men who had no wives had this work to do themselves, so trappers had a strong inclination to take an Indian wife.

When the trappers were not hunting meat, feeding their horses cottonwood bark, cleaning their guns, mending saddles or bridles, sharpening knives or axes, building corrals or forts, or doing whatever other tasks they felt desirable or necessary, they did as they pleased. Impromptu horse races would develop, with bets, intrigues, and coaching, until the horses were in place; the whole village lined the track, cheering and shouting advice to the riders. Shooting matches would grow out of an argument about the accuracy of their rifles, which they named and cared for as tenderly as if the weapons were indeed dearly loved friends. They wrestled, ran foot races, danced or sang or played music on jew's harps or harmonicas or some homemade instrument. If the weather was bitter or stormy, they drifted into one of the cabins or lodges to tell over their adventures, real or imaginary; or they played seven up, euchre, or poker. Some carried a book or two in their possible sacks and spent enchanted hours reading, sometimes aloud. Since many of the trappers were illiterate, those who could read were always sure of an attentive audience. In the winter camp at the mouth of Clark's Fork in 1836–37, the intellectual element became so articulate that they dubbed themselves "The Rocky Mountain College." Osborne Russell wrote, "I doubt not but some of my comrades who considered themselves Classical Scholars have had some little added to their wisdom in these assemblies however rude they might appear."

In January 1833 occurred one of those events that show Carson most vividly as an impetuous young adventurer, for whom danger and daring swelled the heart irresistibly. A party of men had been out hunting and returned about dark. Their horses, very poor from a diet of cottonwood bark, were left free to forage for whatever they could find. During the night about fifty Crow Indians came to the camp and ran off nine horses. The next morning twelve of the trappers set out on their trail.

The Crows ranged from the Wind River Mountains to east of the Bighorn Mountains and from the North Platte to the Yellowstone. They were skilled horse thieves, usually having for trade a number of animals they had recently stolen. Breaking a trail through deep snow, they were heading home with their trophies when Carson and his companions caught up with them. Crisscrossing buffalo paths had confused the trail, and after a ride of forty miles, the horses of the trappers were worn out. As night came on, they saw, two or three miles ahead, a grove of trees, which looked like a good place to camp. When they reached the grove, they could see fires about four miles ahead, almost certainly the camp of the Crows.

They tied their animals to trees, waited until it became dark, then circled around the Indians so as to surprise them by approaching from the opposite direction. Cover was poor, visibility good in the snow. In order to get near enough to ascertain the layout of the Indians' camp, the trappers had to crawl through the snow for a long distance. At about a hundred yards they could see that the Indians had divided into two equal forts.

They were dancing and singing, . . . passing the night jovially in honor of the robbery committed . . . on the whites. We saw four horses . . . tied at the entrance to the fort. . . .

When we thought they were all asleep, six of us crawled towards the animals. . . . By hiding behind logs and crawling silently towards the fort, . . . we finally reached the horses, cut the ropes and, by throwing snow balls at them, drove them to where was stationed our reserve.

At this point the men paused to decide what to do next. Those who had recovered horses wanted to secure the animals and return to camp. Carson and two others wanted satisfaction for the cold and fatigue the Indians had caused them. "The peace party could not get a convert to their [side]. Seeing us so determined for a fight (there is always a brotherly affection . . . among trappers and the side of danger always being their choice) . . . all agreed to join us in our perilous enterprise."[18]

Sending three men back to grove with the horses, the other nine marched toward the fort. When they had almost reached it, a dog began to bark. The Indians hurried out of the fort, and the trappers opened fire, picking them off as they came, killing nearly every Indian in the fort. A few who were wounded escaped to the other fort, from which the Indians began firing. But the trappers stayed behind trees and fired only when sure of their target.

The night was almost gone. As it began to get light, the Crow Indians saw how few attackers there were and charged from the fort. Waiting until they were very close, the trappers fired, killing five. The others fled to the fort and seemed to be considering the situation. After a time they charged again. The trappers retreated, darting from tree to tree until they reached their camp. With all twelve men together again, they awaited the approach of the Indians, but none came. The trappers took the back trail and arrived at Gantt's camp in the evening, excited at winning the battle, recovering the horses, and sending "many a redskin to his long home."[19] The remainder of winter camp was peaceful.

In the spring of 1833 they cached around four hundred pounds of beaver on the Arkansas, then headed north to the Laramie. To make a cache, the trappers first dug out a space of turf or topsoil large enough to admit the body of a man and placed it to one side. Then they dug deeper, enlarging the diameter of the hole as they went down so that it was shaped somewhat like a jug. They piled the soil on a blanket, carried it to a stream, and scattered it in the water so it would not be conspicuous. The furs were carefully arranged in the hole, protected from the earth by brush and leaves and packed tightly to avoid danger of a cave-in. On top of all this they placed the turf or topsoil in the same position it had occupied before. Often they staked their horses or built a campfire on top of the cache, trying to hide all traces of it. Upon their return, they hoped to find the cache undisturbed.

This time they were unfortunate. When they reached the South Platte, two men deserted, taking three of the best horses. Suspecting that they were going back to the cache, Gantt sent Carson and another man in pursuit. With the best horses and a head start, the deserters easily reached the cache first, dug up the beaver, and loaded it on a canoe they had used during the winter for crossing the river. Signs at the river bank were the last; men and beaver had vanished. Never hearing from them again, Carson assumed that they had been killed by Indians: "Such a fate they should receive for their dishonesty. The animals we recovered . . . they being of much more service to us than men we never more could trust."[20]

At this point, Carson's memoirs lead to two questions: Were Kit and his companion instructed to wait at the winter camp for Blackwell? While they were waiting, did they have a memorable adventure with Joe Meek that Carson forgot to mention?

Joseph L. Meek, two months younger than Carson, had come to the Rockies with William Sublette in March 1829. Robert Newell and several other lifelong friends were in the party, and in the mountains Joe cared for Milton Sublette after the latter had been stabbed by an Indian, thus making another devoted friend. He claimed that he and his brother Stephen accompanied Joe Walker to California in July 1833. After many adventures, some of them shared by Carson, he left the Rockies by wagon in 1840 with Robert Newell and took his Indian wife and their children to Oregon, where he prospered and became a leading citizen.

In his later life he recounted his adventures to Mrs. Frances Fuller Victor, who made of them a famous book, *The River of the West*. Many years after the events, his memory was often faulty concerning dates and details. He told of an excursion into Comanche country with Carson, Levin Mitchell, and three Delaware

54

Indians, Manhead, Jonas, and Tom Hill, in the spring of 1834. Carson was not in that area at that time, and if Meek went to California with Walker, neither was he. This remarkable event may have occurred in the spring of 1833.

According to Meek's story, the trappers were attacked south of the Arkansas by about two hundred Comanches. As the Indians came pouring over a rise in the prairie, chilling the blood with their wild yells, the whites came to a desperate conclusion. Maneuvering their mules into a circular formation, they jumped off and each man cut his mule's throat with his hunting knife. The mules dropped where they stood, making a low barricade, behind which the men took shelter. As the Indians circled them at a dead run, yelling boasts and threats and flourishing their weapons, the whites looked to the priming of their guns and dug as well as they could to deepen their fort, keeping a sharp lookout lest the Indians come near enough to shoot down at them.

Whenever an Indian hungry for renown dashed toward the "mule" fort, the trappers carefully picked him off. They had to conserve ammunition, and they had to be sure some guns were loaded all the time, so they took turns shooting and tried to be sure of their mark. In this way they shot forty-two of the enemy. The Indians conferred from time to time and concluded to make a concerted charge, but their horses, maddened by the scent of mule blood, refused to approach close enough for them to shoot with any effect.

Finally darkness closed in, and little fires of sage and buffalo chips appeared around them on the plain. The trappers slipped out of their fort and crawled away, hugging the ground, watching the horizon for any moving form. They carried only their guns, leaving bridles, saddles, and other gear for the Indians. As soon as they were safely outside the circle of little fires, they set off at a trot for camp.[21]

Meek told Mrs. Victor that a trapper named Guthrie was killed by lightning soon after this battle. Leaning against the lodgepole in Fraeb's lodge, the trapper was struck by a bolt and died instantly. Fraeb dashed out, shouting, "Py Gott, who did shoot Guttery?"

"God a' Mighty, I expect," drawled a trapper named Hawkins. "He's afirin' into camp."

In a letter of November 13, 1833, Fitzpatrick tells of Guthrie's death, fixing the date of the supposed Comanche attack before that time. If this battle occurred, it would explain the careful preparations Carson and his companion made for defense, for the Comanches would be out for revenge: "We took possession of one of the buildings . . . built during the winter . . . not having the remotest idea how long we should have to remain. Being by ourselves we never ventured very far from our fort unless for the purpose of procuring meat. We kept our horses picketed near and . . . slept in the house, always keeping a good lookout."[22]

After about a month Blackwell arrived from Missouri with ten or fifteen men, and shortly thereafter four trappers from Gantt's party came to find out what had happened to Carson and his companion and to report that Gantt's camp was in South Park. Less flat than North Park, this high mountain valley was a favorite hunting ground because of numerous beaver streams and an abundance of other game. Winding southeast between flat banks through extensive meadows, the South Platte unobtrusively gathers its tributaries as they come down from the mountains, sometimes meandering around pleasant knolls topped by evergreens. As the mountains begin to rise between it and its appointed course to the east, it enters Eleven-Mile Canyon, is swung around to the northeast, and plunges through the winding canyons of the Front Range to the edge of the High Plains.

A few days after the arrival of Gantt's men, Blackwell started the party up the Arkansas. For four days they saw no sign of Indians. One morning they turned the horses loose to graze while they got ready to leave camp. As they sat eating breakfast, they noticed a disturbance among the horses and jumped up at once, guns in hand. Seeing Indians creeping among the herd, they rushed toward them. The Indians ran, all except two. One was killed before he could get away. The other, already on one of the horses, galloped out of range before they could stop him.

The Arkansas boils through the Front Range in a granite canyon with sheer walls over a thousand feet high.[23] Here the men climbed to the summit of the mountain, followed a difficult, winding route for a few miles, and camped on a beautiful tributary coming in from the northwest. They staked their best animals and posted a heavy guard. Their dog barked continually during the night, keeping the guards alert, but they saw nothing.

The next morning Carson and three others left to investigate a fork of the stream not far off to check for beaver sign. About an hour after they had left, a party of Indians charged the camp and ran off all the loose animals. Four men mounted four of the best horses, overtook the Indians, and recaptured all of the animals, but one of the men was severely wounded. An Indian was killed.

In the meantime Carson and his party were making their way over a difficult mountain to the fork. When they arrived, they found no beaver sign. Taking a different route on the way back, they came around a spur and saw four Indians near their former trail. Carson suggested charging them, and the other agreed.

We started for them, but . . . found we had caught a tarter. . . . upwards of sixty Indians surrounded us and our only chance to save our lives was a good run, . . . the Indians firing on us from all directions. We run the gauntlet for about two hundred yards, the Indians were often as near as twenty yards. . . . We durst not fire, not knowing what moment our horses might be shot from under us and the idea of being left afoot, your gun unloaded, was enough for to make any man retain the shot which his gun contained.

By some miracle, no one was killed, but one of the men was severely wounded. When they arrived at camp and heard about the horse raid, they understood how the ambush had been set up. Having seen them leave camp, the Indians, disappointed at losing the stolen horses, decided to get the scalps of Carson's group as they returned to camp. "They made a very good attempt, but thank God, failed."[24]

With two men severely wounded, they had to fort up for the night. The next morning one of the wounded was able to ride. They made a litter for the other one and in four days reached Gantt's camp, where they rested the horses and trapped neighboring streams while the wounded men recovered. When the wounds were sufficiently healed, they rode over the Continental Divide to the Old Park.

Old, or Middle Park collects the mountain streams forming the headwaters of the Colorado River, often called the Grand River in

Carson's day. Less well defined than North Park or South Park, it lies between them, the only one of the three west of the Continental Divide. Surrounded by lofty peaks, the park is a jumble of large and small hills separated by little streams.

Finding the area too crowded and beaver scarce, Carson again took advantage of his independent status. With two other men he rode away from Gantt's rather haphazardly managed brigade and ranged through the mountains, trapping nearly all the streams, avoiding the plains because of the vulnerability of so small a party. Either their luck changed or they exercised better judgment in selecting their terrain. The streams began to yield plenty of beaver.

After amassing a large quantity of furs, they rode down to Taos to sell them "and then have the pleasure of spending the money that caused us so much danger and hardship to earn. We arrived at Taos in October, 1832 [1833], disposed of our beaver for a good sum, and everything of mountain life was forgotten."[25]

Chapter 6

Kit Takes a Wife

Carson's celebration of his first excursion into the Rockies was brief. Before the month was out, he made arrangements to guide Captain Richard Bland Lee on a journey into the mountains. Lee was acting as an associate of Bent and St. Vrain.

Charles Bent and Ceran St. Vrain were rapidly establishing a financial empire in the New Mexico–Colorado area. Using trapping and trade as a foundation, they became active in acquiring land and in politics, and in all they were successful. St. Vrain became a Mexican citizen in 1831, handled his business, personal, and political affairs with great skill, and steadily grew in wealth, power, and influence.[1] Bent, equally able but more ambitious and less tactful, was less fortunate in the end. He was appointed civil governor of New Mexico in 1846, but through his personal and land dealings he had early antagonized some of the local people, notably Padre Antonio José Martínez. A number of lawsuits were directed against him, and at one time he was held in jail until his fine was paid, and he barely escaped an angry lynch mob. Although María Ignacia Jaramillo, of a prominent Taos family, was known as Mrs. Bent, no official record of a marriage is known to exist.[2] It is possible that Padre Martínez refused to sanctify this union unless Bent joined the Catholic Church. At any rate, the enmity of this influential priest was believed to be an indirect cause of Bent's assassination in 1847. Although Bent became Carson's brother-in-law in 1843, the two men had had little social contact at the time Kit worked with Captain Lee.

Lee's relationship with Bent and St. Vrain is not clear. A cousin of Robert E. Lee of Virginia, he may have had personal connections with some leading families of St. Louis. He returned to St. Louis with a Bent and St. Vrain caravan in 1834.

As a career army officer, however, Lee was at this time on an unspecified mission for the War Department.[3] In the northern Rockies Captain Benjamin L. E. Bonneville, ostensibly heading a trapping expedition, was also on a secret mission. There are strong indications that both men were gathering such data as the army might need in case of hostilities with Mexicans, Indians, or British. The British, under the guise of the Hudson's Bay Company, made strenuous efforts to keep Bonneville from the Oregon country.[4] Lee's ostensible aim was to bring trade goods for barter with the trappers wherever he found them. This activity gave him plenty of opportunity to observe the terrain and the Indians, and the trappers were excellent sources of information on both.

Carson was one of twelve men who accompanied Lee from Abiquiú on November 19, 1833, following the Old Spanish Trail toward the northwest. This part of the trail had been laid out in 1776 by Padre Francisco Atanasio Domínguez and his secretary, Silvestre Vélez de Escalante. A Ute guide, Awat-Apaw-gai (The Talker), or Silvestre, led them by the safest route he could devise, crossing the White River well to the east of Ouray—"The Place Where Waters Meet" (the White, the Green, and the Uintah, or Duchesne) and therefore a likely place to run into Indians who might be hostile—and crossing the Green just south of the Uintah Mountains before turning west toward the Wasatch Range and Utah Lake.[5]

Later travelers shortened the trail, going straighter and not so far north, missing the White River and Ouray altogether, and turning southwest east of the mountains bordering the Great Basin. But Carson, looking for trappers he had heard were near the Wasatch Mountains, followed the Dolores River and the northern trail, or nearly so. At a Ute village he asked for a guide. A chief's son, who had only an old, useless Spanish rifle, offered to go in return for a good rifle. Kit accepted. This young guide took the party up the Bookcliff Range by way of Westwater, crossed the summit and struck Twowater Creek, a branch of Bitter Creek, which led them to White River. The White took them to Ouray, where they found an adobe fort. The young guide received a new rifle, which he carried proudly back to his village and related how he had earned it. Kit Carson was an easy name to remember, and these Utes always did remember it: the name of an honest white man.[6]

The fort at Ouray belonged to Antoine Robidoux, one of the most important fur traders of the St. Louis family of that name.[7] With him were about twenty trappers and traders as well as a number of Indians. Kit says nothing about carrying any goods of his own, but the Indians remembered him under a huge cottonwood tree near the Uintah, his goods spread out for trade.

The season was getting late. Snow began to fall, and the traders had to build shelters for the winter. They chose a spot at the mouth of the Uintah where, Kit reported, they passed a very pleasant winter.[8] An incident occurred during these months that speaks strongly of Kit's rapidly growing reputation for courage and responsibility. "A California Indian of the party of Mr. Robidoux run off with six animals, some of them being worth two hundred dollars per head. Robidoux came to me and requested that I should pursue him. I spoke to Captain Lee and he informed me that I might use my pleasure."[9]

From a nearby village, Carson chose a Ute to accompany him. Robidoux furnished them with two fine horses, and they took the trail down the river. At Ouray and probably as far as Carson had to pursue the Indian, the Green winds through a vast, dry plain, broken by low mesas, backed on the horizon by mountains. The men were pushing their horses hard, giving them little time to graze even when they could descend the canyon wall to the bank of the river. The animal of Carson's companion gave out and Carson went on alone, determined to finish what he had begun. The thief, encumbered by six horses, began to lose ground. When Kit came in sight and the Indian saw that only one man was after him, he turned to fight. Kit "was under the necessity of killing him."[10]

After Kit returned to Ouray with the horses, some trappers

from upriver arrived and reported that Fitzpatrick and Bridger were on the Little Snake River. These two were important partners of the Rocky Mountain Fur Company. Although illiterate, Bridger was one of the more accomplished of the mountain men. He became famous for his story telling around the campfires and was one of the best loved of the brigade leaders.[11] Carson sought him out time after time.

Hearing that these important captains and their brigades were not far away, Lee decided in March 1934 to go looking for them. The Little Snake, arising in the Park Range near the Elk River, joins the Yampa about thirty miles from its confluence with the Green. After fifteen days, Carson found the trappers. Lee traded the remainder of his goods to Fitzpatrick for beaver and started for Taos.

Carson joined Fitzpatrick, but before the month was out, he decided that he would prefer working with a smaller group, even though the danger from Indians was greater. Finding three men of like mind, he headed for the Laramie. They passed the spring and early summer along the gentle valley between the Medicine Bow Mountains and the Front Range of the Rockies, trapping on the head of the Laramie and its tributaries, avoiding the plains and the danger from roving bands of Indians. They expected to join Bridger for the journey to the rendezvous on Ham's Fork of Black's Fork of the Green River, and as summer advanced, they moved nearer the east-west trails that might bring someone with news of him.

One evening after Carson had chosen a good campsite, he gave his horse to one of his companions and set out up the side of the ridge to find meat for supper. After going about a mile, he saw some elk, maneuvered into a good position, and shot one. Immediately he heard a noise, looked behind him, and saw two huge grizzly bears charging at him. There were too near for him to re-load. He could do nothing but run, hoping to beat the bears to a clump of aspens not far away. As he approached the grove, he could hear the bears so close to his heels that he dropped the gun and jumped for a sturdy tree. He climbed frantically, got ten or fifteen feet from the ground, and clung there. He was confident that the bears would not be able to uproot the tree he was in, and they were too big to climb it (grizzly cubs can climb trees, but mature grizzlies cannot), but he had no idea how long they would keep him treed or whether they might, in their fury, break his gun, for grizzlies had the reputation of knowing the use of guns and of feeling a vengeful antagonism toward them.

One of the bears soon gave up and ambled away. The other tore at the smaller trees around him, attacked the one he was in, and stood upright at its foot roaring with fury. At last it gave up and lumbered away, still growling. After waiting until he felt sure that the bears were out of hearing, Carson dropped limply to the ground, retrieved his rifle, and hastened to camp. By that time it was too late to send for the elk, so the men had nothing to eat before morning, when they feasted on fresh beaver tails.[12]

Ten or fifteen days later Bridger came along. They joined him and rode to the summer camp on Ham's Fork, Carson's first experience at an annual rendezvous. Nathaniel Wyeth of Boston had contracted to bring three thousand dollars worth of goods for the Rocky Mountain Fur Company, but William Sublette was racing to get there first. Neither having arrived, the men were bartering their beaver to other traders for supplies. Because of the labor and expense of bringing supplies to the mountains and the high risk of losing either the goods on the way out or the furs before arriving safely in St. Louis, prices were exorbitant. The wealth in furs with which the men approached the rendezvous diminished rapidly as they paid two dollars a pint for coffee, sugar, or gunpowder, a dollar a bar for lead, fifteen to twenty-five dollars for a woolen blanket.

Besides the necessities, there were liquor and tobacco, and an array of delightful "fooforaw" was spread to entice their generous impulses toward their Indian sweethearts or wives and children— or themselves. Whatever the traders could think of that they might buy was there, and the men were like boys at their first carnival, eager to exchange their earnings for whatever caught their eye.

Ashley had instituted the rendezvous in 1825 as a meeting of the trappers and their company representatives, a practical means of distributing the yearly store of goods. By saving the trappers a trip to the settlements, the rendezvous created the mountain man. Before many years the rendezvous had grown beyond the company.

It attracted Indians by offering goods for trade[13] and was an ideal resting place for travelers. At the rendezvous of 1834 were Jason Lee, Methodist missionary for Oregon, and Sir William Drummond Stewart, Scottish baronet touring the Rockies for pleasure, who attended all the rendezvous from 1833 to 1838.

This rendezvous was also the first for Osborne Russell, a young man of broad and active intelligence and observant and poetic mind, who took detailed and accurate notes on what he saw and did, enjoyed and suffered during almost nine years of trapping in the Rockies. After settling in Oregon, he used these notes to write *Journal of a Trapper*, one of the most fascinating and trustworthy of the firsthand accounts of life as a mountain man. Russell and Carson were companions on many hunts, and events related in Carson's spare prose are sometimes considerably enriched by Russell's colorful, detailed, and often humorous descriptions and observations. Since the book relied on the daily notes describing and dating events as they happened, it is also important in correcting errors that crept into the memory of Carson and Meek as the years passed. Curiously, neither Carson nor Russell ever mentions each other, even though they shared many perilous adventures.[14]

Russell came west as an engagé of Nathaniel Wyeth. When they arrived, William Sublette was already there, pressuring his brother Milton to buy from him and repudiate his agreement with Wyeth. The contract depended upon the continued existence of the Rocky Mountain Fur Company. Fraeb and Gervais were prevailed upon to sell their shares, and the company was dissolved. Having no way of enforcing his contract, Wyeth sold whatever goods he could at the rendezvous and built Fort Hall on the Snake River Plain as a base from which to sell the remainder. He then rode on to Oregon to stake a claim there and meet his ship, the *May Dacre*, which was bringing supplies to trade to the Indians for fish. This project also failed. When he was finally squeezed out of the western trade in 1837, Fort Hall was purchased by the Hudson's Bay Company. Foreign ownership did not prevent this outpost from becoming the main way station west of Fort Laramie for travelers, trappers, and traders.[15]

Competition for beaver pelts had become extremely keen, even unscrupulous, among the traders. Latecomers such as Wyeth,

Gantt, Blackwell, and Bonneville had almost no chance against Bent and St. Vrain, the Hudson's Bay Company, or Astor's American Fur Company. Astor retired in 1834 and sold his Western Department to Pratte, Chouteau and Company of St. Louis. After the Rocky Mountain Fur Company was dissolved, the remaining partners reorganized with Lucien Fontenelle and became Fontenelle, Fitzpatrick and Company. In 1836 Fontenelle and Fitzpatrick could not meet their bills and had to sell out to Pratte, Chouteau and Company.[16] Bridger had been kept as a partner to the last because he was a hard worker and the best of the brigade leaders, one whom the trappers liked and trusted.

Carson joined him as camp was broken up at the end of the rendezvous of 1834. In early September they started for the headwaters of the Missouri—Blackfoot country. About fifty men were in the party, a number of whom were camp keepers. These guarded the equipment and animals and took care of various work about the camp while the other men tended the traps. The party was safe as long as they kept together, but profitable trapping was a solitary trade. At most, only two or three men could work near one another. When the men split off into such small groups, they stood a good chance of stopping Blackfoot arrows or fusil balls. Carson remembered 1834–35 as a poor hunting year: "The Indians were very bad. We had five men killed. A trapper could hardly go a mile without being fired upon. We found that we could do but little in their country, so we started for winter quarters."[17]

In November they camped on the Snake River, where they lived quietly until February 1835, when the Blackfeet came and stole eighteen horses. Carson, Tom Biggs, Mark Head,[18] and nine others followed them about fifty miles through heavy snow. The Indians could force the horses no farther. They had been breaking a trail through the snow, and the trappers were gaining. A few shots were exchanged, but the two parties were not near enough to do each other any damage. The Blackfeet, who had snowshoes, drove the horses to the side of a hill where there was little snow. When the trappers tried to follow, they sank to their waists.

The Blackfeet, though wishing to stay out of range of the trappers' rifles, were determined not to leave the horses. The trappers could not flounder through the snow without putting themselves in danger of a fusil ball; yet they were determined to get back the mounts, one of which was "Bridger's favorite racehorse, Grohean, a Comanche steed of great speed and endurance."[19]

This seemed a time to try diplomacy, and the trappers asked for a parley. The Indians agreed. One man from each side advanced halfway and tried to reach an agreement without losing advantage. The Blackfeet claimed they had not wished to steal from the whites; they had thought the horses belong to Snake Indians. The whites insisted that if they were friendly, they would lay aside their arms and have a smoke and talk. The Blackfeet agreed to this. Both sides laid down their arms and all met between the lines to smoke and talk.

There were thirty Blackfeet, twelve trappers. The Blackfeet finally sent some of their men to bring the horses. The trappers were not ready to relax their guard, but they began to hope that their persistence had brought success. Then they saw the Indians returning, driving the five poorest horses before them. The trappers began protesting, raising their voices and gesticulating toward the animals on the hill. The Blackfeet stoutly insisted that they would bring no more. Peace and friendliness vanished as each side sprang to their arms and sought cover.

Carson and Head were in the advance. Each had picked out an Indian in the rear. From behind trees the two Indians were trying to get a shot at them without exposing themselves. Mark Head's attention was distracted for a moment, and Carson saw Head's Indian raise his gun to fire. Forgetting the danger he himself was in, Carson swung his gun on Head's Indian and fired. As the Indian fell, he remembered his own danger, but he had no time to reload. The other Indian was sighting for his breast. As the Indian fired, he dodged. The ball grazed his neck and passed through his shoulder.

The trappers retreated for a mile and camped for the night in the snow. They dared make no fires, which would reveal them as targets for the Indians. They had no covering but their saddle blankets. Carson's wound ached unbearably, frozen blood clogging the wound. When daylight came, they could see the Indians in the same place, but they were not strong enough to attack. Dismally and painfully they led the five poor animals and rode toward camp.

When they arrived, Bridger took thirty men and rode back to the scene of the battle, but the Indians had gone to the plains.

The camp settled back into its quiet pattern while Carson recovered from the wound. On February 26 he and Biggs visited Fort Hall, Biggs bought sugar and coffee and paid with beaver. Carson also made some purchases, which he paid for with "one gray horse, unbroken." Abel Baker, Jr., storekeeper for Captain Wyeth, perhaps pitying Carson's painful shoulder, treated the two men to a half-pint of rum.[20] Baker may have hoped to even scores with the Sublettes by luring these two mountain men into Wyeth's camp. He may simply have been reveling in a little companionship. Being storekeeper at Fort Hall could be one of the loneliest and dreariest situations in the mountains.[21]

Bridger seems to have felt a particular regret about Carson's wound, received while trying to recover Grohean. Meeting a party of Wyeth's men on Salt River in May, Bridger told them that the country was much infested with Blackfeet, with whom his men had had several skirmishes. Although this was three months after the event, and Carson was probably completely well, Bridger mentioned his having been wounded in the shoulder by a fusil ball.[22]

The brigade was well into the spring hunt by that time. This hunt, by taking the beaver mothers before the young were able to care for themselves, was to a large degree responsible for the rapid decline of the beaver. It was also largely responsible for the painful rheumatism suffered by many of the trappers as they grew older. The traps were set under water, and the men waded sometimes as deep as their thighs while setting them. The cold was numbing, especially at the beginning of the spring hunt, when the streams were barely above freezing, with sheets of ice along the banks and chunks often floating in midstream.

After reporting the fight, Carson says nothing more about the wound. He seems to have been actively engaged in the hunt as the brigade trapped the tributaries of the Snake and the Green Rivers, getting a good supply of beaver ready for the rendezvous before going into summer camp on the Green.

The rendezvous of 1835, like all those Carson attended except that of 1834 and the 1838 gathering on the Popo Agie, was held at the mouth of Horse Creek on the Green River, a geographical center of the trapping area.[23] Realizing the strategic value of this green valley, Captain Bonneville had here built a fort that the other traders dubbed "Fort Nonsense." Even before he removed himself from competition by returning to active duty, however, they recognized his logic and designated his fort as the site for the next rendezvous.

Outsiders present at this rendezvous were Dr. Marcus Whitman, who removed an iron arrowhead, three inches long, from Bridger's back where a Blackfoot warrior had lodged it three years before; Sir William Drummond Stewart; and the Reverend Samuel Parker, who, in his *Journal of an Exploring Tour Beyond the Rocky Mountains*, first brought the name Kit Carson to public notice.[24]

The summer of 1835 was a significant one for Carson, who recounts the following incident with some agitation:

There was in the party of Captain Drips a large Frenchman, one of those overbearing kind and very strong. He made a practice of whipping every man that he was displeased with, and that was nearly all. One day, after he had beaten two or three men, he said that for the Frenchmen, he had no trouble to flog, and as for the Americans, he would take a switch and switch them. I did not like such talk from any man, so I told him that I was the worst American in camp. Many could t[h]rash him, only [they did not] on account of being afraid, and that if he made use of any more such expressions, I would rip his guts.

He said nothing but started for his rifle, mounted his horse, and made his appearance in front of the camp. As soon as I saw him, I mounted my horse and took the first arms I could get ahold of, which was a pistol, galloped up to him and demanded if I was the one which he intended to shoot. Our horses were touching. He said no, but at the same time drawing his gun so he could have a fair shot. I was prepared and allowed him to draw his gun. We both fired at the same time; all present said but one report was heard. I shot him through the arm and his ball passed my head, cutting my hair and the powder burning my eye, the muzzle of his

*gun being near my head when he fired. During our stay in camp
we had no more bother with this bully Frenchman.*[25]

Some accounts state that Kit killed Shunar (the trappers' pro-
nunciation of the bully's name).[26] Kit's account implies the contrary. *'Dear Old Kit'* quotes the *Journal* of Parker, who states that
"Kit 'went for another pistol' but 'Shunar begged that his life
might be spared.'" Parker continued that "the Mountain Men
'would see "fair play" and would "spare the last eye"; and would
not tolerate murder, unless drunkenness or great provocation
could be pleaded in extenuation of guilt.' . . . there is no indication that Carson was drunk and Shunar was giving no provocation
when begging for his life."[27]

Friends have testified that Carson could never tell of this duel
without renewed resentment toward Shunar. He had seen drunken
men make fools of themselves before this without great excitement. Higgins had shot Lawrence on the road out of Los Angeles.
Although Carson did not actually see that episode, he showed no
emotion in his style of telling it. Carson seemed certainly to have
felt a personal resentment toward the Frenchman in addition to
his disgust at the man's braggadocio.

Captain Smith H. Simpson, who knew and served under Carson
in later years, said that Carson told him that he and Shunar were
rivals for the favor of an Indian girl, and he understood it was the
Arapaho girl that Carson married soon afterward.[28] Such a situation, with Carson in love with Waanibe and the big Frenchman
making unseemly advances to her, would have the young man
seething with fury that would need little to cause an explosion.

Kit and Waanibe[29] were probably married shortly after his victory over his rival. Kit never mentions an Indian wife and children
in his memoirs, but he acknowledged among family and friends
that Adaline was his daughter, and many years later Lieutenant
Beale reported a conversation denoting Carson's loyalty to the
memory of his Indian wife.[30]

Chapter 7

Blackfoot Country

Twice Carson left the rendezvous in late summer with Bridger. For both years he traced the same route—the Yellowstone and Bighorn and their tributaries—but in 1835 Bridger led the brigade directly to the Three Forks. On September 9 they came upon signs of another party of trappers on the Madison.[1] With a group of fifteen, Carson rode forward to investigate. On a small branch about three miles from the river, they came upon a party in charge of Joseph Gale, trapping for Nathaniel Wyeth. Osborne Russell, a camp keeper with Gale, left an account of a fight they had had with the Blackfeet, in which three horses were killed, six were stolen and two men were wounded. One of the wounded was Richard Owens who was to become Carson's very good friend.

Though known throughout his mountain career as Dick Owens, at his birth near Baltimore on October 14, 1812, he was named Richard Lemon Owings. Richard Owings, Dick's father, had felt the same westering urge that had carried Lindsey Carson to Missouri, but he had settled on a farm among the wooded hills near Zanesville, Ohio. Less than two years old at the time, Dick could remember no other home. The eldest of six children, he quickly acquired a sturdy self-reliance, endurance, and daring. Apprenticed to a gunsmith at sixteen, Dick could make a flintlock rifle as well as shoot one with accuracy and speed by 1834, when he headed for the Rocky Mountains with an experienced mountaineer named Caleb Wilkins. At Independence they met Nathaniel Wyeth, who was hiring men for his second expedition. Owens, carrying a rifle he had made himself, accompanied Wyeth to Oregon and returned with Captain Joseph Thing, who had been hired to take charge at Fort Hall. Thing took a small party, including Owens, and set out in April 1835 to trade with the friendly Flatheads and Nez Perces on the Salmon River. The Blackfeet attacked and were repelled, but not before they had captured all the trade goods.[2]

About a month later, Owens was a member of Gale's party at Pierre's Hole when sixty completely naked warriors charged the camp. Fifteen or twenty mounted Indians dashed back and forth in front of the camp, brandishing weapons and small poles with dangling scalps and confounding some of the greenhorns by their skilled riding, their paint and feathers, and the weird and ceaseless ululations of their yells. Fusil balls soon sent the Americans to cover, but they retaliated, and after two hours the Indians retreated with mournful lamentations.

Owens was found under an old, overhanging root. Balls had hit the shinbone and passed through the calf and the thigh of one leg. The other foot was pierced by an arrow.[3] Gale took him on a rough and painful journey over the Tetons, across Jackson's Hole, over mountains and down cliffs to Wind River, then over the mountain in a snowstorm to Stinking River,[4] back over the mountains to the Yellowstone, the Gallatin, and finally the Madison. Although the men gave him the easiest gaited horse, handled him as gently as possible ascending and descending the steep slopes and fording the rivers, and paused to rest after especially hard days, Owens suffered greatly. He was still on crutches September 9 when Carson's small band rode up to the camp on the Madison.

Expecting Bridger to follow shortly, Carson's group remained with Gale, sitting late by the campfire telling tales and exchanging news. The next morning some of them went out to set traps. About two miles from camp, eighty Blackfeet attacked, driving them back. They quickly hid the animals in some brush and concealed themselves, preparing to fight. High bluffs towered above the camp, the western side covered with thick groves of aspens, the eastern side very steep and rocky and covered with tall pines. From these bluffs the Blackfeet showered fusil balls upon the camp, doing damage only to Gale's horses in a corral in the open. Ignoring the Indians' taunts and their aimless shooting, the trappers lay quietly in the brush for about three hours, watching alertly for the Blackfeet to expose themselves within range.

The frustrated Indians set fire to the dry grass and rubbish—brush and leaves left by spring floods. A south wind whipped the flames, and in a few minutes flames and smoke were curling over the heads of the trappers. Russell wrote:

Death seemed almost inevitable . . . but all hands began immediately to remove the rubbish around the encampment . . . setting fire to it to act against the flames that were hovering over our heads. . . . Scarce half an hour had elapsed when the fire had passed around us and driven our enemies from their position. At length we saw an Indian whom we supposed to be the Chief standing on a high point of rock and give the signal for retiring which was done by taking hold of the opposite corners of his robe and lifting it up and striking it 3 times on the ground. The cracking of guns then ceased and the party moved off in silence.[5]

Unaware of the setting of a backfire, Kit considered the escape from the flames miraculous. "It was the hand of Providence over us that was the cause. It could have been nothing else, for the brush where we were concealed was dry and easily burned as that which had been consumed."[6] He also believed that the Indians had heard of the approach of Bridger's men and decided to leave before they were surrounded and wiped out.

As soon as the Indians were out of sight, Carson's group prepared to return to the main camp, now about six miles away. In the two battles Gale had lost twelve animals, and five had been badly wounded. Seeing that his party could no longer travel without help, he followed Carson to Bridger's camp.

At sunrise on September 12 the men looked up and saw a line of Indians on a ridge to the west. In their center stood a small pole, and from it waved an American flag. They were Piegans, a branch of the Blackfeet, now eager to be friends although some of them had been present when Owens was wounded. As they sat and smoked, the chief related that the mournful cries with which they had departed from that fight were for four men killed and many wounded. Eight of these had died before reaching their village.[7] Carson does not mention this encounter, one of the few instances of Blackfeet wishing to be friends with Americans. He may have been out trapping, or the two parties may not have camped very close together.

The next day the two brigades left the Madison Fork for Stinking Creek.[8] Carson, riding about eight miles ahead of the brigade, saw a number of ravens hovering in the distance and rode forward to look for the cause. Near the carcass of a bear that had lately been killed, he saw a fresh Indian trail taking the course he planned to go. Immediately he turned back to join his companions. The day Bridger's men arrived at Stinking Creek, a trapper was killed by the Blackfeet. For eight days the Indians watched them constantly, sniping at them daily, especially if they rode away from the group. Hunting being impossible on Stinking Creek, they headed for the Jefferson.

About four days' march up the Jefferson, they caught up with a large band of Flathead and Pend Oreille Indians, northern tribes living mostly west of the Rockies. Both tribes were friendly toward whites. As the trappers moved south, they were joined by several of these people and their chief, probably Insala, whose daughter had recently become Bridger's wife. On the Beaverhead, they found Francis Ermatinger of the Hudson's Bay Company "endeavoring to trade every Beaver skin as fast as they were taken from the water by the Indians."[9] At the headwaters of the Jefferson they came to high, rolling hills, which they descended to a smooth valley about eighty miles in circumference and full of buffalo herds. After a day hunting and feasting on fat hump ribs, boudins, and other delicacies, they crossed the mountains to Camas Creek, so named for a small plant with a nutritious root highly prized by Indians and trappers.

Gale had been using some of Bridger's animals to replace those killed by the Blackfeet. At this point he sent Russell, alone, against the urgent advice of Bridger and his men, to Fort Hall to bring more horses so that he could dispense with Bridger's help. Not having received clear directions, Russell followed the creek until it sank into the dry, rocky ground, then tramped without water for two days until his way was blocked by lava beds. His horse was exhausted and lame, its hoofs worn to the quick. Leading the animal, he turned back west and reached one of the lost streams[10] of the Salmon River Mountains, its valley teeming with buffalo.

As he was reveling in the cool water and shade, a band of Indians came streaming through a gap in the mountains. He lay hidden among the willows, wondering at the Indians' skill with bows and arrows. "Upwards of a Thousand Cows were killed without burning a single grain of powder." Near him, a hunter "let slip an arrow" into a galloping cow and she fell. Recognizing the man as an acquaintance of the Bannock tribe, met while he was keeping store at Fort Hall, Russell rose to his feet. The hunter stopped and spoke to him in Shoshone.[11] He replied in the same tongue. The Indian invited him to remain with the camp, and placed a piece of clothing on a stick to show his wife where she was to set his lodge.

When Russell left this village a week later, carrying a good supply of boiled buffalo tongues, he rode due east to the Snake River. After another week with a Snake chief, who enjoyed as much as he did exchanging jokes and stories in the Shoshone language, he rode on to Fort Hall to await the arrival of Wyeth, from whose service he was eager to resign so as to try his luck as a free trapper. When he rejoined Bridger on the Snake River in February, Carson was about ready to go off with a Hudson's Bay Company leader, Thomas McKay.

McKay was the stepson of Dr. John McLoughlin of Vancouver. His half-Cree mother, Marguerite, had married McLoughlin after having been deserted by Alexander McKay, who had later died when the supply ship *Tonquin* was destroyed by the Indians of Nootka Sound.[12] McKay's callous attitude toward his wife had not extended to his son, whom he had given a good start in the fur trade. When McKay let it be known that he was taking a brigade south of the mountains to Mary's River, Carson, Antoine Godin, and four others joined him.[13] Carson had not seen Mary's River, but he had heard that beaver were plentiful there, and it was relatively near to Fort Hall.[14] He may have been influenced by the fact

74

that the Hudson's Bay Company encouraged wives of the trappers to accompany the brigades.

This was altogether a disappointing excursion. Mary's River, first explored by Peter Skene Ogden and named for his Indian wife, wound across a flat plain between eroded ridges, both plain and slopes covered by stunted brown sage.[15] Here and there the river supported a clump of willows or a cottonwood; looking across the plain in other places, one would not know that a river was there. The adaptability of the beaver is shown by the fact that this lover of the cool, swift streams of the mountain canyons was also at home in the Mary's and the lower Gila, winding between bare banks through desert sands under a relentless sun.

The brigade followed the river to where it flows into Mary's Lake, then ascended it some eighty miles, but took few beaver. Turning across the mountains to the north, they reached the Snake River, which McKay followed toward Fort Walla Walla.[16] Carson and the others turned upstream toward Fort Hall. "On our march we found no game; the country was barren. For many days the only food we [had] was roots and we would bleed our horses and cook the blood. About four days travel before we got to the fort, we met a party of Indians. I traded with them for a fat horse, which we killed. [We] feasted for a couple of days and then started for the Fort."[17] That the six men found enough roots to keep them alive suggests that Waanibe may have been with them, as does the fact that no purchases of beads were charged to Kit in his absence.

Wyeth's people at Fort Hall received them with kindness and treated them well. After a few days of rest, they started to hunt buffalo, which they found in abundance within a day's ride. The Blackfeet must have seen them hunting and followed them back to the fort in order to carry out a bold and ingenious plan. During the night, when the sentinel saw two men approach the corral, let down the bars, and drive out the animals, he assumed that they were some of the owners turning out the stock to graze. The next morning the trappers easily recognized the moccasin prints of the Blackfeet. Being now afoot, however, they had to remain at the fort while the Indians rode their horses up the Snake toward the mountains.

In about a month Thomas McKay came by. Carson bought some animals from him and accompanied him to the rendezvous at the mouth of Horse Creek on Green River.[18] Dr. Marcus Whitman, H. H. Spalding, their wives, and W. H. Gray, Presbyterian missionaries on their way to devote their lives to the Indians of Oregon, had come to the rendezvous with Fitzpatrick's caravan. Narcissa Whitman and Eliza Spalding, the first white women to cross on the Oregon Trail, excited much curiosity among the Indians and much acting-up among the trappers.

Meek stated that he, Newell, and Carson accompanied Drips and a small party of trappers along the trail toward the Laramie to meet the caravan. They were so pestered by Indians that, after the second night, they turned back. All had lost their mounts except Carson and Meek, who had slept with their horses tied to themselves with long ropes. They found Newell wandering on foot, helped him find his horse, and all rode back to the rendezvous.

Meek then got up a party of trappers dressed as Indians and, as the missionaries approached, rode out to meet them at a dead run, yelling, making threatening gestures, whooping. Racing down beside the caravan, they fired a volley over the heads of the travelers, then raced into a circle to show off their horsemanship. Meek had had the forethought to carry a white flag, reassuring the ladies that the parade was all in fun.[19] Although alarmed at first, Narcissa and Eliza were soon watching the antics with amusement, but they were more deeply interested in a welcoming committee of Indian women, who shook their hands and each gave them a hearty kiss.[20] No mention is made of a meeting between them and Carson.

In August, Carson and five others returned to Fort Hall and joined a party of the Hudson's Bay Company that was on its way to the Salmon River, where Kit had spent his first winter in the Rockies. They trapped the Salmon to its head in the Sawtooth Range, crossed over to the head of the Malade River,[21] and followed it to the Snake. Ascending the Snake, they trapped Goose Creek and Raft River, then took the furs to Fort Hall and disposed of them before the middle of October.[22]

Carson remained at the fort for a month, then headed across the

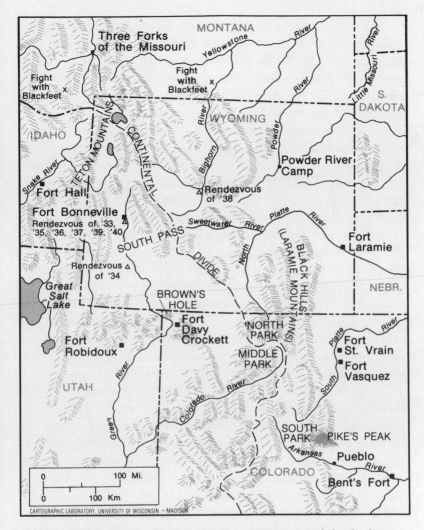

Carson in the Rendezvous Country, 1831–41: Carson attended only the rendezvous from 1835 through 1840.

mountains to the Yellowstone, where he found Bridger at Clark's Fork. The route of his fall hunt and the month's pause at the fort are both puzzling, for he obviously wished to be with Bridger's brigade. It is possible that, since Adaline, his first child, was born about this time, he left Waanibe at the fort so that she would be near other Indian women, and upon his return from the Salmon, remained long enough to see that she was provided for.

When he reached Clark's Fork, a dramatic confrontation with the Blackfeet was about to take place. On January 29, 1837, a few men were out hunting not far from camp when suddenly the Blackfeet were all around them. Isaac P. Rose was wounded in his right arm with a poisoned ball. His rifle fell, and an Indian snatched it up and shot after the trappers as they scampered away. Rose's arm bled copiously, thereby saving his life.[23] A few days later a party of twenty Indians were seen crossing the plain. A party of trappers, Carson among them, set off in pursuit. The Blackfeet took refuge on an island in the Yellowstone, where they ran into some old Indian forts. The trappers surrounded them and kept up a constant fire until sunset. Again one man was wounded, the Delaware, Manhead. A poisoned ball lodged under his kneecap. He lived in agony for four days, then died.

The morning after the fight, the trappers returned and found that the Indians had left. The conical forts were spattered with brains and blood, and a trail led to a hole in the ice where the Indians had disposed of their dead. Another trail showed where the wounded had been dragged away on travois. Bridger began to prepare for the Indians' return. "Now, boys, the Indians are close," he told the men. "There will in a short time be a party of five or six hundred return to avenge the death of those . . . slain."[24]

Not far from the camp a large butte made a convenient observation post. Someone was stationed there during all daylight hours. Bridger often took his spyglass to the top and surveyed the plain and the adjoining hills. On February 22, when he came down, the men learned that the Indians were on the move. Bridger had seen them coming across the hills to the timber about ten miles below.

The Yellowstone and Clark's Fork come together gradually, leaving a broad valley to the north, a range of steep bluffs to the south. The tongue of land between was low and marshy, covered with an open growth of large cottonwoods. Bridger set everyone to work felling trees and building a breastwork of logs and brush six feet high, enclosing a square 250 feet on a side.

The Indians were also making fortifications. They kept coming for three days, until the plain was alive with them. When the last of them arrived, they had constructed 111 small, conical forts, which would accommodate about eleven hundred warriors. "They had a war dance. We could hear their songs and we well knew that in the morning they would attack."[25]

The trappers numbered about sixty, but they wanted the Indians to attack. With the assistance of their fort, which Carson thought nothing but artillery could damage, they were completely confident that victory would be theirs. At sunset a double guard was mounted. Russell, who had the watch from nine until midnight, noted that the night was bitterly cold, the stars unusually bright, the trees popping like pistol shots as sap froze under the bark. About ten o'clock the northern lights commenced streaming upward, "darting, flashing, rushing to and fro like the movements of an army. At length the shooting and flashing died away and gradually turned to a deep, blood red, spreading over half the sky." After two hours the color slowly faded.[26]

On February 23 the men continued working on their fort, expecting an attack any hour. About two o'clock Bridger and six men rode out to reconnoiter and found the enemy encamped about three miles away on the river. The night again passed without disturbance. About sunrise of the twenty-fourth, a solitary Indian crept up behind the trees and shot at Bridger's cook who was gathering firewood. Marcelino Baca, ordered to the butte to look out, found an Indian in the observatory. As the Mexican approached, the Indian rose up. Marcelino wheeled and ran. The Indian shot him in the heel as he leaped over the bluff and took a fifty-foot slide on the snow to the bottom. This was the only casualty and the extent of hostilities.

About half an hour later the Blackfeet in close columns started marching across the Yellowstone on the ice, turned off into the plain at about four hundred yards, and called a halt. A chief wearing a white blanket came forward a few steps and gave the signal that he would not fight but would return to his village. The Indians then turned and streamed across the plain toward the Three Forks of the Missouri.

After much discussion the trappers came to the conclusion that the display of the aurora borealis a few nights previously, with half the sky blood-red and the other half clear and serene, had convinced the Indians that they had a negative sign from the Great Spirit, a conviction strengthened by the impregnable fortifications around Bridger's camp.

Three days later the brigade left the fort and rode toward the Bighorn. Around Beauvais Fork, wrote Russell, they found plenty of buffalo, "and then began to slay and eat, but we slayed so much faster than we eat that our meat scaffolds groand under the weight of fat buffalo meat."[27] They camped here until March 14, when a Crow village under Long Hair arrived. This dropsical old chief had kept gluing loose hair to his queue until in 1837, at the age of eighty, he had hair eleven and a half feet long that gave him great power among his tribe. After studying the grim faces of the trappers, Long Hair decided that at present he was for peace.

When Bridger turned toward the Bighorn, Carson turned west and "trapped the tributaries of the Missouri to the head of Lewis Fork, and then started for rendezvous on Green River, near the mouth of Horse Creek."[28] This statement was a camouflage for family matters that Carson did not wish to share with his readers. He did turn toward the head of Lewis Fork of the Snake. He doubtless set traps and took a beaver or two if he camped in a promising spot. But whatever had kept him near Fort Hall during the spring and fall was now drawing him swiftly back there.

Entries in the *Fort Hall Account Books* show that Waanibe had not been idle while he was away. On January 23, 1837, nine bunches of cut beads were charged to Carson's account.[29] At three dollars a bunch, this was a considerable piece of extravagance for a young wife whose husband's income was uncertain. She may have been ornamenting with beadwork some things she had made for her baby, her husband, or herself. She could have been wearing all the strings at once around her neck to impress the other women and increase her status among them.

Carson had returned by April 10, when he bought a pound of tobacco at the fort. On May 27 he traded two beaver skins and some castoreum for supplies, but by June 6 he had to fall back on trading in a trap, and again on July 5. His spring trapping had been meager.

The rendezvous of 1837 was momentous and dramatic. Russell states that nearly every tribe of the Rocky Mountains was represented. Waanibe probably set up her lodge with the Arapahoes at some distance from Bridger's camp, for Kit makes no mention of the fight with the Bannocks. Nor does he mention Sir William Drummond Stewart and his artist, Alfred Jacob Miller, who was painting Jim Bridger wearing a full suit of armor, with the great plain of the Green River, dotted with teepees, in the background.[30]

The fight with the Bannocks demonstrated the loyalty of the trappers as well as the ferocity of punishment they could deal out when aroused. Some of the Bannock Indians had been stealing horses and traps and had killed two white trappers. Now the thieves were camped within three miles of Bridger, brazenly riding about on stolen horses. Four or five whites and two Nez Perce Indians went to their village while the men were out hunting and brought back the stolen animals, one of which belonged to Insala.[31]

Soon thirty Bannocks came galloping up, armed for war, and demanded the horses the Nez Perces had taken (the latter, being only six in number, had given the horses to the whites for protection). As brigade leader, and also as son-in-law of Chief Insala, Bridger was obligated to protect the Nez Perces in his band, and he refused to give up the horses. A fierce-looking Bannock called out in his own tongue, "We came here to get the horses or blood and let us do it." Russell understood him and repeated what he had said. Those whites who were not already armed made haste to get ready.

Bridger stood holding Insala's horse by the bridle. One of the Bannocks rushed through the crowd, seized the bridle, and attempted to drag it from Bridger's hand. He was instantly killed.[32] The others wheeled to run, but twelve were downed before they could get out of rifle range. In the confusion Umentucken, the Indian wife whom Joe Meek had inherited from his friend, Milton Sublette, was shot through the breast and instantly killed by a stray Bannock arrow.[33] The trappers jumped on their horses, followed the Bannocks, and fought them for three days until they begged to be left alone and promised good behavior in the future.[34]

Chapter 8

Decline of the Mountain Men

Pratte, Chouteau and Company, still widely known as the American Fur Company, had absorbed its last competition among American traders in the northern Rockies in 1836, when the successors of the Rocky Mountain Fur Company succumbed. Its long-standing representative in the Rockies, Lucien B. Fontenelle, had been associated with Bridger as a partner in 1834.[1] When the rendezvous of 1837 ended, Fontenelle, with Bridger as pilot, started for Blackfoot country with a hundred ten men, among whom were Carson and Russell.

This was a good year for Carson. With a strong force of fifty trappers and fifty camp keepers, the men were determined to trap wherever they pleased and were prepared to fight for the right to do so. They trapped the Yellowstone, Otter, and Musselshell Rivers and then turned up the Bighorn. Crossing over to Powder River, they made winter camp, puzzled because the Blackfeet had not attacked. A Crow village camped near them and remained during the winter. From these Indians, who respected and feared Bridger, they learned that smallpox had broken out among the Blackfeet, and they had fled north of the Missouri.[2]

Powder River arises in the Rattlesnake Range near Casper Creek, which flows into the North Platte about a hundred fifty miles northwest of Fort Laramie.[3] Most tributaries of the Powder arise in and cross the plains and contribute little water or none at all. Crazy Woman Creek and Clear Creek "speedily lose their mountain exhilaration" after leaving the Bighorns and add but little to the volume of the Powder as it winds northeast to its junction with the Yellowstone. Much of its bed is quicksand, but during the winter of 1837–38, one of the coldest Carson had ever experienced, the river was frozen. Corralling the animals to keep them from the Indians and to protect them from the buffalo, the men spent much of their time pulling bark from the sweet cottonwood trees and throwing it by large fires to thaw it out for the horses. These fires also served to keep away the buffalo, which came in such large droves that Carson said, "Our horses were in danger of being killed by them when we turned them out to eat the bark."[4]

If Joe Meek is to be believed, the buffalo were not always so available. He tells of going hunting on the Powder with Carson and a little Frenchman named Marteau. Meek stayed with the pack animals. Marteau rode Meek's horse, which was a good buffalo hunter; Carson rode his own, which was not. The horse fell with Marteau, knocking him unconscious. Kit caught Meek's horse, left his own, and killed four fat cows. When Meek came up, he asked Kit why he had changed horses. Kit explained and asked Meek if he had seen Marteau, who could have been killed by the fall.

> "You go over to the other side of yon hill, and see," said Kit.
> "What'll I do if he is dead?" said I.
> "Can't you pack him to camp?"
> "Pack h——l!" said I; "I should rather pack a load of meat."
> "Waal," said Kit, "I'll butcher, if you'll go over and see, anyhow."
> So I went over, and found the dead man leaning his head on his hand, and groaning; for he war pretty bad hurt. I got him on his horse, though, after a while, and took him back to whar Kit war at work. We soon finished the butchering job, and started back to camp with our wounded Frenchman and three loads of fat meat.[5]

Meek did not feel that he was being callous about Marteau;

peace or war, it was each man for himself. "Being compassionate war not our business. We had no time for such things. Besides, live men war what we wanted; dead men war of no account." Meek often talked more harshly than he acted, but his attitude hardly conforms to Carson's concept of brotherly concern among mountain men.

Around the first of April, the brigade turned northwest from the camp on the Powder, crossing the plain to the Yellowstone. They trapped upstream to the mouth of Twenty-Five Yard River, turned upstream, then crossed over to the Three Forks of the Missouri, trapping the small streams as they went until they reached the Gallatin.[6]

Although he does not say so, Carson followed the pattern of trapping practiced by a large band of men, as depicted by Russell. About thirty men left the camp at a gallop. As they saw a likely place to set their traps, they silently dropped off one or two at a time. By sunset the last two would be setting their traps and getting ready to camp. The next morning they set the remainder of their traps as they dropped downstream. Soon they came upon two more trappers and camped with them. By the end of the day, the camp would grow to ten or twelve men. Thus they ranged the mountain valleys, climbing over a ridge when necessary, keeping loosely in touch but not actually together, for about a week. The main camp caught up with them; they moved on with it to another likely place and made another foray along the streams.

When the brigade reached the Gallatin River, they turned upstream, took a tributary to the west, crossed the mountain to the Madison, and came upon the trail of a village of Blackfeet. There was still smallpox among these Indians. The trappers passed a lodge standing abandoned in the prairie near the river. Three dead bodies lay inside. Bridger thought to bypass the Indians, but the men objected so strenuously to trying to avoid Blackfeet who outnumbered them only three to one that he turned back to the Madison.[7]

Carson and five others rode ahead to observe the Indians' strength. Finding them driving in their animals and making preparations to move their camp, the trappers rode back to the main party, who had arrived within four miles of the village. Determined to prove who had a right to hunt in this country, forty men, including Carson, started for the village, leaving sixty men to guard the camp. At the first attack, the Blackfeet began a slow retreat while the village moved ahead. The trappers pushed after them, firing at will. When the ammunition began to give out, the Indians quickly became aware of their advantage and turned to the attack. The trappers ran for camp. The Indians charged after them. Whirling back, the trappers fired into the onrushing crowd, driving them back, then retreating as far as they could before the Indians recovered and charged again.

As they were passing a point of rocks, the horse of "Cotton" Mansfield fell, pinning him down. As six Indians made for him, he called out, "Tell Old Gabe that Old Cotton is gone!"[8] Carson dismounted, fired, and killed one Indian. The others ran, giving Cotton's horse time to get to its feet. Cotton quickly mounted and headed for camp. When Carson fired, his horse broke away and joined the retreat. A man named White was passing. Carson called. White turned, saw the danger, pulled up to let Carson jump up behind, and raced for camp.

The Indians ran among a pile of rocks about a hundred fifty yards away and the firing continued. "Finding that no execution could be done," Carson recalled, "we concluded to charge them; done so. It was the prettiest fight I ever saw. . . . I would often see a white man on one side and an Indian on the other side of a rock, not ten feet apart, each dodging and trying to get the first shot."[9]

After losing several men, the Blackfeet retreated to their village. The next morning they stationed themselves across the bench along which the trappers were riding to bypass the village, but a sudden and determined charge dislodged them, and the brigade continued up the Madison.[10]

Where the Madison came in from the east, they crossed the mountains over an undulating plain and descended to camp at Henry's Lake.[11] There they discovered another village of Blackfeet, consisting of fifteen lodges. They prepared to wipe it off the face of the earth, but when about two miles from the village, they met six men coming unarmed to invite them, "in the most humble and submissive manner to their village to smoke and trade. This proceeding conquered the bravest in our camp."[12]

After stopping to trade with these Blackfeet, they followed an Indian trail through the pine woods to the plain of Snake River, cut across to Pierre's Fork, and crossed the Tetons to Jackson's Hole. Across the mountain on the head of Green River, an express overtook them and they learned that the rendezvous was to be at the mouth of the Popo Agie. Crossing the divide, they came upon the headwaters of Wind River and followed it to the plain.

At this rendezvous of 1838 the Swiss adventurer, Captain J. A. Sutter, bought an Indian boy from Bill Brown, who said he had bought him from Carson.[13] Where, how, and from whom Kit acquired the boy is a mystery, but the trappers frequently bought children who had been captured by enemy tribes to save the children from maltreatment or death. On the Popo Agie Sir William Drummond Stewart was attending his last rendezvous. Carson remembered him at this time as "a man that will be forever remembered by the mountaineers that had the honor of his acquaintance for his liberality to them and for his many good qualities."[14]

Jason Lee, on his way to visit the States, rode up with Francis Ermatinger. Nine other missionaries bound for Oregon had come with Andrew Drips, who had brought twenty horse carts loaded with supplies, but a rumor was going about that the American Fur Company planned to bring no more supplies to the Rocky Mountains. The trappers were uneasy, and many of them left the brigade.[15]

Whether for this reason or because of anxiety about his family, Carson did not depart with Drips and Bridger on the fall hunt of 1838. With seven other men he rode to Brown's Hole, a portion of the Green River Valley about thirty miles long and six miles wide and almost enclosed by the Uintah Mountains. The river entered the valley through Red Canyon from the northwest, ran smooth and broad through the valley, then plunged into Lodore Canyon on the southeast. Vegetation stayed green all year, and the climate remained mild, making the valley a favorite wintering place for Indians. The Arkansas trappers under Alexander Sinclair wintered there in 1831–32.[16]

Here, about four years later, Alexander's brother, Prewett Sinclair, Philip Thompson, and William Craig opened a trading post just above the confluence of Vermillion Creek and Green River. It later became known as Fort Davy Crockett. During the years 1839 and 1840, with the decline of the fur trade setting many trappers to a rather aimless wandering in the mountains, this post became a sort of perpetual rendezvous. Thompson, Sinclair, and Craig brought their own goods from St. Louis and took laden packhorses to the Indian villages. Other traders also brought goods for trade with the Indians who wintered in this sheltered valley by the Green.

In 1838 Carson joined Thompson and Sinclair's party on a trading expedition to the Navajo Indians. Nineteen-year-old Seth Ward, who later became a leading financier in the region, went on this expedition as camp keeper.

The acquaintance between Carson and Ward soon ripened into a strong friendship, each recognizing the traits of manhood in the other. Mr. Ward's first horse was a present to him from Carson, who had won it upon a wager with Philip Thompson, who maintained that no greenhorn could bring down a buffalo at first dash. Ward accomplished the feat, but his horse coming in collision with the wounded buffalo he was thrown heavily to the ground and carried to camp in an unconscious condition.[17]

It seemed only fair that the horse should go to the youth who, with pluck, skill, and suffering, had won it.

After the trading expedition, Carson, as hunter for the fort, had to keep twenty men in venison. Since the valley was secluded from main routes of travel, finding game did not take him far from the fort. He records having hunted for the fort during the winter, but his reconstruction of the events of the following year does not appear to be accurate.

In the Spring, I joined Bridger. In the party there was myself, Dick Owens, and three Canadians. We five started for the Black Hills to hunt.[18] We trapped the streams in the vicinity of the hills. We separated; Owens and myself taking one course, and the Canadians another. We trapped for three months, made a good hunt,

and then started to find the main camp. We found it on a tribu-
tary of Green River. We remained with the main party till the
month of July, and then went into rendezvous on the Popoaghi, a
tributary of Wind River. About the 20th of August, we started for
the Yellowstone, trapped all the streams within the vicinity of the
Yellowstone and on it went into Winter quarters.[19]

Of all this, only two things seem likely. He and Dick Owens
may have trapped in the Laramie Mountains during the spring of
1839 and taken their furs to the rendezvous on Green River—not
the Popo Agie; only one rendezvous was held there. But the remainder of this account appears to be filler, or camouflage for
events Carson had no wish to relate. Bridger is believed to have left
the mountains for St. Louis late in 1838 or early in 1839 and returned with the supply train of 1840.[20] Carson and Owens spent
the latter part of 1839 at Brown's Hole.

One of Carson's strong characteristics was a sense of duty.
When he took Waanibe to wife, he assumed responsibility for her.
During her first pregnancy, he trapped near Fort Hall, went to join
Bridger for a time, but left the brigade and hurried back to Fort
Hall. During the period from 1839 to 1841, Waanibe gave birth to
another daughter and died not long afterward, some say of a
fever.[21] Since his policy appears to have been not to share with his
readers his memories of his family life, he had little to relate during the winter of 1839–40.

Carson and Owens were certainly in Brown's Hole that winter.
On August 11, 1839, Robert Newell, Andrew Drips, and several
others left Fort Hall for Brown's Hole with five horse loads of
goods to trade with trappers and Indians. On August 23, they
crossed a rise in the sage-covered hills and found Carson and
Owens on Muddy Creek, a tributary of Black's Fork. They all rode
on to Brown's Hole together. Soon Abel Baker, Jr., arrived to trade
for Bent and St. Vrain and Thomas Biggs to trade for Vasquez and
Sublette.[22]

On October 1, 1839, E. Willard Smith, traveling to see the country, arrived at Brown's Hole and found it a noisy and busy place,
with about twenty lodges of Indians as well as the trappers and
traders.[23] Near the Little Snake River, Smith had seen a camp left

by buffalo hunters, with racks for drying meat, and the skeletons of four horses, killed in a fight with Indians. A breastwork of logs stood where the hunters had defended themselves. Smith spoke to a small, blue-eyed, mild-looking man at the fort, found that his name was Kit Carson, and asked him about the battle. Kit told him the following story.

Seven white men and the Indian wives of two of them had been at the spot for several days and had dried a large quantity of meat. One morning, while it was still dark, they were attacked by about twenty Sioux, who fired mostly at a man named Spiller as he lay asleep and pierced him with five balls. The rest of the men began to strengthen a horse pen they had made of logs, digging holes for the men to stand in. At daybreak they commenced firing at the Indians, killing and wounding several. The principal chief rode toward them and made offers of peace. One of the hunters went outside and induced the chief, with several others, to come nearer. When the Indians were within range, the white man fell back behind some trees and gave the signal to fire. The chief and two others were killed. The Indians fired for some time and then retreated. Smith did not record the names of the hunters.

Smith does not mention Carson again by name, but he does report a horse-stealing incident, to which Doc Newell also refers, in which both Carson and Joe Meek became involved in restoration of the stolen horses.[24] Apprehending no danger, the trappers and Snake Indians were in the habit of letting their animals run loose in the valley. According to Smith, on the night of November 1, ten Sioux came into the valley—from the east, access was an easy descent from the plain—and drove off a hundred fifty horses. At first the trappers were determined to follow and retrieve the animals, but considering that severe weather was to be expected at this time of year and the Sioux could easily beat them across the mountains, they abandoned the idea. The next morning twelve men rode to Fort Hall, belonging now to the Hudson's Bay Company, and stole several horses as they left. On their way back, they stopped at a Snake Indian encampment of three lodges. At the lodge of a very old man they were treated hospitably and invited to eat. At evening they left the old man, taking all his horses.[25]

Many trappers were outraged, both from sympathy with the Indians, who came protesting to the fort, and from knowledge that the Indians were more accomplished thieves than the whites, all of whom would probably be punished for the thieving of a few. Craig, Newell, Carson, Meek, and twenty-five others, under the command of Joseph Walker, followed the trail to the mouth of the Uintah River, where the thieves had driven the horses to an island in Green River and made themselves at home in Robidoux's old adobe fort.[26]

Walker made an effort to get the horses off the island undiscovered.

But while horses and men were crossing the river on the ice, the ice sinking with them until the water was knee-deep, the robbers discovered the escape of their booty, and charging on the trappers tried to recover the animals. . . . Walker made a masterly flank movement and getting in Thompson's rear, ran the horses into the fort, where he stationed his men, and succeeded in keeping the robbers on the outside.[27]

Thompson then started giving the horses away to Utes living in the neighborhood, on condition that they help retake them. Walker threatened the Utes with dire vengeance if they interfered. The Utes refused to take sides, and finally, with Thompson and his party looking on, Walker marched men and horses back up the Green and returned the animals to their owners. Carson and the others under Walker were concerned to see justice done, but they did not attempt to punish the horse thieves. Nor did Carson allow the fact that Dick Owens was among the horse thieves to disrupt their friendship, which continued as long as Owens remained in the West. Kit does not mention this affair in his *Memoirs*.

Newell and Meek took three hundred beaver to Fort Hall in February, the deep snow and lack of game keeping them on the trail for forty-five days. Ermatinger arrived the first of June, and Newell went to the American rendezvous at Horse Creek, where Bridger, Drips, and Fraeb brought goods from St. Louis. Harvey Clark, Philo R. Littlejohn, and Alvin T. Smith were on their way to Oregon as missionaries, as was the Catholic priest, Father Pierre Jean De Smet. Newell engaged to guide the Protestants over the mountains in their wagons. He persuaded them to sell the wagons at Fort Hall, but later in the year he returned, and he and Joe Meek acquired the wagons and used them to move their families westward. One lasted for the entire journey, making Newell the first man to bring a wagon all the way over the mountains to Oregon.[28]

In recounting events of that spring and summer, 1840, Carson begins vaguely, "Bridger and party started for rendezvous on Green River. Jack Robison and myself for the Utah country, to Robidoux's fort, and there disposed of the furs we caught on our march."[29] Though he was not with Bridger, who was out on the plains with the caravan from St. Louis, Carson probably was with Robertson. If Waanibe died during the winter of 1839–40 at Brown's Hole, Carson had to make arrangements for the care of his two little girls. The Indian population around Fort Davy Crockett was composed of wandering tribes. If he left the children with one of them, he might never see them again. Robidoux, on the other hand, had a fairly stable household of Indian women, and Jack Robertson, who had a cabin on Black's Fork and is known to have been of kindly disposition, may have offered to help Carson take the children to the fort on the Uintah.[30] His Indian wife, Marook, may have taken care of the children on the journey.

After, or possibly before, taking the children to Fort Uintah, Carson rode to the rendezvous at Horse Creek. He speaks with great affection and admiration of Father De Smet. "Among the missionaries was old father de Smitt . . . if ever there was a man that wished to do good, he is one. He never feared when duty required his presence among the savages and if good works on this earth are rewarded hereafter I am confident that his share of glory and happiness in the next world will be great."[31] Carson remembered his meeting with the priest as having happened in an earlier year, but Father De Smet was not in the West before 1840. Carson must have had more than a mere glimpse of him. Perhaps, in his perplexing situation, he asked the good father's advice. De Smet had many children to baptize; Carson's may have been among them.[32] The priest later became famous as a missionary among the Flatheads.[33]

Carson's account of activities after the rendezvous of 1840 is brief but accurate:

In the fall, six of us went to Grand River, and there made our hunt and passed the winter at Brown's Hole on Green River. In the Spring [1841], went back to the Utah Country and into the New Park and made the Spring hunt. Returned to Robidoux Fort and disposed of our Beaver and remained till September [1841].

Beaver was getting scarce, and, finding it was necessary to try our hand at something else, Bill Williams, Bill New, Mitchell, Frederick, a Frenchman, and myself concluded to start for Bent's Fort on the Arkansas.[34]

All of these, except Carson and possibly the Frenchman, had gone on the great horse-stealing jaunt to California. After the abortive attempt to become horse thieves on the Green River, Thompson, Mitchell, New, Owens, and the other frustrated robbers had started for California, their party increased by Old Bill Williams, "Cut-Nose" Frederick, Peg-Leg Smith, Jean B. Charlefoux, and other men of various nationalities. They stole several thousand horses from missions and ranches. Finding themselves pursued by law-enforcement officers of California, Williams and his faithful retainer, Jesús Archuleta (Pepe), stalked the camp of the officers and stole all their horses. The next day they negotiated with the Californians, agreeing to return the officers' mounts if the pursuit were abandoned.

Thereafter the flight across the desert was less headlong, but half the animals died before reaching the plentiful grass and water of the Rockies. Williams is said to have turned his share of the animals into the corral at Bent's Fort and settled for a barrel of whiskey.[35]

This jaunt, though wild enough, was not quite so criminal as it sounds. Since the republic of Mexico had secularized the missions, many horses were roaming unclaimed, so the mission horses the thieves brought back were not necessarily stolen; those from the ranches indisputably were. After disposing of the horses, many of them at the rendezvous of 1840, the men gravitated to the forts and talked of the condition of the fur trade and of opportunities open to former trappers. From these discussions came the first steps toward a return to life outside the mountains, where each of them followed the way chance and his former life seemed to point, driving for freighters, guiding emigrants and soldiers, trading or running ferries on the trails.

The future must have appeared perplexing and rather awesome to the men who started for Bent's Fort in the fall of 1841, their Indian wives probably having charge of Carson's two small daughters. Carson tells briefly of this journey:

Arrived on the Arkansas about one hundred miles above the fort. Mitchell and New concluded to remain; they apprehended no danger from Indians. We continued on for the fort, arrived in a few days. Ten days after our arrival, Mitchell and New came. They were naked. The Indians run off all their animals, and stole from them everything they had.

I was kindly received at the fort by Messrs. Bent and St. Vrain, offered employment to hunt for the Fort at one dollar per day. Accepted this offer, and remained in their employ till 1842. I wish I was capable to do Bent and St. Vrain justice for the kindness received at their hands. I can only say that their equals were never in the mountains.[36]

An interesting development in Carson's memories of this period is the appearance of expressions of profound gratitude for favors received, first from the people at Fort Hall in 1836, later from Stewart at the rendezvous of 1838, then from Father De Smet in 1840, and finally from the people of Bent's Fort in 1841. He had expected no special favors as a single man and apparently received none. The conclusion seems to be that these expressions of gratitude are in recognition of kindness shown Waanibe and the two children. An unwonted note of pathos sounds in his farewell to the life of a trapper. "It has now been 16 years I have been in the mountains. The greater part of that time passed far from the habitations of civilized man, and receiving no other food than that which I could procure with my rifle. Perhaps, once a year, I would have a meal consisting of bread, meat, sugar, and coffee; would consider it a luxury."[37]

In charge at Bent's Fort, William Bent, a younger brother of Charles, became a devoted friend to Kit. He was married to a Cheyenne, Owl Woman, whose children may have been playmates of Carson's daughters, and who may have helped Kit find someone to care for his children. Sometime during the eight months he hunted for the fort, he also took a Cheyenne wife known as Making-Out-Road.[38] The role of stepmother may not have suited her. Something caused the marriage to be uncongenial, and Making-Out-Road put Carson's belongings out of her lodge, thus dissolving the relationship. Again Carson had the problem of how to take care of his daughters and at the same time make a living for them.

Chapter 9

Carson Meets Frémont

In seeking a solution to his problems as a parent, Carson found a new and more rewarding use for his talents without compromising his essentially simple integrity. Alert, percipient, and responsive, he had become more adaptable as he matured, and his responsibilities became more permanent and binding. After eight months as hunter for Bent's Fort, he decided to take Adaline and visit his relatives in Missouri. The child needed proper training and regular schooling. His sister, Mary Ann Carson Rubey, agreed to take care of her.[1]

He had another reason for wishing to place Adaline in a good home. At Taos on January 28, 1842, he had been baptized into the Catholic Church by Padre Antonio José Martínez, a preliminary step toward marriage with Josefa Jaramillo, which took place a little over a year later. During his eight months as hunter for Bent's Fort, Carson had made occasional trips to Taos. On one of these he had met and fallen in love with Josefa, a strikingly beautiful young lady of fourteen. Doubtless the romance made considerable progress by January, and he had come to an understanding with Josefa and her parents by the spring of 1842. His trip to Missouri had an unforeseen result, beginning a new phase of his life in which, after a year or two, he would be thrust into fame.

After visiting his relatives and friends in the Boonslick area, Carson took a trip to St. Louis, with the possible hope of finding work as a guide. A few days in this trading center and Mississippi River port were enough. Tired of the settlements, he took a steamer up the Missouri, "and—as luck would have it—Colonel Frémont, then a lieutenant, was aboard of the same boat."[2]

John Charles Frémont had been working with the U.S. Corps of Topographical Engineers since 1837. In 1838, with no military training at all, he received a commission as a lieutenant in this service. He was gaining valuable experience with Joseph Nicolas Nicolet, distinguished French astronomer and geographer, who was mapping the northwest country between the Mississippi and the Missouri Rivers. He enjoyed both the adventurous and the scientific aspects of exploration, being well fitted by temperament for the one and well prepared by education for the other.[3] His energies were practically boundless, matched only by his self-confidence.

In 1841 he was in charge of an expedition to survey the Des Moines River from the Raccoon Fork to its mouth.[4] Not long after his return, he and Jessie Benton were secretly married by a Catholic priest after two Protestant clergymen had refused to perform the ceremony.[5] Jessie, only seventeen at the time, was the daughter of Thomas Hart Benton, one of the most powerful men in the Senate and certainly the most influential advocate of western expansion.

Benton's interest in the West was shared within bounds by Colonel J. J. Abert, chief of the Corps of Topographical Engineers. On April 25, 1842, Abert sent Frémont an order "to make a survey of the Platte or Nebraska River, up to the head of the Sweetwater."[6] Although no other set of orders has been found, Benton claimed in later years that Frémont had requested Colonel Abert to extend his explorations to the Rocky Mountains and that Abert had done so.

When Frémont started west, the Rockies were his goal. Understanding that he needed a guide, Carson saw him on the deck of the river boat and spoke to him. "I told him that I had been some time in the mountains and thought I could guide him to any point he wished to go," Carson recalled.[7] After making some inquiries, Frémont offered to hire him at a hundred dollars a month. Carson accepted and made arrangements to leave for the mountains. His pay compared favorably with that of other members of the expedition and was three times what he had received as a hunter at Bent's Fort.[8]

Three accounts exist of the journey across the plains. Frémont's journal, reflected in his *Report*, is full of enthusiasm, *joie de vivre*, and reports on plants and minerals seen. Carson, to whom this was familiar ground, merely mentions that they arrived at South Pass, Frémont did what was required of him, and they returned. Charles Preuss kept a private diary, full of complaints about the food, the discomforts, the montony, the men. His vicious stabs at his companions are startling, especially those directed at "that childish Frémont . . . a foolish lieutenant," "that slut-born Frémont," an "American blockhead," who neglected, among countless other things, to provide Preuss with a mosquito net, though everyone else had one.[9]

His antagonism toward Frémont probably had two main sources: he owed his very livelihood to the extreme kindness of Frémont, and the temperaments of the two men were as different as those of a German and a Frenchman could be. Born April 30, 1803, in Höhscheid, Germany, Preuss never lost his sense of superiority over the French and the Americans.

Frémont was born January 21, 1813, in Savannah, Georgia. His French father, Charles Frémon, and his Virginia mother, Ann Beverly Whiting Pryor, had been unable to marry legally because the Virginia legislature refused Pryor's petition for divorce. The family was living in Norfolk, Virginia, where two more children were born, when the father died. The mother moved to Charleston, South Carolina, where John Charles distinguished himself in Latin, Greek, and mathematics at the College of Charleston. After falling in love with a young Creole girl named Cecilia[10] and spending most of his time picnicking, boating, and roaming the woods with her and her brothers, he was dismissed from the college for "incorrigible negligence."

He became a teacher of mathematics and also worked as a surveyor. Joel Poinsett, former minister to Mexico and an amateur botanist for whom the poinsettia was named, undoubtedly gave impetus to Frémont's intense interest in identification and classi-

fication of plants. As a trustee of the College of Charleston, Poinsett helped in 1838 to assure acceptance of Frémont's request for a
belated B.A. degree.[11]

Frémont's life had already brought him many rewards by the
time Preuss, ten years his senior, came one stormy evening near
Christmas in 1841 with a request that Frémont help him in secur-
ing work. Frémont took care of the immediate needs of the Preuss
family and offered Preuss the post of topographical assistant when
he was preparing for his first expedition to the Rockies, a position
that Preuss could not avoid accepting. He must have exerted rigid
outward control, for Frémont seemed unaware of Preuss's hostile
feelings.[12]

The expedition was on its way to Chouteau's Landing when
Carson asked to be taken on as guide. Frémont described Carson
thus: "I was pleased with him . . . at our first meeting. He was a
man of medium height, broad-shouldered and deep-chested, with
a clear steady blue eye and frank speech and address; quiet and
unassuming."[13] Carson rose in the esteem of both Frémont and
Preuss with time and shared experiences. He would later declare
that he was "under more obligations to Colonel Frémont than to
any other man alive."[14] On this journey, however, the radically
different personalities of the two men did not achieve perfect
harmony.

As they traveled farther west, Frémont's passion for exploration
and his hasty judgment sometimes brought them near disaster.
Some problems arose in utilizing an inflatable rubber boat with
airtight compartments that the explorer had designed. The boat
was first inflated to ferry baggage and supplies across the flooded
Kansas River. All went well until, with night coming on, Frémont
doubled the load. The man at the helm lost control, and the boat
capsized. Carson, Maxwell, and all others who could swim jumped
into the water, racing floating boxes and bales, diving for articles
that had sunk to the bottom. Carson and Maxwell worked so hard
in the water that they became ill, and the expedition halted for a
day while the men recovered and the supplies were spread out in
the sun to dry.

Whatever hardships occurred were shared alike by greenhorns
and mountain men. Randolph Benton, Frémont's twelve-year-old

brother-in-law, and Henry Brant, a nineteen-year-old relative of the Bentons, had come along "for the development of mind and body." After reaching Indian country, these two took their first night watch with Carson. Randolph called out from time to time to direct Carson's attention to some sound as the camp settled down, and in the immensity of the prairie every yip of a coyote seemed like a cry of terror. The next morning Brant, too much keyed up to danger, came spurring from the rear, shouting that he had counted twenty-seven Indians beyond the river. Kit sprang upon one of the hunters and crossed the river. "Mounted on a fine horse, without a saddle, and scouring bare-headed over the prairies, Kit was one of the finest pictures of a horseman" Frémont had ever seen. Beyond the river were six elk, but no Indians.[15]

One evening three Cheyennes approached the camp. Carson and Maxwell started a conversation with them in sign language, to the astonishment of Preuss, and learned that they had been on a horse-stealing expedition among the Pawnees. Unsuccessful because the Pawnees had kept their horses shut up in the lodges at night, they were returning to their own people. They had not eaten for six days. After being invited to share the men's supper, they settled down for the night. They were still with the group when they met their own families far up the South Platte.[16]

In late June a dull and confused murmuring sounded far off, and dark masses began to flow across a distant rise—a great herd of buffalo. As they approached the herd, the hunters rode away from the caravan, which crawled slowly forward. Carson had shot a cow and was dashing after another when his horse stumbled and fell headlong, flinging him to the ground. The horse jumped up and joined the stampeding buffalo, with Maxwell after it. As he was getting ready to shoot it to save Kit's silver-mounted bridle, he discovered that his horse could outrun it. Presently he led it back and found Kit on his feet, ready to start butchering.

The next morning Frémont, riding a famous buffalo-hunting horse named Proveau, joined Carson and Maxwell as they approached the herd. When they were about three hundred yards away, the buffalo near them wavered, and the outer ones began charging to and fro. A crowd of bulls at the rear turned about from time to time as if to fight. The three hunters charged, and the bulls joined the stampede. At about thirty yards the hunters gave a shout and broke into the herd, the buffalo swerving away before them.

Frémont singled out a fat cow, and the horse, with scarcely a tug on the rein, foam flying from his mouth, "sprang after her like a tiger." In a few moments Frémont was alongside, rising in the stirrups a yard away, aiming at the end of the long hair for the heart. He fired, and the cow fell. Reining up, he saw Kit tying his horse to the horns of a cow, getting ready to butcher her. Quite a distance below, a wreath of smoke curled silently away from Maxwell's gun.[17]

When the expedition reached the forks of the Platte, Frémont took Maxwell and a small group west toward St. Vrain's Fort while the main party, under charge of Lambert, headed northwest along a well-marked road with signs of the recent passing of an emigrant train. Carson rode at the front of the caravan, with scouts to left and right of the party and other vigilant riders behind. Three days later, he saw dust rising on the trail and spurred ahead to reconnoiter. Upon recognizing his old friend Bridger, he put his horse into a run and shouted with joy.[18] Bridger had left his new fort on Black's Fork of the Green unattended and was taking a caravan of furs to Missouri. Having recently passed a good camping place with plenty of grass, he and his men turned back to have supper with Carson and camp nearby.

The Indians were on the rampage. Henry Fraeb, with whom Carson had ridden to the Salmon River eleven years before, had been dead for nearly a year, killed by hostile Sioux, Cheyennes, and Arapahoes at a trading post he was building on the Little Snake. The Sioux had also lost some men and were eager for revenge. Gros Ventres and Cheyennes had joined them, and eight hundred or more lodges were stationed at the Red Buttes. The Indians were ready to annihilate any party of whites who came along the trail.

The emigrants were still proceeding toward Oregon—more than a hundred men, women, and children led by Dr. Elijah White and Lansford Hastings. For five hundred dollars, Fitzpatrick had agreed to pilot them to Fort Hall.[19] He had persuaded and bribed the Indians to let them pass, but they had sworn that no other whites should go along the trail. Bridger had evaded them by taking a little-known trail through the mountains, but he advised Carson not to go beyond Fort Laramie.

This news threw the exploring party into a state of acute alarm. Preuss reported that they sat up all night around the fires, ruefully discussing the danger into which they were headed, exclaiming from time to time, *"Il n'y aura pas de vie pour nous!"*—roughly equivalent to "We're done for!"[20] Gloom continued to hang over them as they parted from Bridger and rode past Chimney Rock and Scott's Bluff and on to Fort Platte, the new adobe fort at the mouth of the Laramie. A mile and a half farther, among a cluster of Sioux lodges, the white-washed and picketed walls of Fort Laramie rose above the left bank of the Laramie River. Bastions at opposite corners gave the fort a reassuring appearance of military vigilance, but anxiety about the trail ahead still hung over the camp.

Two days later Frémont arrived. He had enjoyed the Cheyennes, who at parting had shown their appreciation of his hospitality by some discriminating thievery. He had viewed a buffalo surround and had been feasted by the Arapahoes, whose display of their arms in front of their lodges reminded him of the days of chivalry.[21] On an island in the South Platte, he had met Jean Baptiste Charbonneau, Sacajawea's son, who had welcomed him with a very good mint julep.[22]

His pleasure tour of the prairies came to an abrupt end when he found the men at Fort Laramie in their doomsday mood. He optimistically tended to dismiss their fears, but Carson had been in too many tight places with Bridger to doubt his estimate of the dangerous temper of the Indians. After arriving at the fort, he had made his will, a proceeding that Frémont deplored because of its effect on his men.[23] However, before heading into danger under a captain inexperienced in Indian fighting, Carson needed to make sure that whatever he possessed would be used for the benefit of his children.

The Sioux at the fort tried to stop Frémont, emphasizing the danger that the hostile Indians would destroy his party.

Frémont informed them that he was directed by his government to perform a certain duty, that it mattered not what obstacles were in his advance, that he was bound to continue his march in obedience to his instruction, that he would accomplish that for which he was sent or die in the attempt; and if he failed, by losing his party, his government would eventually punish those that caused his failure.[24]

This is a good resume of the oration Frémont delivered to the assembled chiefs.[25] With a flair for drama equal to that of the Indians themselves, Frémont appears to have adopted their style of oratory. He no doubt made a vivid impression. As the party progressed toward the mountains, they met several Sioux who told them that the gathering of Indians had disagreed among themselves and had broken up. When the explorers reached the Red Buttes, their only remaining enemy was a severe drought compounded by a plague of grasshoppers that had eaten most of the scanty grass. In a thick grove of willows on the river, they unloaded their carts, took them apart, and hid the pieces in the thicket. They cached everything else not absolutely essential.

The road left the Platte soon after, but Frémont decided to follow the river to its confluence with the Sweetwater, hoping for better grass and also wishing to map the rivers more accurately. Above the Red Buttes, however, the river boiled over hidden rocks between precipices. Carson advised camping on an island in the Platte and cutting across the rugged hills to the Sweetwater the next day, and for the time being Frémont agreed. Three bighorn sheep were brought in for supper, and Frémont named the place Goat Island.

As soon as they reached the Sweetwater, buffalo appeared. For several days they made short treks so as to dry meat, but this project ended on August 2, about sunset, when rain began. The next day they came within view of the Wind River Mountains, a low, dark mass seventy miles away. These were a disappointment to Frémont, and especially to Preuss, who had expected something like the Swiss Alps, with glaciers, ice lakes, avalanches, and waterfalls. Two days later the men were still slogging forward through driving rain.

As the party filed up the gradual approach to South Pass, the sun appeared and the mountains again came into view, dazzling with a new coat of snow. The explorers left the wagon road and headed northwest, and the scenery became grander. On August 10, between two ridges covered with pines, they came upon a beautiful lake glittering in the sunlight, the yellow sand and light foliage of the aspens along its shores glowing against the dark pines, snow-capped peaks gleaming above.[26]

The peaks challenged Frémont and Preuss irresistibly—the most "magnificent, grand rocks" the latter had seen anywhere, even in Switzerland.[27] As the mules forded the outlet of the lake to reach a convenient campsite, the cistern of the barometer was broken. With ingenuity and persistence, Frémont worked for two days and finally mended it with a piece of powder horn, bits of leather, and glue made from a buffalo.

Leaving ten men in the base camp, Frémont took Carson and thirteen others and set out on mules August 12 with enough meat for two days. The first day they searched among the rocky slopes for a way to the peak that appeared to be the highest. The next day they rode only two or three miles and left the mules, blankets, and provisions in charge of a few men. The rest started toward the peak. From this point it seemed so near and so easily accessible that all expected to be back before dark.[28]

Carson, as guide, took the lead. The way led to the top of ridge after ridge, only to dip again and again into a valley or a ravine. The men clambered over rocks and waded streams. Unused to so much exertion at this altitude, Frémont began to be sick and called to Carson that he was going too fast. Thinking the aim was to get to the top as soon as possible, Carson retorted in such a way as to anger Frémont, who designated "a young chap" to take the lead. Confusion followed. "Frémont got excited, as usual . . . developed a headache," and the party stopped about eleven o'clock for the day. Distressed at the result of his sturdy leadership, Carson explained during the afternoon that "he had not meant it as the other had assumed, and the headache was relieved."[29]

The group spent a cold night at the edge of the pines without blankets or food. Only Preuss, "a more experienced mountaineer," had a piece of dried meat he had stuck into his pocket. His boast may have been more valid than it sounds. During their years in the mountains, Carson, Maxwell, and the voyageurs had in general sought the lowest passes between beaver streams, not the highest peaks.

The next day was no better. Frémont was ready to give up and estimate the height of the mountain, but Carson, scouting alone, reached one of the snowy peaks of the main ridge, from which he had a good view of a promising approach to the high peak towering 800 to 1,000 feet above him.[30] Lajeunesse had brought up some mules with provisions. After eating and discussing what had been observed, Frémont decided that Carson should take all but four or five men and set out at daybreak to return to the second camp. The rest of them would try for the peak.

Soon after daybreak the men got started. Leaving their mules to graze on a bench about a hundred feet above three little lakes,[31] Frémont's group climbed safely to the summit, a narrow crest about three feet wide, overlooking an immense snow field five hundred feet below. In a crevice they fixed a ramrod and unfurled a special flag: the national emblem with an eagle superimposed upon the field of stars.[32] As they descended among the rocks, there was some confusion and delay. Waiting at the Camp of the Mules, Carson decided they had gone down another way and started his party back to base camp. Finding the second camp deserted, Frémont again lost his temper, but by the time he reached base camp, his anger had subsided.[33]

Their mission accomplished, the expedition packed up and started east. At the mouth of the Sweetwater, most of the men, including Carson, were sent to Goat Island. Frémont took the instruments, some of the records, and six men and readied the rubber boat to ride the Platte over the rocky stretch between the precipices, intending to complete the survey.

The boat was unequal to this demand.[34] After a tremendous struggle with the current, rapids, and rocks, it was caught by a submerged rock and overturned, throwing everything into the water. Lajeunesse jumped into the boat, and he and Lambert paddled downstream until the river had to find its way through a mass of rocks that filled its bed from bank to bank. After gathering all the lost articles they could find, they climbed out of the canyon and started for Goat Island, where pieces of fresh buffalo stood around the fire cooking for breakfast.

When the expedition reached Fort Laramie in September, Kit left them. No record has been found of his whereabouts from September to January. Perhaps he trapped the mountain streams to earn money for his wedding, relishing the solitude after the sometimes tense atmosphere among the explorers. He had much to think about. Although not much had happened on the expedition, the potential had been there. Frémont's oration to the Sioux chiefs, a refinement Carson had not yet used in dealing with Indians, may have helped avert serious trouble. Frémont's delight in the voyageurs, whose light-hearted élan was more congenial to him than the more sober and responsible manner of his guide, also opened new vistas, for the American trappers had been inclined to think of the French as frivolous and inconsequential, a less intelligent and lower breed of men, somewhere between the Indians and the whites. Yet all the men responded to Frémont's wishes with cheerful good humor. He seemed to control them by his candid revelation of the dangers they faced and an equally candid declaration of his attitude toward quitters and cowards.

Being his guide was not easy. He would listen, or appear to, then likely decide to go some other way, seemingly on a whim or sudden curiosity to see what was there. He would become irritable if he thought someone was not cooperating; yet he was kind and understanding with men who were honestly trying. As a mountain man, dependent solely on his own skills, Carson appreciated his persistence and ingenuity in repairing the barometer. Like a strange new country, the explorer attracted Carson irresistibly; even a developing awareness of Frémont's weaknesses would not undermine his loyalty. Carson was a new type for Frémont, too, who would perhaps never fully understand or appreciate him. But on this first journey he made enough progress in that direction to welcome his former guide and hunter when they met again.

As Carson returned to Bent's Fort, he also had his approaching marriage to think about. It was by no means certain that he would find the welcome in Taos that he hoped for. Josefa was very young, and her family might easily prefer that she marry a young man of her own people rather than a mountaineer twice her age with two half-Arapaho children. Nothing of this appears in Carson's memoirs, however, only the statement "I went to Bent's Fort, in January

1843 departed for Taos. In February of the same year got married to Senorita Josepha Jaramilla, a daughter of Don Francisco Jaramilla.[35] . . ." The custom was for the groom-to-be to furnish the bride with a complete trousseau. . . . The wedding feast took place in the home of the bride, but the bridegroom's family was completely in charge, and furnished everything for the occasion."[36] Perhaps Ignacia Bent, Josefa's older sister, took over Carson's responsibilities on this important occasion.

Josefa, born March 19, 1828, was almost fifteen at the time of her marriage. Four years later, Garrard described her as a "beauty . . . of the haughty, heart-breaking kind—such as would lead a man with a glance of the eye, to risk his life for one smile. . . . I could not but desire her acquaintance; . . . dress and manners . . . bespoke a greater degree of refinement than usual."[37]

By that time she was nineteen, and her husband had spent most of the intervening years with Frémont in the West. He remained in Taos only two months, because he had a living to make, and his particular talents could not be employed near his home. In April he was engaged as hunter for the wagon train of Bent and St. Vrain, headed for Missouri, a trip that led finally back to the explorer. Josefa had to content herself with the knowledge that she was the magnet that always drew him back to Taos, no matter how far his wanderings might carry him or how famous he might become.

Chapter 10

Lost in the Great Basin

When the Bent and St. Vrain caravan reached the mouth of Walnut Creek at the Great Bend of the Arkansas, they found Captain Philip St. George Cooke encamped with two hundred dragoons. Not far beyond was a caravan of traders under his protection.[1] A West Point graduate, Cooke had patrolled the western frontier since 1829, first as a junior officer under Major Bennet Riley, later with his own company of dragoons. His present purpose was to avert a showdown between Mexicans and Texans on the soil of the United States.

With the Battle of San Jacinto, April 21, 1836, the war for Texan independence had ended, but friction continued. Feeling that the Texans, invited to settle on Mexican lands, had broken their faith, the Mexican government refused to acknowledge their independence. The Texans claimed sovereignty up to the east bank of the Rio Grande. Rebuffed in early attempts to be annexed by the United States, unable to stop Mexican raids in the south, the government of Texas issued what amounted to letters of reprisal to Charles A. Warfield and Jacob Snively. They were to attack Mexican posts and raid Mexican traders in what Texas considered its northwestern province. Calling themselves the Invincibles, they expected to attack the caravan, mostly Mexican, when it crossed the Arkansas.[2]

The traders offered Carson three hundred dollars to carry a letter to Governor Manuel Armijo at Santa Fe. Carson agreed, and he and Dick Owens started for Taos by way of Bent's Fort. Hearing that the Utes were on the warpath to the south, they decided that Owens should remain at the fort; one man would be more likely than two to elude the Indians. William Bent furnished Carson a fine horse to lead. If attacked, he could switch horses and outrun the Utes. He became aware of the Indians without their seeing him and slipped by them in the night. After delivering the letter to the alcalde to be forwarded to the governor, he went home to Josefa to await a reply.

Armijo had sent ahead a party of about a hundred militiamen and Indians. With five hundred or more men he himself marched out on May 1 to meet the caravan on the Arkansas. On the way he met a man of his advance party, mounted on a horse he had managed to steal from the Texans. The remainder of the vanguard had been either killed or captured. Reported Carson, "When the general heard of the defeat of his brave soldiers, his heart failed him, and he returned for Santa Fe in all haste."[3] After waiting four days in Taos, Carson received the dispatches from Armijo and left for the Arkansas, accompanied by one Mexican. Neither he nor Josefa suspected that he would not return for a year.

The third day on the road, a large body of Indians appeared so suddenly that there was no way to avoid them. They were Utes, painted for war. Thinking that the Indians would be less likely to harm a Mexican, his companion urged Carson to take the dispatches and escape on Bent's horse. Carson thought the advice good, since it would ensure that the dispatches reach their destination. As he was about to mount the horse, he changed his mind. "I . . . thought how cowardly it would be in me to desert this man that so willingly offered to sacrifice his life to save mine. I told him no, that I would die with him."[4]

The Utes came racing toward them. One, some distance in the lead, smiled as he approached and offered Kit his hand. Kit reached for it, but instead of shaking hands, the Indian grabbed Kit's rifle and tried to wrest it from him. A struggle ensued, and as Kit regained possession of his gun, the body of Indians surged around them. They talked loudly among themselves, examining their guns, opening the pans and knocking the priming of their rifles, as they rode threateningly around Kit and the Mexican, trying to break their nerve. They could not escape Kit's unwavering stare, which told them plainly that the first to raise his gun would be killed. After half an hour, seeing that they would lose two warriors before they could hope to win any scalps, the Indians reined about and rode away.

When he arrived at Bent's Fort, Kit learned that Cooke and his dragoons had disarmed Snively's "Invincibles" on American soil and sent them back to Texas, and the caravan had continued on its way. He also learned that Frémont had passed on his way to the mountains, with a small carriage for the instruments, a howitzer, baggage carts, and nearly forty men. Unable to resist the allure of this amiable greenhorn whose work seemed so much like light-hearted play, Carson set out toward El Pueblo, intending to exchange greetings, have a talk, and return. Frémont had already hired Thomas Fitzpatrick as guide and two Delaware Indians as hunters, and he thought that Lucien Maxwell, who had ridden with him from St. Louis, would join him as hunter. But when he saw his "good buffalo hunter of 1842, Christopher Carson," he could not let slip a good opportunity and asked Kit to go along. Kit could not refuse. Frémont listed him as a hunter, though he served equally as guide.[5]

Fitzpatrick, acting as trail boss and camp superintendent, had taken the provisions, the heavy baggage, and twenty-five men to proceed at a convenient pace to Fort St. Vrain.[6] As soon as Carson agreed to accompany the expedition, Frémont sent him back to Bent's Fort for mules and supplies, with instructions to meet his party at Fort St. Vrain as soon as possible. When Frémont arrived at the fort, Fitzpatrick was waiting, the provisions intact, and his "true and reliable friend," Kit Carson, had brought ten good mules with packsaddles.[7] In spite of the efficiency and reliability of Fitzpatrick and Carson, finding food for the rather large expedition was to be the most pressing problem during much of the journey. At the fort an excellent hunter and lasting friend of both Frémont and Carson was added to the party. When the Delaware Indians decided to return to their homes, Alexis Godey, a St. Louis Creole who had hunted and trapped in the mountins for six or seven years, agreed to go along as hunter for Fitzpatrick.[8]

Visiting the springs at the head of the Fontaine Qui Bouille, Frémont had noticed a very good lodge trail over the mountains to the Bayou Salade.[9] Unable to follow it because most of his men were ahead, he decided to go directly over the Front Range from the fort, even though none of the experienced mountain men would recommend it. Sending Fitzpatrick with the supplies and most of the men north to the Oregon Trail, he took fourteen men, with Carson as guide, and headed into the mountains on July 28 by way of the Cache la Poudre.[10] A Snake woman, whose husband had been killed July 4 at Fort Lupton, was allowed to join the party with her two half-white children and her half dozen pack horses with baggage. They had not gone far before their way was blocked by the sheer walls of a narrow canyon, through which the river boiled over hidden rocks. As they climbed the steep slopes to bypass this obstruction, they unknowingly left the main stream.[11] When they descended, they met the north fork of the river splashing through little meadows of wild flowers. They ascended the stream to a ridge above the Laramie Plain and followed a tributary of the Laramie to the valley, where Carson brought in an antelope, the first meat they had had in two days.

Soon there were plenty of fat cows, and Carson guided the party to the North Platte, where they camped among the cottonwoods to dry meat. As the men were cutting off thin slices of buffalo and hanging them on racks, one of the guards caught a glimpse of an Indian peering over a neighboring ridge. The horses were driven into camp, the howitzer was wheeled into position, and the men hid themselves among the cottonwoods, rifles ready. With a yell, about seventy Indians galloped into the bottom. Seeing the little cannon, they pulled up and made signs of peace. Arapaho and Cheyenne, they explained that they thought the camp was that of hostile Indians. No one believed them, but the pipe was passed, food was spread, and small gifts of tobacco and other goods were presented for the honor of the United States government.

West of the Platte, the party passed through a region of dry and barren hills leading to an unfamiliar saline plain with little vegetation other than scattered clumps of greasewood.[12] Carson found a creek flowing north, which led them to the Sweetwater and the Oregon Trail. A multitude of emigrants had worn the sage brush down and made a broad, dusty highway across the plain. The explorers rode rapidly across the southern end of South Pass and on August 15 camped on the Green, the Seeds-ke-dee Agie, or Prairie Hen River, of the Crow Indians. Expecting to find some of her people at Fort Bridger, the Shoshone woman left the party.

Sent ahead to Fort Hall to get a supply of provisions ready, "to avoid every delay not absolutely necessary," Carson found himself traveling among the emigrants. The valley of Bear River was dotted with white covered wagons, with women about the fires preparing the evening meal, children playing in the grass, and herds of cattle grazing about the bottom. August 26 a diarist wrote, "Kit Carson, of Fremont's company, camped with us, on his return from For Hall, having been on express."[13]

Henry Lee was on the trail somewhere with a note for Carson. Frémont had followed the Bear as it turned around the mountain at Soda Springs and flowed south to Great Salt Lake.[14] Avoiding the plain Indian-trapper trail, he had led the men through canyons and over ridges. Finally rejoining the Bear, he had inflated the rubber boat and started toward the lake with Basil Lajeunesse, but found the terrain around the mouth of the Bear impenetrable with swamps and thickets. He returned upstream and started some men to moving baggage across the Bear, while others forced the reluctant animals to swim. Here on September 4 Carson and Lee found them.

The emigrants had exhausted supplies at Fort Hall, and Fitzpatrick had not arrived with the provisions. Carson had been able to buy only enough food for two days, but waterfowl were thick in the marshes. The guns of the hunters boomed from time to time, followed by a noise like distant thunder as thousands of birds rose from the water. Exhausted by their long day of struggling with the mules and the baggage, the men camped beside the Bear and feasted on ducks, geese, and plover.

The next day they rode south. Climbing a butte, they saw the lake stretching beyond the horizon to the west.[15] After moving their camp to a grove of trees on the Weber River, they built a corral for the animals and a fort to protect Badeau, Derosier, and Jacob Dodson, the campkeepers. François Lajeunesse and seven others were sent to Fort Hall to try to obtain provisions.[16] With some misgivings, Carson, Preuss, Bernier, and Basil Lajeunesse prepared to accompany Frémont to one of the islands in the lake. The rubber boat was repaired, inflated, and loaded with bags of fresh water, blankets, and instruments. On September 8 they left the camp at sunrise, but it was sunset before they reached the inlet of the lake, and they camped on a low point among the willows. Around them throughout the night, the wildfowl splashed and chattered.

The next morning they took off their clothes and, surrounded by screaming plover, dragged the boat over the soft, foul-smelling mud until they came to a small black ridge on the bottom. Beyond this the mud was replaced by sand, and the water became salty and began to deepen. They paddled away with high spirits over the clear, green water, its depths sparkling in the sunlight like the heart of a vast emerald. When they noticed that white patches of foam moved to the south, indicating a current in that direction, the men recalled stories of suckholes and underground channels and became quiet.

Carson pointed out a band of white near the island—waves breaking into whitecaps as a strong breeze began coming up the lake. Two of the divisions between the cylinders of the raft gave way, and the bellows had to be pumped constantly. The boat rode the waves like a water bird, but the paddles seemed to gain little headway across the rough sea of the open lake. It was noon before they reached the island.

Frémont named the place Disappointment Island because it was perfectly barren except for prickly pear and a few saline plants, mostly greasewood that grew to heights of seven or eight feet.[17] No guard being necessary, all the men climbed the rock to the highest point. While Frémont and Preuss used their glasses to examine the shores of the lake and took readings with the instruments, Carson, possibly aided by Bernier, cut a large cross under a shelving rock, a landmark visible for many years.

After a night on the beach, they filled one of the rubber bags with water from the lake, loaded their equipment, and started back.[18] Storm clouds started rolling toward them. The boat was leaking air, and one man worked continually at the bellows. Frémont directed the men to pull for their lives. As they reached shore, the storm broke. Soon waves were pounding eight or ten feet high on the bushes and rocks where they had landed.[19]

September 11 they boiled down the five gallons of water they had brought from the lake, getting fourteen pints of very fine-grained salt. Roots were their only food that night and the next morning before they started toward Fort Hall. At the end of the day's march, Carson brought in several seagulls, a meager supper for hungry men. September 13 the howitzer was fired with the hope of attracting to the camp the men they had sent for supplies. The next day they forded the Bear and met Snake Indians who traded them a fat young horse. All had a feast except Preuss and Frémont, who were not yet ready to eat horsemeat. September 15 they traded for a small amount of kooyah root from the Indians. As they approached the Malad, a lone hunter came along. Behind his saddle was slung a freshly killed antelope, which he traded to them for powder and balls. They were settling down to enjoy their feast when François Tabeau rode up to their fire with the news that Fitzpatrick was not far away.

But Fitzpatrick awaited them at Fort Hall, as directed. On September 16 Frémont gave an Indian boy a knife to show him the kooyah plant, and the men managed with roots and left-over meat as they ascended the Malad, crossed over a steep pass to the Bannock River, and crossed to the Portneuf and descended to Fort Hall. Supplies at the fort had not been replenished, but Richard Grant, the British factor, was able to let them have several poor horses and five good oxen, one of which they butchered at once. The difficulties with supplies had convinced Frémont that he would be better off with fewer men. When he explained that the journey would continue throughout the winter, probably with severe hardships, and announced that those who wished to return would be paid until November 20, eleven men decided to go back.

On September 22 the diminished party started down the Snake. The emigrant road led along a high plain, covered with sage and scattered with fragments of obsidian. Far to the north the men could see the Salmon River Mountains beyond a plain so broken into chasms and impeded by beds of lava that Fitzpatrick told Frémont it was impassable, even for a man on foot.[20]

When broken, rocky cliffs slowed them down, Fitzpatrick was left to follow with the slower baggage carts, while the exploring party rode ahead. The Snake was gradually sinking into a trough-like canyon, with walls so precipitous that for long stretches they could not get down to the water. Where the canyon gave room, Indians had built villages. Paddling happily in boats made of rushes, they always converged upon the explorers, eager to trade fish for any kind of garment, for there was no game to furnish skins for clothing.[21]

The explorers were cordially welcomed at Fort Boise, where François Payette of the Hudson's Bay Company and his single engagé regaled them with fresh butter and garden produce and sold them a bullock, which they butchered, leaving half of it for Fitzpatrick. After crossing the Malheur River, the road left the Snake, where branch canyons had become impassable. Entering the Blue Mountains, it became dangerously rough and precipitous. When the men came to a large, fertile valley called the Grande Ronde, Frémont decided to leave the road and follow an Indian trail described by Payette. The men had to clear away smaller growth to make a road for the howitzer and the instrument carriage as they climbed through magnificent forests, where larches, spruces, and pines as much as twelve feet in diameter towered two hundred feet above the ground. In spite of every precaution, the barometer was broken. At one camp, Carson, Preuss, and several others had to take rubber buckets and clamber a half-mile down the mountain to find water for coffee, which together with bread made their supper. When at last they came out from among the great trees, they saw Mount Hood standing, white with snow, high above the surrounding country a hundred eighty miles away, not a lone peak as it appeared, but one of several volcanic cones in the Cascade Mountains.[22]

Dr. Whitman was away when they reached his mission at Waiilatpu. The flour mill had burned down, but potatoes were plentiful. After having them for supper and as a bedtime snack, Carson put another potful on the fire before going to sleep.[23] The party stocked up on these and rode on to Fort Walla Walla, where the Columbia spread its vast waters before them, twelve hundred yards wide and apparently deep enough for navigation. On its bank Jesse Applegate was busily building Mackinaw boats.

For a week, with an intelligent Indian boy as guide, the men jogged along the barren sand beside the river or climbed over the grassy, steep hills, crossing the John Day River and the Deschutes, which roared and tumbled through a gorge to join the Columbia. As Applegate's fleet glided by, they watched with envy. Everywhere they stopped, Indians gathered. A very old man, nearly blind, with long, white hair, was among the visitors. Frémont made him a present of tobacco. His people, impressed by this show of respect, assured Frémont that he need feel no uneasiness about his horses, and all went quietly away.

November 4 the men came over the hills to the Dalles, where the Columbia must pass through a chasm only fifty-eight yards wide, forcing the water into many whirlpools and counter currents. The men learned with horror that one of Applegate's boats had gone under the black, swirling waters, drowning his twelve-year-old son, the boy's cousin, and a man who was attempting to guide the boat.

Carson was left at the Dalles to oversee mending the equipment, making packsaddles, and guarding the camp, while Frémont, Preuss, Bernier, and Dodson enjoyed a sometimes perilous boat ride down the Columbia to Fort Vancouver to purchase supplies. With this trip, and as a part of Frémont's orders, they completed the junction with the 1838 voyage of Captain Charles Wilkes. A note was sent to Fitzpatrick at Walla Walla, instructing him to make packsaddles, put all the baggage on his animals, and leave the carts with the missionaries. Frémont was starting home, not along the Oregon Trail, as Colonel Abert had ordered, but by way of the Great Basin.[24]

By the time Frémont returned, Carson had moved to a better camp upriver, where grass was more plentiful, and had new packsaddles ready and all equipment repaired. At the request of Mr. Perkins, the missionary, a young Chinook was allowed to join the expedition so that he could learn more about the whites. Perkins also recommended two Indians as guides to Klamath Lake.

November 21 Fitzpatrick arrived with the baggage packed on

mules. Four days later, twenty-five men, a hundred four horses and mules, some California cattle, and the three Indians started south. Enough flour, peas, and tallow for cooking were packed on the animals to feed the party for three months. When these ran out in February 1844, the party was a thousand miles from the Dalles in the deep snow at the summit of the Sierra Nevada.

Perkins accompanied the expedition for several miles. Numerous Indians tagged along, many of them remaining during the night. Two rough-looking men who were caught stealing were tied up, laid by the fire, and guarded all night. This unusual but mild punishment impressed the Indians without obligating them to seek revenge. At first many men walked, climbing to Tygh Prairie, high and hilly. They gradually left the white cones of Mount Rainier and Mount Hood behind to the north, while coming nearer to Mount Jefferson on the southwest. The tributaries of the Deschutes ran clear and sparkling through narrow valleys separated by high, rounded hills, which the horses climbed and descended day after day.

On December 3 they reached more level ground, a stony, elevated plain which soon gave way to a pine forest, alternating with meadows as the ground gradually rose. A week later, they came to a broad, grassy marsh, with ponds of ice scattered among the grasses. The Indian guides told Frémont that this was an arm of Klamath Lake.

Having heard that the Klamath Indians were treacherous, the explorers camped in a pine grove and kept close watch on the animals. When no Indians appeared, they rode into the marsh and found the Indians collected on the tops of a few large huts of mud and grass on the edge of a river. A fine-looking chief and his wife were walking out to investigate the strange visitors. The guides reassured them by signs, and the Indians allowed the men to approach the huts. Great quantities of small fish from the marshy river hung inside the lodges. From the lush grasses were woven shoes, hats, and baskets. The men traded for mats for bedding, and Frémont traded for a young dog. The men named the pup Klamath.[25]

The Indians assured Frémont that a lake lay a few days' travel to the east. He assumed this to be Mary's Lake, which, together with the Buenaventura River, was his next objective.[26] Although they refused to act as guides, several Indians accompanied the party through the pine forest as far as a stream flowing south, which they said had many affluents and became a great river. As the falling snow became thicker, the Indians turned back to their huts.

Convinced that he had reached the headwaters of the Sacramento, Frémont pushed on toward the east. Because this country had never been explored by white men, the maps he had were of little use. As they rode through the silent forest on December 16, the men saw an opening ahead, hurried forward through the snow, and found themselves at the edge of an abrupt drop of a thousand feet or more. At the foot of the mountain a lake surrounded by greenery shimmered in the sunshine. The ridge where they stood they named Winter Ridge; the lake below, Summer Lake. After a rough and precipitous descent, they found the lake surrounded by a margin of deep mud, edged with saline deposits. They were in the Great Basin.[27]

Continuing to search for Mary's Lake to the east, they discovered and named Lake Abert, walled in by black precipices, surrounded by mud. By digging holes and waiting for the water to seep in, they obtained barely potable water. Signs of Indians were everywhere. In spots, women looking for roots had grubbed up the ground until it looked like a field ready for planting.

December 22 the black ridges to the east seemed impassable. Filling two India-rubber bags with water, the men turned south. December 24 they named the pond beside which they camped Christmas Lake.[28] During the night a horse was stolen. The men celebrated Christmas by firing the howitzer and the guns, and Frémont gave each man a little brandy. This and coffee with sugar was their Christmas feast.

For the next sixteen days they wandered through a forbidding country of sage and barren ridges, southeast, sometimes south, generally following Indian trails but seeing Indians only once. It is generally believed that they reached the western edge of the Black Rock Desert.[29] December 26 Carson's horse, one of the best in the camp, was stolen. Frémont decided that, if another horse were stolen, they would pursue the thieves into the mountains. But their contact with Indians was of a different kind.

Riding quietly over the snow, they noticed smoke rising above the sage. They spurred ahead, but the Indians had seen them first. As they came upon two huts built loosely of sage, several Indians were scrambling up a ridge, while others looked back, shouting, "Tabibo——bo!"—the Snake word for "white." Carson and Godey rode up the hill after them, but they ran like deer. As Carson returned, he became aware of a woman and two children hiding behind a sage bush. The woman shut her eyes and started screaming, but after she was brought back to the huts and calmed by kind words and presents, they learned that she was of the Snake nation and shared the two huts with sixteen to twenty others. They lived on seeds, roots, and rabbits.

In early January, the men started south through heavy morning fog along a ridge of white granite.[30] All walked. They had lost fifteen animals since leaving the Dalles, most of them left on the trail, too weak to walk farther. It was decided that henceforth they would not leave a patch of good grass until another had been found. Frémont, Carson, and Godey took some of the better horses, rode to the southwest, and found a broad, plain trail that led through a ravine with grass and good springs shaded by sweet cottonwoods. The same day Fitzpatrick discovered excellent grass and pure water in a hollow a few miles away, a godsend for their jaded horses.

On January 10 Carson and Frémont found good bunch grass in a valley, left a signal for the party to camp there, and continued up the hollow to see what lay beyond the mountain. The hollow ascended gradually for several miles, forming a good pass. Beyond, a defile dropped rapidly two thousand feet to a broad lake, waves curling its dark green water and the snowy Sierra Nevada sweeping up from its western shore. As the howitzer and baggage were brought up and the animals put out to graze, some of the men butchered the last of the cattle from the Dalles. Others examined the lake, especially the massive rock rising six hundred feet from its surface, from which Frémont named it Pyramid Lake.[31] Ducks and large fish swam in the slightly salty water, and mountain sheep watched from a safe distance along the cliffs.

January 15 a few poor-looking Indians showed themselves, and one was induced to come into the camp. He was dressed in a tunic of rabbit skins and spoke a dialect of the Snake language, which Carson could not understand perfectly. He lived in the rocks nearby, but he went with the explorers as they moved toward the end of the lake, where he said there was a large river. Near the end of the lake, three or four Indians met them. They could make themselves understood only by signs, but the Indians told them that the river flowed into the lake, which had no outlet. The chief spoke in a loud voice, and groups of Indians, armed with bows and arrows, emerged from thickets. After the men had selected a place for their camp, an Indian brought a large fish to trade. Seeing the eagerness with which goods were offered in exchange, the Indians brought many more, which the men boiled, fried, and roasted in the ashes, having a great feast. These salmon trout, from two to four feet long and of excellent flavor, were the exclusive property of the Indians at the southeastern end of the lake, who were fat and happy looking. The Indian who had accompanied the explorers up the lake was given a fish, which he carried back to his people.

The Indians had a few articles of civilized manufacture, such as brass buttons, but it was not certain that they themselves had seen white men. Carson had to tell them not to bring their bows and arrows into camp, and a third of the exploring party was kept on guard at all times. The Indians were full of curiosity about the whites, but when Frémont tried to persuade some of them to guide the party, they looked at one another and laughed.

January 16 the explorers started up the river, which Frémont named the Salmon Trout River.[32] When they came to the mountain, they left the stream and continued south along an Indian trail, Frémont looking in vain for the Buenaventura River, Carson looking for beaver, of which he found no sign. After twenty miles they found another stream flowing from the mountains.[33] With Fitzpatrick and Carson, Frémont rode out to reconnoiter. Smokes were visible all around on the heights, indicating that the Indians were watching them continually and informing neighboring tribes of their whereabouts.

When they returned to camp, Frémont examined the feet of the animals and found them so cut up by the rocks that it would be impossible to cross the rough, barren country to the Rocky Mountains. He announced to the men that they were going to cross the Sierra Nevada to the Sacramento Valley. This decision, he reported, filled them with joy.

Chapter 11

Across the High Sierra

The obvious approach to the Sierra would have been the Carson River, which was at hand, but snowstorms darkened the peaks to the west, promising a difficult crossing. For four days the men rode south among the broken hills, still hoping they might find a trail through the peaks along the fabled Buenaventura River. The peaks were still covered with snow clouds when they came to another large river (Walker River), which was obviously flowing into the Great Basin. They ascended the east fork of this river and entered the mountains. For five days they crossed ridges with lofty pines along the crests and nut pines on the lower slopes. The days were warm, but at night along the little valley streams they had to chop holes in the ice so that the animals could drink, and their moccasins, wet from tramping through the snow, threatened to freeze to their feet. Curious Indians were constantly with or near them, communicating by signs, offering pine nuts for trade, but showing no animosity.

So far the animals were able to paw away the snow and find enough grass, but at the end of January three of the mules gave out. By that time the expedition had crossed three rivers or one river three times, for the rivers often curved around spurs of the mountains and met them again in the next valley. Unable to maneuver the howitzer through the snow and over ridges, they abandoned it.[1] The cold nights and the deep snow added to the perpetual distress of hunger. They had seen deer tracks, but no deer. Provisions were low. No grease of any kind remained, and they were out of salt.

When asked about the trail, the Indians said it would be impossible to cross the mountains this time of year. They held their hands over their heads to show the depth of the snow. Carson tried to cheer the men by talking about the warmth, the rich grass, and the abundance of game in the valleys beyond the mountains. But the peaks rising between them and those valleys were still hidden in clouds of snow.[2]

They descended to another river, where they found a sheltered camp with plenty of grass. Their fires soon drew a crowd of Indians, carrying the usual bows as well as nets for catching rabbits. Frémont held council and was again told that it was impossible for anyone to get through the mountains. However, one thinly clad and nearly barefoot young man had gone all the way to the dwellings of the white people. An offering of a warm green blanket and lengths of blue and scarlet cloth induced him to join the expedition as guide. With two companions he was persuaded to sleep inside the lodge. Carson lay across the entrance, his gun beside him.

February 1, Frémont talked to the men, repeating Carson's descriptions of the beautiful valley of the Sacramento with its rich pastures, abundance of game, and summer weather. A supreme push of seventy miles would bring them to this valley. Though all were aware of the difficulties and dangers of the passage, none guessed that five weeks of incredible labor and suffering lay between them and Sutter's Fort.

The men set to work on their leggings, moccasins, and clothing, making everything as warm and sturdy as possible. They also made warm clothing for the guide and gave him skins for new moccasins. A dog that had taken up with the men on Bear River and had grown fat on their scraps was butchered, and the Indians brought in two or three rabbits to trade. These small animals made a meager feast for the men the night before they started up the mountain.[3]

On February 2 they crossed the river on the ice and headed up the nearest tributary coming from the west.[4] The snow deepened rapidly as they scrambled upward along steep slopes and over spurs. Ten men on the strongest horses opened the road. As the first horse and rider became exhausted, they moved aside and the next in line took over, each falling in line after the others passed. In this way the party traveled sixteen miles the first day. The second day they reached some springs sheltered by the boughs of a lofty cedar.[5] This would be their base camp for two weeks as they struggled to reach the pass over the ridge. Carson scouted for patches of bunch grass cleared of snow by sun and wind, and each evening the animals were sent back under guard to the nearest pasture.

A few Indians came on snowshoes, watching the men curiously as they beat down a road to a steeper grade a mile or so away, where another hollow led upward toward the summit. The third morning Fitzpatrick started with the baggage along the newly beaten road while Frémont and two or three others, each leading a horse, struggled forward along the steep mountain side. They cut a footing in the icy crust as they advanced and trampled a road for the horses. In spite of all their care, a horse would plunge outside the road from time to time and slide a hundred yards down the frozen snow to the bottom of the hollow. One of the men would climb down, get the horse, and laboriously make his way up again, leading the reluctant animal.

Toward evening they reached a bench in the hollow and crossed a short stretch of ground that was fairly level before it dropped away to a basin ten miles across. At the western side of this basin rose a range of naked peaks above slopes dark with evergreens. The guide pointed out a pass among the peaks, and the men tried to force a road, but after plunging through the snow for two or three hundred yards, the strongest horses, completely exhausted, refused to make any further effort. The guide considered the project hopeless, and so did many of the men.[6]

Frémont and Carson did not even consider the possibility of defeat. Fitzpatrick carried out his responsibilities with unflagging perseverance and courage. Even Preuss rose to the occasion and showed remarkable fortitude and sensitivity to his surroundings. After they passed, he made a sketch of these majestic peaks—one of the major documents of the crossing. His allusions to Frémont in the diary are sometimes almost friendly.[7]

Halted by the snow, Frémont returned to the bench in the hollow, where he met Fitzpatrick. Between the springs and the bench, the road was strewn with horses floundering in the snow and with equipment and provisions. Fitzpatrick was sent back to the springs, and Tabeau and a strong guard took all the animals back to the pasture of the night before.

The vanguard camped on the bench with a huge fire around the trunk of one of the great pines, spreading on the snow small boughs on which they placed their blankets. A strong wind made the ten-degree temperature one of the bitterest they had experienced. Two Indians joined them. By now they knew a few words of the Indian language, and they half understood when an old man began pleading with them in a loud voice to return. If they would go back, he would show them a better way across the mountain. Before them were "rock upon rock—rock upon rock—snow upon snow—snow upon snow." They and their animals would surely die. The Chinook who had come with them from the Dalles understood the old man better than the whites did. Covering his head with his blanket, he began to weep.[8]

Early the next morning the guide, draped in all his finery, stood shivering by the fire. Frémont threw one of his own blankets across the young man's shoulders. A few minutes later he slipped away from the fire, and the explorers never saw him again. That day they did not try to go forward. While part of the men brought up some of the baggage, the rest were busy making snowshoes and sledges.

On February 6 a reconnoitering party on snowshoes, marching in single file and trampling the snow as hard as they could, crossed the valley and climbed a peak to the left of the pass indicated by the guide. About a hundred miles to the west they could see a valley bounded by a low range of mountains. Suddenly Carson exclaimed, "There is the little mountain—it is 15 years ago since I saw it; but I am just as sure as if I had seen it yesterday."[9] El Diablo in the Sacramento Valley was at last in sight, but many miles of snow and broken ridges had to be traversed before they would reach it, exactly a month later.

On the way back to camp, the men made fires at the base of dead trees and stumps. The hike had encouraged them. Far off though it was, their goal was within sight once they crossed the valley. The next day Frémont and a party of men dragged the sleds loaded with baggage about four miles along the trail and camped at the first of several high spots, cleared of snow by wind and sun, revealing grass for the animals. Another day dawned bright, with the mercury reading three degrees below zero. Fitzpatrick sent more loaded sleds, and Frémont moved some of the baggage another mile and a half. When snow clouds began to rise in the southwest, he sent everyone back to Fitzpatrick except Preuss, Carson, Talbot, and Dodson, with directions to send for the animals the next morning.

During the night the wind rose to a gale. Snow began falling before daylight, and all remained in camp. This storm, the only one to hit the explorers on the heights, abated sufficiently toward evening for Fitzpatrick to send four sleds with bedding for the men. The next morning Frémont's party with three sleds moved part of the baggage to the foot of the great mountain.[10]

Two of the burning stumps along the trail had left sheltered holes eight feet deep. These were now put to use, one for sleeping, the other for cooking. Preuss snuggled down on a bearskin to watch the fire and keep plenty of water in a large pot of pea soup and mule meat and a small pot of dog meat, for which Preuss's mule and the dog Klamath had been sacrificed. Some of the horse guard, going to a nearby Indian hut to trade for pine nuts, had also been able to obtain some salt.[11]

The other men had been out tramping down the snow to make a road that would hold up the animals. At the first attempt, the mules broke through, plunged off the trail, and almost lost themselves in the deep snow. After extricating them, the men took them back to their pasture, then made mauls and shovels for beating down the snow. Leaving them working on the road, Frémont and Preuss climbed the highest peak, from which they discovered at their feet a beautiful lake, about fifteen miles long, completely surrounded by mountains. With field glasses they could distinguish snow on the mountains far to the west. To the east a terrible mass of broken mountains stretched as far as they could see, fading off to blue at the horizon.[12]

Two days later, Frémont took Dodson and reconnoitered the other side of the mountain. The snow there was rapidly melting. When they returned the next day, the remaining animals, fifty-seven in all, were safe at the grassy hill near the camp. On February 20 the whole camp, with all animals and equipment, arrived at the pass, 9,338 feet high, a thousand miles from the Dalles.[13]

The next morning Carson aroused the camp with an early fire so that they could cross the beds of snow before the sun softened the crust. A spectacular sunrise flushed the eastern sky, fading as they got into motion, and a little later they heard the sound of thunder and saw lightning flashing below them as a rainstorm built up in the valley to the west.

Picking their way along the ridges was still difficult, for in some shady spots the drifts were so deep that they had to be cut through.[14] On February 23, Frémont and Carson scouted ahead. Reaching a small stream, Carson sprang across. Frémont leaped after him, but his moccasin slipped off the icy rock and he fell, dropping his gun. Seeing him floundering in the current, Carson thought he had been hurt and jumped in after him. The stream was not deep, and they were soon out again, with Carson hastily building a fire. Frémont gave up looking for his gun, came to the fire, and began planning the descent of the mountain.

The next day one of the men found the gun under the ice. The little stream ran almost directly west. Its north bank, sloping south, was almost free of snow. The party made such good time along this slope that Frémont decided the bad traveling was over. Leaving Fitzpatrick to bring along the baggage and the weaker animals, he took seven men, including Carson, and rode ahead to get fresh animals and food from Sutter's Fort to bring back to the weaker party.

Only the ragged edges of their great adventure are left to record. Charles Town became light-headed, wandered into the forest, and was rescued by Jacob Dodson. The next day he plunged into icy water foaming over rocks as if it were a quiet pond in summer.

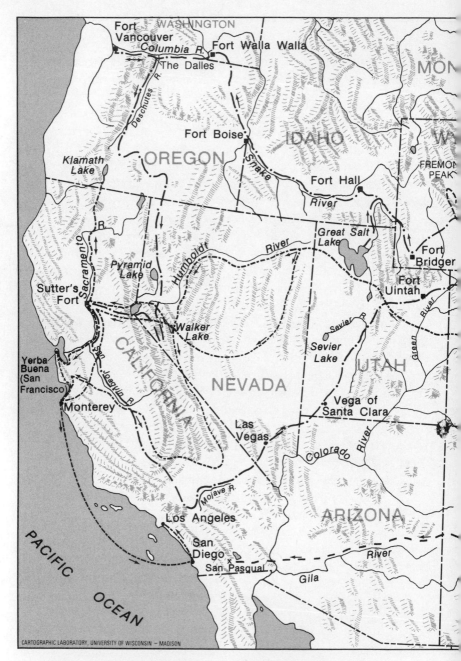

Frémont's First Three Expeditions and Kearny's Route:
Carson served on Frémont's first three expeditions
and guided Kearny west from Socorro, New Mexico.

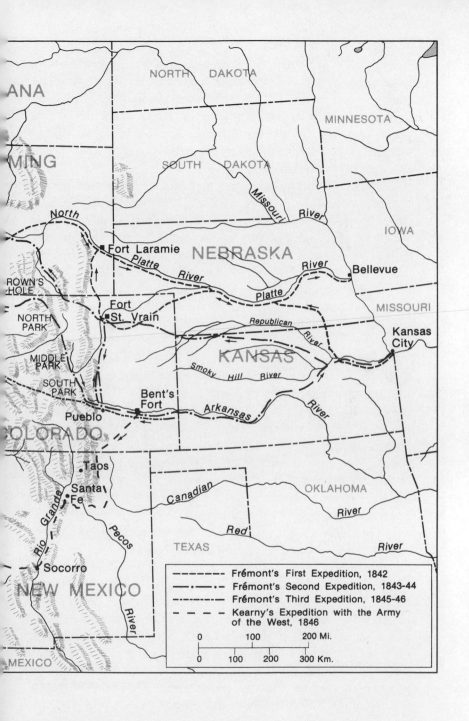

NORTH DAKOTA

MINNESOTA

ANA

MING

SOUTH DAKOTA

Missouri River

IOWA

North Platte River

Fort Laramie

NEBRASKA

Platte River

River

Bellevue

ROWN'S HOLE

NORTH PARK

Fort St. Vrain

Platte

MISSOURI

Republican River

MIDDLE PARK

KANSAS

Kansas City

SOUTH PARK

Smoky Hill River

Bent's Fort

Arkansas River

Pueblo

OLORADO

Taos

Santa Fe

Rio Grande

Canadian

OKLAHOMA

River

Pecos

Red

River

TEXAS

Socorro

NEW MEXICO

River

MEXICO

——————— Frémont's First Expedition, 1842
—·—·—·— Frémont's Second Expedition, 1843-44
—··—··— Frémont's Third Expedition, 1845-46
— — — — Kearny's Expedition with the Army of the West, 1846

0   100   200 Mi.

0   100   200   300 Km.

Perhaps the shock cured him, for he showed no further symptoms of derangement. Preuss, following his inclination to go off alone, wandered for four days, living on wild onions, little frogs, ants, and acorns some Indians gave him. Proveau, the great buffalo-hunting horse, gave out and was left behind. Derosier, going to look for him, got lost on the mountain, went without food, and returned to camp mentally disturbed.[15]

On March 6 the vanguard reached Sutter's Fort near the junction of the Rio de los Americanos and the Sacramento. The next day they took fresh horses and food and returned on their road. When they met Fitzpatrick and the remainder of the party two days later, all the men, weak and emaciated, were on foot, each leading a horse or mule as pitiable as himself. Many of the animals had slipped and fallen on the steep slopes, some losing their packs as well as themselves. Only thirty-three animals, including those brought in by the advance party, reached the camp near Sutter's Fort.[16]

One morning while the men were making new packsaddles and replenishing their stock of provisions and goods, Derosier jumped to his feet, convinced that his mule, which was tied nearby, had been left on the mountain. By the time the men realized that he had gone, he could not be found. Even the Indians had not seen him. Sutter's people finally found him and cared for him until he was well enough to be sent home.[17] Five other men were also left at the fort. Samuel Neal wished to remain and take advantage of the great demand in the country for mechanics. Four others "were discharged with their own consent."[18]

On March 24 the expedition started homeward, forced south by continuing heavy snow on the Sierra Nevada. The large cavalcade—twenty five beef cattle, five milk cows, one hundred thirty horses and mules—was forced by the half-wild mules and horses to rush headlong through valleys and across prairies bright with blue lupines and golden poppies. Frémont could not pause to take astronomical or topographical readings or to indulge in his study of plants. Carson found a good road through the sandhills and over the juncture of the southern Sierra and the Coast Range, and Frémont approached the Mojave Desert convinced that no Buenaventura River ran from the Great Basin to the Pacific. When exhaustion slowed the animals down on the Mojave River, the cavalcade rested while the men dried meat.

Two Mexicans rode in from the east, Andreas Fuentes and Pablo Hernandez, a boy of eleven. About eighty miles away in the desert, they had been encamped with the wife of Fuentes, the parents of Pablo, and Santiago Giacome, waiting to join the great yearly caravan of traders in order more safely to take their *caballada* of about thirty horses to New Mexico. Fuentes and Pablo had been on horse guard when about a hundred Indians charged into the camp and surrounded the horses. At a shout of command from Giacome, Fuentes and the boy drove the horses over and through the Indians and did not stop, except to change horses, until they reached the Agua de Tomaso. Leaving the horses there, they had ridden the next twenty miles to Frémont's camp.

Frémont took the two Mexicans into his mess and promised to do what he could to help them. When the party reached the Agua de Tomaso, they found that the Indians had driven off the animals.[19] Carson relates vividly what happened next:

The Mexican requested [Frémont] to aid him to retake his animals. Frémont stated to the party that if they wished to volunteer . . . he would furnish animals for them to ride. Godey and myself volunteered with the expectation that some men of our party would join us. They did not. We two and the Mexican took the trail of the animals. . . . In twenty miles the Mexican's horse gave out. We sent him back. . . . During the night it was very dark. [We] had to dismount to feel for the trail. By sign on the trail we became aware that the Indians had passed after sunset. We were much fatigued, required rest, unsaddled, wrapped ourselves in the wet saddle blankets and laid down. Could not make any fire for fear of its being seen. Passed a miserably cold night. In the morning we arose very early, went down in a deep ravine, made a small fire to warm ourselves and as soon as it was light, we again took the trail.

As the sun was rising [we] saw the Indians two miles ahead of us, encamped having a feast. They had killed five animals. We were compelled to leave our horses; they could not travel. We hid them among the rocks, continued on the trail, crawled in among the horses. A young one got frightened; that frightened the rest. The Indians noticed the commotion . . . and sprung for their arms. We now considered it time to charge on the Indians . . . thirty in number. . . . I fired, killed one. Godey fired, missed, but reloaded and fired, killing another. . . . The remainder run. I took the rifles and ascended the hill to keep guard . . . Godey scalped the one he had shot and was proceeding towards the one I had shot. He was not yet dead [and] was behind some rocks. As Godey approached, he raised [and] let fly an arrow. It passed through Godey's shirt collar. He again fell and Godey finished him.[20]

With a war whoop Carson and Godey rode into camp that afternoon, driving the fifteen remaining horses and waving the two scalps, to the disgust of Preuss. His attitude would change after the senseless death of Tabeau, which occurred almost two weeks later.[21] In the meantime the men had discovered the naked and mutilated bodies of Hernandez and Giacome at the Archilette and assumed that the two women had been carried off. A little lapdog of Pablo's mother was ecstatic at seeing the boy, but Pablo could only cry inconsolably, *"Mi padre! Mi madre!"*[22] Another party later found the bodies of the two women, mutilated and staked to the ground.[23]

As the explorers rode on, Fuentes pointed out a cactus called *bisnada* by the Spaniards. The cactus has a slightly acid, juicy pulp, that gives some relief from thirst, and the men ate this and moistened their mouths with the acid of the sour dock as they made another dry *jornada* on May 4—between fifty and sixty miles without a drop of water, the heated air seeming to draw the moisture from their bodies. They kept going into the night. About midnight the wild mules began running ahead, and in a mile or two they reached "a bold, running stream," where they remained during the day.

Indians crowded nearby bluffs, tried to surround the horses, shouted and threatened. A man who appeared to be a chief forced his way into the camp. "Why, there are none of you," he said. He counted the men. "So many," he sneered, showing the number with his fingers, "and we—we are a great many." His gesture swept the hills and mountains. "If you have your arms, we have these!" He twanged his bowstring.

The bold, aggressive insults of this man filled Carson with fury. "Don't say that, old man!" he cried. "Don't you say that! Your life's in danger!"[24]

Early that morning before the Indians appeared, men had been sent to bring in several animals that had been left behind near the camp. Finding the animals already killed and cut up, the meat drying on bushes a short distance from the trail, they knew the Indians were watching and hurried back to camp. That evening when Frémont gave a worn-out horse to some of the Indians for a feast, he started a chorus of complaints from those who had been given none, for they would not share with one another. They could not be discouraged from crowding up to the camp. With long sticks hooked at the end, some hauled out lizards and other small animals from their holes and came up to the fires to roast and eat these small creatures.

The Diggers continued to follow the explorers stealthily. The bottom of the Rio Virgen was thickly covered by their tracks. No horse or mule could be left behind to rest and be brought up later. On May 9 Tabeau, with a strong guard, took the horses to a nearby hollow. Frémont, who had been arranging plants, dropped off to sleep. He was awakened by Carson. Tabeau had gone back to the former camp a mile away to look for a lame mule and had not returned. While Carson was speaking, a smoke rose suddenly from a cottonwood grove below them. The Indians had struck a blow and were warning neighbors to be on guard. Carson and several others rode back down the river to look for Tabeau. The mule was several miles away, standing among some bushes, mortally wounded. Not far away they found a dark pool on the ground. They were now sure that Tabeau was dead, but in the darkness they could find nothing more. The next morning Frémont and several men returned to the spot and saw where Tabeau had struggled among the bushes before he fell at the pool of blood and died. His body had been dragged to the river bank and thrown into the torrent.

The men had all liked Tabeau and wished to avenge his death, but the animals were too weak to pursue the Indians into the mountains.[25] Preuss, in particular, was filled with horror, remembering the times he had wandered off from camp, the foolhardiness of his naive trust in the Indians. "They lurk like wolves between the rocks along the road. Often we are surrounded by thirty or fifty of them without knowing it. One hears nothing, yet one is watched by a hundred eyes. Woe to him who moves too far away from the party or accidentally remains somewhat behind."[26]

Their twenty-seven days in the desert ended May 12 when they climbed a ridge to Las Vegas de Santa Clara, a mountain meadow about a mile wide by ten miles long, with water and grass for recovering the animals' strength. Still the men could not relax their vigilance. The caravan moved all day in a state of alertness. They were constantly dogged by swarms of Indians, some of whom came up to the camp, shouting taunts and threats. After their long day of toil, the men kept guard all night, a third of them on duty at all times. They were convinced that a debate was going on among the Diggers as to whether the party should be attacked.[27]

Their anxiety was relieved when Joseph Walker appeared with a party of nine, for Walker was the one best acquainted with this part of the mountains. As he had been riding with the great caravan, he had seen signs that the Frémont expedition had passed and had hurried after it. Several of his horses had been wounded, and he had had to kill two of the Indians to make them keep their distance.

The white crests of the Wasatch Mountains appeared to the east. With Walker as guide, the party traveled along parallel to these mountains, on May 17 leaving the Spanish Trail when it bore off to the southwest. Three days later they met Wakara, the Ute robber chief, on his way to exact tribute from the great caravan. As tokens of friendship, he proposed an exchange of gifts between him and Frémont, giving a Mexican blanket and receiving a fine one from Vancouver. "You are a chief, and I am one, too," Preuss quoted him as saying, "It would be bad if we should evaluate exactly the price of one or the other. You present me with yours, and I present you with mine. Fine!"[28]

On May 23 François Badeau, pulling a gun toward himself by its muzzle, accidentally discharged it and was shot through the head. He was buried on the bank of the Sevier, the second casualty of the long journey. Three days later, the long preoccupation with hunger ended when the men reached Utah Lake, where they were able to buy dried fish from the Indians. An old acquaintance also gave Carson a piece of venison. Walker guided them through the Wasatch Mountains, sometimes hugging the cliffs so closely that the going was difficult for the pack animals, but leading to an open and easy pass. From there the trails were familiar to Carson, along the Strawberry, the Duchesne, the Uintah.

Carson enjoyed a little joking with Preuss, who reported:

Kit bought an Indian boy of about twelve to fourteen years for forty dollars. He is to eat only raw meat, in order to get courage, says Kit, and in a few years he hopes to have trained him, with the Lord's help, so that he will at least be capable of stealing horses. He actually eats the raw marrow, with which Kit supplies him plentifully. He belongs to the Paiute Nation, which subsists only on mice, locusts, and roots, and such a life as the present must please him very much."[29]

It pleased them all very much. They reached Fort Uintah, where Auguste Archambeault, a hunter in the class of Carson and Godey, joined the expedition.[30] To the north lay the Uintah Mountains, crested with snow, their upper slopes wooded with aspens and evergreens. Beyond these they descended by a rocky and narrow ravine to Brown's Hole, where the hunters killed several bighorn sheep.[31] Carson merely mentions these old haunts as points touched on the way to Bent's Fort, with no hint of what memories they may have evoked.[32]

Ascending the Little Snake and St. Vrain's Fork,[33] they entered a pine forest, through which they rode easily to the summit and looked out across the Medicine Bow and Sweetwater Mountains. No buffalo grazed along the placid streams and broad meadows of New Park, and on the way to the pass toward the south, Carson noticed that an Arapaho village had gone before them into the heavy groves of fir, spruce, and pine. The Arapahoes descended before them into Middle Park, and Carson remained constantly on the alert. Coming from the country of the Utes, their traditional enemies, he did not want the Arapahoes to see his party first. Riding ahead on June 18, he saw the Indians coming and dropped back to join his party. Before long thirty Arapahoes rode up. They said their main camp was in the park on Grand River,[34] and they were on their way to the hills to hunt and dig roots. However, as soon as they received presents, they turned and hurried back to their village.

Carson quickly sought the most protected place he could find for the cavalcade—an opening among the willows, the Colorado behind, the flooded bottoms in front. The men had no time to fort up before about two hundred well-armed Indians galloped up to the edge of the bottom. The Stars and Stripes was planted between the explorers and the Indians. A short parley and a large number of presents brought about a truce. About twenty Sioux were among them, including an old chief who, having seen the expedition on its way west, had tried to restrain the warriors.

The Arapahoes told Frémont that he could cross the Colorado near their camp. Though not convinced, he was too vulnerable to refuse to take their word, but he put several sloughs between his camp and theirs and forted strongly on the bank of the river, which was rapid and deep. In spite of the explorers' vigilance, Indians swarmed about the camp and several things were stolen. The next morning Frémont crossed the river lower down, landing on the left bank of a tributary that came from the south. Large numbers of buffalo herds began to appear, driven from the Bayou Salade by the Indians. The river divided into three forks. Since the one on the right had no buffalo, Carson concluded that no pass was to be found there and led the party up the middle fork into the pines, where they put up a strong fort.

The next morning six trappers walked into camp. Two of their companions had already been killed by the Arapahoes, and they wished to join the explorers. Carson and the other hunters returned with them to their camp to bring their animals and baggage. Suddenly they were surrounded by Arapahoes, who told them that their scouts had discovered a village of Utes in South Park and that a large war party was going to attack them. The main body of warriors had already gone up the left fork of the river. This group had followed the explorers to add them to their force. Carson told them the men were already too far up the mountain to turn back, but would join them in Bayou Salade.

When the men reached the Continental Divide[35] that afternoon and descended into South Park, they saw a group of horsemen coming over a spur. These proved to be Ute women, who said that beyond the ridge their warriors and the Arapahoes were fighting. They begged the whites to help their men, but joining an Indian war was no part of Frémont's plan. He and Carson took council on how best to avoid the Indians. Keeping the ridge between themselves and the battle, they hurried along until they were fifteen miles south of the village.

The next day they left the South Platte where it turns abruptly toward Pike's Peak. Over a gentle rise they entered the broken spurs of the mountains bordering the plains. Small tributaries of the Arkansas ran through grassy and open hollows, but in a few miles descended into deep canyons. For several days the party traveled laboriously across this broken country.

On June 28 they rode out of the mountains, and on July 1 they emerged from the trees along the river at Bent's Fort. George Bent, who was in charge, ran up the flag, fired the guns, and gave them a cordial welcome. "On the 4th," Carson recalled, "Mr. Bent gave Fremont and party a splendid dinner. The day was celebrated as well, if not better, than in many of the towns of the States."[36]

On this expedition Carson had been of inestimable service to the explorer and had become the trusted guide in unfamiliar terrain, the epitome of courage and high morale in crossing the Sierra, the indispensable adviser in dealing with the Indians. The report of the expedition subsequently brought him to the attention of a world eager to hear about the untamed West, and he became a symbol of the daring and intelligence by which the frontier was being extended.

Chapter 12

Waiting for War

Carson reported that he remained in Taos until March 1845, but he thought nothing of riding a hundred miles any given day, so it can be assumed that Taos was his base. A trader name Webb, camped about sixty miles north of Taos on the Culebra River in the fall of 1844, had a vivid glimpse of Kit, Maxwell, and Tim Goodale:

They approached at a brisk gallop, each with a led horse. They dismounted, unsaddled, and in a few minutes had a fire kindled, and the coffeepot over the fire. . . . As soon as they got dinner cooking (coffee boiling, a prairie dog dressed and opened out on a stick before the fire), Carson and Maxwell came to our camp. . . . They left Pueblo that morning and expected to reach Taos that night. They soon left, ate their dinner, saddled their horses, caught their led horses, and were off, Kit galloping up to the trail rope, or lariat, of his horse and, stooping in his saddle, picked it up and was off without breaking a gallop, giving us this word of caution: "Look out for your har, boys! The Ute are plenty about here!"[1]

Pueblo was over a hundred miles to the north and beyond the Sangre de Cristos.

In March 1845 Carson and Dick Owens crossed the Sangre de

Cristos to the Little Cimarron, chose a site on the Beaubien–Miranda Land Grant of 1841, built themselves little huts, put in grain, and began getting out timber for building.[2]

Frémont, with some of his former men and a dozen Delaware Indians, was hurrying west, ostensibly on an expedition for the Topographical Engineers, but prepared to accept whatever role circumstances required. Congress had voted early in 1845 to annex Texas, a step that many believed would result in war with Mexico. Theodore Talbot and Alexis Godey were with Frémont, and he counted on getting Carson, who had given his word the year before that he would join if Frémont went exploring again. At Bent's Fort Frémont heard where Carson was and sent an express that reached the Little Cimarron in early August. Without hesitation, both Carson and Owens sold out for about half the value of their crops and equipment and hastened to Bent's Fort.[3] Frémont was glad to see them both.

This was like Carson, prompt, self-sacrificing, and true. . . . That Owens was a good man it is enough to say that he and Carson were friends. Cool, brave, and of good judgment; a good hunter and good shot; experienced in mountain life; he was an acquisition, and proved reliable throughout the campaign. . . . Godey had proved himself during the preceding journey, which had brought out his . . . resolute and aggressive courage. Quick in deciding and prompt in acting he had also the French élan and their gayety and courage. . . . I mention him here because the three men come fitly together . . . under Napoleon, they might have become Marshals . . . Carson, of great courage; quick and complete perception, taking in at a glance the advantages as well as the chances for defeat; Godey, insensible to danger, of perfect coolness and stubborn resolution; Owens, equal in courage to the others, and in coolness equal to Godey, had the coup-d'oeil of a chess-player, covering the whole field with a glance that sees the best move.[4]

From Bent's Fort the expedition went up the Arkansas to the canyon, climbed the mountain to meet a tributary, and ascended it between evergreen forests toward the Bayou Salade. Beyond the park, they crossed the rugged western ridge to rejoin the Arkansas and followed one of the forks to its head high in the mountains. After crossing the Continental Divide, they rode down Piney River and on northwest to the Colorado, crossed the river and climbed Sheep Mountain to the head of the White River.[5] Following the White as it flowed west to the Green, the trail led through gentle green valleys, with plenty of buffalo, elk, deer, and mountain sheep. Here they met Joseph Reddeford Walker, who joined the expedition as guide. In the mountains they also encountered Old Bill Williams, who traveled with them until he learned that they intended to cross the desert to California. This he refused to do.

After crossing the Green, they rode up the Uintah and the Duchesne, crossed the Wasatch Mountains, and followed the Provo River to Utah Lake. Turning north, they encamped on October 13 by the Great Salt Lake, where they remained for two weeks, exploring and surveying.[6]

This was a low-water season for the lake, with crusted salt around the edges. Frémont, Carson, and a few others rode through the water over a bed of salt to the largest island. They stayed two days, killed several antelope, and named it Antelope Island. On the shore an old Ute was waiting. He reproached them for killing his antelope and demanded payment. Frémont cheerfully had a bale of goods unpacked and gave him a red cloth, a knife, and tobacco, at which he nodded and grunted with pleasure.[7]

Frémont was determined to try crossing the desert, which all the men thought had never been crossed by a white man. Even the Indians were not aware that Jedediah Smith and two men had crossed it from west to east in June 1827, sometimes burying themselves in the sand in order to endure the great heat and dessicating air.

Although Carson knew nothing of this part of the Great Basin, he was willing to help Frémont carry through his plan to attempt a crossing. Far across the desert a peak-shaped mountain rose above the sandy waste. Carson, Archambeault, Maxwell, and Basil Lajeunesse started toward this peak at night, taking a pack mule carrying water and food. If they found water or grass, they were to make a smoke that Frémont could see with his telescope from the mountain near his camp.

For about sixty miles they rode over terrain "as level and bare as a barn floor."[8] When they reached the mountains, they found small streams trickling over the bare rocks, their banks green with grass. They sent up the smoke signal, and Archambeault started back to guide Frémont across. As he approached the camp, the jingle of his spurs in the darkness was welcome music to the men. The next day at dark they reached Carson's party. Only a few animals had died of heat, thirst, and hunger. The mountain, which Frémont named Pilot Peak, became a prominent landmark on the Hastings Cutoff.[9]

After a day's rest for the animals, the expedition started forward. November 8 they encamped on a small tributary[10] of one of the main forks of Mary's River, which Frémont now renamed the Humboldt. Placing Edward Kern, his topographer, in charge of a large body of men, he directed him to survey the Humboldt and its valley to the sink where it was lost in the sand. Walker was to guide this group to a rendezvous at Walker Lake near the foot of the Sierra.

With Carson and nine other men, Frémont set out directly westward across the Basin. They had three unusual encounters with Indians. One day as they rode along the foot of a mountain, they saw a light smoke curling up from a ravine. Riding quietly up, they found a single Indian, entirely naked, standing in deep thought before a small earthen pot that hung over a little sagebrush fire. A bunch of sagebrush squirrels lay on the ground nearby with his bow and arrows. The men were right upon him before he became aware of them. When a wild look around showed him that escape was impossible, he offered with a deprecating smile to share his squirrels with them. Frémont reassured him with a shake of the hand and a small gift. After riding away, he discovered that the Delawares had taken the bow and arrows, which were excellently made, the arrows tipped with obsidian nearly as sharp as steel. He made the Indians return them to the solitary hunter, reminding them that without these weapons he would be in danger of starvation.

Another time the Delaware Saghundai found a spring for the night's camp. In the mud near it, he saw the print of a woman's naked foot, but he saw no other signs of human life. Carson had shot an antelope, and after making a good supper of its meat, the men were lying around the fire enjoying their pipes. Suddenly Carson, who was lying back with his arms behind his head, half rose up, pointing across the fire and exclaiming, "Good God! Look there!"

Shading her eyes from the glare of the fire by her bony, gnarled hands, an ancient woman stood peering at them, her grizzled hair hanging down over face and shoulders, her body nearly naked. Terrified at sight of the white men, she turned to run, but the men gathered around her and brought her back to the fire. They gave her about a quarter of the antelope, expecting her to roast it by their fire, but she clutched it and darted off into the darkness. Someone grabbed a firebrand and ran after her, but calling her brought no response. The next morning fresh tracks showed that she had come to the spring for water. They left a little food for her and left the fire burning. Nut pines and junipers grew on the mountain. She would have both food and fire even after the snow came. Frémont named this place Saghundai's Spring.

On the third encounter with Indians nothing happened, nothing at all. The men had reached one of the lakes near the foot of the Sierra Nevada. As they turned a point of the lake shore, a party of twelve or fourteen Indians came into view, advancing single file, their heads bent forward and eyes fixed on the ground. When they met the whites, they neither raised their eyes nor turned their heads. The explorers likewise passed on without halting or speaking.

November 24 they camped at the rendezvous on Walker Lake. Three days later the Talbot–Kern party arrived. The great mass of the Sierra Nevada loomed to the west. Frémont now divulged to his men that they were going to California, as no doubt they had already surmised.[11]

Having sat in on many discussions of Thomas Hart Benton and his colleagues in the government, Frémont felt that he understood clearly what would be expected of him when hostilities with Mexico began, as they seemed certain to do. "For me, no distinct course or definite instruction could be laid down, but the probabilities were made known to me as well as what to do when they became facts. The distance was too great for timely communication; but failing this, I was given discretion to act."[12] His band of brave and skilled riflemen would be invaluable to supplement the navy forces in the harbors along the Pacific Coast, and his activities seem to have been designed to keep them as near as possible to the area in which they would be needed. Since his position was confidential, he was not at liberty to discuss it with anyone.

An interesting aspect of this military and political position, into which Frémont with so much enthusiasm allowed himself to be maneuvered, is that he had no training whatever in either field. His sole political experience had been in listening to Benton and his friends. His education had been in science and mathematics. He had entered the army as a lieutenant with in-the-field training in surveying and topography, with no notion of military rules and procedures. Though brave, he was a poor shot with a rifle.[13]

When they met at Walker Lake, both parts of the expedition were low on provisions. Knowing how slow and hazardous crossing the Sierra could be at this time of year, Frémont sent the larger party under Kern and Talbot, with Walker as guide, around by the southern tip of the Sierra Nevada, while he took Carson, Owens, Maxwell, Godey, and eleven others to attempt a crossing to Sutter's Fort before snow blocked the passes.

This time they approached the peaks by way of the Salmon Trout (Truckee) River along a road already established by emigrants. The weather continued fair and mild. When on December 5 they climbed the rocky ridge to the crest of the divide, 7,200 feet above the sea, the thermometer at sunrise read twenty-two degrees. Now they turned from the emigrant road and traveled along a broad ridge. The straight red boles of the pines lifted tufted crowns to incredible heights and filtered the sunshine to a "dim religious light."[14] Great cedars lifted their lacy crests among the pines. Descending among the long-acorned oaks, they reached Grimes Ranch near Sutter's Fort on December 9.

The crossing of the Sierra Nevada had been so easy, the supply of grass and game so plentiful, that neither animals nor men needed prolonged rest. After buying some animals, a small drove of cattle, and other needed supplies, the men started south to meet Kern. The rivers were low. They met no difficulties until they tried to ascend the Merced and cross over to the head of the Lake Fork of the Tulare, known to the Californians as the Rio de los Reyes

(Kings River). Near the headwaters of the Mariposas River,[15] they came upon scattered bones dragged about by wolves and bears. They were among the Horse-thief Indians.

Dick Owens, Maxwell, and two Delawares were sent forward to reconnoiter. Frémont made camp in a little glade where a clear brook ran over a bed of slate through clumps of oak trees. The men had barely removed the saddles when they heard the crack of rifles, shouting, and dogs barking. Within minutes they were galloping toward the sounds. They found the four scouts at bay among rocks and bushes on top of a knoll, with more than a hundred Indians creeping up the slopes. Shouting in Spanish, the Indians had almost surrounded the knoll and captured the horses, while their women and children at the nearby village screamed and shouted encouragement. As the explorers galloped into view, the Delawares yelled and dashed out to retrieve their horses. Owen and Maxwell fired at the same time, dropping one of the leaders of the assault. Taken aback by this loss and the sudden appearance of reinforcements, the Indians withdrew a little, and Frémont started the men back to camp. The Indians surrounded them, shouting threats from the rocks and bushes, but pressed no nearer.

Half the men remained on watch through the night, and when morning came, they turned back down the mountain. They had not gone far when an Indian was seen galloping toward the plain. Maxwell, riding ahead, spurred forward to cut him off. Frémont, Godey, and two of the Delawares followed, hoping to capture him, but before they could come up, Maxwell and the Indian were exchanging shots. The Indian fell, and the Delawares captured his horse.

On December 22 they reached the Lake Fork, where Walker had been instructed to bring the Kern–Talbot group. After two days, still seeing no sign of their friends, they turned up the mountain, thinking Kern might have camped higher up among the sugar pines and cedars. Indians crowded them all the way to the divide, preventing the cattle and horses from grazing. Finding no trace of Kern's party, they began their descent. The animals, gaunt from lack of food, were becoming lame from continued riding on the rocky slopes. When snow began to fall heavily on January 1, the men had to leave the cattle and get themselves and the horses down before snow blocked the way. They returned through the San Joaquin Valley, which had plenty of game and was already green with spring grass. January 15 they reached Sutter's Fort.

Carson and Owens rode back to search for the Kern–Talbot party, while Frémont took Sutter's launch to Yerba Buena, where he called on Vice-consul Leidesdorff, who rode with him to Monterey. Consul Thomas A. Larkin took him to pay his respects to the commanding general, Don José Castro; the prefect, Manuel de Jesús Castro; the alcalde, Manuel Díaz; and the former governor, Alvarado. Frémont readily obtained permission to survey the nearest route from the United States to the Pacific Ocean, and the Mexican officials treated him with every courtesy.

Meanwhile, Carson and Owens had met Walker, who was out looking for them, and had conducted the party back to the Laguna Rancho, just east of San José, where the reunited expedition settled down to rest and refit. For over a month they remained in the vicinity of Monterey, climbing Wildcat Ridge to marvel at the redwoods, descending to the coast to enjoy the sea air and the picturesque rocks and cypresses.

On March 3 they camped at Hartnell Rancho, about twenty-five miles from Monterey. Lieutenant Chavez came to them there, introduced himself in an abrupt manner, and handed Frémont a letter from General Castro, dated March 5, 1846. The Americans were ordered to leave California and were threatened with force if they did not comply at once.[16]

Frémont told Chavez to tell Castro that he refused to comply with an order insulting to his government and to himself. The next day he moved his camp to Gavilán Peak, a hill a few miles away, built a strong fort of solid logs, and set up a tall sapling on which the American flag was raised amid the cheers of the men. Their reaction to the whole affair is expressed succinctly by Carson: "We remained in our position . . . for three days, had become tired of waiting for the attack of the valiant Mexican General."[17] The third day the flagpole fell over, and Frémont told the men it was time to move the camp.

They "retired slowly and growlingly"[18] over undulating country toward the Bear River settlements in the Sacramento Valley, crossed the Feather River, reached Butte Creek and the ranch of

Samuel Neal, the former blacksmith who had stayed with Sutter on the second expedition. Neal gave them a fat cow, and some of the Indians ran races for the head and offal of the animal. March 30 they camped on Deer Creek, opposite the house of Lassen's ranch. Peter Lassen, a native of Denmark, also made them welcome, and they stayed until April 5. The men thought they were preparing for a journey to the Columbia. Frémont expected to go as far as Klamath Lake.[19]

As they turned up the Pit River, Mount Shasta, over fourteen thousand feet high, rose above the forest to the north. Game was plentiful. A fierce hailstorm struck while they were on Cow Creek, whitening the ground and surrounding peaks and scattering the animals. Frémont turned back to Lassen's ranch, where he remained for another two weeks, taking temperature readings and again establishing the latitude and longitude.

April 24 they again left Lassen's, ascended the Sacramento for two days, then turned up a small tributary. Soon they were climbing steeply among mingled oak and long-leaf pine, with mariposa poppies waving in grassy meadows. The mountain rose rapidly into the area of snow and sugar pines as they approached the pass between the Sierra Nevada and the Cascade Mountains. At Klamath Lake on May 6 they traded with the Indians for fish and for the use of canoes to cross the Klamath River, then started north between the lake and the mountains.

On the night of May 7 as Frémont stood alone by the fire, he heard the sound of horses. From the forest into the light of the fire rode Samuel Neal and Levi Sigler, sagging with weariness. Behind them on the trail, Lieutenant Archibald Gillespie of the U.S. Marines was bringing letters to Frémont from Washington. With the officer were Joseph Stepperfeldt, Peter Lassen, and Ben Harrison.[20] Because of the great danger from Indians, Gillespie had sent Neal and Sigler ahead on their best horses. The Indians had tried to cut them off at the upper end of the lake. Neal doubted that Frémont could reach Gillespie in time to save him.

At dawn the next morning Frémont took Carson, Owens, Godey, Basil Lajeunesse, Maxwell, four Delawares, and one other man and started on the back trail. At the end of a day's hard riding, they stopped at one of their former camps, the nearest water to the

1. Carson first went to the rendezvous country from New Mexico in the employment of *Thomas Fitzpatrick* in 1831. Later they were both on Frémont's Second Expedition. Photograph courtesy of the Kit Carson Memorial Foundation, Inc., Kit Carson Home and Museum, Taos, New Mexico.

2. Although Carson worked for *William Bent* for only eight months as a hunter for Bent's Old Fort, the two men were friends in later life and sought to influence government policy favorably toward the Indians. Photograph courtesy of Kit Carson Memorial Foundation, Inc., Kit Carson Home and Museum, Taos, New Mexico.

3. Carson trapped for furs and fought the Blackfeet under *Jim Bridger*. Bridger and Thomas Fitzpatrick are both considered rivals of Carson for first place among the mountain men. Photograph courtesy of the Kit Carson Memorial Foundation, Inc., Kit Carson Home and Museum, Taos, New Mexico.

4. *Alexis Godey* was the hero of Frémont's disastrous Fourth Expedition. Frémont said that under Napoleon, Carson, Owens, and Godey would have been marshals. Godey settled in California. Illustration from the *Century Magazine*, 1891.

5. *Lucien B. Maxwell*, half French, half Scotch-Irish, became the greatest land owner of that time in the United States. He and Carson were close friends throughout Kit's life. Photograph courtesy of the Kit Carson Memorial Foundation, Inc., Kit Carson Home and Museum, Taos, New Mexico.

6. *Richard Lemon Owings* (Dick Owens) was Carson's favorite trapping companion. After the conquest of California, Owens joined his family in Indiana and married there. This picture was made when he was seventy-five or eighty years old. Photograph courtesy of Richard Owings.

7. *George D. Brewerton*, author of
the article "A Ride with Kit Carson"
(1853), thought of writing Carson's
biography. It is too bad he did not do
so, for he was a more talented writer
than Dr. Peters, who did write one.
Photograph courtesy of the Kit Carson Memorial Foundation, Inc., Kit
Carson Home and Museum, Taos,
New Mexico.

8. *Edward Fitzgerald Beale,* a naval lieutenant who made several transcontinental crossings, was genuinely fond of Carson. Along with Jessie Benton Frémont, he wrote and thought of Carson as "dear old Kit." Courtesy of the Collection, National Trust for Historic Preservation.

9. Carson reluctantly guided *General Stephen Watts Kearny* to California from Socorro, New Mexico, for it was Kearny who brought Frémont to court-martial. Photograph courtesy of the Kit Carson Memorial Foundation, Inc., Kit Carson Home and Museum, Taos, New Mexico.

10. *John C. Frémont* craved fame and power, which he had and then lost. Carson was one whom he advanced, along with himself, and Carson repaid him by his loyalty through thick and thin. Photograph courtesy of the Kit Carson Memorial Foundation, Inc., Kit Carson Home and Museum, Taos, New Mexico.

11. *James H. Carleton* was an admirer of Kit Carson and his early exploits. He determined to make Carson into a military officer and finally succeeded to a considerable degree. Photograph courtesy of the Kit Carson Memorial Foundation, Inc., Kit Carson Home and Museum, Taos, New Mexico.

8

12. Josefa Carson's older sister, *Ignacia*, was usually known as Mrs. Charles Bent, though no marriage record has been found. She was also mother-in-law to Carson's friend Tom Boggs, who became guardian of the Carson children in 1868. Photograph courtesy of Kit Carson Memorial Foundation, Inc., Kit Carson Home and Museum, Taos, New Mexico.

13. *Jessie Benton Frémont* took a special interest in Carson and wrote of him after his death with great perception about his character. Photograph courtesy of the Kit Carson Memorial Foundation, Kit Carson Home and Museum, Taos, New Mexico.

14. This sketch of Carson was made by Lieutenant George D. Brewerton in 1848. The signature may be Carson's, but the writing above it is not his. The sketch has merit but is not widely known. Photograph courtesy of Kit Carson Memorial Foundation, Inc., Kit Carson Home and Museum, Taos, New Mexico.

15. This may be the earliest daguerrotype of Carson if it was taken in Washington, as Jack K. Boyer believes, in 1847 or 1848. It may, however, date from the period 1854–56, when he was Indian agent. The beaver hat might be the one presented to him by Major Carleton, but we have no proof of this. Photograph courtesy of Kit Carson Memorial Foundation, Inc., Kit Carson Home and Museum, Taos, New Mexico.

16. Probably photographed in St. Louis in 1865, this likeness of Carson is one of the most familiar. It was used for a commemorative Carson medal in 1968. Kit, who is wearing the uniform of a colonel, had not yet begun to lose weight at that time. Photograph courtesy of Kit Carson Memorial Foundation, Inc., Kit Carson Home and Museum, Taos, New Mexico.

17. Brigadier General Carson, 1866. Carson appears as a very handsome man in this picture, which is probably a photograph, although there is a crayon portrait that is very similar. Photograph courtesy of the Kit Carson Memorial Foundation, Inc., Kit Carson Home and Museum, Taos, New Mexico.

18. This is one of two pictures made on Carson's trip east in 1868. In this one he is all slicked up for a picture but showing the ravages of his aneurism. It is one of the best-known Carson pictures. Photograph courtesy of Kit Carson Memorial Foundation, Inc., Kit Carson Home and Museum, Taos, New Mexico.

19. This photograph, also taken on his trip to the East in 1868, shows him on a visit to Mrs. Frémont in New York and was apparently taken for the Frémont family only. He has made no attempt to put on a good appearance and his clothes hang loosely on his frame and his hair is uncombed. This "candid" shot has seldom been reproduced. Photograph courtesy of Donald Jackson and Mary Lee Spence.

place where Neal had left Gillespie. If he was still on the trail, he would stop at this camp. As the sun was sinking behind the trees, the lieutenant and his three companions rode from the forest.

Gillespie had come by the quickest way across Mexico as confidential agent of Secretary of the Navy Bancroft "to ascertain the disposition of the California people, to conciliate their feelings in favor of the United States . . . with a view to counteracting the designs of the British."[21] He brought a letter of introduction from Bancroft and said that he had been told to reveal his instructions to Frémont. He had also brought letters and papers from Senator Benton and the family and had been instructed to find Frémont wherever he might be. He had followed six hundred miles into the mountain wilderness and into serious danger.

Both parties were exhausted from their long ride, and Frémont was doubly so from having slept little the night before. The communication from Senator Benton, guarded in expression because of the danger of its being intercepted by the Mexicans, required interpretation; and on the basis of that interpretation, Frémont had to make decisions. He felt that he was being told that the United States intended to take California, that this must be done before England made any move to do so, that he was being relieved from further duties as a military topographer to take up other duties as an officer of the army; and he realized that he was the only such officer in California.[22] Since war was inevitable, he decided that his course was to return to the Sacramento Valley and use his men and his influence to the best advantage of his country.

Having come to this decision, he lay down under an overhanging cedar without posting a guard. He was jarred awake by Carson's voice, calling to Basil, "What's the matter over there?"

Out of the menacing silence came a groan, followed instantly by a cry from Kit and Owens, "Indians!"[23]

The Delawares, who were lying near their fire, sprang to cover, rifles in hand. Crane was jumping from side to side, trying to shoot, but the rifle he had picked up was not loaded. As the Klamaths charged into the open, he stood erect, swinging the butt of the rifle at them until he fell with five arrows in his breast. The evening before, Carson had accidentally broken the tube of his rifle. Rushing at the Klamath chief, he fired his pistol and cut the string that held the Indian's tomahawk. Maxwell fired and hit the chief in the leg. Stepperfeldt fired a fatal shot into the chief's back, and he fell in front of Crane. The rest of the Indians ran into the forest.

Denny had been killed with arrows. Basil's skull had been split by a tomahawk, the sound of the blow waking Carson. Now someone threw a blanket over Crane, and Owens brought the animals up as the other men, keeping up a constant fire, concealed themselves among the trees and flung blankets across the boughs to deflect the arrows. The Indians poured arrows into the camp and made several attempts to recover the body of their chief, but were stopped by rifle fire.

Suddenly Carson cried out, "Look at the fool. Look at him, will you?"[24] Godey had stepped out to the light of the fire to look at his gun, which was not working to suit him. He turned resentfully to Carson, but did not hurry with his examination of the gun, and the whirring arrows did not touch him. Before morning light the Indians went away, leaving their dead chief. Gillespie recognized him as the man who had given him a salmon the day before. In his quiver were forty arrows, the most beautiful and warlike, Carson said, that he had ever seen. The heads, probably obtained from the Hudson's Bay Company on the Umpqua, were lancetlike pieces of iron or steel, poisoned for about six inches.

In the camp, in addition to three men dead, another Delaware had been wounded. All the men were full of grief and anger. Carson seized the tomahawk that had killed Basil and split the chief's head, and Saghundai scalped him. Yet over the years Carson remembered him with admiration. "He was the bravest Indian I ever saw. If his men had been as brave as himself, we surely would all have been killed. . . . If we had not gone to meet Gillespie, he and party would have been murdered. The Indians evidently were on the trail for that purpose."[25]

Even Frémont, usually intent on avoiding violence, was outraged. "For the moment I threw all other considerations aside and determined to square accounts with these people before I left."[26] After burying their dead among the laurels on the mountain, the party rode back to meet the main camp. That evening the Delawares painted their faces black and sat brooding by their fire, filled with rage and grief. Frémont went to sit with them. After a time he asked Swanok what could be done. Swanok and Saghundai conferred, then suggested that Frémont take the others down the trail a little way in the morning, leaving the Delawares behind.

The next morning the men started out as if leaving, but stopped about a quarter of a mile away to wait for the Delawares. They presently heard the crack of rifles from the camp and shortly thereafter the Delawares rode out of the woods. Swanok spoke to Frémont, "Better now; very sick before, better now." The Klamaths, seeing the party leave, had rushed into the campground. The Delawares had taken two scalps, and others had been wounded but had escaped.

For two days the men continued warily up the lake. The third day, as they approached the village at the inlet of the lake, Carson and Owens were sent ahead with ten chosen men to reconnoiter, with instructions to avoid fighting, if possible, until the main party arrived. They found about fifty lodges, beautifully woven of flag. The Indians were running about excitedly. Concluding that they had been warned of the approach of the whites, Carson led the men in an attack. At the sound of firing, Frémont and the rest hurried forward. Above the mouth of the river was a rapid, where the rocks near the surface made a ford. Plunging in without drawing rein, Frémont's group joined the others, who were hard pressed by a large band of Indians. Scattered throughout a field of sagebrush behind the village, the Indians had little cover. They lost fourteen men before they broke for the shelter of the woods.

About a mile from the village the explorers built a strong corral in an opening in the woods and drove the horses there without unsaddling them. Scouts were posted on all sides. In the afternoon Indians were reported coming through the woods. With Carson, Saghundai, Swanok, Stepperfeldt, and Archambeault, Frémont rode out to intercept them. Riding through the timber in close formation, they came to an oak tree that had blown over. Frémont gave Sacramento rein, and the horse cleared the green mass with a beautiful jump. Carson called out, "Captain, that horse will break your neck some day."[27]

A few minutes later, the horse's love of jumping saved Carson's life. As they emerged from the trees, they came upon an Indian scout drawing his arrow to the head. He aimed at Carson, who was in the lead. Carson tried to fire, but his rifle snapped. Frémont fired but missed. Swiftly he turned Sacramento and jumped him directly at the Indian, knocking him to the ground. The arrow went wild. Saghundai threw himself from his horse and killed the man with his war club.[28]

Now the men wanted only to make their way out of the mountains, but for many miles they were harassed by Indians. Two days later, as they rode down the lake, Archambeault and Maxwell met a lone warrior. Upon seeing the white men, the Indian took from his quiver some young crows he had tied there, laid them on the grass, and let fly an arrow at Maxwell, who flung himself from his horse just in time. After an exchange of arrows and rifle balls, the Indian was killed, and his scalp was hung on an arrow stuck in the trail to warn the others that Indians were near and hostile. Another day Owens, Stepperfeldt, and Dodson, while riding ahead, were attacked. The remainder of the party hurried forward and dispersed the Indians, killing one. After they struck the Sacramento, they came to a place where the trail led through a canyon. Because of the hostility they had been meeting, they rode off the trail along the ridge. Indians swarmed from the rocks and bushes along the canyon, arrows flying. The Indians were quickly driven back, with the exception of one who hid himself behind a large rock and commenced firing arrows very rapidly. Retreating out of range of the arrows, Carson moved to a point from which he could see the Indian and fired. "My shot had the desired effect. He was scalped. He had a fine bow and beautiful quiver of arrows, which I presented to Lt. Gillespie. He was a brave Indian, deserved a better fate, but he had placed himself on the wrong path."[29]

This battle ended their ordeal with the mountain Indians. They crossed the Sierra Nevada into the magnificent forest of redwoods, sugar pines, and cedars, dropped down the slopes to oak and pine forest, on to open groves of oak and low, rolling hills, finally into a profusion of flowers. May 24 they were back at Lassen's ranch, and two days later they reached Neal's.

Chapter 13

The Conquest of California

War had been officially declared on Mexico on May 13, 1846. Official word did not reach Frémont until August,[1] but belligerent actions of *Californios*[2] convinced him that war had begun or would begin soon.[3] His silence concerning his position caused people to believe he had authority. In response to a proclamation by Castro against Americans, a group of settlers came to ask his protection, and he agreed not to leave while they were in danger. Believing him to be under secret orders, Gillespie supported him in every way. Supposing that he had discretionary powers as the ranking army officer on the Coast, Commander Montgomery of the *Portsmouth*, at anchor in the harbor at Yerba Buena, (San Francisco Bay) offered him every assistance that did not interfere with his own duties. Commodore Sloat, Commander in Chief of U.S. Naval forces in the Pacific, was "very anxious to know if Captain Frémont" would cooperate with the Naval forces when, having received official notice that a state of war existed, the commodore decided on July 6 to hoist the American flag at Monterey.[4]

Three days later Sloat wrote to Frémont, bringing him up-to-date on developments and asking him to bring a hundred men to Monterey as a protective police force. Frémont immediately did so. Sloat asked him the basis of his authority. Frémont's statement that he had no expressed authority appalled the naval officer, who quickly dropped all support for the irregular enterprise.[5]

By then it was much too late. Carson recalled that, at Lassen's ranch,

Some Americans . . . came in stating that there were about 1,000 Indians in the vicinity making preparations to attack the settlements; requested assistance of Fremont to drive them back. He and party and some few Americans that lived near . . . found them to be in great force . . . and attacked. The number killed I cannot say. It was a perfect butchery. . . . it would be long before they ever again would feel like attacking the settlements.[6]

Another member of the expedition said that Frémont discharged all the men who wished to try to drive the Indians away, promising to rehire them afterward; four declined and were left to keep camp. After a three-hour fight, they counted over 175 killed. The rest ran away to the mountains.[7]

Carson correctly placed the event just related before the march to Oregon. Martin's account makes this clear by relating the precautions taken by Frémont in requiring the men to resign and be rehired so as not to involve the government. Nor could Frémont himself participate, when war with Mexico was not yet assured. The news of this aggressive action spread north like wildfire and explains the hostility of the Klamaths, who had been peaceable during the first visit to their country. After receiving the letters from Gillespie, Frémont regarded war as certain and could act openly. In writing his memoirs years later, Frémont said the Indians were incited by Castro and depicted himself as leading his men against them to save the crops of the settlers from destruction.[8] No corroboration has been found for a second attack on the Indians. It is unlikely that the attack described by Carson was justified, and Carson must take his share of the blame for it.

Aggressive acts had also been directed against the *Californios*. Ezekiel Merritt, with Frémont's encouragement, had captured horses bound for Castro. Forty settlers had captured Sonoma and its arsenal. General Guadalupe Vallejo, Colonel Salvador Vallejo, Colonel Victor Prudon, and Jacob Leese were prisoners of war at Sutter's Fort, where Frémont had placed Edward Kern in command.[9] William B. Ide and others had drawn up a declaration of independence at Sonoma, and a flag was fluttering there displaying a crudely painted grizzly bear and a star on a field of white. A battle had been fought, with the settlers defeating seventy *Californios* and rescuing two prisoners. Frémont had taken possession of the undefended fort at Yerba Buena and incidentally had named this majestic passage the Golden Gate. The settlers had formed into four companies with 224 men and had asked Frémont to take command. He had not only willingly complied and eloquently reminded them of their obligation to do nothing that would embarrass their country, but had quickly sent out parties to bring in horses from the estate of General Vallejo to mount his men.[10]

Headquarters had been established at a camp on the American River near Sutter's Fort. To the men who took part in them, the actions being directed from there were serious and important. Carson believed that Frémont had definite news of the declaration of war.[11] Only one man of the exploring party had resigned. Declaring that Frémont had acted as a coward in the confrontation at Gavilán Peak, Joseph Walker had demanded his release, gathered four or five hundred wild horses, driven them through Walker Pass, and headed along the Humboldt toward Green River.[12] The remainder of the men stuck loyally to Frémont until they were disbanded at the end of the war, and Dick Owens and Alexis Godey, though not called as witnesses, were at the court-martial, ready to give testimony in Frémont's favor.

No one was in Frémont's confidence; he continued to feel that his authority was so secretly given, some hint of it coming from President Polk himself, that he could discuss it with no one. At one point he drew up his resignation from the army and sent it to Benton to be used if the government found it expedient to repudiate his activities.[13] His actions had more definite and far-reaching effects that he anticipated, and he was to discover, to his chagrin, that his government did not need his resignation from the army to disavow him. However much those in power profited from the results of his decisions, he made it convenient for them to let him bear the blame for irregularities in the actions of all concerned.

One happening of small impact on the war is a matter of reproach to Frémont and involved Carson. Two Americans, on the road from Sonoma to Bodega with news of the Bear Flag Revolt, had fallen into the hands of *Californios*, who had tied them to trees and killed them with knives. A wave of anger and vengefulness swept the Americans, resulting in the death of three apparently innocent men. Frémont recorded that "letters were intercepted which required De la Torre to send horses to the Point the next morning to meet troops from the other side. . . . My scouts, mainly Delawares, influenced by . . . feelings [about the murder of the two Americans], made sharp retaliation and killed Bereyasa and de Haro, who were the bearers of the intercepted letters."[14]

Carson did not mention the event in his memoirs, but in 1853 William Boggs asked him why the men were killed when they were already prisoners. Boggs recorded that "José de los Berreyesa and his twin nephews, Ramon and Francisco de Haro, were captured by Carson, Granville Swift, Jack Neil, and others at the *Embarcadero*, where they had just landed. Carson rode back to ask Frémont what should be done with them. Frémont replied, 'I want no prisoners, Mr. Carson, do your duty.' Carson reported to his companions, and the men were shot."[15] This was one of the instances in which Frémont's judgment, never so trustworthy as he believed, was unequal to the demands growing out of a role for which he had no real talent and no training at all.

Sloat's abhorrence of Frémont's irregular victories had little effect. When the hundred men requested rode into Monterey, the Englishmen of the *Collingwood*, newly arrived flagship of Admiral Seymour of the British Navy, and the Americans of the three U.S. Navy ships watched them with excited interest. One of the Englishmen later wrote

A vast cloud of dust appeared first, and thence in long file emerged this wildest wild party. Frémont rode ahead, a spare, active-looking man. . . . He was dressed in a blouse and leggings, and wore a felt hat. After him came five Delaware Indians . . . they had charge of two baggage-horses. The rest, many of them blacker than the Indians, rode two and two, the rifle held by one hand across the pommel of the saddle . . . one or two . . . enjoy a high reputation in the prairies. Kit Carson is as well known there as the duke is in Europe.[16]

Officers and men of both the British and American ships often visited the camp on the ridge between the town and the bay, eager to see as much of the men, especially the Delawares, as possible.

Frémont and Gillespie visited the frigate *Congress* to talk with Commodore Stockton, who was waiting for Sloat to pass on to him the rank of commander in chief. The cautious Sloat was reluctant to hand such power to his second in command, but he finally turned the *Cyane* over to Stockton, who immediately notified Frémont and Gillespie that if they would place themselves under his command, he would form a battalion and appoint Frémont major and Gillespie captain. Thus the Navy Battalion of Mounted Riflemen was created. Owens was named captain and Carson and Godey lieutenants.[17] Acceptance of the commission under command of a naval officer facilitated the conquest of California but complicated Frémont's later difficulties with the army.

The Battalion was immediately ordered to embark on the *Cyane* for transportation to San Diego. The plan was to obtain horses for the men, return to Los Angeles, and force Castro to surrender. On this little voyage of the man-of-war, which the men had expected to be a pleasant and easy change from their rugged life in the mountains and the deserts, nearly everyone was seasick. Carson was so miserable that never again was he willing to board a ship when he could ride a mule.

The end, at least, was easier than they expected. When they arrived in San Diego July 28, they were received as friends by Don Juan Bandini, the chief citizen, and Don Santiago Arguello, captain of the port. Even with the help of these men, a week was needed to find mounts for the Battalion. Leaving a garrison of marines and about fifty of the Battalion in San Diego, Frémont rode toward Los Angeles August 8 with 120 men, Carson among them. August 13 they met Stockton before reaching Los Angeles and entered the town without opposition. Castro had fled to Mexico, and his men had scattered. All his officers were released on parole as soon as they understood that they were expected to aid in keeping the peace.

Stockton was eager to wind up affairs in California and collect volunteers to help in the conquest of Mexico. Thinking that peace was established permanently, he appointed Frémont military governor of the territory and Gillespie commandant of the southern district, promising to meet Frémont in San Francisco October 25 to confirm him as governor. On August 28, 1846, records of all Stockton's acts as governor and commander in chief in California were sent to Secretary of the Navy Bancroft.

To ensure the safety and speedy delivery of these important papers, and

as a reward for brave and valuable service on many occasions, we decided to make Carson the bearer of these despatches. . . . He was to go direct to Senator Benton at Washington, who would personally introduce him to the President and Secretary of the Navy. . . . It was a service of high trust and honor, but of great danger also. . . . Going off at the head of his own party with carte blanche for expenses and the prospect of novel pleasure and honor at the end was a culminating point in Carson's life.[18]

With Lucien Maxwell and fourteen other men, Carson started across the desert to the Colorado River, pushing the animals hard. Some of the mules died from heat and exertion and some were killed for food as they ascended the Gila. The men were tormented by hunger. They had left California with only twenty-five pounds of dried meat and a quantity of pinola (a mixture of parched corn meal and the sweet flour of mesquite beans). They had traded with Indians for corn, which the men could parch by the fire, but they could not take time for hunting.

When about ten miles from the Santa Rita del Cobre mines, Carson discovered an Apache village. Whether he remained still or tried to pass them, his party would almost certainly be seen. He and Maxwell discussed the situation—both had learned something from Frémont about co-existence with Indians—and decided "to take for the timber and . . . be as close as possible" before the Indians became aware of them. They were about a hundred yards from the village when the Indians showed signs of alarm. Carson made signs of peace, said he and his men were friends en route to New Mexico and wished to trade animals. The Apaches agreed and brought enough horses for a remount, and Carson and his men rode on.

On October 6 at Socorro, New Mexico, they met General Ste-

phen Watts Kearny, on the way to California, and Frémont and
Stockton lost their personal emissary to Benton and the president.
Carson informed Kearny that California had been conquered by
Frémont and Stockton, which was exactly what the dispatches he
carried told President Polk. Kearny quickly decided to send his
guide, Thomas Fitzpatrick, to Washington with the dispatches and
ordered Carson to guide him to California.[19]

Frémont overestimated the importance to Carson of the honor
of meeting the powerful men in Washington, but no one could
overestimate the importance to him of carrying to successful completion a significant task that had been entrusted to him. He protested vehemently against Kearny's demand:

*I told him I could not turn back—that I had pledged myself to
Commodore Stockton and Colonel Fremont to take their despatches through to Washington City, and to . . . carry them all the
way back if I did not find some one at Santa Fe that I could trust
as well as I could myself; . . . besides that I was under more obligations to Colonel Fremont than to any other man alive. . . .
When General Kearny could not persuade me to turn back, he
then told me that he had a right to make me go with him, and
insisted on his right. . . . I guided him through, but with great
hesitation, and had prepared everything to escape in the night
before they started . . . Maxwell . . . urged me not to do so.[20]*

Maxwell's friendly counsel probably saved Carson the conse-
quences of desertion. Mere disobedience would have invited
punishment.

Carson reported, "More than twenty times on the road, General
Kearny told me about his being a friend of Colonel Benton and
Colonel Fremont and all their family, and that he intended to
make Colonel Fremont the governor of California, and all this of
his own accord, as we were traveling along or in camp, and without
my asking him a word about it."[21]

In spite of his awkward relationship with Kearny, Carson
guided the small army without untoward incident from the Rio
Grande over the mountains and along the Gila. As they approached its mouth, they came upon a camp of Mexicans with five
hundred animals. The traders gave different accounts of the desti-

nation of the horses and the state of the country, but one man said that the Americans had been driven from Los Angeles and that eight hundred armed *Californios* were in possession of the town. Kearny, under orders to conciliate the Californians where possible, bought remounts for his men and let the Mexicans go. The next day Lieutenant Emory brought in a solitary rider. Having him searched, Kearny found a wallet of mail from California to Mexico, telling of the revolt.

Deciding not to approach Los Angeles with his small force, Kearny asked Carson to guide him to San Diego. Carson led the column to a ford about ten miles below the mouth of the Gila and entered the dry sand, rocks, and heat of the California desert. Late in November the men—most of them ragged and some of them barefoot—were clambering through the hills east of San Diego. On December 2 they reached Warner's Ranch. Edward Stokes, an Englishman, came in and reported that Stockton was at San Diego. Stokes took a letter from Kearny to Stockton, asking for news and an escort.[22]

At first news of the revolt, Stockton had rushed to the aid of the besieged garrisons, only to find that he could not leave the ship without meeting well-mounted *Californios*. Extremely skillful with lances, they immediately drove his unmounted men back to the ships. All mules, horses, and cattle had been driven away from the Coast. By the time Kearny reached Warner's Ranch, Stockton had procured from a merchant ship enough horses for forty men. He was ready to send Gillespie to attack fifty *Californios* at San Bernardo when the dispatch from Kearny arrived. Gillespie's force was sent to Kearny with the infrmation that the garrison at San Bernardo had been reinforced to about a hundred fifty men.

A few days before, Carson had gone with Lieutenant John W. Davidson and twenty-five dragoons to intercept a party of *Californios* en route to Sonora. They had brought back seventy or eighty horses and mules, among which Captain Benjamin Moore had found forty horses gentle enough for mounts for some of his men.

Gillespie's forty men, which included Godey from the Battalion and Edward Fitzgerald Beale from the navy, met General Kearny December 5 in the mountains between Santa Maria and Santa Isabel. When Gillespie told the general about the *Californios* at San

Bernardo, he decided to attack. That evening he sent Lieutenant Thomas C. Hammond with a few dragoons to examine the enemy position. The *Californios*, camped in the Indian village of San Pasqual, discovered the scouts watching them.

Around one o'clock in the morning of December 6, the Americans packed up and moved out. When about a mile from the enemy's camp, they saw scouts watching the road and charged them. With his dragoons, Moore was sent to attack the main body of the enemy, while Captain Abraham R. Johnston with fifteen mounted men, including Carson, rode ahead to capture the animals. Carson, in the advance, was about a hundred yards from the enemy camp when his horse fell, throwing him to the ground and breaking his rifle. As the remainder of the troop passed over and around him, he could see the flying hoofs striking within inches of his head. He managed to crawl to the side, got to his feet, and ran forward. A dragoon had been killed. Carson took his rifle and cartridge box and joined the battle. The *Californios* were fighting mostly with their deadly lances. Johnston and two or three more dragoons were killed before the *Californios* retreated, pursued by Moore. The forty men on horses got ahead of the others, who were mounted on mules. Seeing this, the enemy wheeled, cut off the advance, and killed or wounded thirty-six. Captain Moore and Lieutenant Hammond were killed. Nearly every officer of the command was killed or wounded. General Kearny was so badly wounded that Captain H. S. Turner took command.

Lieutenant Davidson brought up two howitzers, but before his men could do anything, all of them were killed or wounded and one of the howitzers was lassoed and dragged off. The *Californios* stopped about three hundred yards away and tried to fire the gun at the Americans, but they did not know how. The survivors gathered among the rocks of a nearby hill and stayed there during the night, not daring to move. Between midnight and one o'clock they managed to bury the eighteen men who had died. Godey and two others were sent to Stockton to ask for help.[23]

The next morning Carson was given fifteen men and ordered ahead. The *Californios* would show themselves on every hill in front of the advancing Americans. Late in the evening, when Carson was about four hundred yards from the water where he intended to camp, the *Californios* charged. The Americans were forced back about two hundred yards to a rocky hill. The enemy took the hill next to them and opened fire, but Emory and Turner led the remaining dragoons in a charge that drove them off, leaving the two hills in possession of the Americans.

When Godey and his men returned, the Americans had to watch helplessly while they were surrounded and taken prisoner. Later in the day the *Californios* sent a flag of truce with a package Gillespie's servant had sent by Godey, a note offering Gillespie, who was wounded, medical care if he wished to visit the camp of the *Californios*, and an offer to exchange prisoners. The Americans had taken only one prisoner. None of Kearny's men was willing to trust the flag of truce, but Lieutenant Beale volunteered to parley, hoping he could obtain the release of Godey. Knowing Godey's worth, the *Californios* released Thomas H. Burgess, who knew nothing of the plans of Stockton for the relief of the Americans.[24]

The camp of the Americans had barely enough water for the men to drink, and not a sprig of grass grew among the rocks. Provisions were exhausted; the only food was mule meat. Because the animals were suffering acutely from lack of food and water, some were turned loose to go to a stream five hundred yards away. As soon as they were out of range of their owners' rifles, the *Californios* drove them off to join their own *caballada*.

Feeling that conditions could not be worse, Kearny decided to burn everything the men could not carry and march on. The *Californios* formed a line five hundred yards in their rear, placing the men ten feet apart to make poor marks for the artillery. Kearny discussed with his officers this novel disposition of the enemy troops, decided the *Californios* would attack as soon as they left the rocks, and concluded that they were in no condition to fight and that their best course was to send to San Diego for reinforcements.

When volunteers were called for, Lieutenant Beale again stepped forward. Asked whom he would like to accompany him, he requested his Indian servant and Carson. Kearny said that he could not spare Carson. Beale said that in that case he would go with the Indian. Kearny relented, and the men gathered a handful of parched peas and corn and some pieces of mule meat and waited for dark. Seeing that the Americans were not leaving after all, the enemy were again stationed around them.

Learning from the prisoners that Carson was with the army, Don Andrés Pico urged extra caution by his sentinels, now sitting their horses in three rows. "Carson is there," he told them. "*Se escapará el lobo.*"²⁵ After pulling off their shoes, which scraped on the rocks, the men slithered downhill, watching for a chance to pass between the guards, who were sometimes so close that the smoke of their *cigaritos* drifted down to the messengers. Beale brought his lips close to Carson's ear and whispered, "We are gone; let us jump up and fight it out." The Indians had long believed that Carson had "Strong medicine," a faith shared by Carson himself. He whispered back, "No; I have been in worse places before, and Providence has always saved me."²⁶

At last they were out in the open valley, but their shoes had slipped out of their belts and lay somewhere behind them among the rocks and cactus. They had thirty-five miles to cover in their bare feet through rocks and prickly pear before reaching San Diego. About twelve miles from the town they separated, each to try on his own to get through the guard the *Californios* had thrown around Stockton's forces. The Indian reached Stockton first, Beale second. Carson was last, but in the best physical condition. Beale collapsed when he reached the American sentries, who had to carry him to Stockton. After reporting, he was taken aboard the *Congress* for medical care. He did not fully recover from this ordeal for two years.²⁷

The cruel irony of the excruciating journey was that before the messengers reached Stockton, he had already sent the reinforcements Godey had requested. As these approached, the *Californios* departed, leaving Kearny free to move forward to meet the relief force. He could say with some degree of truth that the enemy had left the field; on this slender base he built a claim that victory had been his. When the Army of the West came limping into San Diego on December 12, Stockton walked to meet them, not having a horse fit to ride.

Meanwhile, hearing of the shortage of horses, Frémont had returned to Monterey to get the horses and artillery he had left near his camp.[28] After a short skirmish, he was able to proceed south to San Luis Obispo. There he arrested José de Jesús Pico, who had broken his parole. Señora Pico pled so eloquently for her husband that he was pardoned. After promising to devote his life to Frémont, he followed him toward Los Angeles.[29] They reached Santa Barbara soon after Christmas.

On January 8, 1847, Stockton and Kearny defeated Andrés Pico at the Battle of Los Angeles.[30] January 12, Frémont camped at the Mission of San Fernando and sent Jesús Pico with a message to the camp of his brother, two miles away. The next day Frémont and Andrés Pico met and signed the Treaty of Cahuenga, establishing a lasting peace between the Americans and the *Californios*.[31]

Kearny grew more bitter. Having missed the glory of victory, he was now denied the prestige of making peace, and the honor he felt his rank should command among the men of the Battalion eluded him. As soon as Frémont entered Los Angeles, he reported to Stockton, then went to the quarters assigned to him by Stockton, finally called upon Kearny, who felt he had been slighted.

Carson reported at once to Frémont and continued in his service during the winter. When Kearny ordered Frémont to suspend the execution of orders he had received from Stockton, Frémont replied that he would continue to take orders from Stockton until the question of rank was settled. Leaving the letter with Talbot to copy and asking Carson to bring it to Kearny's office,[32] Frémont went ahead to meet his erstwhile friend. Carson, who left after delivering the letter, was not aware of its contents.[33] All the men were conscious of tension among the leaders, but Carson did not understand its basis or its seriousness. The impasse ended with Frémont's court-martial and resignation of his commission, but Carson was himself a civilian before it reached that stage.

Chapter 14

Famous Dispatch Rider

February 25, 1847, Carson again started toward Washington with dispatches for the war department and letters for the Benton family, as well as other mail. With him rode Theodore Talbot and Lieutenant Edward Fitzgerald Beale. Beale was still so ill from exposure, strain, and fatigue incurred during the journey from San Pasqual that Carson had to lift him on and off his horse.[1] Twenty-five years later Beale vividly recalled those desperate days,

> When I lay on the burning sands of the great desert, under a mesquite bush, where you had, as tenderly as a woman would have put her first born, laid me, sore from wounds and fever, on your only blanket. I see the dim . . . mirage . . . the waving sands ripple with the faint hot breeze . . . and break upon our scattered saddles. I see the poor mules famishing of thirst, with their tucked flanks and dim eyes, and hear their sad, plaintive cry. . . . I see the men dogged and resolute or despondent, standing around or seeking such shelter as a saddle blanket thrown over a gun afforded.
>
> Without a thought of ever seeing water again, you poured upon my fevered lips the last drop in camp from your canteen.[2]

Carson remembered this association with great pleasure, and added, "I was trebly repaid by the kindness and attention given me by his mother, while I was in Washington."[3]

While encamped on the River Gila, the party was attacked at night by Indians. Now the important consideration was not who was in the right, but how to get through rapidly and safely. Carson had learned from Young as well as Bridger that it is sometimes more effective to mystify the enemy than to meet him with brazen courage. "I directed the men to hold before them pack saddles and not to speak a word, so that the Indians could not direct their aim by hearing us, for them not to return the fire but let the Indians approach, and then use our rifles as clubs."[4] A rare example of Carson's colloquial narration was preserved in the Beale family:

Things whirrin like birds on the flight wuz flyin over us as I was tryin to sleep by the campfire and Ned wuz sleepin or leastwise he was snorin. Then suddenly he sits up and says, "What's that Don Kit?" and I says "Them's arrers" and they wuz and would you believe it before I could hold him down Ned wuz wrapping his buffalo robe about him and standing in the fire kickin out the embers. "Now," says he, as them arrers came whizzin along like a raft of geese goin south before er north wind, "Now," says he, "Don Kit, they won't be able to get our directions any more and you know they don't dare rush us;" and then he tumbled down on the ground and went on with his sleepin.[5]

Beale was right. Whatever the Indians thought of the utter silence and unresponsiveness of the camp, no rush occurred.

Although Carson dismissed further manifestations from the Indians, Beale remembered the journey otherwise:

Oh, Kit . . . on bloody Gila, where we fought all day and traveled all night, with each man his bit of mule meat and no other food, and when worn from a hurt I could go no further, I begged you to leave me and save yourself. I see you leaning on that long Hawkins gun of yours (mine now) and looking out of those clear blue eyes with a surprised reproach as one who takes an insult from a friend.[6]

About the close of the first week of April, they reached Santa Fe and the shock of the news of the Taos massacre: the death of Governor Charles Bent, Carson's brother-in-law; Sheriff Stephen Lee; Cornelio Vigil, Josefa's uncle; Pablo Jaramillo, her brother; Narcisse Beaubien, friend of Lewis Garrard and son of Judge Charles Beaubien and brother-in-law of Lucien Maxwell; Beaubien's slave-companion; and Circuit Attorney J. W. Leal. At Arroyo Hondo, Simeon Turley, miller and distiller, and six of Carson's friends had been besieged in the mill, burned out, and slain. At Mora, Lawrence Waldo had been killed. Mark Head, for whom Carson had taken the Blackfoot ball in his shoulder, and a companion named Harwood had been captured on the trail as they rode down from the mountains with their furs. As the men rode along single file, Harwood had been shot in cold blood. Head had ridden imperturbably forward until a second ball knocked him from the saddle.

Bent had been warned of the plans for revolt, which was to have occurred about Christmas, and had made a few arrests. Thinking the insurrection defused, he had ignored further warnings and had ridden up from Santa Fe together with Leal to visit his family and to issue a proclamation. Early in the morning of January 19, he was aroused from sleep by a mob in front of his house, trying to force the door and digging at the earthen roof. Ignacia begged him to escape by a back way, but he considered it his duty to protect his family—expanded, as Mexican families often were, by relatives Josefa Carson and Rumalda Luna Boggs, Ignacia's daughter and wife of Tom Boggs. Believing that he could quiet the mob, Bent opened the door, but the tumult drowned his voice as the leaders forced their way in.

Rumalda and Josefa had retreated to an inner room and were digging at the adobe wall with a poker and a heavy iron spoon. The Mexican woman who lived in the next house, which shared this wall, started digging on her side. As the women broke through, Bent, mortally wounded, retreated to the inner room, pushed his family through the hole, and crawled through himself. Taking a paper from his pocket, he tried to write, but his strength was rapidly failing. Commending his family to God and his brothers, he died. "Rushing in and tearing off the gray-haired scalp, the Indians bore it away in triumph."[7]

The women and children, in their night clothes and without food, stayed where they were, the lifeless body beside them, the rest of the night and the next day and night. Before daylight the second morning a Mexican friend smuggled them away to his house, gave them shabby clothing, and put them to work as servants. There they were safe until a relief force arrived from the south.[8]

Out in the streets the horrors continued. Leal was scalped alive and dragged through the streets before he was killed. Lee was killed in front of his own house. Narcisse Beaubien and his Indian slave hid in the hay in a trough. The insurgents, thinking they escaped, were leaving when a woman servant called from the housetop, "Kill the young ones, and they will never be men to trouble us." The mob rushed back, found them, and killed and scalped them.

Charles Town, who had been a hunter on Frémont's second expedition, was the only American in Taos to escape the slaughter. He rode all night to bring the news to Ceran St. Vrain, safe at Santa Fe. Quickly gathering sixty volunteers, St. Vrain joined Colonel Sterling Price and his soldiers and marched north. At La Cañada, twenty-five miles out of Santa Fe, they met fifteen hundred insurrectionists and sent them scurrying back toward Taos. Reinforcements arrived from Albuquerque, and the combined forces again defeated the rebels at El Embudo. At Taos they found that the Mexicans had either fled or taken refuge in the big church at the pueblo.

Price's cannon hardly dented the thick adobe walls of the church. The troops stormed the building with axes and ladders. Many, including Captain Burgwin, died as they chopped and dug at the wall then charged into the dim church. When a hole was opened, most of the rebels darted out and fifty-one were slain. Others, including "Big Nigger," a Delaware trapper from the Purgatoire, fought desperately to the end.[9]

Some of the rebel chiefs were captured alive, tried by Judge Beaubien, and sentenced to be hanged for murder or for treason, the latter a charge that seemed to young Garrard abominably lacking in justice, "when its distorted meaning is warrant for murdering those who defend to the last their country and their homes."[10]

Garrard left after the first round of hangings on April 9. Carson arrived and left before the second round on April 30. The rebellion had been finally and completely quelled, but the shock and agony of the bereaved families endured without respite. After twenty months away from Josefa, Kit found her stunned with grief and horror. Though unable to resist completely the urge to see what lay beyond the horizon, Kit felt more protective concern for Josefa after this time and chafed when forced to remain too long away from home.

Now he was under orders to deliver the dispatches to Washington. After a delay of ten days, he set out again. On the Purgatoire he met the party of Garrard, who watched as he shook hands with John L. Hatcher, a trapper and raconteur whose campfire Garrard had shared for several weeks, and who impressed Garrard as a mountain man as strongly as the nationally famous Carson.[11]

After leaving Bent's Fort, Carson soon dropped off part of his escort. "The same day Mr. Ruxton joined us," wrote Garrard, "Davis, Brackenridge, Step, and a California Indian, members of Kit Carson's escort, . . . added somewhat to our numerical, and incalculably to our fighting strength. . . . With Brackenridge and party were left the broken-down mules, to recruit by rest and grass."[12]

Toward the end of May, Carson arrived in St. Louis, where he found Senator Benton furious over gossip and newspaper stories, suspected to have originated with Lieutenant Emory, damaging to Frémont and Stockton and hailing Kearny as conqueror of California and heroic leader at a great victory at San Pasqual. Emory, who supported Kearny, and Gray, who supported Stockton, had already arrived in Washington with dispatches from the two commanders, each of whom claimed the honor of having brought the conquest successfully to completion. The letter Frémont had written in February gave his version of events, a version at last fleshed out and completed by his own trusted emissary. Senator Benton read the letter avidly and, after asking all the questions he could think of, sent letter and emissary on the Washington by steamboat, stage, and steam cars.

Notified of his coming, Jessie met Carson at the railroad station. She recognized him instantly by her husband's description and startled him speechless by rushing up and taking him in charge. The senator had invited him to make the Benton home his own while in Washington. For the most part he did so and "received the very kindest treatment."[13]

He also spent part of his time with the Beales, where Ned's mother took him on his own terms and allowed him to sleep on a couch on the verandah. Aside from being used to sleeping in the open, he would find the weather in Washington in June such that the verandah was more comfortable at night than a well-furnished and curtained bedroom. He seems to have been perfectly at ease with this understanding and indulgent lady. If he actually "shed tears of gratitude and joy"[14] at her allowing him to sleep in the open, he must have felt oppressed unbearably by the exigencies of Washington society.

Though in his memoirs he never mentions Jessie Benton Frémont, she devoted her efforts for some weeks to making him comfortable, amusing him, reading to him, and helping him with his errands. Unlike Mrs. Beale, Jessie took him in hand, introduced him to the Benton and Frémont friends, and joined them in making much of him. His own exploits, tempered by his modesty and gentleness, as well as his eagerness to recount Frémont's accomplishments, quickly earned their esteem. The simplicity and quaintness of his speech delighted them. But all this attention from Jessie's polished friends made him ill at ease.

Asked to find out what was troubling him, Lieutenant Beale learned that he felt that the Washington ladies might not like to associate with him if they knew he had had an Indian wife, and he did not like seeming to conceal his life with Waanibe. "She was a good wife to me. I never came in from hunting that she did not have the warm water ready for my feet."[15] This observation probably provoked the mirth of Washington society. Only men who had waded up to their thighs in mountain streams at the edge of the melting ice and snow to tend their beaver traps could comprehend the immense value of such devotion.

Jessie introduced him to great literature, which he enjoyed having her read to him. Byron's "Mazeppa's Ride" appealed to him particularly, with its patient, implacable evening up of scores. "That's so, that's so!" he exclaimed. "He knows how a man feels! That's the way I felt. Until I paid them back after the Blackfeet destroyed my câches and carried off all my furs and skins. . . . I had to wait for the right men to help. . . . Then . . . we left mourning in their tribe."[16]

He was able to talk frankly with her on some subjects. He objected to being kept in Washington, when he believed that Frémont was eagerly awaiting his return with letters and dispatches. Disillusioned with the men of power in the government, he said to Jessie, "They are princes here in their big houses, but on the plains *we* are the princes. What would their lives be without us there?"[17]

Finally on June 7 Jessie accompanied him to call upon President Polk to deliver Frémont's letter of February 3 addressed to her father, relating events and describing conditions in California. That night he saw the president again and had a "full conversation with him" concerning affairs in California and especially regarding the collision between Stockton and Kearny.[18]

Both Kit and Jessie did their best for Frémont, but Kearny held the rank as well as the latest orders from Washington. The difficulty arose from a conflict of orders and a deviousness of approach to the California problem on the part of the government, aggravated by slowness of communication and swiftness of developing events on the West Coast. Frémont and Stockton had achieved what Polk wanted. Much as he desired "to put an end to this most unfortunate controversy," the president could not openly admit to purposeful ambiguity.[19] He wanted the conflict dropped, not resolved. Benton insisted on a total clearing of Frémont's name, either by a retraction of the charges or by an airing of the whole affair in a court-martial. The report Frémont had prepared for Secretary of State Buchanan, giving details of the civil government and outlining the desperate need of funds to support its functions, was turned over to Secretary of War Marcy, who would deal only with Kearny and who had already ordered that the expenses of civil government in California were to be kept within the revenues collected at the ports. Frémont was headed for both disciplinary and financial trouble.[20]

At Buchanan's suggestion, the president appointed Carson second lieutenant in the regular army, and on June 14 he received orders to carry dispatches to the commanding officers in Santa Fe and in California, retrieving on the way the United States mules

Talbot had left at Fort Leavenworth.[21] He was heartily glad to be at last free to go. Everywhere in Washington, people had stared, asked questions, wanted to shake his hand, pushed after him when he tried to escape by going into the street. He was perplexed, bored, and finally exhausted by the pressing attention of strangers. The newspapers had kept curiosity and interest alive. That summer the *Washington Union* printed a short narrative of his life, based on personal interviews.[22] It also reported his appointment as lieutenant, and on June 15 the following appeared in the same paper:

This singular man left Washington this morning, in company with Mrs. Frémont, for the West. On entering the War Office yesterday, we were asked: "Have you seen Kit Carson? He has this moment left my room; and a singular and striking man he is! Modest as he is brave . . . with the bearing of an Indian, walking even with his toes turned in."[23]

Ned Beale accompanied Jessie and Kit to St. Louis, where he had to turn back because of ill health. In addition to dispatches, Carson carried letters and—a special treasure for Frémont—a miniature of Jessie painted in 1845 after the momentous third expedition had departed. He carried encouraging news from Mexico, where Zachary Taylor had defeated Santa Anna at Buena Vista on February 22, Winfield Scott had conquered Vera Cruz and Cerro Gordo in March and April, and Doniphan had occupied Chihuahua March 1. Nicholas P. Trist had been sent in April to negotiate for peace, and the capital was optimistic about his success.

After reporting to Senator Benton, Carson visited his relatives in Howard County, where he was reported to have said that he planned to take his family, including Adaline, and settle in California.[24] The Taos Massacre, added to the supposition that Frémont would remain on the West Coast, made this move seem attractive at the time.

At Fort Leavenworth, Carson picked up fifty raw volunteers, who were to accompany him as escort through the Comanche country, for they were now on the warpath. At Pawnee Rock they camped about three hundred yards from Lieutenant S. D. Mullowny's company of Missouri Volunteers. The next morning as

Mullowny's men were leading their horses out to picket them in the new grass, a band of Comanches topped a rise and came galloping and whooping toward the *aballada*. Twenty-six horses and all their cattle ran with the Indians. The cattle swerved toward Carson's party, who cut them off and brought them back. Two of Carson's volunteers, eager for a shot at the Indians, dropped their lead ropes, and their horses scampered after the captured band. Three of Mullowny's men were wounded.[25]

When Carson reached Santa Fe, Josefa was waiting there to meet him. This unexpected pleasure may have influenced him to choose the Spanish Trail for the next part of his journey. By taking the more northern route, he could see Josefa safely home and spend a little more time with her. He would also be less likely to meet hostile Indians, and he would be traveling a part of the mountains that he loved.[26]

On the more northern route, he met no problems until he reached the edge of the Great Basin. At Muddy Creek, a tributary of the Virgin River, about three hundred Indians were gathered, probably Paiutes. They wanted to come into the camp. Carson told them no, they had killed seven Americans the fall before, and he would not allow them to come near enough to kill his party. If they did not retire, he would fire on them. "I was compelled to fire," he reported. "One Indian was killed and the balance went off."[27] On this journey they troubled him no more. He ran out of provisions as he crossed the Mojave Desert and had to butcher two mules to feed his men.

During Carson's absence, things had changed in California. General Kearny had left for Washington May 31, taking Frémont with him under arrest. The Battalion had been disbanded, men and officers discharged without pay, because Frémont's request for funds had been deferred until the muster rolls should be received in Washington. Dick Owens and Alexis Godey had gone east. Major Gillespie, in company with Commodore Stockton, had also left for Washington. When Carson arrived in Los Angeles in October, he had to saddle up and carry the dispatches on to Monterey, where Colonel Richard B. Mason was now governor.

One man at headquarters had been looking forward eagerly to

his arrival. A red-haired first lieutenant of artillery, William Tecumseh Sherman, adjutant-general to Mason, introduced himself as soon as Carson rode up. He later wrote:

His fame was then at its height, from the publication of Frémont's books, and I was very anxious to see a man who had achieved such feats of daring among the wild animals of the Rocky Mountains, and still wilder Indians of the Plains. I cannot express my surprise at beholding a small, stoop-shouldered man, with reddish hair, freckled face, soft blue eyes, and nothing to indicate extraordinary courage or daring. He spoke but little, and answered questions in monosyllables. I asked for his mail, and he picked up his light saddle-bags containing the great overland mail, and we walked together to headquarters, where he delivered his parcel into Colonel Mason's own hands. He spent some days in Monterey, during which time we extracted with difficulty some items of his personal history.[28]

Throughout the territory, his arrival and the news he brought were matters of importance. After some weeks at Los Angeles, he was assigned twenty-five men and ordered to Cajón Pass to prevent Indians from taking stolen animals through the mountains.[29]

In the spring he was again ordered to Washington. With twenty-seven men he left Los Angeles May 4, 1848, carrying government dispatches and private letters, including the news of the discovery of gold at Sutter's Mill. With him rode Lieutenant George Douglas Brewerton, a writer of considerable ability, who later published his impressions of the journey across the desert and along the Old Spanish Trail to Taos.[30] Like Sherman, he had formed a romantic concept of the celebrated mountaineer. He was astonished to find the "real Kit to be a plain, simple, unostentatious man; rather below the medium height, with brown, curling hair, little or no beard, and a voice as soft and gentle as a woman's . . . one of Dame Nature's gentlemen."[31]

Several days ahead of Carson's party traveled the great trading caravan, whose animals had drunk practically all the water and eaten the grass at the camp sites. While on the trail, Carson seldom spoke, seeming preoccupied with his responsibility for the safety of men and mailbag, his gaze constantly alert to any movement or other sign among the rocks or along the horizon. He was pushing forward to get ahead of the caravan, and in eight days he passed it.

Though relatively peaceable, the Indians were known to be skulking among the rocks. At night the men took turns guarding the animals; Carson's mess guarded the camp. Except now and then to light his pipe, Carson did not expose himself to the full glare of the fire. "No, no, boys," he would say, "hang around the fire if you will . . . but I don't want to have a Digger slip an arrow into me, when I can't see him."[32] His ritual at bedtime was always the same. He used his saddle for a pillow, placing it so as to shield his head. Above it he placed his pistols, half-cocked. His rifle lay beside him under the blanket, where, protected from the damp, it was within easy reach.

At first light, when he called, "Catch up!" all moved quickly.

Kit waited for nobody; and woe to the unfortunate who discovered to his sorrow that packs would work, bags fall off, and mules show an utter disregard for the preservation of one's personal property. A man . . . soon learns to pack a mule as it should be done, at first, put on his saddle as it ought to be put on, and keep his arms in serviceable order."[33]

This was the discipline of the trapper, who was absolutely responsible for himself, his animals, his equipment, and for maintaining his connection with the group.

To cross the *Jornada del Muerto*, the party started about three o'clock in the afternoon and traveled most of the way by moonlight. On some stretches the feet of the mules made no sound in the deep sand. The men, with tangled hair and beards and shapeless clothing, whitened by the fine dust, moved wraithlike among the dark rocks hanging over the dimly gleaming sands.[34]

Along the Old Spanish Trail the Diggers could not be ignored, but in 1848, Brewerton saw them as more humorous than dangerous. While resting after the long night's ride, Carson raised himself on his elbow and asked Brewerton if he saw any Indians. Brewerton could see none.

"Well," said Kit, "I saw an Indian's head there just now, and there are a party of at least a dozen more, or I am much mistaken."[35]

Suddenly, from the rocks at the top of one of the steep, gravelly hills, an Indian stood straight up, gesturing excitedly and shouting, "Tigabu! Tigabu!"

Carson rose to his feet and shouted back, "Tigabu! Tigabu!"[36]

The Indian turned to speak to his companions still hidden by the rocks, then moved hesitantly toward the camp, repeating his assurance of friendship. Carson walked to meet him and soon reassured him with a small present. His companions came in two or three at a time, indicating that they were hungry. They finished off a residue of moldy beef and the coffee in the pot and sat down to smoke, one old man with such hunger that he pulled the smoke into his mouth and held it until he seemed about to suffocate. When accused of murder and robbery, these Indians protested that they held the whites in high esteem and hinted that a gift of a horse would be welcome proof of Kit's esteem for them.

When, about sunset, Carson cried, "Catch up!" and everyone became busy packing up to leave, a young Indian snatched a tin cup from the pack of an old mountaineer and flung it across the creek into a patch of rushes. The mountaineer caught him by the hair and one leg, plunged him headfirst into the creek, and ordered him to swim across, find the cup, and return it, if he did not wish to die. The Indian obeyed, and for two days the Diggers watched from the hills, but none approached the camp.

When a party of them finally approached, they acted so suspiciously that Kit kept as hostage a young warrior, who sat at ease talking and sharing their supper, while his friends howled dismally from the hills. At bedtime, Kit called to them, and the young man added his reassurance before wrapping himself in a borrowed blanket. When morning came, he was given a few presents. Someone donated a pair of worn-out pantaloons, which gave him great pleasure.[37]

Brewerton heard the tales of this stretch of the trail: the massacre of the Hernandez and Fuentes party; the murder of Tableau; the great horse-stealing expedition, which explained the great number of bones, where the hard-driven horses had died. An excit-

174

ing chase ensued when Indian tracks were discovered near the *caballada*. Concluding that the Diggers were spying with the intention of stealing the animals, several men followed along the river bottom, up one of the steep sandhills to the top of the bluff.

"There he goes!" shouted Kit. The Digger, his bow and arrows at his back, was bounding across the deep sand, throwing himself from side to side to present a poor target. Kit, Brewerton, and Archambeault fired at him in turn, but missed. Lewis dropped to one knee and raised his long Missouri rifle, exclaiming, "I'll bring him, boys!" At the crack of the rifle, the Digger bounded forward and his arm fell suddenly to his side. Though evidently wounded, he escaped.[38]

Near Little Utah Lake, the men had hardly sat down to breakfast, their only meal of the day, when Wakara and his Ute warriors joined them. Embarrassed to eat in front of the hungry-looking Indians, Brewerton decided to share his plate of atole with one of them. The Ute outate him badly, and at the end, when Brewerton thought to get one more mouthful from the plate, his guest grabbed it and passed it to an Indian behind him, who literally licked it clean. The same happened to the lieutenant's cup of coffee. He was so disgusted that he said nothing about it for several days. Finally he told Carson, who "thought it one of the best jokes he had ever heard."[39]

In the Rockies their adventures became more alarming. When they arrived at the Grand River, they found it in flood. "In his shirt sleeves, working hard himself—instructing here and directing there," Kit got a few logs cut, notched, and rolled into the water, where the men tied them together with their reatas (braided leather ropes). The wind was cold, and the water had just come down the mountains from the melting snow. Kit ordered the swimmers to pull the raft. Archambeault would steer. The nonswimmers could hold on. Whatever happened, they must not lose the mail bags.

The water, roaring and boiling over hidden rocks, caught the raft as it left the bank, whirled and bounced it along for about a mile, and deposited it on the same side from which it had started. As Brewerton tried to anchor it with a reata tied to a tree, it swung about and knocked him senseless. Archambeault seized his hair and dragged him out of the water, and all returned upstream through rocks and brush, carrying the baggage. The next raft got across safely, but Archambeault worked so hard in the cold water that he was convulsed with cramps until the others thought he would die. They rolled him in the sand and rubbed him until he recovered. Finally all the men and animals had crossed safely, but the last raft was ripped apart in midstream, losing six rifles, a number of riding and pack saddles, much of the ammunition, and nearly all the remaining provisions.[40]

With only three days' frugal rations per man, several men without rifles, two without pantaloons, and several without saddles between them and the bony backs of their mules, they rode glumly eastward. Several days later Kit aroused some cheer when he brought in a deer, but as Indian sign became more threatening, the men became silent and wary. Mexican traders told them a party of trappers farther on had been defeated and deprived of their animals. When about fifty miles from Taos, they saw a large village ahead. The valley was becoming narrower, and they could do nothing but continue close under the mountain, hoping to pass unobserved. It was soon evident that they had already been seen. A freshly painted Indian came galloping up, pulled his horse back on its haunches, and asked for the *capitán*. Carson recognized him as a Ute and spoke to him in his own language, which the Indian pretended not to understand.

Turning at once to one of the men, Carson ordered him to get the mules together and head for a patch of chaparral, while he followed with the Indian. Before they reached the place, "about a hundred and fifty warriors, finely mounted, and painted for war, with their long hair streaming in the wind," charged at them, brandishing lances and spears. They were Apaches and Utes.

At the little grove of stunted trees, Kit sprang from his mule and called out to his men, "Now, boys, dismount, tie up your riding mules; those of you who have guns, get around the *caballada*, and look out for the Indians; and you who have none, get inside, and hold some of the animals. Take care, Thomas, and shoot down the mule with the mail bags on her back, if they try to stampede the animals."[41]

As the men took their places, he turned, took a few paces forward, and began to harangue the Indians. "His whole demeanor was now so entirely changed that he looked like a different man; his eye fairly flashed, and his rifle was grasped with all the energy of an iron will." He told them his party was destitute and could give them nothing. But he cried, "There is our line, cross it if you dare, and we begin to shoot. . . . You say you are friends, but you don't act like it. . . . so stand back, or your lives are in danger!"[42]

While the Indians hesitated, a rider galloped up on a foam-flecked horse with information for the chief. After a moment's consultation, the chief gave a shrill whistle and the warriors drew back a few paces. Carson immediately called out, "Now, boys, we have a chance, jump into your saddles, get the loose animals before you, and then handle your rifles, and if these fellows interfere with us, we'll make a running fight of it."[43]

They retired slowly, followed by the Indians, who finally dropped away and returned to their village. Carson then rode as hard as the state of the animals would allow and about midnight reached a collection of shepherds' huts, where he learned that two hundred volunteers were on the way to punish the Indians for outrages committed in the area. News of this pursuit brought by the lone horseman had saved Carson's party from attack.

The next day, June 14, they reached Taos, where Brewerton was "hospitably entertained by Carson and his amiable wife, a Spanish lady, and a relative . . . of some former Governor of New Mexico."[44] The former governor was Josefa's uncle, Juan Bautista Vigil, acting governor after the flight of Armijo. Her cousin, Donaciano Vigil, was acting governor at the time of Brewerton's visit.[45]

After spending a few days in Taos, Carson took his party to Santa Fe, where Brewerton had already gone. Colonel Edward Newby, in command there, informed Carson that his appointment as second lieutenant had not been approved by the Senate. Some of Carson's friends advised him to delivery the dispatches to Colonel Newby and go on about his own affairs. Carson remembered that he

considered the matter over, and as I had been entrusted with the despatches, chosen as the most competent person to take them through safely, I determined to fulfill the duty. . . . Having gained much honor and credit in performance of all duties entrusted to

my charge, I would on no account wish to forfeit the good opinion
of a majority of my countrymen because the Senate . . . did not
deem it proper to confirm on me an appointment . . . that I never
sought, and one . . . I would have resigned at the termination of
the war.[46]

Now a private citizen, Carson discharged all his men but Archambeault and nine others, returned to Taos and hired seven
more men, including Jesse Nelson and Louis Simmons. They
crossed the mountains at the Sangre de Cristo Pass, rode up a tributary of the Arkansas, followed the Bijou-Platte-Republican route
to Fort Leavenworth, and finished the journey safely and quickly.

While in Washington, Carson renewed his friendship with the
Bentons and the Frémonts. Jessie's first son was born in late July.
When the baby was baptized on August 15, Carson was sponsor.
He warned Jessie that the frail, sickly baby could not live, but his
words did not prepare her for the overwhelming grief she felt when
the baby died.[47]

Eight years later Carson stated:

I was with Frémont 1842 to 1847. The hardships through
which we passed I find impossible to describe, and the credit
which he deserves I am incapable to do him justice in writing.
But his services to his country have been left to the judgment of
impartial freemen, and all agree in saying that his services were
great and have redounded to his honor and that of his country.

I have heard that he is enormously rich. I wish to God that he
may be worth ten times as much more. All that he has or may
ever receive, he deserves. I can never forget his treatment of me
while in his employ and how cheerfully he suffered with his men
when undergoing the severest of hardships. His perseverence and
willingness to participate in all that was undertaken, no matter
whether the duty was rough or easy, is the main cause of his suc-
cess. And I say, without fear of contradiction, that none but him
could have surmounted and succeeded through as many difficult
services.[48]

Joe Meek, also in Washington at this time, had come to report
the Whitman Massacre, in which his daughter, Helen Mar, had

died. As a representative of Oregon, he was also requesting aid from the federal government in dealing with the Cayuse Indians. He reported seeing Carson. Short of funds, no longer on the army payroll, Kit may have borrowed some money from Meek, who, as cousin of the president's wife, could obtain what he needed.[49]

Carson soon returned to St. Louis, where he remained a few days, then visited his relatives in Howard County. Adaline, now eleven, was growing up and may have been hard for Elizabeth to manage. Carson took her to Fayette and entered her in the Howard Female Seminary, where her cousin George, William's son, saw her several times in 1849.[50] Again Adaline had to watch her father start west without her.

Chapter 15

Farmer and Scout

When Carson returned to Taos in October 1848, the complexities of life in a civilized community settled around him. He had a living to make. He had responsibilities and emotional ties as husband and father. However, frequent calls upon his highly developed skills as scout, tracker, and Indian fighter conflicted sharply with his efforts to stabilize his home life and develop a permanent occupation, efforts in which he was never very successful.

At this time, Frémont was on his way to attempt a winter crossing of the San Juan Mountains.[1] He intended to prove that a railroad could operate at a latitude of thirty-eight degrees, even in a winter as harsh as the mountaineers foresaw in 1848 from the abnormally early low temperatures and the heavy snow in the mountains. This expedition he had planned as early as March 1848, counting on governmental support. When he learned in August that this would not be forthcoming, private financing was hastily arranged with St. Louis businessmen. Carson, returning from Washington, spent several days in St. Louis in September. The expedition set out on October 3. Neither Carson nor Frémont, in his memoirs, mentions any discussion, offer, or refusal concerning the expedition,[2] but Carson was later reported to have said that he had advised Frémont against going into the mountains that winter, telling him that he "could not get through or over them at that period of the year."[3]

As Frémont passed Big Timbers,[4] thousands of Cheyennes, Arapahoes, Kiowas, Comanches, and Prairie Apaches were gathered to exhibit their social skills and to promise one another and their agent, Thomas Fitzpatrick, that thenceforth they would live at peace with one another and with the whites. Although not convinced of the good intentions of the Indians, William Bent decided to take advantage of the temporary lull in hostilities to reopen the trading post at Adobe Walls.[5] This fort had been built on the Canadian River in the Texas panhandle in the wake of Lieutenant Abert's survey in 1845, but the hostility of the Comanches had caused its abandonment. Bent asked Carson to try to reestablish trade there. With him to the Canadian went Lucien Maxwell, John Smith, Robert Fisher, and Lucas Murray—all experienced in dealing with Indians—and two Mexican herders.

The broad valley was rich in tall grass, and the walls of the fort enclosed a square eighty feet on a side, ample for containing the animals at night. The little party succeeded in establishing themselves at the fort, and the Comanches traded in a few buffalo hides and a large herd of horses and mules. Then the Jicarilla Apaches swooped into the valley, killed the herdsman, and stampeded the *caballada*. Only two mules, tied inside the fort, were saved.

To remain in this hostile country without horses was unthinkable. The trade goods were buried, the ammunition and camp gear were packed on the two mules, and the men set out at night on the long walk through sand, rocks, sage, and cactus to Bent's Fort. The direct distance was no more than a hundred fifty miles, but handicapped as they were, they probably followed the Canadian, touching the river frequently for water and grazing.

Early one morning as they trudged toward the northwest, a band of Kiowas appeared over a rise, caught sight of the men, and, whooping and flourishing spears, charged upon them at a dead run. Carson placed the mules together and the men around them, facing the Indians. As they approached, the men fired carefully, one at a time. When the first horse fell, the Indians shied away, circling the whites, at too great a distance to do any damage, but not out of range of the rifles. Several other horses fell, and three riders. That was enough. Collecting their fallen warriors, the Kiowas slipped out of sight over a rise in the prairie. Carson's little band reached Bent's Fort without further trouble.[6]

The Jicarilla Apaches were raiding widely in the adjacent plains and mountains. In December, Colonel Benjamin Lloyd Beall sent a small command in pursuit of a raiding party, which fled into the mountains. The same severe cold and deep snow that were defeating Frémont farther north drove these dragoons back to Taos. Determined to teach the Indians a lesson, Beall himself headed a larger command, with Carson as guide, that succeeded with much hardship in crossing the Sangre de Cristos. Failing to find the Indians and running out of provisions, they were returning through Sangre de Cristo Pass when they came in sight of a village of Apaches. The charge was sounded, but the horses were too jaded to catch the Indians. After plundering the village and taking two prisoners, Beall called a halt. Carson advised that the greatest advantage to be gained from the prisoners, both of them chiefs, would be to impress upon them the fairness and liberality of the United States government and the benefits they could expect from peace, then to let them go. The colonel followed his advice, and the command hurried out of the mountains and back to Taos, which was comparatively free from the severe cold and snow of the storm.[7]

On January 21, 1849, Frémont entered Beaubien's store in Taos and found Carson, Dick Owens, and Lucien Maxwell passing the long winter evening at their ease.[8] So changed was he that Owens failed to recognize him. Maxwell, more alert, pleased him by exclaiming, "Why, don't you know the captain?" Godey was with him. Their faces were drawn, their eyes sunken from the horrors endured by the party in the heights of the San Juans. In some places the snow up there was eighteen feet deep. The horses and mules had all frozen, and the men, many of them with frozen feet, were dying helplessly of cold and starvation. Carson had been aware that Frémont had launched a fourth expedition, but his sudden appearance in Taos brought the first news of the disaster that had overwhelmed him.

Carson and Maxwell helped outfit a relief party. The next morning, with four Mexican muleteers, thirty animals, food and blankets, Godey rode back toward the mountains. He succeeded in bringing about three fourths of the men to safety. Ten of the forty-four had died.[9]

Frémont allowed himself the luxury of submitting to the ministrations of Kit and Josefa, who, following the custom of the country, served him his morning chocolate in bed and sought constantly to distract his mind from the horrors he had experienced and to make him comfortable. Dick Owens and Kit's youngest brother, Lindsey, were also staying at the comfortable adobe house at the northeast corner of the plaza. Ceran St. Vrain and Francis X. Aubry came to visit, and on January 29 St. Vrain dined with the Carsons.[10]

These diversions helped, for Frémont, the optimist, accustomed to dashing into danger and achieving at least some show of success, could not face the heartbreaking events of the past month.[11] Realizing, perhaps, how much his success in crossing the Sierra Nevada in the dead of winter had depended on Carson's cheerful optimism, alertness, and expertise, he blamed his failure in the San Juans on Old Bill Williams. In the deep snow and almost constant storm, Williams had turned up Alder Creek, twenty miles short of Willow Creek, which led to the pass he intended to cross.[12] But Frémont was not an easy man to guide, and the disaster resulted in large degree from his faulty judgment in trying to force his way through the mountains in the terrible storm.

Rumor linked Old Bill with something even more horrible. As the defeated expedition returned, he was sent ahead with an advance party to seek help. Henry King died, and Charles Taplan, who came along later, reported that King's body was more than half eaten by his companions. Old Bill was too craggy a person to have been universally loved by the trappers, and Frémont reported many years later when he was writing his memoirs that Carson had remarked, "In starving times no man who knew him ever walked in front of Bill Williams."[13]

Kit's and Josefa's efforts to distract him helped Frémont to turn his mind to his plan to proceed to California. He needed men to replace those who had died as well as several who refused to go any farther. Owens let him believe that he would meet him in California after returning to Missouri to get married. Frémont wrote to Jessie, "Carson is very anxious to go there with me now, and afterwards remove his family thither, but he cannot decide to break off from Maxwell and family connections." He would be especially reluctant to leave Josefa, who was well into her first pregnancy.

Godey continued with Frémont to California on February 13 and settled there. Lindsey Carson and Tom Boggs, lured by news of rich gold strikes, also went with him. Kit and Josefa were briefly left with their few servants, Dick Owens, and six-year-old Teresina Bent, who had lived with Josefa since the death of her father. Owens soon went to his family in Indiana, where he married. He moved to Tama County, Iowa, during the Civil War and to Jackson County, Kansas, in 1872, where he died in 1902.[14]

With Maxwell, Kit was planning his second farming venture. In marrying Maria de la Luz Beaubien, Maxwell had become involved with one of the most extensive of the Mexican land grants, the Beaubien–Miranda grant claimed by his father-in-law, Charles Beaubien, and the latter's Mexican friend and business associate, Guadalupe Miranda.[15] At the outbreak of the Mexican War, Miranda had fled to Mexico and later sold his share of the grant to Maxwell. When his son Narcisse was slain in the Taos uprising of 1847, Beaubien lost enthusiasm for establishing a family seat in his adopted country.

By 1849 Maxwell was already well on his way to becoming the sole owner of the grant on the Little Cimarron, with the concomitant responsibility for developing it.[16] He and Carson were making plans for opening up a stock farm when, in February, Colonel Beall again required Kit's help with the Indians.[17]

The treaty of Guadalupe Hidalgo at the end of the Mexican War had stipulated that captives held by the Indians would be returned to their respective countries. Hearing of a large encampment of Indians on the Arkansas, Beall set out to visit them and receive from them the Mexican captives held in their villages. The Indian agent, traders, and interpreters all urged him not to make the demand at that time. Two thousand Indians would protest violently, for intricate relationships bound the Indians to their captives.

For half a century or more the Indians of the southern plains, mountains, and deserts had been professional raiders, stealing horses and other moveable property that looked useful to them, and carrying off many young children. These children were adopted and trained with the Indian children, later marrying among them. Some of the identifiable captives had grown old in the villages and knew no ties except those to their Apache kinsmen. Even recently captured Mexican boys were often unwilling to give up the free, wild life and the honored position bestowed by the Indians. The status of girl captives was little above slavery, but they shrank from a return to their native villages, where, they believed, they would be despised. Colonel Beall finally decided that his wisest course would be to await the making of a treaty, which could include as one of the articles the delivery of the captives.

By April Carson and Maxwell were again ready to start farming. Carson had accumulated two thousand dollars over the years of trapping, guiding for Frémont and the army, and soldiering. Half of this he lent to Maxwell.[18] They bought stock, seeds, and supplies and, with the help of a few Mexican laborers, started building and making improvements on Rayado Creek some miles south of the farm Carson and Owens had started in 1845 on the Little Cimarron.

Because the Rayado was about fifty miles away and across the Sangre de Cristos from Taos and was dangerously exposed to raids by Apaches, Utes, Comanches, and Cheyennes, Carson did not move his family during the first year. On May 1, Josefa's first child was born prematurely and was named Charles, in memory of Charles Bent. The baby, too frail to risk the journey across the mountains, died within a year.[19]

The settlement, strategically located on the mountain branch of the Santa Fe Trail, began to grow almost at once. In the spring of 1849 Maxwell and Luz and her sister Petra and Jesús Abréu established their homes there. Bill New, Robert Fisher, and several land-hungry pioneers took up land along the little rippling tributaries of the Canadian. During the winter of 1849–50, Captain Grier sent Sergeant William Holbrook with ten dragoons from Taos to establish a post for the protection of the Santa Fe Trail and of Maxwell and his settlers.

Kit, meanwhile, had been called away. In October 1849, several travelers, including J. M. White and his wife, their little daughter, and a woman servant, pulled ahead of their caravan on the Cimarron Cutoff. The dead bodies of the men were later found sprawled beside the road at Point of Rocks. Nearby, the wagon in which the women and the child had ridden lay on its side, broken in pieces. Some Pueblo Indians said they had seen at the Apache camp a white woman and a little girl, suspected to have been Mrs. White and her daughter. Rescue efforts were slow in materializing. In November Captain Grier set out from Taos with a company of First Dragoons, guided by Antoine Leroux, Robert Fisher, and Dick Wootton. On the Rayado he picked up Carson but unfortunately did not give him much authority.

At the springs where the murder was committed, Carson found "trunks . . . broken open, harness cut . . . everything destroyed."[20] The trail was one of the most difficult Carson had ever tried to read. At each camp, they would find some of Mrs. White's clothing. The Indians separated each morning, creating several trails.

At the end of a week and a half, Carson saw the Indian camp and broke into a gallop, calling for the others to follow. Grier, thinking it advisable to call for a parley, ordered a halt. Carson had to pull up. He was given to understand that Leroux had advised the halt, but this was an error. The guides shouted and swore at the delay. The Indians took advantage of the pause to grab their arms, take a shot at the whites, and get to their horses. A ball hit Grier low in the chest, doubling him up and knocking the wind out of him, but not hurting him seriously. The men left his side and charged furiously at the fleeing Indians. By the time they reached the camp, only one Indian was left. When he plunged into the Canadian River nearby, he was shot. About two hundred yards away lay the body of Mrs. White, still warm, an arrow through her heart.

Carson believed that a sudden charge as soon as the camp was sighted would have saved her life, though

the treatment she had received from the Indians was so brutal and horrible that she could possibly last but a short period. . . . In camp was found a book, the first of the kind I had ever seen, in which I was made a great hero, slaying Indians by the hundred, and I have often thought that as Mrs. White could read the same, . . . she would pray for my appearance and that she might be saved.

Not having been able to live up to her expectations was a sore point with Carson, who found it hard to forget Captain Grier's ill-judged hesitation. The child and the servant were never found.

As the rescue party returned, they ran into the worst snowstorm Kit could remember, in which, as he heard later, many of the Indians perished. On November 23 Grier tried to reach Barclay's Fort on the Mora, but the force of the wind drove the men off course, and only Fisher and a few others succeeded. One man froze to death. Near Las Vegas they arrived at a patch of timber which gave them some shelter from the blizzard. Two days later Grier, Carson, and Leroux reached Barclay's, exchanged news, and returned to Las Vegas.[21] After returning with Grier over the mountains to Taos, Carson rode back to the Rayado, where further problems developed with the Indians.

In late March or early April a band of Jicarilla Apaches charged upon two herders about two miles from the ranch house, seriously wounded them both, and drove off a herd of horses and mules. One of the herders was able to reach the Rayado. Sergeant Holbrook immediately mounted his men. Carson, Fisher, and New saddled up and joined the soldiers in a hard ride through the dusk to the scene of the attack. At dawn the next morning they picked up the trail. For twenty-five miles they followed it at top speed and, when fresh tracks indicated that they were nearing the marauders, moved up cautiously, surprised the Indians, and killed five. Four made their escape on four of the horses.[22]

On May 5, 1850, Carson and Tim Goodale started a band of forty or fifty mules and horses to Fort Laramie, following the trapper-Indian trail up the plains east of the Rockies.[23] Fort Laramie had been purchased by the army on June 26, 1849, but in 1850 a number of former mountain men and traders were scattered along the Oregon Trail from Ash Hollow to North Fork Ford, offering goods and services to dusty, exhausted emigrants. Over fifty thousand arrived at the fort that year, riding in wagons, on carts, on horseback, or plodding afoot through the dust. One was pushing a wheelbarrow. Most were bound for the gold diggings of California, but some were settlers on their way to Oregon. Around thirteen thousand Mormons were following their religious leaders, chiefly to Utah. Three hundred sixteen emigrants had died east of the fort, most of them from cholera.[24]

By the time they reached the fort, many emigrants were short of provisions; nearly all had equipment that needed mending; many oxen, mules, and horses were too broken down to continue. As the trail neared the fort, the wagons turned aside, the emigrants trading, bartering, and paying from scanty hoards of hard cash to make themselves roadworthy for the second half of their long journey.

Carson and Goodale disposed of their horses and mules with ease. The emigrants were eager to see and speak to Carson, expecting him to be the wild-eyed fighter of the dime novel. The mountain men gleefully pointed out as the famous scout whatever unlikely person struck their fancy. When given a straight answer, the emigrants were the less satisfied.

One walked up to Kit and asked, "I say, stranger, are you Kit Carson?"

His blue eyes twinkling, Kit replied, "I reckon I am."

The man studied him in perplexity for a long moment, then gave a skeptical shake of the head. "Look 'e here, stranger," he finally asserted, "You can't come that over me. You ain't the kind of Kit Carson I'm alookin' for."[25]

The tide of forty-niners carried Goodale to California, while Carson, accompanied by a Mexican herdboy, turned toward home. Where the Greenhorn River crossed the Taos road about twenty-five miles south of Pueblo, several trappers had settled with their Indian wives and their children. When Carson stopped there to rest his horses, talk of Apaches waylaying travelers to the south caused the herdboy to refuse to ride farther. Charles Kinney, an old mountain man of the settlement, was the only one willing to accompany Kit across the mountains.

They traveled by night, crossing Sangre de Cristo Pass and reaching the Trinchera River. Carson hid the animals some distance from the road, then climbed the highest cottonwood to watch for the Apaches. There he remained all day, sometimes falling into a doze, jerking awake just as he began to topple from his perch. Near evening he saw a half a mile away a large body of Indians riding without particular attention to the trail. Knowing that they were unaware of his presence, he and Kinney saddled up and traveled in the brush some distance from the road until dark. They took the road at nightfall and arrived at Red River at daybreak. That evening they rode on to Taos.[26]

When Carson reached the Rayado a few days later, he learned that the Indians, catching Bill New working alone in his field, had knifed him to death. A large band had run off every head of stock from the settlement, but Major Grier and a detachment of soldiers had overtaken them, left several Indians lying on the prairie, and brought back all the stock except a few head the Indians had killed.

The settlement was quiet during the summer, but Carson was soon asked by Lieutenant Oliver Taylor of the First Dragoons to go on the trail to arrest a former dragoon named Fox for evading a debt. When Carson refused to take the assignment, Lieutenant Taylor disclosed the following: Two Santa Fe traders, Elias Brevoort and Samuel Weatherhead, and a lawyer named Tully had left for Missouri, each carrying a large amount of gold. Traveling with them were Fox and about thirty other men. Another stranger in Taos, thinking himself on his deathbed, had confessed that Fox had asked him to join in a plot to murder the men when they reached the Cimarron, take their gold, and ride hard for Texas. Carson immediately agreed to lead a posse to the relief of the traders. With ten dragoons he galloped across the plains until one o'clock in the morning. Meeting Captain Ewell with recruits for New Mexico, he explained the errand of his little band, and Ewell and twenty-five men joined him.

As they approached the camp of the traders, all was quiet, the traders unsuspecting. Dumbfounded, Fox was taken into custody and turned over to Captain Ewell, who returned with him to his own camp. Weatherhead and Brevoort selected fifteen men in whom they had confidence and told the rest to leave. They then asked Carson to claim whatever reward he wished and it would be his. He declined, "considering having done a good act, thereby saving the lives of two valuable citizens, was reward sufficient."[27] However, the following spring Carson received from Brevoort and Weatherhead a pair of splendid, silver-mounted pistols, specially made at the Colt factory and inscribed to commemorate the event.

The Rayado having been quiet for some months, Carson decided in November to bring his family across the mountains. Many years later Teresina Bent Scheurich told about the journey up the canyon east of Taos and across the pass when she was nine years old. For the first time, the family had several months together, uninterrupted by alarms or violence.

In the spring of 1851 Maxwell proposed that Carson go to St. Louis for provisions and merchandise. In addition to the money to be earned, Carson had an important personal reason for wishing to make the trip. He planned at last to bring Adaline to New Mexico. With Jesse Nelson he left the wagons at the village of Kansas,[28] went to St. Louis to purchase goods and order them delivered up-river, then returned to Howard County to visit relatives and friends. The announcement that Adaline was going with him caused a flurry of excited activity. Nelson became aware of Robert's daughter, Susan. Time was short, the attraction flourished, and before the wagon train started west, the two were married. Susan was to have a more exciting honeymoon than her Uncle Kit anticipated.[29]

Having the two young women in his care, Carson planned to go by Bent's Fort. He expected to find better water and grass and less danger from Indians than on the Cimarron Cutoff. When the wagons were about fifteen miles below Chouteau's Island,[30] they came upon a village of Cheyennes. Supposing them to be friendly, Carson took no special precautions for safety. But while he was in Missouri, an officer of Colonel Sumner's command, about ten days' march ahead, had had an Indian chief flogged for having stolen his wife's ring. Being beaten was an insult of the worst kind, and Carson's party, the first whites to come along, became the object of the Cheyennes' revenge.

The Indians allowed Carson's wagons to pass, but when the train was about twenty miles from their village, they began to come into his camp by ones, twos, and threes. After about twenty arrived, Carson invited them to sit down and smoke and talk. Not realizing that Kit understood Cheyenne, they began discussing in their own tongue how best to kill the party. Carson could be killed with a knife, they decided, when he was smoking and off guard, and the Mexican drivers could be dispatched as easily as buffalo.

With two young women under his protection, Carson could not afford a fight. Suddenly he sprang to his feet and started talking.

"So you wish to take my scalp! Why? I have done you no injury! You came to me as friends. I asked you to smoke with me and talk as friends. Now I hear that you wish to do me injury, and you must leave this camp. Any that refuse to leave will be shot. If any of you return, I will fire on you."

Two vivid eyewitness accounts were given of this tense situation. A Frenchman called Pete, a member of Carson's party, later gave this report:

Why, Kit knew just what was to be done and did it too. With any other man, we would have gone under. The Indians were more afraid of him than all the rest of us put together. There were red devils enough there to eat us up, and at one time I could almost feel my hair leaving my head. We had two women traveling with us and their crying made me feel so bad that I was sartain there was no fight in me. Women are poor plunder to have along when going out on a war party, but Kit talked to them and then to the Indians, and put them both finally on the right trail. Wah! but them were ticklish times.

Nelson pictured a dramatic tableau with a big Indian brandishing a hatchet over Kit's head, Nelson's gun leveled at the Indian, and another Indian threatening Nelson with drawn bow and arrow. This dangerous impasse was broken by Chief Old Bark's son, Ah-man-nah-ko, who recognized Carson and called a warning to the Indians.[31] The crisis eased temporarily, the Indians, with what dignity they could muster, stalked away to join their friends on the sand hills. Ah-man-nah-ko paused to warn Carson that they would try to ambush him later.

Carson ordered his men to hitch up and hurry on toward Bent's Fort, keeping their rifles ready in one hand, their whips in the other. At dark, he started one of the young Mexicans, an exceptionally good runner, to the Rayado, where Major Grier was now stationed.

The next morning Carson started early and traveled until noon, when five Indians appeared. He placed the train on the alert, stepped forward, and ordered the Indians to halt at a distance of a hundred yards. When they obeyed, he allowed them to come nearer and told them that he had sent an express the night before to Rayado to get the troops stationed there, who would surely come to his relief, and that if he were killed they would know on whom to avenge his death. The Cheyennes returned to his camp of the night before and found the moccasin prints of his messenger, who had by then gone too far to be overtaken. Impressed by his sagacity in getting the messenger on the road without their knowledge and by the retribution sure to strike if they harmed him, they did not again approach his train. About twenty-five miles from Bent's Fort he met the troops.

His messenger had caught up with Colonel Sumner the third day and had delivered the letter, but Sumner would not send any aid. When the messenger reached Rayado the next day, Major Grier immediately detailed Lieutenant Robert Johnson with a small force to Carson's relief. When Johnson met Sumner, the latter sent Major James Henry Carleton and thirty men along, wishing, Carson believed, to share credit for the rescue. Whatever resentment Carson still held concerning Grier's failure to cooperate effectively in the effort to save Mrs. White was eradicated by this prompt response. Toward Johnson and Carleton he felt immediate gratitude and admiration, as much as if they had actually fought the Indians by his side. This esteem was wholeheartedly returned. In years to come, Carleton would be the means of pushing Carson to fame in his final role as a soldier.

Fort Union was being established on the Santa Fe Trail forty miles south of the Rayado, whose military establishment was soon removed. Carson bought the military hospital, and he and Jesse Nelson made homes in it for their families.[32] During the winter of 1851–52, he lived undisturbed as family man and rancher. Maxwell was developing a very profitable business supplying the army post with feed and produce from the ranch, and Carson shared in this enterprise.

The ranch was not, however, totally peaceful. Teresina Bent Scheurich recalled two occasions when the Indian threat seemed very real to herself as a young girl.[33] Once when Carson and his herders were the only men on the ranch, about three hundred Indians came in and camped. For two days and nights Kit had to exercise all his talent and skill in diplomacy to maintain the delicate balance between friendship and merciless pillage and massacre. At last the Indians left, on the warpath for Utes and Apaches. Should they be unsuccessful, and return filled with fury and looking for scalps, the settlement would lie in their path. Carson took his women and children and joined the other families in a temporary exodus to Taos.

On another occasion Carson was away and Tom Boggs was in charge. A party of Cheyennes demanded food and were fed, but one of them tried to trade horses for Teresina, to whom he had taken a fancy. Boggs managed to stall him off, but the Indians did not leave until Carson returned in company with some soldiers from Fort Union.

Maxwell kept open house at his headquarters on the Rayado, and Carson spent many winter evenings with him and his guests, playing seven-up, Kit's favorite game, euchre, billiards, and other games of chance and skill, talking over old adventures and planning new ones. They worked up a spring hunt of eighteen former mountain men, with Carson as captain.

In March 1852 they saddled their horses, loaded their beaver traps on their led mules, and started up the Arkansas.[34] They trapped the Bayou Salade, down the South Platte to the plains, through the Plains of Laramie to New Park, finding the streams rich in beaver. Trapping up the tributaries of the North Platte, they crossed over to the headwaters of the Colorado in Middle Park, crossed the Divide to the head of the Arkansas, followed it to "where it goes out of the mountain,[35] then followed on under the mountain, thence home to Rayado through Raton Mountain, having made a very good hunt."

In October of that year his second son was born and named William, called Julian by Josefa and her people. Adaline turned her wayward eyes on Louis Simmons, about twenty years her senior, who asked Kit for her hand in marriage.[36] Whether she and Louy lived in the hospital or found a home apart is of small importance, for they would soon leave New Mexico for good.

Word had reached the ranch that a fortune could be made by delivering sheep to California, where the burgeoning population had activated a tremendous demand and driven prices sky-high. In 1852 Dick Wootton had rounded up nine thousand head and with twenty-two employees had driven them across the mountains and deserts to Sacramento. The next year Carson, John L. Hatcher, and Lucien Maxwell organized a drive, partially financed by two young Taos merchants: Henry Mercure, Canadian born, a former comrade in the California Battalion; and Juan Bernadet, a Spaniard.

In early February 1853, Carson rode to the Rio Abajo, the settlements along the Rio Grande south of Santa Fe, where he was able to buy sheep for fifty cents a head or less. Rounding up about 6,500, he and his helpers drove them to the Rayado. After seeing Josefa and the children settled at Taos, he was ready to begin the drive in late February or early March.

Hatcher took charge of the first drove, Carson the second, and Maxwell the third. With Carson and his herders went Mercure and Bernadet and their men, Adaline and Louy, Tom Boggs, and probably Tim Goodale. Progress was slow. From Fort Laramie on, the trail had to be varied from that followed by Hatcher and emigrant trains so as to find forage for the sheep. The herders had to be constantly on the watch to keep them from straying, to prevent laggards from being picked off by wolves, and to prevent them from drowning as they forded streams. Close guard was necessary at night to protect them from mountain lions and other predators. Probably a few sheep were traded to the Indians from time to time, but no raids occurred, and Carson reported "no serious loss."[37]

Following a new trail from the Sweetwater as he searched for grass for the sheep, he reached a new ferry over Green River, about six miles above the regular crossing, and the ferrymen crossed his animals gratis. Naming the new trail "Kit Carson's Cutoff," they hoped to attract other passengers because of his patronage.[38]

The progress and arrival of the drive were reported by the newspapers of northern California, for Carson was known there not only as the famous scout, but also as a member of the California Battalion who had helped to win independence from Mexico. An emigrant train arriving August 9 reported having passed him in Carson Valley in the Great Basin as he neared the Sierra Nevada.[39] He seems to have followed the 1843 route through Carson Pass, for on September 2 he brought the first flock of fifteen hundred to the Cosumnes River.[40] September 6 he reached Sacramento.[41] Samuel Norris, a Californian since 1845, paid $5.50 a head for the sheep, giving each of the partners a substantial return for eight months' work.[42]

An express from Maxwell, who had followed his trail along the Carson River, overtook him at Sacramento, asking him to wait so that the two parties could return together along the Gila. While waiting, he viewed with astonishment the rapidly growing town. Tents and shanties housed a population of twelve thousand where, seven years before, Frémont's men had camped on the open prairie and prepared for war. Business blocks sheltered the exploiters and developers upon whom the population depended for services and supplies.

Carson was again harassed by celebrity seekers. "His society was constantly courted by men he had never seen; he was passed free on steamboats and to all places of amusement. . . . He was pointed out wherever he went as a man who had done the State great services. . . . Men sitting next to him at table would speak of him and Kit would quietly eat his meal and walk off, signaling his friends not to give him away."[43] Tom Boggs enjoyed teasing him about this when they rode over to the Napa Valley and then to the Russian River to visit relatives, for plain old Kit's discomfort in the face of this adulation pleased and amused his friends. Many years later an old timer in the Napa Valley recalled this visit with the same amused approval.[44]

The folks from home delighted in their own way to do honor to their guests. Lilburn Boggs, Tom's father and former governor of Missouri, was starting to build the first brick home in the valley and Kit was remembered as having laid the cornerstone. William Boggs sat talking with Tom and Kit far into the night. Lindsey and his family were ranching about forty miles north of Sonoma on the Russian River, and Moses was in the same vicinity. Robert, father of Susan Nelson—Robert, eldest son of Rebecca and black sheep of the family—may also have been there. Accompanied by Moses Briggs, son of his sister Nancy, "Old Bob" had walked into the valley two years before during the rainy season, drunk and destitute. William Boggs had given young Briggs five dollars and told him how to reach his Uncle Lindsey, whom they were seeking.[45]

Adaline and Louy accompanied Carson to the Sonoma Valley, and there he saw for the last time this child of his mountain years.

The next year Lindsey wrote and said that he had not heard from them for some time, but that they had been well the last he heard.[46] Later Simmons left Adaline because, as Jesse Nelson reported, "she was a wild girl and did not behave properly."[47] Adaline seems to have gravitated to the gold fields. In 1859 with George W. Stilts and a Wilson family, she came to the new diggings near Mono Lake in eastern California. As Adaline Carson Stilts she was buried there about 1860.[48]

John L. Hatcher accompanied Kit to the Russian River Valley, settled there for a time, later moved to Oregon. Tom Boggs also remained in California for a time. With Maxwell, Carson rode the steamer across the bay to San Francisco, now a great port with a population of forty thousand. Only his visits with Frémont to Yerba Buena in 1846 made it possible for him to recognize the terrain where now a conglomeration of adobe huts, frame shacks, tents, and business blocks staggered down the hills to the bay.

Maxwell wished to take a steamer down the coast to Los Angeles. Remembering the misery of his one ocean voyage with the California Battalion, Carson chose to ride overland. Maxwell arrived fifteen days before him and began making preparations for the homeward journey. Before they left, they probably saw Alexis Godey, who was in southern California, Ned Beale, newly appointed Indian agent, and Kit's former master, David Workman.

Jake Beard of Taos, who had accompanied Hatcher, intending to try his luck at panning gold, looked wistfully on as Carson and Maxwell prepared to depart. "Kit, on seeing you, I feel homesick," he exclaimed, "and I think I ought to go back with you."

"Well, Jake," replied Kit, "we have only one life to live, and . . . we should make the most of our opportunities."

Beard returned to the ranch where he was employed, settled his affairs, saddled up, and overtook Carson. For many years he lived contentedly in New Mexico.[49]

At last the party rode east across the San Bernardino Mountains, through the Mojave Desert, and up the Gila. "We came to the Pima village and, on account of the scarcity of grass, we continued up the Gila to the mouth of the San Pedro, up it three days and from there we took a straight course for the copper mines and then [on to] the Del Norte, thence home through the settlements of the Rio Abajo. Arrived at Taos Decr. 25th, 1853."[50]

This was the last time Kit would set forth on an odyssey to far places. In Santa Fe he met Jacob Bernhisel, delegate to Congress from Utah Territory, who informed him that Kit had been appointed Indian agent for the Mohuache Utes. Thereafter his choices were more strictly limited by the course of events, more rigorously determined by his stern sense of responsibility.

Chapter 16

Agent to the Utes

Twice Carson had decided that he had roamed enough and had made some effort to settle down. On Christmas Day, 1853, when he rode into the village where, twenty-seven years before, he had spent his first winter in the West, he seemed to have succeeded. Josefa had waited over ten years for this to happen. To William, now over a year old, he was a stranger.

Also awaiting his homecoming was a copy of *Harper's New Monthly Magazine* of the preceding August, containing a well-written article by George D. Brewerton, "A Ride With Kit Carson Through the Great American Desert and the Rocky Mountains."[1] When the article was read to him, Carson was deeply impressed.

On January 6, 1854, following the festivities of Christmas and the New Year, Kit posted $5,000 bond, endorsed by Charles Beaubien and Peter Joseph.[2] With prospects for a steady income at work he understood and liked, he rode to Santa Fe to report to David Meriwether, territorial governor and ex officio superintendent of Indian Affairs for New Mexico.[3] To his agency for the Mohuache Utes, Meriwether added the Jicarilla Apaches and the Pueblo Indians.

Three days later Carson dictated a letter to Brewerton, who immediately sent back a reply, excerpts from which follow:

Brooklyn, N.Y., March 12th, 1854

My dear Kit:

   *You can scarcely conceive the pleasure which I derived from
the reception of a letter from yourself dated Taos, N.M., Jany. 9th,
1854, which reached me some four days ago. . . . Among all the
complimentary notices which my first essay in prose writing for
the press—the "Ride with Kit Carson" has received, I have heard
nothing which gave me as much gratification, as the remarks contained in the last four lines of your letter. . . . As regards your offer
to give me a sketch of your life up to the present time I can only
say that you could not possibly do me a greater favor. . . . it
would be both a pride and a pleasure to give your history to the
world.*

Urging Carson to get started as soon as he could and to send an
installment by each mail, Brewerton ended, "If my business would
permit—and a wife & youngsters did not anchor me down at
home, I should most assuredly cross the Grand Prairie once more
if but to shake you by the hand."[4]

The arrangement seemed to hold out much promise, but Carson had first to establish himself as Indian agent. Because of econ-
omies ordered in federal expenditures, the Jicarilla Apaches had
taken to supporting themselves by robbing the citizens of New
Mexico.[5] Much of Carson's time during his first years as agent was
spent in helping the army to bring the Indians under some measure of governmental control.

In February 1854, Colonel John Garland, commandant of the
U.S. military department of New Mexico, ordered that any Indian
who should commit depredations upon the citizens must be pursued and punished.[6] In March the Jicarillas ran off stock not far
from Fort Union. Lieutenant David Bell with sixty men of the Second Dragoons was ordered after them. He overtook them in a canyon of the Red River north of Taos, recovering twenty or thirty
horses and killing a number of Indians. Among those killed was
White Wolf, leader of the band that had abducted Mrs. White. Two
soldiers were killed and several wounded, and the patrol was so
hard pressed as reinforcements rushed to join the Jicarillas that an

express was sent to Lieutenant Colonel Philip St. George Cooke, who went to their rescue.[7]

A few days later a large body of Apaches came within twenty miles of Taos. Still busy setting up his office, Carson had started to Santa Fe. He stopped and talked with several of the chiefs, who pretended friendship. While he was gone, the Indians commenced raiding near the village of Cieneguilla.[8] Lieutenant J. W. Davidson, Carson's old comrade in the desperate fight at San Pasqual, was ordered to take sixty dragoons and "watch and restrain" them.[9] Davidson found them in the Embudo Mountains, strongly placed among huge boulders on the side and top of the mountain.

Leaving his horses under guard of a few men on the bank of a small stream, Davidson and the remainder started up the mountain in the face of the Indians' arrows and lances. Darting from rock to rock, the Indians retired before them, but it soon became evident that instead of running away, they were dropping back along the flanks of the dragoons. His men falling around him, his horses threatened with capture, Davidson ordered the dragoons to withdraw, taking what cover they could. Disregarding his own danger, he led them back to the horses, fighting his way through the Indians. Twenty-two men lay dead on the field. Most of the others, including himself, were wounded, but he fought through to the main road to Taos, several times wheeling about and charging the pursuing Indians before shaking them off. This Battle of Cieneguilla was a grievous defeat for the soldiers, "one of the most desperate fights in our Indian record," according to Colonel James F. Meline.[10] Returning to Taos the day after the fight, Carson stopped to help bury the dead soldiers. The Indians had ridden west across the Rio Grande, carrying their dead with them.

More clearly than most whites, Carson saw, as early as 1854, that game in the Ute country was becoming so scarce that the Indians could no longer support themselves by hunting, and he concluded that "the government has but one alternative, either to subsist and clothe them or exterminate them." He was not unsympathetic to the Indians, but he knew they would have to be defeated by military means before they would become permanently peaceful.[11]

When Cooke, now in command at Fort Union, took the field on

April 4, 1854, Carson volunteered to accompany him as chief guide.[12] He needed to find out which Indians were involved as well as to determine their condition. James H. Quinn and forty Pueblo Indians and Mexicans were employed as scouts to stay in front and keep on the trail of the Indians. The command crossed the Rio Grande at the mouth of Arroyo Hondo, about ten miles northwest of Taos. The river was swollen with melting snow. Taking the lead, Carson urged his horse into the surging waters, where the animal floundered among the large rocks covering the bottom. The troops followed, each dragoon making several crossings to help the infantry across. Carson crossed and recrossed about twenty times, and several dragoons nearly drowned as their horses lunged and slipped on the rocks while a foot soldier clung behind.

Having deduced where the Indians were headed, the scouts led the soldiers across country, gaining two days. April 8 they came upon a fresh trail in two feet of snow and climbed among snow showers through a chaos of steep slopes, rocks, snow, and bog. The Apaches had taken a position among crags, with precipices falling away to the churning waters of the Agua Caliente.

When the body of troops arrived, the scouts were exchanging shots with the Indians. Captain George Sykes of the infantry had kept up the morale of his troops by wading with them through mush ice and snow, leading the horse he could have ridden. Upon hearing that the Indians were just ahead, he and his men "raised a run and entered the Indian village in company with the Dragoons."[13] The one man killed and one wounded in this battle were of Sykes's Company. Greater loss was prevented by the daring of Lieutenant Bell and his dragoons, who galloped to the left through the Indians' fire into an angle of the cliffs commanding a view of the enemy position. The Apaches, seeing their danger, streamed away to the right. Cooke and Blake surged forward with the entire firing line, now on foot.[14] As the Apaches fled, Sykes and Moore pursued them up the mountain and into the woods, where they scattered and vanished.

At the village, some men brought in the Apaches' horses while others destroyed lodges, robes, skins, clothing, equipment, and provisions. Carson questioned the prisoners and learned that the Indians had lost four or five killed and five or six wounded, and that seventeen women and children were missing, probably lost and frozen during their night flight through the snow.[15] "Mr. Carson showed his well known activity and boldness," Cooke wrote in his report of the battle.[16] At sundown Major James H. Carleton and his command joined the expedition.

A corporal and a party of privates were detailed the next morning to escort the wounded man back to Abiquiú. The rest of the command took up the pursuit of the Indians, but the Apaches had separated into small bands and their trails led in all directions, often over tangles of trees downed by storms and half-covered with snow, leaving everywhere signs of desperation. Many dead horses lay along the trail, some ridden to death, others butchered for food. "Tracks of bare and diminutive feet" in the mud and snow displayed vividly the suffering of women and children.[17] By April 11 the trails of the fugitives disappeared among bare rocks high in the mountains; others were followed into the plains, where the trail vanished. Assured that further pursuit would uncover no more than two or three Indians, Cooke abandoned the chase.[18]

Those prints of small, bare feet in the snow and mud were eloquent signs to Carson that the battle was not simply against a band of reckless adventurers, but against a people—old and young, mothers and children. April 12 he wrote from camp on the Rio Puerco to William S. Messervy, acting governor, giving his opinion that the Indians had been driven to war by the actions of officers and troops in the vicinity of Taos, that the recent pursuit through the worst mountains he had ever seen had led them to believe that no quarter or mercy could be expected. He asked Messervy to send for them and make with them a fair and just treaty, but Messervy replied that the Indians had begun hostilities and he could not make overtures of peace.[19] This was the beginning of a revision of Carson's attitude toward the Indians. The change did not appear abruptly, but signs of it became more frequent and striking. Though interrupted by what he considered to be necessary punitive acts to convince the Indians of the advantages of peace, this change was manifested by his deep sense of responsibility and sympathy for the Indians in his agency and his recognition of their individual human qualities, by his disregard of Carleton's more extreme orders in the Navajo War, and by his strenuous efforts at Fort Garland to avoid more bloodshed.

When Cooke's command reached Abiquiú, it was discovered that new trouble threatened. The party detailed to bring back the wounded soldier had met a Ute and had taken him prisoner, confiscating his arms and his horse. He had escaped. A man was sent to request that the leading Utes come to Taos for a talk, and Carson hurried home to meet them. After he explained that the soldiers had thought the Indian was an Apache, assured the chiefs that the Americans wished to be friends, and returned the property confiscated, the Utes agreed to stay out of the war.[20]

Carson's memoirs are high in appreciation of Cooke, "as efficient an officer to make campaigns against Indians as I ever accompanied . . . brave and gallant." Cooke had taught the Apaches that they were not safe from the soldiers in any part of the mountains, no matter how rugged or distant.[21] This lesson was reinforced when, late in May 1854, Major Carleton led an expedition against the Jicarillas. Serving as chief guide, Carson led the main body of troops over Sangre de Cristo Pass, while Quinn led his scouts along the base of Old Baldy and Sierra Blanca to the Sand Dunes and across Mosca Pass. Apache sign was found in both passes. Near the Huerfano River, Carson found the main trail. Across canyons, ridges, and ravines the command followed the Indians into the Raton Mountains. Carleton held the soldiers back and kept them hidden in the timber as much as possible to give the trackers time to untangle the trail. On June 4 Carson remarked that if they met with no accident, they would find the Indians by two o'clock. Surprised at such precision, Carleton replied that if they did, he would buy his guide one of the finest hats that could be produced in New York.

About two o'clock Carson looked over the edge of a deep amphitheater on the east side of Fisher's Peak and saw a band of horses and the lodges of the Indians. As the Mexicans and Pueblos started down the steep side of the basin, whooping and firing, the Jicarillas fled in panic to the deep woods. They took only one horse and one mule, for Davidson and his men were galloping to cut them off from the horses while Quinn and the scouts continued to the creek to capture the herd. Moore's dragoons were ordered back to the mesa to cut off the Indians as they emerged from the hollow, but none emerged. Davidson's and Johnson's[22] men, pursuing the Indians on foot, also saw none. The Indians had scattered throughout the wood and hidden among the boulders.

Food was cooking on the fires. That and all else belonging to the Apaches was destroyed. One man was shot after being lured from the wood by the Apaches' rallying call. Following the headwaters of the Canadian down the south slope of the Raton Mountains, the expedition found no further sign of Indians.[23] Few had been killed, but their suffering had been great, and they had again seen that the soldiers could and would follow them to their hiding places in the mountains, no matter how rugged, and leave them even more wretched and destitute than before.

Officers and scouts had cooperated perfectly. Each gave credit to the other for the success of the campaign. In his report, Carleton wrote that Carson,

justly celebrated as being the best tracker among white men in the world, says that . . . he never saw such wonderful trailing . . . as was made . . . by Captain Quinn and his Mexican and Indian spies . . . that these had kept on the track when he himself would have given up. . . . Therefore, to Carson and Quinn and the spy company is due all the credit . . . for whatever success this column may have had in finding the Apaches.[24]

Carleton, a man of many interests, wrote to a friend in New York, and one day a fine hat arrived in Taos, inscribed on the inside band:[25]

At 2 o'clock
KIT CARSON
from
MAJOR CARLETON

In August Carson traveled about two hundred miles to visit the Utes and arrange for them to meet Meriwether at Abiquiú in October.[26] In September he reported to Meriwether that the Utes were poor and game was scarce, that they complained because Indians of the North were receiving presents, while they received none. He respectfully suggested that the superintendent call them together as early as possible and make presents of blankets and shirts before cold weather began. "I deem this to be a matter of great importance," he concluded.[27]

At the council Meriwether gave away a number of blanket coats, with disastrous results. At the meeting, however, the Indians had only one grievance. Some Mexicans killed an Indian to get his coat. The Utes asked for animals as compensation. Meriwether refused their request, but promised that the murderers would be arrested and punished according to law. Although one of the murderers was apprehended, he soon escaped and was not retaken. Nothing further was attempted to satisfy the Indians.[28]

As they returned to their hunting grounds, smallpox broke out among them, and every man to whom a blanket coat had been presented paid for it with his life. Believing that the coats caused the disease and that Meriwether had purposely injured them, the Mohuaches joined the Jicarillas in a cruel and bloody campaign, attacking the settlement at Costilla, killing men and driving off stock.[29]

Fort Pueblo suffered the most terrible of the raids, the climax of the Indians' fury. While Mrs. Sandoval, wife of the trader, was preparing the Christmas feast with the help of her two young sons, Dick Wootton stopped and warned her husband, Benito, of Indian sign in the vicinity. Tierra Blanca, a chief of the Mohuache Utes, showed up at the fort some time later, made friendly signs, said his men were out hunting buffalo, and was invited in.[30] Soon other Utes came and were admitted. Friendly contests began. At Blanco's suggestion all went inside the cabin for a friendly smoke. Suddenly the Indians seized the guns and killed everyone at the fort except Romaldo, a herder. After shooting him through the jaw, they cut off his tongue and left him for dead. He managed to reach the Baca ranch two miles below the fort before he died.

News swiftly reached Fort Union and was carried on to Santa Fe. General Garland put Colonel Thomas Fauntleroy, commander at Fort Union, in charge of regular troops and called upon Governor Meriwether for five companies of mounted volunteers.[31] More citizens offered to serve than were needed, especially after Meriwether appointed Ceran St. Vrain commander of volunteers. "In fact," reported Carson, "it was the only appointment of the Governor that met with the approbation of the people. Many were surprised at his sound judgment in making such a noble choice."[32]

Carson was chief guide when, early in March 1855, the command left for Fort Massachusetts. Lucien Stewart of Taos headed the scouts. The weather was severe, with frequent snowstorms. The soldiers had cleared brush and trees and removed haystacks from near the fort. Guards were kept constantly on the alert, but the Indians, having now all the stolen sheep and cattle they could manage, had driven them into Saguache Valley.

An advance party of scouts and dragoons met the Indians, who thought this small group was the entire force coming against them. Blanco, conspicuous in a red woolen shirt, rode back and forth, haranguing the warriors and giving orders. The Indians charged, were repulsed by the dragoons and irregulars, rallied and charged again and again. Lucien Stewart and his scouts surged forward with a flanking attack. Confused, the Indians drew back. The arrival of the main body of troops, bugles sounding the charge, put them to flight. The troops pounded after, killing and wounding a number of Indians, and the rest immediately scattered.

The last of March, Fauntleroy returned to Fort Massachusetts, and the command dispersed among the settlements to recuperate where forage could be furnished the horses. Three weeks later, Fauntleroy was crossing Poncha Pass, where the San Juans and Sangre de Cristos merge north of the San Luis Valley. In a punishing pursuit of Blanco's band, the soldiers destroyed baggage, took many animals, and killed forty-four Indians. The Utes scattered into the mountains.[33]

Meanwhile St. Vrain, with Carson as scout, had gone east over Sangre de Cristo Pass on the trail of the Jicarillas. Coming up with them on the Purgatoire, the volunteers routed them, capturing animals and baggage. Day after day the pursuit continued, with warriors killed and women taken prisoner. Carson reported this campaign as if he were not there, though Rafael Chacon reported that he was active in the beginning.[34] Perhaps after locating the Jicarillas on the Purgatoire, Carson obtained leave to return to Taos. About this time, his half brother Moses visited Jesse and Susan Nelson and then stayed with him for a time before moving on, leaving him with some bills to pay. On June 23, Carson's daughter Teresina was born.[35]

That year for the first time, Carson's annual report appears in the records of the Bureau of Indian Affairs. In Meriwether's report for 1854, he gave Carson credit for "judicious management" in preventing the Utes from taking sides with the Jicarillas, but failed to send in Carson's September letter. To Carson's 1855 report, Meriwether appended a note lamenting Carson's not having specified which tribe of Indians was still committing depredations, though "the last part of his report would leave the impression that they were committed by the Jicarilla Apaches," an impression reinforced by Carson's memoirs. Meriwether chose to reject this impression, which implied that the Indians, who met him in council a few days later, were not properly in awe of his power. He reported a suspicion that the depredations were committed not by the Jicarillas, but by the Comanches, who were based largely in Texas.[36]

At the council near Abiquiú in September 1855, a few prisoners were exchanged and treaties were signed, setting aside for the Mohuache Utes a reservation of a thousand square miles, including part of the San Luis Valley already occupied by whites, and promising the Utes $66,000; the Jicarilla Apaches were promised $36,000 and a hundred sixty thousand acres. The Indians were to give up claims on other territory.[37] Apparently Meriwether was promising the Indians whatever he thought would keep them quiet.

Carson disapproved of the treaties. While he favored a reservation for the Indians, keeping them away from white settlements and giving them training and encouragement in farming, he considered the terms both too generous and unenforceable, because the Apaches could not be trusted.[38] His opinion was shared by most New Mexicans. Diego Archuleta, agent for the Jicarillas at Abiquiú, wrote directly to Washington, protesting the making of treaties with Indians, who owed no sovereignty to anyone with whom a treaty could be made and who considered treaties as temporary arrangements while they recouped, never hesitating to kidnap children, run off stock, and murder villagers as soon as self-interest impelled them to do so.[39] The Utes Carson considered more trustworthy, but whether the protests of Archuleta and others were effective, or whether the Senate was simply trying to cut costs, the treaties were never ratified.

At this council or the next, something occurred to widen the rift between Carson and Meriwether. Having opposite attitudes toward human relationships, they would inevitably become antagonistic. Meriwether's memoirs show him to have been mainly interested in establishing his authority in whatever situation he found himself. Carson had little respect for authority *per se* and was too independent to suit the governor. The lack of sympathy between the two precluded any but the most elementary cooperation, but Meriwether's two references to Carson in the reports to Washington have been noted. Neither shows resentment.

We do not know whether Carson was punished as Meriwether stated thirty years later, or whether the former governor's memory was distorted by fantasies of punishment he wished he had heaped on the unimposing little agent who could not be made to knuckle under.[40] His account seethes with long pent-up anger and frustration. He had had a hundred sheep driven to the place of meeting, ten or fifteen to be released to the Indians morning and evening. When Carson arrived, the herder was directed to turn the sheep over to him, with strict orders to deliver to the Indians no more than ten or fifteen each morning and evening. Having no herder and no pen for the sheep, Carson turned them over to the Indians. This led to some unfriendly remarks between governor and agent. Meriwether remembered great alarm and confusion among the Indians the next day, with Carson urging him to take cover beside the river bank. He refused, saying that he was not afraid, and ordered Carson to go among the Indians and try to quiet them. Instead, Carson took cover. When the governor implied that he was a coward, he said that Carson became very abusive "and said that he was not a damn fool, as I was, to risk his life in the manner I did." Thereupon, Meriwether remembered, he discharged Carson as Indian agent, and when Carson became "boisterous" put him under arrest; Carson begged to be allowed to continue as Indian agent, but he vowed to report Carson's conduct anyway. No such report is on record.

Nothing of such a disturbance was mentioned by either Meriwether or Carson in the report of 1855. In September 1856 Carson reported that a Tabeguache Utah Indian, receiving an old, worn blanket, tore it up and "wished to kill the Superintendent but was hindered by the other Indians."[41] A report circulated that Carson instigated the disturbance. Carson wrote to Meriwether September 17, 1856, stating that he was not present when the event occurred. Meriwether replied that he had heard nothing of the report and the disturbance had been a mild one.[42] Somewhere between his letter to Carson and the dictation of his memoirs when he was eighty-six, a metamorphosis seems to have occurred.

Contrary to the expectations of Carson, Archuleta, and others, both the Jicarillas and the Utes learned an enduring lesson from the pursuits and fights, destruction and suffering of 1854 and 1855. By 1856 Carson was able to concentrate his activities largely in Taos, where he received visiting Indians in front of his house as often as at the agency. Whenever the came to the village, they would have a smoke and talk with him. For the first time he became aware of himself as a person of authority, for more and more they listened to him and heeded his advice.

Carson now had time to think of his plan to give Brewerton the story of his life, and he now had the means to do it. Because of his meager skills in reading and writing, he had to have a clerk. The Bureau of Indian Affairs made no provision for a clerk, but did allow for an interpreter. Carson hired several young men as interpreters over the years. They wrote letters and reports for him and kept the accounts of the agency, not always to the satisfaction of his superiors. Occasionally he forgot that his young helper was supposed to be an interpreter. Once Meriwether objected to "Charges for expenses for *self and clerk* at Santa Fe $13 when I am ignorant of any regulations which authorize an Agent to have a clerk."[43]

John W. Dunn had taken charge of the agent's office when Carson was serving as guide in 1854 and 1855. Other clerks were Charles Williams, J. P. Esmay, John Mostin, and John Martin. During 1856, Mostin wrote in longhand as Carson sat dreaming aloud of glorious days along the beaver streams in the high valleys of the Rockies, of Indian fights that, looking back, seemed sometimes to have been no more than a rough kind of play, of rugged comrades as true and brave as could be found anywhere, of those strange journeys with Frémont, and the California Battalion of Mounted

Riflemen who had helped bring that rich country into the Union. The salient facts were recorded in Mostin's smooth, flowing script. Only occasionally were they fleshed out with details when some event vitally interesting to the narrator welled up in his memory.

When he came to recent wars with the Indians, his indignation was again aroused by injustices laid upon them and by the cruel retaliation of the Indians upon the New Mexico communities, which only brought more misery upon themselves.

I frequently visit the Indians, speak to them of the advantages of peace, and use my influence with them to keep them satisfied with the proceedings of those placed in power over them. . . . I cannot see how the Superintendent can expect Indians to depart satisfied that he has called to see him from a distance of two or three hundred miles, compelled to go several days without anything to eat, unless they have carried it with them. They are given a meal by the Superintendent, then the presents are given. Some get a blanket; those that get none are given a knife or hatchet or some vermillion, a piece of red or blue cloth, some sugar, and perhaps a few more trinkets. They could more than earn the quantity they receive in one day's hunt, if left in their own country. . . . They should not be allowed to come into the settlements, for every visit an Indian makes to a town, it is of more or less injury to him.[44]

On this note he ended his memoirs. Perhaps he had Brewerton in mind when he began, but something happened to his negotiations with the young writer. When the manuscript was finished, Carson turned it over to Jesse B. Turley to use "as he may deem proper for our joint benefit." Turley planned at first to make the memoirs the basis of a biography that he himself would write. Later he approached Washington Irving as a possible writer of the biography. Finally he made an agreement with army surgeon D. C. Peters, who had known Carson during the wars of 1854 and 1855.[45]

Peters was to write the life of Carson, the profits, if any, to be divided equally by Peters, Turley, and Carson. In 1858, with the help of C. Hatch Smith, a Brooklyn hack writer, Peters published *The Life and Adventures of Kit Carson, the Nestor of the Rocky Mountains, from Facts Narrated by Himself.* Although Peters probably made a modest amount from the book, there is no record that either Carson or Turley received any financial return. When the book was read to Carson, he remarked, "Peters laid it on a leetle too thick."[46]

That Carson should end his memoirs with a plea to keep the Indians away from the settlements is significant. Each year, beginning with the report for 1857, he reiterated his belief that the only salvation for the Indians was to be settled on reservations as far as possible from white settlements and taught agriculture and mechanic arts, with a military fort nearby to protect them from encroachment by unauthorized white traders and settlers and by unfriendly Indians. The commander of the military post was to serve as their agent, counselor, and protector because practice of dual supervision by civilian agents and military disciplinarians produced confusion. Carson's predecessor, E. A. Graves, reported in 1853 that when depredations were committed by the Indians, the citizens reported to the Indian agent, who reported to the superintendent, who investigated the incident then reported to the military command. If a difference of opinion existed, nothing was done.[47]

Through his years as agent, Kit slowly gained the confidence of the Utes, as well as their affection. With the Mohuache chief, Ka-ni-ache, he shared mutual respect and trust, though Blanco, the chief who led the Pueblo massacre of 1854, hated and mistrusted all white men. He may have acquired his terrible smallpox scars during the epidemic that preceded that attack. Although he had met with Carson in council, all were aware that the agent was not altogether an exception to his hatred. One day when Ka-ni-ache and several others of the tribe were talking and smoking with Carson in front of his house, Blanco rode up and sat his horse, glowering, probably primed with Taos Lightnin' and bolstering his courage by brooding on his wrongs. Suddenly he raised his gun, aiming at Kit. Alert and wary, Ka-ni-ache sprang for him and wrested the gun away before he could fire.[48]

In November 1857 the Mohuaches were accused of stealing some animals on the Arkansas River. Applying for military aid at Cantonment Burgwin, Carson was given five men. With this escort he rode to the Indian village on the Conejos, where he found the Utes destitute. He gave them sixty-four fanegas of wheat[49] and recovered the animals, which he returned to their owners. During that winter he was authorized to exceed his estimated supplies and increase provisions to the Utes, whom Brigham Young was threatening to incite against the army command being sent to Utah. On the way to Fort Massachusetts to ascertain the disposition of the Indians, he met a band of Utes with an Arapaho and a Blackfoot coming to Taos to conclude a treaty of peace and friendship. On January 22, 1858, a tentative treaty was made. None of Carson's charges joined the Mormons.

Meriwether resigned in 1857. James L. Collins, whom Carson had known since they came down the Santa Fe Trail together in 1826, succeeded him, and friction between agent and superintendent ceased. Carson was able to bring about some of the reforms he had worked for, such as taking the yearly presents to the Conejos instead of bringing the Indians to the settlements. "It would promote the advance of civilization among the Indians if . . . I could live with them," he wrote that year. But that would be impracticable "until agency buildings are built. . . . the Indians . . . settled on reserves, guarded by troops, and made to cultivate the soil."[50]

Still many chose to visit him in Taos. Sometimes he had to use his own meager wealth to eke out the provision allowance of the government. "Scarcely a day passes but I have five to twenty-five to feed and take care of their only resource is upon Government."[51]

Because he understood the principle of compensation practiced by the Indians, he was more successful than most agents in keeping the peace. At the 1859 gathering for presents on the Conejos, an Indian picked an ear of corn from the field of a Mexican. Taking a club, the owner almost beat the Indian to death. The Utes were ready to massacre the whites when Carson arrived and pacified them by talking and giving presents to the injured man.[52]

Carson sent two reports for 1859, eloquently urging that the Indians be removed from the influence of whites and taught farming so that they could support themselves, the "one mode of saving them from annihilation. . . . They are as uncivilized as when the government first took them under her care, and . . . they will continue to sink deeper into degradation, so long as a generous government, or their habits of begging and stealing, afford them a means of subsistence."[53]

The discovery of gold in the mountains made conflicts inevitable, for when the miners swarmed into the Bayou Salade, the game left. Seven miners were murdered, and many Indians were killed. The Tabeguache Utes, who had been added to Carson's agency the year before, refused to come to the Conejos for their presents. Camped on Grand River, they sent word that the murderers of some miners were with them and if the troops wanted them, they should come and get them. Because the soldiers were busy with the Navajos, nothing was done. In October, after a fight with the miners in which five Americans and three Utes were killed, the Tabeguaches sent word to Carson that they were ready for peace. When he met them northwest of Abiquiú, they professed innocence and received their presents, but Carson thought letting them go unpunished would lead to trouble.

However, the next year he reported that his Indians had been on friendly terms with all citizens. Two things were wrong: the Mohuaches were falling victim to whiskey, to which the Apaches were already addicted, and the game upon which the Tabeguaches depended was exceedingly scarce. Again he urged the removal of the Indians from white settlements and the provision of training and tools to make farmers of them.[54]

The outbreak of hostilities between North and South in the spring of 1861 brought Carson's work as Indian agent virtually to a close, but his influence with the Indians he had served for almost eight years continued. He had been a better-than-average agent, taking his responsibilities seriously, deeply concerned about the Indians he supervised. He never withheld any part of the annuities for his own enrichment. He was never arbitrary in his assertion of power, but smoked and reasoned with the Indians. The illiteracy that annoyed his superiors in government was no handicap with the Indians. He was acquainted with their customs and their ways of thinking, and these he respected. He would listen to them with attention and would respond in ways they could understand, and he told them the truth as he saw it.

When he left the agency at the end of May, W. F. N. Arny, his successor, moved the agency to Maxwell's Ranch to get the Indians away from the distillers of Taos Lightnin'. Arny reported that the Indians continued to be peaceful.

Busy as he was with the Indians, Carson probably had more time to spend with his family during these years than at any other period. On June 13, 1858, another son was born and named Christopher, or Cristobal, after his father.[55] William, almost six years old, had already started to school at the Lux Academy in Taos and had been commended by his instructor for good conduct.[56] In addition to the two boys and their sister Teresina, a toddler of three, the family included Teresina Bent, a Navajo girl, and possibly two other Indian children whom Kit and Josefa were bringing up. Charles Carson later wrote that his parents educated Nicanor Jaramillo, Josefa's brother's son, and reared three Indians from childhood.[57]

Even though Carson became very uneasy if he had to be away from his family for long, he clung only lightly to his home. He rode frequently to Santa Fe on agency business, delivering his reports in person instead of dictating them in Taos.[58] John Ward, a very intelligent man in the office of the superintendent, probably wrote most of these reports and dated them Taos. Smith H. Simpson, a friend who claimed also to have helped with the accounts, related how he persuaded Carson to sit for a tintype, his first photograph. One day when Kit suggested mildly that they get to work on the accounts, Simpson pointed out that he did not feel like working on the accounts any more than Kit felt like sitting still for the tintype. Carson saw the point and allowed his photograph to be made.[59]

On a trip to Santa Fe, Albert D. Richardson, the star reporter of his time, noticed at the hotel supper table "a stout middle-aged man, with straight brown hair, mild eye and kindly face. He wore a suit of gray, and looked like an Illinois farmer." It was Carson, and Richardson struck up an acquaintance and rode back with him to Taos. At noon, sitting on the grassy bank of a stream, they talked as they ate bread and dried buffalo meat while their horses grazed nearby. Richardson was impressed by Kit's reluctance to speak of his own exploits.[60] In reply to questions, he told of life along the beaver streams, the limited diet and the wading in icy water, the absence of sickness. "I lived ten years in the mountains, with from one to three hundred trappers, and I cannot remember that a single one of them died from disease." He told of his daring and reckless youth, of learning to be vigilant through seeing many of his comrades killed by Indians because of carelessness.

He told of being outwitted by some Sioux disguised in wolf-skins. In a party of six hunters who had had pretty good success after buffalo, Carson, lying by the fire, heard wolves, and the dogs began to bark.

I saw one or two big wolves sneaking about camp—one of them quite in it. Gordon wanted to fire, but I would not let him, for fear of hitting some of the dogs. I had just a little suspicion, that the wolves might be Indians, but when I saw them turn short around, and heard the snap of their teeth, as the dogs came too close to one of 'em, I . . . made sure it was a wolf. . . . Confound the rascal. . . . He had . . . two old buffalo bones in his hand that he cracked together every time he turned to snap at the dogs. . . . We dozed off, and I was awoke by a crash and a blaze. I jumped straight for the mules, and held 'em. If the Indians had been smart, they'd a had us all, but they run as soon as they fired. They killed . . . poor Davis. He had five bullets in his body, and eight in his buffalo robe.

Richardson and Carson spent the night "at a spacious adobe whose swarthy owner received us in great dirt and dignity." After washing up in the little *acequia*, they supped on mutton, frijoles, and eggs and "slept on floor-mattresses with yellow-haired saints and a pink-faced virgin staring down from the walls." Before leaving the next morning, they had breakfast and placed a quarter-eagle on the table. "The hospitable Mexican entertains all travelers, but never demands payment, leaving that question wholly to his guest."

Richardson spent the night as guest of the Carsons, whose "home was brightened by four or five children," and pronounced Josefa "an intelligent Spanish lady" and Kit "a gentleman by instinct; upright, pure, and simple-hearted, beloved alike by Indians, Mexicans, and Americans."[61]

Marian Russell remembered, as a schoolgirl in Santa Fe, having

Carson fall into step beside her and try to engage her in conversation. Referring to her school uniform, he remarked, "Them nuns do a heap of good in this god-forsaken country." Josefa was waiting near the door of a little chapel, heavy dark hair braided, shy, enormous eyes cast down. Kit's eyes were tender when he looked at her and called her Little Jo, the girl remembered. "Carson was lonely and a bit uncouth. Often he was hatless and always coatless and tieless. Always he spoke in the vernacular. His was a great heart and very kind. . . . Only with children and the child-like Mexicans did he seem able to lay shyness aside."[62]

In 1857 Carson testified for Lucien Maxwell, acting for Charles Beaubien, who was in the process of having the Beaubien–Miranda Grant confirmed. Since Maxwell had settled there in 1849, the ranch had flourished. Maxwell became briefly the largest landowner in the United States, with 1,750,000 acres east of the Sangre de Cristos, but he was careless with money. The ranch funds were kept in the bottom drawer of an old, dilapidated pine bureau.[63] Although he knew Maxwell to be both wealthy and honest, when Carson made his will in 1868, he stipulated that if Administrator Tom Boggs could not obtain security for a $3,000 note of Maxwell's that Carson was holding, Boggs was to collect from Maxwell and invest the money elsewhere for top interest and on good security.[64]

Problems of the Jicarillas and the Mohuaches as well as his own business often drew Carson east of the Sangre de Cristos, where he enjoyed the openhanded hospitality of the Maxwell home and the constant stream of guests stopping there. Everyone was welcome, old friends from among the trappers especially so. With these, and sometimes with some of the Utes, Carson went on a fall hunt whenever he could, both for sport and for meat for the table. In 1860, on a hunt in the San Juans, he was leading his horse along a difficult trail when the animal fell, entangled him in the lead rope, and dragged him as it rolled down a steep slope. The injuries he sustained gradually improved, but he was never completely healed from them.[65]

In addition to enjoying swapping yarns, playing cards, and hunting, Carson was an enthusiast about Indian-style horse racing—full speed over short distances. Fans promoted this sport from Las Lunas to Denver. When on business trips to Santa Fe, Carson sometimes rode on south to attend the races. In 1860, in reply to a letter from Carson, R. Jones of Albuquerque wrote back, giving and asking for news of likely horses and their owners.[66]

After the gold rush of 1859, Carson often needed to confer with the authorities concerning encroachments by both miners and settlers upon the hunting grounds of the Utes. The quickest and most efficient way to do this was to saddle up and ride to Denver. A race course there was known as one of his favorites. In Denver he was noticed by both the press and the curious and found to be "a most pleasant and affable gentleman" with a "full, good-natured face, and dressed in a sober suit of black."[67]

Zan Hicklin, husband of Josefa's niece Estefana Bent, had a ranch on Greenhorn Creek near Pueblo, where the old-timers would stop by and stay as long as they liked.[68] Early in 1861 a young miner named Luther Perry Wilmot, who was hunter for the ranch when Carson came by, left an exuberant account of the meeting.[69] The men played poker until midnight. Kit did not play with the "big bugs," but with the workers. Having no money and no chips, they used beans for betting, and Carson and the foreman won all the beans. Shooting matches were arranged between Lew and Hank Hall, "one of the best hearted Gamblers in the west." Kit judged one of the matches, all of which Lew won. Lew wanted Kit to go hunting with him, but reported that Kit said it was too much like work. Kit would not complain to a mere boy, but he was still recovering from his hunting accident. Lew was gratified by Kit's interest in the shooting matches.

Lew was the only northern man employed by the ranch. He was impressed to learn that Kit was a Union man also, and both kept quiet about it. Though both Kit and Lew went on to Denver, it is doubtful that they ever saw each other again. Lew moved to Washington Territory in a couple of years. By that time Kit had helped repel the Texans from New Mexico and was busy subduing the Navajos.

Chapter 17

Kit Fights to Save the Union

After the Mexican War and the discovery of gold, settlement of the West caused communications to develop rapidly. When President Lincoln declared on April 15, 1861, that insurrection existed and called for 75,000 three-month volunteers, the news was not long in reaching New Mexico. The West immediately broke into a ferment no less unsettling than the turmoil in the East. As soon as the Indians realized that the whites were fighting among themselves, they took to the warpath. The Butterfield Southern Express route to California was forced to abandon service. The garrisons on the San Pedro and the Santa Cruz near Tucson retired, leaving the land to the Apaches.

The Texans quickly started up the Rio Grande. Major Isaac Lynde surrendered Fort Fillmore at Mesilla with scarcely a shot fired, but resistance stiffened toward the north. When Confederate sympathizers gathered in Taos Plaza to hoist the Confederate banner, Carson, Smith H. Simpson, and several others nailed the Stars and Stripes to a cottonwood pole, set it in the plaza, and placed a guard to keep it flying day and night, as it has done ever since.[1] That the invaders were Texans probably influenced many New Mexicans to remain loyal, for they did not forget earlier aggressive inclinations by their neighbors to the east. During June, July, and

August, the Union forces in Santa Fe were busy recruiting men and commissioning officers for volunteer units.[2]

May 24, 1861, Carson resigned as Indian agent. In August, as lieutenant colonel of New Mexico Volunteers, he joined Colonel Ceran St. Vrain in signing a protest against the withdrawal of regular troops from the Territory. This was addressed to Major General Charles Frémont, commander at Western Headquarters in St. Louis, urging that the raw volunteers would not be able to hold Fort Union and its valuable stores against the fire-tried Texans. If this post fell, the Territory would be at the mercy of the Confederates. Colonel E. R. S. Canby endorsed this plea and pointed out that most of the volunteers had never handled a gun.[3] Frémont was unable to help.

But men were volunteering faster than they could be equipped and trained. More than a year later, when Carson was directed to hold Captain Hubbell's company ready for action, he replied that Hubbell's fifty-four men had only seventeen rifles.[4]

The First Regiment of Volunteers was being assembled at Albuquerque. Carson brought his family there to share his quarters, and at this post on August 2 Josefa gave birth to another son,[5] named Charles for her first child, who had died. Rafael Chacon, a captain in the regiment, later recalled that Carson showed great affection for his family:

He used to lie down on an Indian blanket, in front of his quarters, with his pockets full of candy and lumps of sugar. His children would . . . jump on top of him, and take the candy and sugar from his pockets and eat it . . . and he derived great pleasure from these little episodes. His wife, Dona Josepha Jaramillo, was called by him by the pet name of "Chipita," and he was most kind to her.[6]

In September, St. Vrain resigned because of ill health. Carson, succeeding him, was commissioned colonel October 4, 1861.[7] Having had no regular army training himself, he was not prepared to put his recruits through a course of training that would quickly make soldiers of them. He seemed to depend on the common sense, self-reliance, and self-discipline that had made working units of the trapper brigades. Several anecdotes tell of his informal approach to discipline.[8]

Mac, the drillmaster, was Carson's adviser in military procedure, but his advice was only roughly followed. A Mexican soldier stole a horse and pistols and was caught trying to desert. When Carson asked Mac what should be done, he was advised to institute court-martial proceedings. Carson demurred. That would be a lot of trouble. How about drumming the culprit out of the service? To this Mac agreed and was proceeding with the punishment when Carson caught sight of the prisoner's face. "Why, Mac," he exclaimed, "you've got the wrong man." Mac had brought out a man arrested for drunkenness, which was not punishable by dishonorable discharge.

One Sunday Mac requested permission to march his company to church. The cathedral in Albuquerque had no seats. Mac marched his men to the front and ordered a "Parade rest" until the priest appeared, whereupon he called, "Attention!," then "Shoulder arms!" and "Present arms!" then again, "Parade rest!"

Some officers, horrified by such behavior in church, reported to Carson, who said, "well now, what if he did present arms to the priest? Mac is a military man and he would be sure to do it according to Army regulations."

Another time a boat loaded with young women on the way to church was starting across the Rio Grande, swollen by the spring thaw, when a rough ranchero jumped into the boat. After he had ignored several requests to leave, Carson struck him with the flat of his cavalry sabre, knocking him into the water. As he sank, Carson plunged in after him and dragged him to shore. Although Carson's approach to discipline was very personal, when given time he established good rapport with his men, and morale was high, as was evident when they were put to trial at Valverde.

By December 1861, rumors were flying fast as the Texans advanced. In January Carson's regiment was ordered to Fort Craig, and the family returned to Taos. Marching toward Fort Fillmore at Mesilla, Canby learned that Sibley's Texans had received reinforcements and were marching north. He retired to defend Fort Craig.[9] Canby hoped the rebels would lay siege to this fort so that he could break in his raw recruits by allowing them to fight from behind the walls. Sibley hoped to avoid the fort as he headed toward the territorial capital at Santa Fe and the government stores at Fort Union. To do this he crossed the Rio Grande at the Panadora Ford below the fort and passed along the broken plain below the mesa three or four miles to the east. About five miles above the fort at the ruinous, deserted settlement of Valverde, he would have to recross the river.

A sally by Captain James "Paddy" Graydon's company and five hundred mounted militia under Pino and Stapleton was thrown into confusion by the enemy artillery, but their presence delayed the rebels for one night. Canby dispatched Lieutenant Colonel B. S. Roberts with regular cavalry and mounted volunteers to guard the ford at Valverde. The next morning Carson's regiment was sent to the ford with most of the remainder of the force. Knowing that his recruits would fight better if they could become accustomed to the situation gradually, Carson asked that they not be committed at the beginning, and Canby agreed. When Canby himself arrived with fresh troops to relieve Roberts, the tempo of the battle quickened. Carson's report follows:

About 1 o'clock in the afternoon I received from Colonel Canby the order to cross the river . . . after which I was ordered to form my command on the right of our line and to advance as skirmishers toward the hills. After advancing some 400 yards we discovered a large body (some 400 or 500) of the enemy charging diagonally across our front, evidently with the intention of capturing the 24-pounder gun, which . . . was advancing and doing much harm to the enemy. As the head of the enemy's column came within some 80 yards of my right a volley from the whole column was poured into them, and the firing being kept up caused them to break in every direction. Almost at the same time a shell from the 24-pounder was thrown among them with fatal effect. They did not attempt to reform, and the column supported by the gun on the right, was moving forward to sweep the wood near the hills, when I received the order to retreat and recross the river. This movement was executed in good order. The column . . . returned to its station near Fort Craig, where it arrived about 7 o'clock in the evening.[10]

This was the extent of Kit's fighting to preserve the Union. His men had fought well, and he was described as waving his pistols as he urged them forward.[11] Although his segment of the line was gaining ground, the tide of battle had turned with charge after charge of Confederates upon Captain Alexander McRae's battery commanding the ford. Many of the volunteers had been of little use, some running, some refusing to fight at all, over a hundred deserting from the field. The main fighting had been done by the regulars. McRae was killed at the guns, and half his men were killed or wounded. The regulars had lost sixty-eight killed, one hundred sixty wounded, and thirty-five captured.[12] The Confederates had lost forty killed and two hundred wounded. The crippled Sibley command moved on north, left their wounded at Socorro, and met no opposition as they headed for Santa Fe.[13]

While regular troops, reinforced by Colorado Volunteers under Colonel Slough and Colonel Chivington, marched south to meet Sibley, Carson remained with Canby at Fort Craig. The advancing rebels fought at Glorieta Pass, Apache Canyon, and Pigeon's Ranch, at the last of which Chivington and Manuel Antonio Chavez surprised the supply train and captured forty men and nearly all the stock. The eighty wagons of supplies they burned on the spot, a loss which forced the Texans to retreat by the route they had come. On March 31, when Canby marched north to hasten their departure, he left Carson with orders to hold the fort "to the last extremity."[14] Far from wishing to make an attack, the Texans found a by-trail that carried them around Fort Craig; Carson and his men saw them no more. They reached Mesilla with less than a third of their men and less than a tenth of their supply train.[15]

Kit had sent word to Josefa to leave Taos with the children and seek safety somewhere else, which she did. She concealed her money and jewels on a Navajo girl she had raised. They met some Utes with a three-year-old Navajo boy. When the Utes said the boy was in their way and they were going to kill him, Josefa gave a horse for him. When the family returned to Taos, Kit adopted him, and he was named Juan Carson. Later he married a Mexican girl but died soon afterward.[16]

At least part of the time during the summer, Carson's family was with him at the army posts.[17] On May 10, 1862, Canby ordered the best men of the First, Second, Fourth, and Fifth New Mexico Volunteer regiments reorganized as First New Mexican Volunteers under Carson's command. By the end of May the remainder of the volunteers would be discharged. Carson's monthly pay was raised to $110, with allowances for food, horse forage, and servants bringing his income to a comfortable $216 per month. Canby kept this regiment stationed along the Rio Grande to the south as a buffer against further attempts at invasion by the Texans.

The great danger, however, was from the Indians. The Navajos and the Apaches had for two hundred years earned a good part of their livelihood by raiding their neighbors, Indian and white.[18] Some had become wealthy, with immense flocks of sheep and large herds of horses. With the arrival of Sibley's Confederate troops, both Navajos and Apaches had commenced ravaging the New Mexican villages and ranches, running off stock, carrying off women and children, murdering men. The Territory was virtually paralyzed with confusion and terror.[19]

In December 1861 Canby concluded that the Navajos would have to be either exterminated or placed in an isolated colony far from the settlements.[20] After the expulsion of the Texans and the reorganization of the volunteers, he ordered four companies of Carson's command armed and equipped immediately for "mounted service in the Indian country, in suppressing bandits and in restoring law and order."[21] He had scarcely begun preparation toward carrying out his plans for resettlement when he was ordered east to a more active role in the war against the South.

The key figure in the campaign then became Major General James H. Carleton, who in 1855 had awarded Carson for his scouting expertise the best hat New York could produce. Early in 1862 Carleton had started east with 2,350 California Volunteers to aid Canby in expelling the Texans. Delayed by the necessity of liberating Arizona in passing, they had reached the Rio Grande just as Canby was ordered to Washington. On September 18, fully aware that controlling the Indians was his most pressing problem, Carleton succeeded Canby in command of the Department of New Mexico.[22] He realized that his greatest asset was having under his command the most famous and most experienced Indian fighter in the country, and he knew that Carson's volunteers and the Indians themselves were aware of their colonel's reputation and respected his character as well as his ability.

Carleton also recognized that his prize Indian fighter had a serious handicap. The idea that a grown man should have to be disciplined was as unthinkable and repugnant to Kit as it would be to an Indian. The brief period he had commanded the regiment had not given him the experience needed to compensate for his lack of formal training, and the recent reorganization had thrown into his command men from other regiments, not all of whom were easy to assimilate. Discipline was certain to be a problem. Carson had neither inclination nor training for it. Carleton liked Kit and thought he could teach him to be a good officer. To do this, he planned to give Kit command in the field while he himself directed operations.[23]

Unaware of the change of command, Carson wrote to Canby September 21 requesting permission to leave the post at Los Lunas and come to Santa Fe for a conference on the approaching Navajo campaign and also, the roads being unsafe, to accompany his family from Los Lunas to Taos. Six days later Carleton issued Special Orders No. 176, directing Carson to take five companies of his command, go to Fort Union to collect necessary supplies, then proceed without delay to reopen Fort Stanton in the White Mountains to the southeast. This fort had been abandoned and partially burned by Union forces as the Texans advanced. Situated in the midst of Mescalero Apache country, it had formerly been a strong influence in assuring the good behavior of these Indians. Carleton added that the "worldwide reputation of Colonel Carson . . . gives a good guarantee that anything that may be required of him [calling for] the peculiar skill and high courage for which he is justly celebrated, will be well done."[24]

Carson left Los Lunas October 5, 1862. It seems likely that he was allowed to see Josefa safely home, for on October 10 he wrote to her from Mora, between Taos and Fort Union, that he was sending her "by the peon who came with me" a hundred pounds of sugar, fifty pounds of coffee, two boxes of soap, and a box of candles. Since trade with the States was disrupted by the Indians, these items were both scarce and expensive. October 18 he again wrote to her from Fort Union, wishing her "every kind of happiness" and asking that she give the children his fatherly love and that she place little Julian in school, assuring him that if he applied himself his father would "have the greatest pleasure in doing for him."[25]

When he arrived at Fort Stanton on October 26, he found the roofs, floors, doors and windows burnt and the walls badly damaged. His men were to make these quarters habitable by their own labor. He saw little prospect of any better shelter than the Sibley tent during the coming winter.[26]

On the way south he had received a confidential letter from Carleton giving details of what was in store for the Mescaleros:

All Indian men of that tribe are to be killed whenever and wherever you can find them: the women and children will not be harmed, but you will take them prisoners and feed them at Fort Stanton until you receive other instructions about them. If the Indians send in a flag and desire to treat for peace, say to the bearer that when the people of New Mexico were attacked by the Texans, the Mescaleros broke their treaty of peace, and murdered innocent people, and ran off their stock: that now, our hands are untied and you have been sent to punish them for their treachery and their crimes: That you have no power to make peace; that you are there to kill them wherever you can find them; that if they beg for peace, their Chiefs and twenty of their principal men must come to Santa Fe to have a talk here; but tell them fairly and frankly that you will keep after their people and slay them until you receive orders to desist from these Head Quarters; that this making of treaties for them to break whenever they have an interest in breaking it, will not be done any more; that that time has passed by; that we have no faith in their promises; that we believe if we kill some of their men in fair open war, they will be apt to remember that it will be better for them to remain at peace than to be at war. I trust that this severity in the long run will be the most humane course that could be pursued toward these Indians.[27]

This autocratic bent, which was at times a problem with Carleton,[28] was so foreign to Carson's nature that he seems not to have taken the directive seriously, but it did strike a responsive note in some of his officers.

Carson did not fight the Mescaleros. Before his arrival, Captain Graydon with an advance unit of the command met the chiefs Manuelito and Jose Largo and their band and, after a brief verbal exchange, fired into the band of Indians, killing the two chiefs and nine other warriors and wounding twenty more. The Indians began to surrender almost as soon as Carson arrived. On November 12, he sent three chiefs—Cadetta, Chatto, and Estrella—to Santa Fe to General Carleton, where they learned that their tribe must move to the Bosque Redondo. At this round grove of cottonwoods on the Pecos River about a hundred fifty miles southeast of Santa Fe, Carleton had already ordered a new fort to be built, called Fort Sumner in honor of his friend, Edwin Vose Sumner.[29] Though some bands fled to the west and south and never did surrender, Carleton was able by March 19 to report that around four hundred Mescaleros were at Fort Sumner and that this tribe had been subdued.[30]

Carson's pleasure in the quick victory over the Mescaleros was tempered by suspicion that Graydon's success may have been based on treachery. Major Arthur Morrison, who had upbraided Graydon for not having taken Manuelito into custody the day before when he had the opportunity, reported that Graydon left the camp early the day of the fight, met the Indians, gave them presents of beef, flour, and other provisions, befuddled them with liquor, then shot them down. As Graydon described it, the killing was in self-defense, with Manuelito demanding whiskey and threatening with his pistol to fight for it. Carson began an investigation, but his intemperate and undisciplined officers moved too fast for him.

J. W. Whitlock, who had formerly served as surgeon under Carson, followed him south, presumably seeking recommendation for employment; but before leaving Fort Union, he had published in the *Santa Fe Gazette* an accusation that Graydon had lured Manuelito and his band into camp with whiskey, got them drunk, then murdered them in cold blood. When Whitlock arrived at Fort Stanton, Graydon challenged him to a duel. Both men were wounded, Whitlock in the wrist, Graydon in the lung. While attempting to flee from the fort, Whitlock was shot from his horse, his body was thrown into a ditch, and the men of Graydon's company pumped a hundred thirty bullets into his corpse. Following a Board of Inquiry that Carson called on November 5, Carson recommended that Graydon be ordered to resign. On November 20, Carleton ordered that he be allowed to resign provided he appear at once at Santa Fe and surrender to the civil authorities for trial. But Graydon, whose wound had at first seemed not serious, had died November 9.[31]

This was only the first of many disciplinary problems to surface in the hastily organized command. Carson was not responsible for the "murder, alcoholism, embezzlement, sexual deviation, desertion, and incompetence" that would cause nearly half of the officers "to resign in disgrace or face court-martial proceedings before the campaign was over."[32] However, on this campaign the command was often divided, and he was not able to control the undisciplined officers when they were away from him. It was these officers, not Carson, who committed the outrages against the Indians for which he has often been blamed by uninformed persons, both Indian and white.

The violence implied in Carleton's directives doubtless aggravated the instability among the officers. Sometimes suggestions he made created troublesome situations. He had specifically requested that Major Thomas Blakeney of the California Volunteers be given a "chance for distinction."[33] When getting ready for his first long scout in August 1863, Carson placed Blakeney in command at Fort Canby. Mutual dislike quickly developed between volunteers and regular army men and between Californians and New Mexicans. Blakeney tried an autocratic approach to his task, the New Mexicans resisted, and he became more rigorous and less supportive. Not only did he take petty satisfaction in arbitrarily interfering with the officers in their work, he also caused an emissary of Navajo chief Herrera Grande to be maltreated and possibly killed. His approach was directly opposed to the policy of Carson, who took every opportunity to talk with captives and, if possible, convert them into willing emissaries to their tribesmen. He resented bitterly Blakeney's performance, which surely deterred other Navajos from coming in to discuss peace.[34] Evidently Carson appealed to Carleton for support in his efforts to protect those Navajos ready to surrender. In his letter of September 19, 1863, Carleton backed him up, but reiterated: "Say to them 'Go to the Bosque Redondo, or we will pursue and destroy you.'"[35]

The hornet's nest stirred up during Blakeney's command was aggravated by liquor. Several officers were arrested for using foul language in the presence of enlisted men, harboring women of bad repute, and homosexuality, and most of them had to resign. But because of the bitter and conflicting accusations, those arrested while Blakeney was in charge were freed. Upon Carson's return, Blakeney was himself arrested and charged with "tyrannical and capricious conduct." Because of the chaotic situation, Carleton suspended charges against Blakeney and transferred him to Los Pinos. In a private letter Carleton reprimanded him for "splitting hairs and quibbling on little points."[36]

Because of his inability to read, Carson unwittingly cooperated in the men's efforts to get whiskey. At Fort Wingate one of the men told the company clerk that he was not feeling well and asked him to write an order on the post commissary for a quart of molasses. He then took the order to Carson, who cheerfully signed it. Returning to barracks, the man told his comrades he did not believe the colonel could read manuscript. To test this, another man took an order for whiskey, complained of not feeling well, and said he wanted to buy molasses. Carson signed the order and the man got his whiskey.

When Carson later stopped by the commissary, he greeted the sutler, John Waters, with "Well, John, how's business?"

Waters replied that it was fine; he had sold two barrels of whiskey to the men of Company H.

"John, don't you know that it's agin regulations to sell whiskey to enlisted men of the post without a written order from the commanding officer?"

Waters showed him his order string holding a foot of orders, all properly signed by Carson.[37] Thereafter he would not sign an order until his adjutant, Lieutenant Lawrence Murphy, had read it.[38]

To Carson's frustrations and distaste in dealing with problems of discipline were added anxiety about his wife and children and an increasing desire and need to be with them. On February 3,

1863, while still at Fort Stanton, he sent Carleton the following letter:

Dear General:

You will no doubt be surprised at receiving my resignation, but the fact is that it is a resolution which I had formed long since, and was only delayed from carrying it into execution by the supposition that there would have been another opportunity of proving my devotion to that Government which was established by our Ancestors.

There is no probability that we shall be again called upon to defend our Territory against hostile invasion. Should it be that I am in this mistaken, the General Comdg may rest assured that it will be my pride and pleasure to serve under him in any capacity in which I can best serve my country. At present I feel that my duty as well as happiness, directs me to my home & family and trust that the General will accept my resignation.[39]

The letter gave Carleton the clue needed to persuade Carson not to resign, for he was at the time acting in the capacity in which he could best serve his country. The Navajos were only slightly less disruptive of the peace and prosperity of the citizens than the Mescaleros had been, and Carleton was aware, if Carson was not, that in all likelihood no one else could be found so well fitted to bring an end to their predatory career.[40] Carleton reinforced his persuasion by allowing Carson to go home on extended leave about the middle of February.

When Fort Wingate was being built, roughly halfway between Los Pinos and Fort Defiance, eighteen chiefs of the peace party of the Navajos, led by Delgadito and Barboncito, rode to Santa Fe to confer with Carleton. To their consternation they were given until July 20, 1863, to prepare to move to the Bosque Redondo; otherwise they would be considered as hostiles, for the soldiers could not tell the difference between peaceful Navajos and those planning depredations. Barboncito told Carleton that he would not go to the Bosque; he would remain peaceably near Fort Wingate even if he had to die for it. The delegation was allowed to return home to deliberate, and Carleton went ahead with plans to send a force of nearly a thousand men against them.[41]

Writing to Carson at Taos April 11, 1863, Carleton authorized the hiring of ten Ute warriors and four Mexicans, all to be the best guides obtainable and familiar with the country of the Navajos. He was leaving for Fort Wingate in two days and expected Carson to be at Santa Fe when he returned April 25. However, general orders did not go out until June 15. On July 1 the expedition was to leave Los Pinos, sixteen miles south of Albuquerque on the eastern bank of the Rio Grande. Beyond Fort Wingate the precise destination of the force was not known. Carleton was sending along a board of officers to select a site for a fort to serve as base and supply depot for the expedition.[42]

Three mounted companies could not be made ready. Captain Francisco P. Abréu was delayed because of a lack of horses. Captain Jules Barbey, a friend of Carleton's, had been ordered to the vicinity of Las Cruces to protect travelers on the *Jornada del Muerto* and had not returned. Captain Albert H. Pfeiffer, a close friend of Kit and of his family, had been stationed at Fort McRae. Just south of the fort was a hot springs, the waters of which Pfeiffer hoped would cure a skin ailment from which he was suffering. On June 20 Indians had attacked Pfeiffer, his wife, two servant girls, and six enlisted men at the springs. Pfeiffer, who was bathing at the time, was hit in the side by an arrow. Two privates were killed; the others hastened to the fort to get help. Pfeiffer's wife and the two servants were later found lying in the trail, so badly wounded and bruised that Mrs. Pfeiffer and one of the girls died of their injuries. Pfeiffer was so badly burned by the sun on his bare skin as he made his way to the fort that he was still very ill when Carson left Los Pinos.[43]

Pfeiffer already had a drinking problem, about which Carson lectured him in a letter written at Santa Fe on May 8.[44] The tragedy near Fort McRae probably aggravated this condition, while at the same time strengthening his courage and determination as an Indian fighter. He was later described as "probably the most desperately courageous and successful Indian fighter in the West."[45]

Chapter 18

The Navajo Campaign

At no point could the Navajo Campaign be called glamorous or heroic. It was a military operation in which few persons were killed and no real battles were fought. A few soldiers were wounded while pursuing Indians. Major Joseph Cummings, the one man killed by the Navajos, went off with a civilian "against positive orders" while on a scout and was shot from ambush.[1]

Carleton's directives for this campaign were the same as for that against the Mescaleros: all Navajo men were to be killed wherever found; the only alternative to endless pursuit and destruction was submission and removal from their homeland. Carson urged that the Utes be allowed to keep their captives. They were accustomed to fight for booty. The women and children taken would be sold into Mexican households, where they would be introduced to the customs of civilization and weaned away from those of their tribe. He seems to have forgotten that trading in human beings was no longer legal in the United States.[2] Carleton, with his New England background, did not forget for a moment. All the prisoners *without exception* were to be sent to headquarters in Santa Fe. A bounty would be paid for each animal captured, but these must be turned over to the army for disposal by the quartermaster department.[3]

The Utes had no use for bounty money. In the middle of the

first long scout, when denied the herds captured by the soldiers, they went home, "much to the satisfaction of everybody in the Command," wrote Sergeant George W. Campbell, Carleton's reporter on the expedition. Since their unrelenting hatred of the Navajos made capture of the latter almost impossible, Carson may have agreed with his sergeant, but he believed that the real reason they left was that they had all the stock and captives they wanted.[4]

The campaign got under way on July 7, 1863, when Carson left Los Lunas. Three days later, already exhausted by the hot, dry march, the command arrived at Fort Wingate. After a rest of three days, they left on another dry march, reaching Ojo del Oso, a major watering place of the eastern Navajos, on July 16.[5] In this green valley bounded by some of the most colorful cliffs in New Mexico, Carson paused for two days, feeding the ripening wheat from the nearby fields to his suffering animals. July 19 he moved on and the next day reached Fort Defiance, abandoned by the army since the spring of 1861.

On July 22, taking the board appointed to select a site for the fort, the Utes, his own field and staff officers, and seventy men, Carson left for Pueblo Colorado.[6] After riding about a third of the way, he took the Utes and pushed ahead. On Rio de Pueblo Colorado they came upon a small party of Navajos and killed three men. A captive Paiute woman told them that a strong party of Navajos with a large herd of sheep, cattle, and horses was spending the night at a pond thirty-five miles to the west. When the rest of the command reached camp at five o'clock, Carson gave them two-and-a-half hours to rest and eat supper. At seven thirty they started west. All night they rode across the barren land, determined to surprise the Indians, round up their herds, and bring back some captives. Eager for revenge and plunder, the Utes pushed ahead. At five in the morning they reached the pond. The Navajos had left the evening before.

After following their trail for two hours, the horses began giving out. Carson and Ka-ni-ache, who was leading the Utes, decided that trying to catch the Navajos would mean traveling ninety miles without water. The jaded horses could not do it. Turning back, they reached camp at five o'clock in the evening of July 23, after thirty-six hours almost continuously in the saddle. The Utes killed eight Navajos on the way back, making twelve since the command left Fort Wingate.

This pursuit had given Carson a good view of the country near Pueblo Colorado, where Carleton had tentatively planned to establish the fort. Convinced that water, grass, and wood were not to be found in the vicinity, Carson returned to Fort Defiance, where roofs remained on enough buildings to store supplies. Carleton agreed that the fort be established there, renamed Fort Canby.[7]

On July 24, after the fruitless march to Pueblo Colorado, Captain Francis McCabe tendered his resignation. Four days later he changed his mind and asked to withdraw it. Carson insisted on sending the resignation to Santa Fe, stating, "I do not wish to have any Officer in my command who is not contented, or willing to put up with as much inconvenience and privations for the success of the expedition as I undergo myself."[8] McCabe had to write to headquarters at Santa Fe, asking that his resignation not be accepted. This request was granted. McCabe became one of Carson's most dependable officers, and there were no further impulsive decisions by the officers to throw up the whole thing.

The first three long scouts were variations of this rather brief one. Sergeant William Need, Carson's clerk, and Sergeant Campbell sent periodic synopses of the campaign, but Carleton was not satisfied.[9] He prodded Carson to furnish fuller and more prompt official reports, but Carson could not scout and send reports at the same time.[10] With his route changing according to circumstances, he could not spare adequate escort for a weekly express, for men leaving him would have no way of rejoining him until he returned to the fort.

Communication was very slow. Carson had let the Utes get away with a number of captive women and children before he received Carleton's letter forbidding them to take any at all. He had called the base by its old name in several letters before he received Carleton's order to name it Fort Canby. Carleton scolded him more than once for lack of news that had already been sent at the first opportunity Carson could arrange. Carson's understanding of the problem and patience with his superior were strong elements in the good relationship between the two men.

On the first long scout, the aim was to go to Zuni, find guides, turn northwest to search for Navajos as far as the Hopi village of Oraibi, and examine the vicinity of the Cañon de Chelly on the way back to Fort Canby. Captains Pfeiffer and Barbey had arrived August 2, but Pfeiffer's horses were so broken down that his company had to march on foot. Five Moqui (Hopi) Indians captured on the way south reported Navajos with large herds near their villages. Doing without the Zuni guides, Carson turned west immediately. Although only the Utes took captive women and children and killed one man, the soldiers captured twenty-five horses and eleven hundred sheep and goats, and Pfeiffer wounded a man. At this point the Utes took their plunder and returned to the mountains.

An Oraibi Indian brought news of a party of Navajos with large herds twelve miles away. Leaving Major Morrison in charge, Carson and Thompson took out after them, chased them for twenty-five miles, and had to give up with the coming of night. While they were away, seven mules strayed from camp and were run off by Navajos. The Indians, so difficult for the soldiers to find, seemed to be seldom out of touch with the command. August 15, about two in the morning, they made a determined attempt to run off the herd, but were driven off by the rifles of the pickets. Three days later they picked off Major Cummings.

August 19, back at Pueblo Colorado, Carson sent to Fort Canby all animals unable to bear the hardships of desert travel. With only sixty animals for nearly three hundred fifty men, the command started toward the Cañon de Chelly, destroying corn, pumpkins, and beans as they went. They arrived at the west entrance to the canyon August 23, but found no water. After finding water and grass for his camp twelve miles away, Carson made a careful examination of the area and concluded that the few Navajos in the canyon had no stock and had depended for their livelihood on the corn he had recently destroyed. He expected actual starvation to drive them either to wealthier kinsmen at Red River[11] or to the Bosque Redondo.

On the way back to Fort Canby, one Indian was killed. Looking back over the month's scout, Carson could see little achievement. The men had destroyed 350 acres of corn, some of which they had fed to the animals, for the wheat had now been largely harvested.

They had captured a large number of animals, but their contact with the people had been negligible. However, Carson felt that the scout had been worth the hardships suffered because of the greater knowledge of the country and a more exact notion of the probable whereabouts of the Navajos.

At Fort Canby Carson found the men in a turmoil after the misrule of Blakeney. His first act to still the tumult was to free the men who had been imprisoned, including Little Foot, an Indian about seventy years old from the Chusca Mountains. After talking with Carson, this old man declared that his people wished to come in and emigrate. Carson let him go. Little Foot was one of the few Navajos who failed to return after having promised to do so.

During his next scout, Carson left Captain Asa B. Carey, chief quartermaster, in charge at the fort. A graduate of West Point who had served in New Mexico since 1860, Carey was the only outsider accepted and admired by the volunteers. He went straight to the root of the trouble, sending two brawling women from camp and ordering on September 28 that the sutler sell no liquor without a permit from the commanding officer of the post.[12] With admirable self-possession and careful attention to all the interests of the command, this energetic and efficient officer then settled down and ran the fort very capably as long as his superior was in the field.[13]

On September 9, Carson set out with over four hundred officers and men and one hundred ninety-two horses. This scout, southwest to the Little Colorado, was even less productive than the first. After making arrangement with the Zunis to buy their surplus corn, Carson moved west with Zuni guides to the region between Rio Pueblo Colorado and the Little Colorado River. The Zunis found the Navajos, took about fifty goats and sheep from them, and returned home while Carson was on a side scout. Pfeiffer's party came upon seven Indians with about fifteen horses, but the worn-out army horses were not able to overtake them. An abandoned village was destroyed. Nineteen animals were captured; but seven wild mares escaped. While trying to recapture them, two men were wounded. Again Carson felt that acquiring a greater knowledge of the country and the haunts of the Navajos was worth the fatigue and hardships suffered. Campbell wrote Carleton that

Carson had "done all that man could do under the circumstances. . . . I have seen him reeling in his saddle from fatigue and loss of sleep, still pushing forward and hoping to come upon them."[14]

After returning from this scout on October 5, Carson remained at Fort Canby until November 15. Apparently Carey continued to manage affairs at the post while Carson concerned himself largely with directing brief scouting expeditions.[15] No Navajos were encountered on these scouts, but destitution was making them bolder. They attacked army herds, and their success in driving away animals greatly embarrassed Carson as well as Carey, who twice had animals run off while he was in command of the fort, once from a wood detail and once from the hay contractor. Both times the guards of the trains, not sufficiently alert, were surprised by a sudden appearance of the Indians.[16]

Carson's capture of the Navajos' stock and destruction of their crops were also pushing them toward surrender. On September 6 Carleton moved fifty-one Navajos, who had been captured or who had surrendered at Fort Wingate, to the Bosque Redondo. He continued to assert that no exception would be allowed: all Navajos must go to Fort Sumner or be considered hostile. Nevertheless, when Delgadito surrendered a month later with a group of 188, he had to change his mind and order that Delgadito, Cha-hay, Chiquito, and Tsee-e should be given passports to return to Fort Wingate to attempt to persuade other Navajos to go to the Bosque.[17] He spread the word that Navajos who came in and surrendered would be allowed to take all their possessions, including animals, to the Bosque with them.

Carson had established a grazing camp at Laguna Negra,[18] twenty-five miles north of Fort Canby. The animals were driven at night into a canyon with a narrow, steep slope at the end. Believing that no animals could be driven up this slope, Major José Sena, the officer in charge, was chagrined on the morning of October 26 to find that the Navajos had driven away eighty-nine sheep. Sena sent a sergeant and two men on their trail. Returning at nightfall, the sergeant reported that they had not seen the Indians or the sheep. By the time Sena arranged a close and adequate pursuit, the rustlers and their prey had disappeared into the Cañon de Chelly.

Carson wrote to Carleton on November 1, 1863, about what were probably his most pressing thoughts during this lull in his scouting: his need to go home to see about his family. Josefa was expecting her sixth child, and he had not seen her for months, certainly not since July. He did not mention his health, which was also showing signs of weakness.[19] While waiting for Carleton's response, he prepared for his third long scout. Captain F. P. Abréu, who had served under Carson since September 1861, arrived at Fort Canby on October 14 and, at Carson's request, was now promoted to the majority left vacant by Joseph Cummings's death. Having proved himself capable in handling troops as well as in protecting the stock, he was left in charge at Fort Canby.[20] Carson had planned to start the scout November 1, but delayed until November 14 so that the men could receive their pay.

Only the officers were mounted. All the cavalry horses except twenty-five had been sent to Los Pinos. Mules carried the baggage. The men walked. Carson evidently hoped to find a large number of Navajos west of the Moqui villages. Early in the march, Sergeant Andres Herrera's company trailed a small party of Indians twenty miles, captured fifty sheep and a horse, wounded two men and killed two. Carson persuaded some men from each Moqui village to join him, excepting the Oraibi, who were in league with the Navajos. Taking their governor and one of the head men as hostages, he marched west sixty-five miles with only one two-hour halt, arriving at "a running stream' " a tributary of the Little Colorado, at 2:00 A.M. November 24.

The next day a boy and seven horses were captured, and an encampment was destroyed. Carson talked earnestly with the boy, explaining the intentions of the government toward the Navajos, then released him to return to his people. Carson's peace effort was nullified, however, by a scouting party that was thrown into confusion when three Indians suddenly appeared. One warrior fired his gun into the air, then rode forward. The soldiers were deterred from shooting him by his gestures of peace, but they could not understand his speech, and the manner of the soldiers was so threatening that when they took from him the two rifles that he carried and made motions that he could leave, he did so. Carson was disappointed, for the Moquis identified one of the rifles as belonging to Manuelito, one of the Navajos' most important lead-ers.[21] Talking with this man would have been worth more than any armed expedition. Another opportunity to talk was missed the same day. In the canyon of the Little Colorado a woman and a child, five hundred sheep and goats, and seventy horses were cap-tured and another encampment was destroyed, but because of the jaded condition of the cavalry horses, the five men with the herd escaped up the side of the canyon.

A few days after his return to Fort Canby, Carson received Carleton's emphatic response to his request for leave: "As I have before written to you, I have no authority to grant you a leave."[22] However, he had a proposal. He wished to discuss the campaign with Carson, and as soon as Carson could capture a hundred pris-oners, he could bring them to Santa Fe, but he should first go through the Cañon de Chelly.

Carson expected little to come of going through the Cañon de Chelly. What he needed was a face-to-face talk with the Indians. In a letter to Carleton on December 20, he expressed again his out-rage at the treatment the emissary of Herrera Grande had received at Fort Canby. "I deplore it the more as I have only one way of communicating with them—through the barrels of my rifles."[23] He also needed a hundred prisoners; it seemed at the time that he would have as much chance to take Carleton a hundred singing birds. Unexpectedly, the opportunity to talk with the Indians and the acquisition of the prisoners came about with the passage of the Cañon de Chelly.

Carson intended to send Major Abréu ahead to reconnoiter, but as orders were being written, stressing that the animals to be used must be guarded carefully, since they were about all that could be procured, a messenger was approaching the fort with the news that Abréu had been promoted to lieutenant colonel of the First Infan-try and transferred to Santa Fe. Not only was Carson disappointed over losing one of his best officers, but he was outraged because Major Sena had assigned an inadequate guard over the stock, and the Navajos had run off forty-eight mules and seven oxen.

The loss would necessitate a postponement of the expedition to the Cañon de Chelly, Carson wrote. Not so, replied Carleton, de-ploring that the command could not protect its own stock. If

Carey could furnish transport for provisions, the men could carry their own blankets and three or four days' rations in haversacks. "The Army of the Potomac carries eight days rations in haversacks. Unless some fatigue and some privations are encountered by your troops the Indians will get the best of it."[24]

About this time Carson received a letter from Frémont, written during the summer and entrusted to Richard G. McCormick, newly appointed secretary of Arizona. Frémont (whose letter has not been found) had reached a low ebb in his fortunes. An enclosure from Jessie gave news of her children and reported having a letter from Ned Beale in which Carson "had large mention." She rejoiced at Carson's success and continued well-being and mentioned the sorrows she had suffered since she had last seen him, including Frémont's failure in 1849, when Josefa had cared for him "so kindly."[25]

McCormick, who had missed seeing Carson on the way west, hoped to get expert advice on the territory to which he was going, but Carson was too busy to visit Arizona as the new secretary wished.[26] He was occupied with many problems in addition to those mentioned above, among them overcoming a shortage of ammunition and conquering a reluctance to take his command into the canyon.

More mystery surrounded the Cañon de Chelly than any other spot he had explored, with the possible exception of the Great Salt Lake. He did not know that the Spaniard, Lieutenant Colonel Antonio Narbona, had led his soldiers down the precipitous path at the timbered eastern approach on January 17, 1805, and, camping one night on the way, had marched them through the canyon to its red sandstone mouth; or that two Americans—Captain John G. Walker in the Cañon de Chelly, the central gorge, in 1859, and Lieutenant Colonel Dixon S. Miles in Monument Cañon in 1858—had done the same; or that Major Henry L. Kendrick and Henry Dodge had traversed the canyon with much interest from west to east in July 1853 and had found Chiefs Fairweather (or Barboncito) and Amagoso not only friendly but hospitable.[27] He was aware that in 1849 Colonel John M. Washington's detachment, led by Lieutenant James H. Simpson and including Henry Dodge, had gone about nine miles into the western end before turning back; and that Colonel

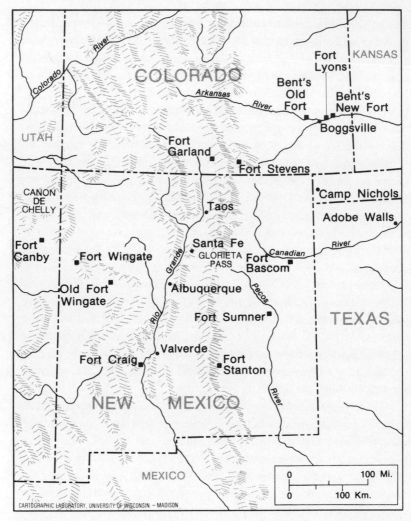

Carson's Civil War and Indian Campaigns: Carson's military career embraced the period from June 1861 to November, 1867, during which time he advanced from Lieutenant Colonel to Brevet Brigadier General of United States Volunteers.

Edwin Vose Sumner had led his command twelve to fourteen miles into the western end in 1851—much of the way under attack of arrows, musket balls, and rocks launched by Indians who remained out of range of the rifles—and when night fell and thousands of little fires glimmered far above him in the darkness, he had commanded the men to saddle up and withdraw in silence.[28] He may have heard report of the warning of Colonel Miles that "no command should ever again enter" the canyon.[29]

The mystery of the canyon could be conquered by courage and common sense. Inadequacy of personnel was not so easy to overcome. While serving as ordnance officer, Major Sena had let the supply of ammunition run low. Lieutenant Murphy, reporting the shortage to Carson, was given instructions to send in a list immediately of the stores needed. Carson understood that for this expedition a direct application was all that was required. When Captain Shoemaker, ordnance officer at Santa Fe, refused to send the stores without a formal requisition, the requisition was sent, but in the meantime all possible balls were saved. Instead of being fired off, the balls were withdrawn and cartridges were made by purchasing powder from the sutler. This was no remarkable feat for an old mountain man, but it added to the multiple responsibilities of preparing for the expedition.

A new problem became urgent when Captains Thompson and Berney returned from scouts with fourteen women and children, almost naked and starving. Only a good crop of piñon nuts had kept them alive. Foreseeing an imminent increase in the number of Indians forced to surrender by hunger and freezing weather, Carson wrote to Carleton on January 3, 1864, describing the condition of the prisoners and asking that the Indian Department send blankets to the forts for issue to the Indians who surrendered. He also reported that the supply train had just left for Pueblo Colorado and Cañon de Chelly, and that he would follow in three days.[30]

He was able to compensate for the stolen mules by commandeering an ox train coming to the post with supplies, ammunition not included. A heavy snow fell just before the expedition started out on January 6, with 14 officers and 375 enlisted men. The officers were mounted. Enlisted men trudged through the snow, carrying overcoats and blankets. Giving Pfeiffer the pack mules and the salvaged bullets, Carson sent him to the east entrance to the canyon. He had expected Major Sena and the supply train to reach Pueblo Colorado and rest the oxen by the time he arrived there with the rest of the men. He was even more disappointed at the end of the second day of march to find that the inept major had taken five days for the twenty-five-mile trip and had lost twenty-seven oxen from cold and exhaustion on the way. Leaving twenty-five men to guard one of the wagons containing ten days' rations for his command, Carson pushed on. By the time he reached Chinle Wash at the west entrance of the canyon on January 12, his escort had killed one warrior.

With his staff and escort, Carson led a brief reconnaissance to the right. Out of range on the north side of the canyon, several Indians watched. The sheer red walls offered no visible route for access to the expanse of red earth a thousand feet below, where a thin sheet of ice glistened, meandering between strips of vegetation. Wondering where Pfeiffer was, Carson returned to camp at the west entrance. Sergeant Andres Herrera brought in two women and two children and a hundred thirty sheep and goats. Sent out with fifty men the previous night, he had overtaken a party as they were about to enter the canyon and killed eleven men.

More important for Carson's purpose, four warriors approached the camp. Their great fear of being killed had given way before their desperate need. "He who appeared to be the most intelligent I furnished with provisions, and evidence of having been in my camp, and he willingly agreed to go to those Indians" still hesitating, many of them with flocks and horses, and assure them of safety with the troops if they would agree to emigrate.[31]

January 13 Captain Berney and his company were sent along the north rim with three days' rations in haversacks. Captain Carey, similarly equipped, marched along the south rim, accompanied by Carson, who was anxious about Pfeiffer's command and also eager to see more of the canyon. At the site of Herrera's encounter, they came upon the eleven dead Navajos. Five warriors lay nearby, desperately wounded. Two of the wounded died, but careful treatment by Dr. Shout saved the other three and demonstrated better than any promises that the army was interested in helping those who submitted. On the fourteenth Carson and Carey continued until they believed that they had an unobstructed view of the eastern entrance. Finding no signs of Pfeiffer's command and no fresh signs of Indians, they returned to the main camp. There they found Pfeiffer, who, having by-passed the entrance to the main canyon in a snowstorm, had arrived after a safe but exciting passage through the Cañon del Muerto, its northern branch. All believed this to be the first transit of the canyon by any white man.[32]

The Navajos, badly beaten though they were, managed to make the passage dramatic for Pfeiffer and his men. Mindful of the sinister reputation of the canyon, Pfeiffer had planned his expedition with care. At the entrance to the canyon, he divided the command into three parties, a lieutenant heading each, with instructions to move together as a body. The vanguard carried picks and shovels, and the pack animals brought up the rear. For twelve miles they marched on the ice of the shallow stream whose channel formed the floor of the canyon. The mules often broke through the ice, and one of them "split completely open under the exhausting fatigue of the march." On this stretch the vanguard caught four half-starved and naked prisoners.

The next day Indians accompanied them on both rims of the canyon, "whooping and yelling and cursing, firing shots and throwing rocks." Two warriors were killed, as was "one old Squaw who obstinately persisted in hurling rocks and pieces of wood at the Soldiers. Six prisoners were captured." Others were chased up a canyon, but they escaped "where nothing save an Indian or a Mountain Goat could make their way." This second night in the canyon they spent in a secure place beneath ancient dwellings solidly and skillfully built of masonry, high on the rocks. Nearby was a large peach orchard, which the aggressiveness of the Navajos kept Pfeiffer from destroying. Many Indians rested far above them on the rim, looking no bigger than crows. The next day Pfeiffer emerged at the west entrance, where three more Indians came in under a white flag while he was in temporary command of the camp.[33]

Wishing to take part in this historic passage, Carey requested and received a command of his own, which he led from west to east through the canyon. Because Pfeiffer had shown the Indians that the canyon was not impregnable, and because Carson had received kindly those who had surrendered, Carey did not go far before the Indians began to gather on the rocks above and to indicate that they wished to approach him. Through a Navajo interpreter, he told them he would talk with them. That night over a hundred fifty Indians joined his camp. He talked with them, then gave them permission to leave and bring in their families. The next day he left the canyon and started the march back to Fort Canby through deep snow, crusted so that nearly every step broke through. January 18 he brought in a hundred five grown Indians and some children. Others followed his trail and arrived in small parties during the next few days.[34] Carson had left his prisoners with Major Sena and the ox wagons while he hurried ahead to welcome Indians who came directly to the fort. Sena arrived January 24 with 344 Navajos, increasing the Indians at the post to more than 500.[35]

Two days later, leaving Carey in command at Fort Canby, Carson was on his way to Los Pinos with 240 Navajos, which was as many as he could transport supplies for at the time. From there he rode north to Santa Fe to consult with Carleton, than hurried home to Taos. During the next six weeks, while he rested and enjoyed being with his wife and children, the tide of Navajos flowed east to Fort Canby and Fort Wingate. Carey allowed those who wished to bring in their families to return to the mountains and canyons. Herrera Grande and Soldado Surdo came in, bringing other Indians, some with plenty of sheep to feed themselves and with horses to ride. By February 21, fifteen hundred were at Fort Canby, arriving faster than Carey could find transportation for them, in greater numbers than he could find provisions to feed them and blankets to clothe them. Many arrived almost dead from starvation and exposure, and many of these died at the fort. Even with wagons reserved to haul the sick and the very old, some died along the trail to Los Pinos. Rations had to be cut because of the unexpectedly large number of Indians arriving; clothing and blankets could not be sent fast enough from the States. Supplies for such an influx of people could not be furnished in the Territory. Lucien Maxwell, beyond the Sangre de Cristos, sent what he could spare to Fort Sumner to care for the Navajos arriving there.

Even after so much suffering, renewed hope made most of the

Navajos optimistic; they were being fed, a better fate than being hunted like starving rabbits in the wilderness. Captain Joseph Barney, who escorted 1,430 Navajos to the Bosque Redondo during February and March 1864, sent in a detailed and graphic account of the journey. The Indians, with rations of a pound of meat and a pound of flour per person, seemed determined to cooperate with the government and make a success of Carleton's experiment. A chief would make a speech each day, encouraging them. Although ten persons died on the way, two strayed from camp, and three boys were stolen, those arriving at the reservation, after a very affectionate reunion with friends and relatives already there, set to work building *acequias*, or irrigation ditches, and clearing mesquite from the fields. Captain Berney concluded, "They seem now to be very happy and contented, and we may look forward to the time when they will all become peaceful, intelligent and industrious citizens."[36]

When Captain McCabe brought 800 Navajos to Fort Sumner March 20 to May 11, pressure on the food supply had caused Carleton to order the rations halved. The Indians did not complain, but many of them deserted and increasing numbers died.[37] The greatest loss occurred in the late winter and early spring of 1864, when 126 Indians died from extreme cold or from dysentery while awaiting transportation at Fort Canby. After Captain John Thompson finally started with 2,400 of them to Fort Sumner, another 197 died.[38]

Carson returned to Fort Canby March 19, "unwell and very much fatigued," Carey wrote.[39] He was doubtless distressed to leave his family, with Josefa's baby expected any day. But his once robust health was deteriorating. The aneurism that eventually killed him had been aggravated by the hardships he had undergone during the past year. Distressed because he assumed his duties at once, Carey regretted "that there should have exhisted [sic] a *necessity* for the *immediate* return of Colonel Carson to this Post."

In a letter dated April 10, 1864, Carson protested that a daily ration of one pound of beef, flour, or corn was decidedly insufficient for an able-bodied Indian.[40] Carleton, however, could not assign rations he could not procure. On April 1 General Henry W.

Halleck, Army Chief of Staff, agreed to forward supplies, but while these were en route the soldiers as well as the Indians had to subsist on reduced rations.[41]

To protect the Indians trying to reach the fort, Carey had stopped sending out scouting parties lest there be a clash and the Indians become afraid to try to surrender, but this truce did not extend to civilians.[42] Before the army campaign could be launched in 1863, New Mexicans had been urged to organize to protect themselves from the depredations of Navajos and Apaches. Now that the Navajos were almost helpless, some New Mexicans were pursuing, robbing, and killing any they could find, whether the Indians were trying to evade the soldiers or trying to come in to the forts. People were also robbing them and kidnapping their children as they passed through the towns and villages along the way. April 13 Carson wrote to Carleton, protesting against these practices and asking that Lieutenant Hubbell and a party of enlisted men be assigned to operate against the marauders. On May 4 Governor Henry Connelly issued a proclamation ordering an end to the citizen campaign, warning that any armed men found in Navajo country were subject to arrest by the army, and forbidding any further traffic in captive Indians.[43]

On March 20 Carleton had ordered that when McCabe reached Fort Sumner, he would remain as part of the permanent garrison. Captain Deus was to bring in the next convoy from Fort Wingate and go on to Fort Bascom. Because of the expiration of enlistments, Fort Canby was, as Carson had advised, being phased out.[44] On April 10, Carson requested removal to Santa Fe, there to be reassigned to a post where his family could be with him or to be allowed to resign from the service.[45] Carleton had anticipated him by two days, writing on April 8 that when Carson came to Santa Fe for court-martial proceedings against Captain Eben Everett, who had ruined his army career by addiction to alcohol, he should transfer his command to Captain Carey.[46] When Carson left Fort Canby on April 21, he was not aware that Carleton had plans for him that appeared to be exactly suited to his experience and talents.

Carleton's plans for settling the Navajos and the Mescaleros at the Bosque Redondo had met with three major obstacles. In addition to difficulties in finding transportation and provisions for the large and rapid influx of emigrants, unexpected opposition had developed from the Department of the Interior, which Carleton had supposed would take charge of the Navajos once the army settled them on the reservation. Dr. Michael Steck, superintendent of Indian Affairs in New Mexico, agreed that the Navajos should be placed on a reservation, but considered the Bosque Redondo inadequate for both Navajos and Mescalero Apaches and believed friction would develop between them.[47] Because of their ancient kinship as Athapascans in the Northwest, Carleton had assumed that the two tribes would feel a bond of kinship and could share the reservation with harmony. Actually, they felt little sympathy for one another. As the Navajos had acquired some arts and customs from the Pueblos, the Apaches had cherished their wildness and freedom. Only extreme necessity could bring them together. Resenting the crowding brought about by the influx of Navajos, the Mescaleros began almost immediately to leave the Bosque. November 3, 1865, all Mescaleros left except the aged and feeble.[48]

In an eloquent plea to Adjutant General Lorenzo Thomas, Carleton outlined the needs and the rights of the Navajos, including supervision by a man uniquely qualified to foresee their needs and advise them in their work.[49] In early July, Carson was appointed military superintendent of Indians at the Bosque. July 12 he met the leaders and found them content, apparently eager to learn the arts of peace, to become a happy, contented people as Carleton had dreamed they would. He recommended that a small flock of sheep and goats be given to each family to supply wool and milk.

The crops appeared to be doing well. No one could foresee that as the shoots grew, moths would lay eggs in the top of each ear. These hatched into inch-long worms that developed unseen among the silk, devouring half the grain before gnawing their way out. The tiny hole they left was unnoticeable, but through it other small insects entered and completed the devastation, so that when the Indians started harvesting their corn, they found husks filled with trash left by the insects.[50] For their labor, the Navajos had little besides the *acequias* and the acres cleared of mesquite. The army fed them. Carleton encouraged them not to despair. The next year they planted again. The Pecos overflowed with the melting of the snow in the Sangre de Cristos. What the floods did not destroy was pounded by hail. Anything left by the storm had to endure severe drought with burning sun and a drying wind that tore earth away from the roots. The Navajos began running away from the Bosque as early as 1865. By 1867 they refused to plant.[51]

June 1, 1868, Lieutenant General W. T. Sherman signed a treaty with them, giving them a reservation on their tribal lands and providing means for their rehabilitation—farmland, implements and seeds, sheep and goats, schools and instructors. Before the treaty was signed, they started west, but the main body, a column ten miles long, left Fort Sumner on June 18, 1868, escorted by four companies of cavalry. At last around seven thousand reached Fort Wingate and their agent, Colonel Theodore H. Dodd, whom they called Gopher.[52]

The Navajos were home; yet Carleton's and Carson's efforts were not wasted. The Navajos had learned one lesson well: not to go to war against the white men. They had learned many other lessons and would continue to learn, for they were and are an intelligent and eager-minded people and their experience had convinced them of the usefulness of the arts of peace that Carleton had wanted them to learn. Hunger had stimulated their ingenuity into making the first steps toward one of their major crafts, the working of silver. Having to depend on the army for food, they had somehow procured metal, made dies, and counterfeited the metal ration tickets issued by the army, thus obtaining more food.[53] Back in their homeland, they began at their own speed and in their own way to develop and cultivate what they had begun to learn, until they became wealthier and more secure than ever before and achieved fame all over the world for their weaving and their silver work.

Having no written language, the Navajos were inclined to be very creative and dramatic in dealing with their past.[54] Their tribal memory of the events of 1863 and 1864 transformed Carson into a symbol of evil, the cause as well as the agent of the sufferings they endured before, during, and after the Long Walk to the Bosque.[55] The foregoing account shows that he was not the cause, that he carried out his orders with as much humaneness as circumstances would allow, and that he was not present during the exodus of the Navajos from their tribal lands.[56]

Carson did not live to hear of the Navajos' return, but Sherman had such respect for his judgment and knowledge of the Indian that he could well have been influenced by him.[57] The final provision for the Navajos closely approximates the recommendations Carson had been making since 1857. Perhaps the greatest result of their period of captivity and exile was to transform them from a people of many small political units into what today can be called the Navajo Nation, with definite political boundaries and a central government.[58]

Chapter 19

The Coup at Adobe Walls

Carson remained at Fort Sumner only a few months. He was not actually in charge of the Navajos. From the post commander, Captain Henry B. Bristol, he had to request both supplies for the Indians and authority to carry out decisions for their welfare. As a colonel of the New Mexican Volunteers, he found this subservience to an army captain intolerable. He tried to resign because his position was not what he had expected, and he considered it not "befitting an Officer of my rank in the Service."[1] Carleton immediately replied that by Article of War No. 62 he could take command at the fort any time he wished, that authority had already been sent for him to come to Santa Fe for a talk, and that "I will always sustain you and give you the best command I can."[2]

This was the third time Carson had submitted his resignation since going to Fort Sumner. Obviously, the position was not to his liking. Carson was too valuable a man to lose, but Carleton had plans more likely to interest him. The plains Indians had been on the warpath all spring and summer. Carson would be the man to subdue them.[3]

By November 6 an expedition of 14 officers and 321 enlisted men was ready to leave Fort Bascom with a train of 27 wagons, an ambulance, and 2 twelve-pounder howitzers. On November 10

Carson rode up with 75 Ute and Apache Indians, including his old friend Ka-ni-ache, ready to begin the campaign. Colonel F. P. Abréu and 75 infantrymen accompanied the wagon train. Carson and the Indian scouts pushed on with cavalry and artillery. On the third or fourth day they passed the site of Mrs. White's death, and the colonel told his fellow officers about that distant and tragic encounter.

The Utes lent color to the march. Several flanked the column during the day. Two were sent ahead each morning. At evening they rejoined the camp and gave Carson their report. From dark until almost daylight they howled their songs of defiance as they danced around their fires. While the soldiers were at supper on November 24, the Indians were lying idly about, some gambling, some sleeping, some watching hopefully for something to be offered them from the soldiers' mess. Suddenly all sprang to their feet and stood gazing east, talking excitedly among themselves. The officers turned to Carson for an explanation. Telling them that the two scouts sent ahead that morning had found the Comanches and were on their way back to report, he indicated two moving specks far away on a hill. When these arrived, they rode leisurely through the camp, looking neither right nor left and ignoring all questions until they came to Carson, to whom they reported that they had found abundant sign about ten miles ahead.

Carson immediately ordered all cavalry and the howitzers to prepare to move without delay. Leaving Abréu to escort the wagon train the next morning, he assembled the remainder—13 officers and 246 men—and gave them orders for the march. During the night march, there was to be no smoking or talking. Four days before, they had ascended from the valley of the Canadian to more rolling, higher ground. By midnight they had descended again to the flood plain of the river, where they found the fresh trail. Halting, Carson had the men dismount but ordered them to stand, neither speaking nor smoking, holding their mounts by the bridle, a position not only tedious but extremely uncomfortable as a heavy frost settled. At the first lightening of the eastern sky, they mounted and proceeded along the trail, Carson at the head of the column with the Utes and Apaches, followed by a portion of the cavalry, the howitzers next, and the rest of the cavalry in the rear. The Indians, the tops of buffalo robes standing high above their heads, their knees drawn up, looked like shapeless bundles perched atop their horses.

Suddenly from across the river they heard a voice call out, "Vene acá! Vene acá!"⁴ Carson ordered Major McCleave to take a detachment across the river. The Indians dashed into a clump of bushes, left their robes, reappeared wearing war paint and feathers, and rode whooping into the river. Carson sent the remainder of the men ahead to strike the Indian village, while he and Lieutenant Heath's detachment remained with Lieutenant George H. Pettis and the howitzers. The cannoneers, unmounted, marched beside the guns to dislodge them when the small wheels caught on the tall grass or driftwood and to set them upright when they overturned.

About nine o'clock the battery passed through a herd of the Kiowas' cattle, then came upon the Utes and Apaches. Each Indian, having rounded up a number of the enemy's horses, taken one to ride, and left his own mount with his chosen herd, was getting ready to gallop forward to join the fight. The firing ahead was increasing in intensity. The cavalry had surprised the Indians among their lodges of whitened buffalo hide, which now became visible. The warriors, far in advance, had lured the soldiers away to give the women a chance to salvage as much as possible of their belongings. Carson, warming to the excitement of battle, threw his heavy military overcoat on a bush, expecting to pick it up as he returned. He never saw it again.

About four miles beyond the village, the battery came in sight of the battle line. Having arrived at the old fort of Adobe Walls, the men had corralled their horses and deployed as skirmishers, trying to pick off the Comanches and Kiowas who, stripped to paint and feathers, were charging back and forth at a run, leaning far over the sides of their horses and occasionally shooting under the animals' necks. The Utes and Apaches were doing the same thing from the near side of the line. Carson and Heath's cavalry spurred ahead. Pettis and his men galloped after and dragged the guns to the top of the knoll where Carson and a few other officers were directing the fight, and Carson ordered, "Pettis, throw a few shell into that crowd over thar."

Twelve or fifteen hundred warriors were being harangued by their chiefs and seemed about to charge the soldiers. The cannoneers quickly unlimbered the howitzers, loaded, and sighted them. At the explosion, all the Kiowas and Comanches rose high in their stirrups and stared in astonishment for an instant before they turned with a long wail of dismay and terror and started at a dead run for a Comanche village about a mile behind them.

Carson ordered the men to eat something and water their horses, after which they would proceed to take the Comanche village ahead of them. A corner of the old fort had been set up as a hospital, where the surgeon was treating the half-dozen or so wounded, among them a young Mexican who had been bitten by a rattlesnake as he crawled through the grass. After dressing the wound, the surgeon gave him a stiff drink of whiskey. The men had finished the bits of raw bacon and bread that they had managed to snatch up before leaving the wagons, and all were trying to tell their tales of the battle when across the plain came the Indians. The horses were quickly corralled, the artillery horses hitched up again, and the cavalrymen again deployed in the grass, the young Mexican with them. Soon the command was surrounded by a thousand well-mounted Indians, some deployed as skirmishers, others circling and firing under their horses' necks.

The fight lasted all afternoon, but the Indians had learned to avoid close formations and the howitzers were seldom fired. Someone behind the Indians' line had a bugle, and every time Carson's bugler sounded a command, the Indian bugler sounded the opposite command, a little game that the soldiers greeted with shouts of laughter.

As far as a dozen miles in advance the Canadian was visible, with several more Indian villages along its banks. From these, bands of warriors continued to join the enemy until their number was estimated at around three thousand. Two or three miles out on the flanks, parties of warriors rode back toward the village the soldiers had passed through during the early morning.

With so many Indians riding to his rear, Carson began to have some anxiety concerning the wagons moving up, protected by only seventy-five men. In spite of the wishes of most of the officers that they press forward and capture the village ahead, he gave orders to fall back and destroy the village they had passed. Forming a column of fours with the cavalry horses, one man riding and leading the other three, he threw the other men out on the flanks as skirmishers, the howitzers guarding the rear, and began a cautious withdrawal.

The enemy swarmed up, attacking on every side. Setting fire to the grass, they rode through the smoke toward the column, firing as they came. The rear hurried forward ahead of the burning grass, and Carson set fire in the advance and took a position on elevated ground where the grass was short. The artillery was quickly placed in position, and as the Indians hurried toward the knoll, the guns were fired into their midst, throwing them back. The one scalp taken in the battle was gained in this maneuver. An Indian had charged forward through the smoke, which was suddenly carried away by a gust of wind, leaving the Indian and the young Mexican only a few yards apart. Both fired. The Indian fell, and the boy ran forward to scalp him. Other Indians galloped forward to save their comrade, but the soldiers rallied to support the boy. Their steady fire kept the Indians at bay until the boy got back to the line with his trophy.

As the column neared the village, the Indians again surged forward to try to rescue the remainder of their property. When the troops reached the village, it was swarming with them. Again the howitzers were fired into their midst, and they fled, yelling, leaving the village in possession of the troops. Each soldier took one or two buffalo robes, but they burned everything else—lodges, dried meat, berries, buffalo robes, powder, cooking utensils, an army ambulance and government wagon, and a countless variety of other plunder taken from some train crossing the prairie.

Now the most severely wounded were placed on the gun carriages and the ammunition carts, and the exhausted column rode back in search of the supply wagons. They came in view of the campfires about eight-thirty, and before long they were unsaddling and picketing their horses. A double guard was stationed, and the men fell into their blankets, too tired to think even about eating. They had been marching and fighting for nearly thirty hours, with less than half an hour of rest and no food except the little snack at Adobe Walls.

In his report Carson regretted that the horses were too broken down to pursue the Indians and capture their horse herds. He recommended that on a future expedition against the Indians no less that a thousand men, with two six-pounder and two twelve-pounder rifled guns should be sent. He also strongly urged that traders not be allowed to approach these Indians, to whom they had been trading arms and ammunition. He was, however, indebted to Mexican traders for information that five white women and two children were prisoners among them and might be exchanged for Indian women if he could capture some. Carson estimated that no less than sixty Indians had been killed or wounded. The Mexicans reported that nearly a hundred were killed and between a hundred and a hundred fifty were wounded. Of Carson's force, two soldiers and one Indian scout were killed, and fifteen men were wounded.

The Battle of Adobe Walls was the most brilliant that Carson ever fought, though it has been called a defeat.[5] To appreciate the skill and good judgment with which Carson controlled a potentially disastrous situation, one may compare it to the Battle of the Little Bighorn, in which Custer faced similar odds. Carson, of course, was guided by motives totally different from those that spurred Custer to the sacrifice of himself and all his men. For Carson the battle was a serious and important task to be performed, utilizing his knowledge of the enemy, his native ability, and his long experience. Without thought of glory, he weighed the situation as it developed, chose the course of action most likely to impress the enemy and most sparing of his own forces, and carried through his plan with economy and precision. In spite of opposition from some of his men, he retained their cooperation and exacted their utmost effort. Carleton had made a general of him.

The Indians were impressed. The battle was exactly in the style they understood: entering enemy territory, inflicting damage, and retiring with little loss—a very impressive *coup*. This battle was one of the decisive factors in making the Kiowas and Comanches seek peace in the autumn of 1865.

Carleton wrote to Carson on December 15, 1864, "This brilliant affair adds another green leaf to the laurel wreath which you have so nobly won in the service of your country."[6] On October 27,

1865, in a letter to the adjutant general in Washington, he added to the other feats of Carson for which he had already recommended recognition "his gallantry in his brilliant engagement with the Comanche and Kiowa Indians November 15, 1864."[7]

Carleton's repeated efforts on behalf of his favorite scout were rewarded March 13, 1865, when Carson was breveted brigadier general, U.S. Volunteers, for gallantry at the battle of Valverde and for distinguished services in New Mexico. Hundreds of brevet ratings were being named as the war drew to a close, and Carson and Carleton remained for some time unaware of the distinction bestowed upon him.

Carson's efforts henceforth would be toward establishing a just and workable peace, using diplomacy rather than armed force. His next orders, however, were to build a base from which to punish the plains Indians. During the spring of 1865, the Kiowas, Comanches, and Cheyennes preyed upon caravans from the States heading southwest across the Cimarron Cutoff. In reply to a letter in early May from Carleton concerning a fort at or near Cold Spring, Carson wrote from Taos endorsing the plan and expressing pleasure that Pfeiffer was to be one of his officers. On May 8, Carleton sent official orders, leaving the exact location to Carson, as well as the plan and construction of the fort.[8]

By June 16, Carson was able to report that Camp Nichols, about halfway between Fort Dodge and Fort Union, was in operation. Breastworks of stone banked with earth had been built, and six sets of officers' quarters, also of stone, were completed. Marian Russell, who as a young girl had known Carson in Santa Fe, had watched the fort being built. Now married to one of his officers, she lived in the tent next to Carson's. Sometimes she noticed with concern that his face was haggard and drawn with pain as he lay on his camp bed, the sides of the tent rolled up, and with unremitting vigilance moved his field glasses around the horizon.

The pain was intermittent. At times he played seven-up with some of his officers, and Marian would hear "his short, sharp bark of laughter, or shout of glee as he won." Having discussed the plans for the fort with Pfeiffer, he gave little supervision to the work of actual building, which progressed rapidly and efficiently. Marian found him exceedingly kind and courteous and was touched when he came by leading his horse to tell her goodbye, warning, "Remember, child, the injuns will get you if you ride alone out thar."[9]

Leaving Pfeiffer in charge, he was on his way to Fort Lyon to give a congressional committee his expert opinion of the Sand Creek Massacre, a controversial attack, November 29, 1864, by Colonel Chivington upon a band of peaceable Cheyennes.[10] Carson agreed with William Bent, four of whose children had been present, that Chivington's attack was a cruel injustice to the Indians and a grave disservice to the country.

Carson did not go back to Camp Nichols. Planned as a protection for the wagon trains, the fort was to have been occupied until November 1, when travel along the trail would virtually cease. Although Carleton's chief quartermaster, Major J. C. McFerran, recommended that a permanent fort be established there, Camp Nichols was not completed.[11] When the troops were withdrawn September 22, 1865, it was never occupied again except as an occasional shelter for passersby.

In reply to General Order No. 19, Carson stated on July 24 that, the war being over, he did not desire to remain permanently in military service.[12] But his combination of integrity, special knowledge and skills, and experience made him indispensable. His appearance before the congressional committee so impressed the chairman, Senator J. R. Doolittle, that he requested, and Carleton's order of August 5 directed, that Carson try to induce the plains Indians living on and south of the Arkansas River, to stop their acts of hostility and to meet commissioners in council the following October.[13]

The Indians knew Carson as the victor of the Battle of Adobe Walls and as a well-prepared adversary who had just built the stone fort at Cold Spring. His offer of a parley was accepted. This success was followed September 8 by notice from Fort Leavenworth that Major General Pope had appointed him one of the commissioners to treat with the Indians on Bluff Creek, about forty miles south of the Little Arkansas, on October 4. William Bent was also a member of this commission.[14]

Carleton had suggested that the negotiations with the plains Indians be opened by Carson and Bent, who would "smoke through" the preliminaries, the congressional commission to arrive when the Indians were ready to complete the treaty.[15] After a few weeks at Fort Union and Taos, Carson rode east in September. Some delay had occurred in arrangements for the parley, and he found himself three weeks early. Others were also early, and interviewers and celebrity hounds took advantage of his leisure and left him no peace. After telling Major Edward W. Wynkoop where he was going, he disappeared. About two weeks later, Wynkoop rode out to Cottonwood Creek and found him contentedly smoking his pipe, and they rode together to meet the Indians.[16]

It was hoped that this council would find means of atoning to the Cheyennes for the injustice at Sand Creek. The Treaties of the Little Arkansas were concluded October 14, 17, and 18, 1865.[17] They did not end the troubles with the Cheyennes. Though contrite enough to make lavish gifts, the government offered none of the benefits—farm tools, training, schools—that Carson and Bent had long advocated. The Indians gave up all claim to the land between the North Platte and the Arkansas, and between the forks of the Platte and a line running roughly from the Red Buttes to the head of the Arkansas. They were not likely to remain contented in the restricted territory promised to them, but their peaceful acceptance of the terms temporarily indicated success. On October 18 was concluded the first treaty ever made with the Kiowas and Comanches. They agreed to a reservation limited to the Texas and Oklahoma panhandles and a part of western Oklahoma, giving up all claim to any land in New Mexico, Colorado, and Kansas and to much of what they claimed in Texas.[18]

From the Little Arkansas Carson had orders to report in person to Major General John Pope in St. Louis.[19] Pope's superior, Lieutenant General William Tecumseh Sherman, who was present at the interviews, probably initiated the orders. The main topic of discussion was doubtless the Indian problem, but Carson's future in the service was under consideration as well. The volunteer units were being phased out, and officers who had won distinction during the war were being reduced to more modest peacetime rank. Carleton had suggested that Carson might become sutler at Fort Union, but Carson did not feel that he had the business ability for such a post. Carleton may have discussed him with Sherman, who had first seen him in 1848 when he arrived at Monterey with dispatches and mail from the East. Sherman had won a lasting place in military history, but he had not forgotten Carson or failed to note his achievements. The business with the generals was over by October 30, when Carson received orders to rejoin his regiment.[20] After a brief visit with his relatives, he rode home.

On November 29 he wrote to Carleton from Taos, announcing his return the day before, "in somewhat better health . . . I think that the peace will be a permanent one. I visited . . . General Sherman and Pope. . . . formed a very high opinion of them both. When we have the pleasure of meeting, I will give you the full particulars."[21] We have no record of that meeting.

In December 1865, Carson received official notice of his appointment as Brevet Brigadier General of Volunteers, a singular honor for a man who had been denied the modest reward of a lieutenancy at the end of the Mexican War. He wrote to Secretary of War Stanton: "Though unsolicited by me, I accept with grateful pleasure, as a memento that during the late rebellion, the exertions of the New Mexico Volunteers, though restricted in its influence to its own territory, have not been overlooked by the United States."[22] His passing the honor on to his men was characteristic, and their reaction was also characteristic. Pleased and proud, they never failed to the end of their lives to refer to him as the General.

His new rating was quickly followed by Special Order No. 13, assigning him to the command of Fort Union.[23] This was a very large post, and Carson was busy there. But because it was a supply depot and the work was largely administrative, Carleton saw that Carson's talents were more suited to another post.

For some time Fort Garland, at the western side of the Sangre de Cristos in southern Colorado, had been neglected. Three bands of Utes and one band of Apaches—about 1,050 warriors in all—lived within a radius of fifty miles. About sixty men were stationed at the fort, a force totally inadequate to restrain so many Indians. Discipline was poor, the buildings in bad repair.[24] Here was a challenge worthy of Carson's talents and training. On April 21, 1866, Special Orders No. 12 directed that "Brevet Brig General *Christopher Carson*, U.S. Volunteers, Colonel 1st Cavy N.M. Vols.

with the Adjutant and Non-Commissioned Staff and records of his regiment, will proceed without delay from Fort Union, New Mexico, and take command of the post Fort Garland, Colorado Territory."[25]

Chapter 20

General Carson and the Utes

When Carson arrived at Fort Garland May 19, 1866, the Utes were restless and resentful. Following the miners surging into the Front Range and the San Juans, ranchers had settled at the foot of the Sangre de Cristos on the east and pushed up the river valleys. Mexicans had already settled in the San Luis Valley.[1] Game had become so scarce that the Indians were near starvation.

Carson quickly organized his command, chose from among his officers a council of administration, and kept Carleton informed of its proceedings. By June 10 he had completed a report on the fort for Major Roger Jones, assistant inspector general for the army at Fort Leavenworth.[2] At the eastern edge of the San Luis Valley, about twenty-five miles southwest of Sangre de Cristo Pass, Fort Garland had been established in 1858 to replace Fort Massachusetts, which was too vulnerable to attack by Indians. After relating the advantages of the site, the beauty of the mountains, the abundance of water and wood and of mineral and metallic ores, the fertility of the soil, and the usefulness of the post in restraining the incessant warfare between the mountain Indians and those of the plains, the report stressed the need to strengthen the fort and increase the garrison. Plans should be carried out to place the Indians on reservations and protect them from contact with the whites, but until that was done, they had to be restrained. Dissatisfied with Governor Evans's treaty of 1863, and outraged to see the country well stocked with white men's animals while they could not find enough buffalo to feed their families, they could be prevented from stealing only by a garrison strong enough to overawe them. A copy of this report sent to Carleton brought immediate promise of reinforcement.

The Indians did not wait. Shavano's band of Utes and some Jicarilla Apaches—over three hundred lodges in all—had gone east of the Sangre de Cristos to hunt buffalo. On the way to the plains they had stolen over seventy horses and many cattle, leaving the settlers in dread of their return. Their hunt was unsuccessful, and on the way back they raided McDonald's ranch and took a horse, two cows, and twenty sheep. They also stole all the coffee, sugar, flour, powder, and lead at the ranch and whipped a herder severely. Three men were reported killed in the area. Lafayette Head, agent of the Tabeguache Utes, came to Carson and asked for soldiers to help him capture or kill Shavano and his band. He was given ten men.[3]

By June 17, nothing had been heard of Shavano or Head. At that time Carson thought it would be fortunate if Shavano were killed, "for he is a restless spirit of quite notorious character."[4] However, he again emphasized the dissatisfaction of the Utes with the treaty, amended by the Senate without their knowledge, and pointed out that they were destitute. By that time, his letters show, he was convinced that the aims of the Indians were impossible to achieve, but he tried to arouse greater recognition of their needs: "Present want appeals more directly to their feelings than prospective punishment, if war ensues it will be forced partly by the Indians necessities," partly by "the weak state of the garrison for some time past and the laxity of discipline maintained."

As soon as the new mounts arrived, he planned to ride to the Utes on Saguache Lake, where he and Pfeiffer would try to convince them that their grievances could be righted. Of the Indians near the post with whom he could "talk and reason" he had nothing to fear, but he had requested Head to furnish food to alleviate their hunger, Head replying that he had neither funds nor credit to obtain provisions for them.

By June 30 nearly five hundred Ute warriors had passed. All were adamantly opposed to Governor Evans's treaty, declaring that they would never give up the San Luis Valley and move west of the Continental Divide.[5] Most of them wished to remain at peace with the whites, but a strong party that Carson believed was influenced by the Jicarilla Apaches was for war. Carson asked that the Apache agent recover all stolen property from the Jicarillas, both to teach the Apaches a lesson and to impress the Utes with the power of the government.

The arrival of reinforcements on June 18 and 24 influenced Shavano to join the Utes encamped near the fort. No more is said of his depredations, and for a time Carson was chiefly concerned with repairing the fort and maintaining discipline. The paymaster had not appeared since April 30, and discontent was rising.[6] By the end of June, a few men were deserting, taking their mounts and equipment.[7]

This relatively peaceful interlude was interrupted by a summons by Major General John Pope, who wished to see Carson in Santa Fe.[8] Though we have no record of his conversations with Pope, the general, tremendously impressed by what he saw of Carson and heard about his understanding of the Indians and their problems, wrote to General Sherman on August 11 from Fort Union. "Carson is the best man in the country to control these Indians and prevent war. . . . He is personally known and liked by every Indian . . . likely to make trouble. . . . Peace . . . is of all things desirable, and no man is so certain to insure it as Kit Carson."[9]

Carson's belief that the Utes were on the verge of war convinced the general, who on July 26 issued from Santa Fe General Field Order No. 5, establishing a fort along the Upper Huerfano, or Cucharas River, to be called Fort Stevens.[10] On the advice of Carson and Ceran St. Vrain, a site was selected on a plateau below the Spanish Peaks, and on August 15 Carleton ordered Colonel Andrew J. Alexander to begin construction. Although the fort was never completed, the presence of Alexander and his men in the area was important in relations with the Indians during the autumn of 1866.

While in Santa Fe, Carson met two men who left records of

their brief acquaintance. Worthington Whittredge, an artist who had come out with General Pope, found Carson unique, "a man who had been born with some gentle instincts and who had lived a solitary life . . . where primitive nature had had full swing of his sensibilities," yet had remained modest and truthful.[11] One day Carson asked Whittredge if he might accompany him up the mountain to watch him sketch. After looking over his shoulder for a time in silence, Carson asked if he would stop sketching and sit down with him, then led the way to a rock. After they were seated, Carson began describing with such graphic detail a sunrise he had once seen high up in the Sangre de Cristos that Whittredge remembered it vividly forty years later when he wrote his memoirs. Having no notion of the lengthy and meticulous work involved, Carson asked if Whittredge could paint the scene for him. "Nature had made a deep impression on this man's mind," wrote Whittredge, who imagined him standing alone on some distant mountain, "worshiping in his way a grand effect of nature until it entered into his soul and made him a silent but thoughtful human being."

Whittredge also remembered him as being so anxious lest he do something not strictly according to polite usage that he went to great trouble to find gentlemen's pumps to wear to a ball given for General Pope. None being available in Santa Fe, he bought a pair of ladies' slippers that fitted him perfectly. Whittredge added, "The officers did not change their boots, but for a moment it was difficult for me to see where in the world in his tight fitting uniform, he had managed to secrete his slippers. On close inspection it was evident he had buttoned one on each side of his breast until his figure was not unlike the figure of many of the handsome 'senoras' whirling in the waltz."

James F. Meline, an officer accompanying Pope, wrote that the pleasantest aspect of his visit to Santa Fe was the society of Carson, with whom he spent three days.[12] Meline found him talkative, "with great distinctness of memory, simplicity, candor, and a desire to make some one else, rather than himself, the hero of the story." Without claiming to be an authority on Indians, he explained why they used short stirrups, as did hunters and trappers. The short stirrups were necessary so that a man could shift his weight, as he had to do in a running fight. They made it possible for the Indian to ride hung over the side of his horse, only a leg showing as he fired from under the horse's neck. He retold the story of the Sioux who had fooled him by clicking two buffalo bones together and creeping around camp on all fours like a wolf. The Utes, he said, were the best shots in the country, whether Indian or white. "I have handled the rifle since I was so high, but some of the Utes beat me." His modesty extended to his recent promotion. When someone apologized for not calling him "General," he replied, "Oh call me Kit at once, and be done with it."

Meline was present when Carleton and Carson held a council with some Zunis and through this association derived much honor from these Indians when, on July 28, he saw them in Albuquerque.[13] By that time Carson was on his way back to Fort Garland, where he felt his presence was needed.

His surmise was correct. August brought one crisis after another with the Utes. On the sixth the children were playing outside the fort when a group of Indians from Shavano's band came riding toward them, painted and feathered for war.[14] The children ran to Kit, who went to meet the excited Indians, already inside the sentry line. They had found a young Indian dead not far from the fort and were clamoring for revenge. The Indians believed that a soldier had mixed a potion for the young Indian that had poisoned him and demanded that the guilty soldier be turned over to them.

Carson asked where the body had been found, and the Indians told him to come and see for himself. He and Dr. Gwyther, the post surgeon, rode back with the Indians and examined the body. The victim had been killed by blows about the nose and ears with a stone, club, or other dull, heavy weapon. These had been given at some distance from where the body lay, and the boy had staggered along until he fell and died. Dr. Gwyther stated that he had been dead about forty-eight hours.

Back at the fort, Carson gravely invited the chief and some of the warriors to come inside and talk. An Indian named Cassadore, together with his wife, had been staying at the fort so that he could receive medical treatment from Dr. Gwyther. As the room filled with Indians, this couple took positions on either side of Carson, each concealing a sharp knife with which they were prepared to defend him to the death. Pfeiffer went quietly about putting the soldiers on the alert, and Josefa herded the children into another room away from the Indians.

Near where the body had been found was a camp of adobe makers, and the Indians began to suspect these men of the murder. Meanwhile Cassadore called Carson's attention to the excited state of a medicine man who sat trembling, nervously grasping his gun. Carson promised the Indians to investigate and, if possible, find and punish whoever was guilty. They left, declaring again that they would have revenge.

Cassadore told Carson that the medicine man, a brother of Shavano, had hated the dead boy because of a young woman, and Cassadore believed he was the murderer. After careful investigation, Carson found no reason to believe that the adobe makers had had anything to do with the death. Cassadore joined some Indians who, believing war was certain, started to Maxwell's. Carson gave him a letter warning Maxwell of probable trouble, for he now believed war with the Utes was inevitable.

A letter from Maxwell asking that he come to investigate conditions at the agency did not lessen his anxiety. Feeling it unwise to leave the fort, he sent Pfeiffer instead, with orders to warn all villages and outlying settlers of the danger. Carson hoped that Shavano, who had become friendly, would help to calm the excited Indians, but the chief had gone to Conejos, and it was rumored that he had got into a fight with a storekeeper. If this were true, he would not be feeling peaceable. Carson urged Carleton to send as many mounted men as could quickly be made ready, as well as plenty of ammunition and two howitzers. On the Cucharas, the Francisco ranch had eight hundred cattle. A company should be sent to protect them, for they would be a great asset to the Indians at war. Apparently Carleton depended on Carson's influence with the Utes to avert war in the north. One company of infantry volunteers arrived at the fort August 31, far short of what Carson requested.

How this matter was settled has not been determined. Kit, Jr., believed an agreement was made at the fort in which the Indians were to receive a hundred dollars in money and a good horse, to be paid a week later on the Saguache. According to his story, when Kit and forty troopers met the Indians, they demanded more money. Kit refused, and a warrior rode forward with a rawhide rope as if to strike. Without taking his eyes off the warrior, Kit told his men, "If he strikes me I will kill him, then we will fight if we all have to die together." At this the Indians accepted the recompense and promised good behavior.

This story, told by Kit, Jr., some sixty years later, seems rather unlikely because Carson in his report stated that the Indians were threatening revenge as they left. When Agent Head reported about a week later that the Indians were perfectly satisfied with the settlement, Carson sent the communication on to Carleton with the comment that he disliked the settlement, which implied that the whites were to blame.[15] An agreement may have been made by Head.

This crisis had barely passed when worse trouble erupted to the south.[16] When hunting in the Red River region, one of Ka-ni-ache's sons succeeded in killing nothing. As he passed a ranch, he demanded a sheep. The Mexican herder told him a band of Utes had come by shortly before, taken one sheep, and wantonly killed two more. He could take one of those. The young man wanted to shoot one of his own choice. When he was told that he could shoot no more sheep, he drew an arrow at the herder, who shot him dead.

The herder fled to Fort Union, closely pursued by Ka-ni-ache, two of his sons, and ten other warriors. The two brothers were bent on revenge, but Ka-ni-ache, seeing additional units of cavalry and infantry come in and camp near the fort, seemed more reasonable. Carleton sent two companies of cavalry to Maxwell's Ranch and units to other danger points. Acting Governor W. F. N. Arny rode across the mountains to Cimarron. Pfeiffer and his escort met him there, and together they tried to persuade Ka-ni-ache to go to Fort Garland until the court at Mora could try the murderer of his son.

The Indians at the Cimarron agency were in a pitiable condition, hungry and nearly naked. They had no agent and had received no goods from the government for almost a year. In June the superintendent of Indian Affairs for New Mexico had instructed Maxwell to give them five hundred dollars worth of food per month, but that was much too little. August 25 Carleton ordered the command at Cimarron to issue a half-pound of wheat meal and a half-pound of meat per day to each man, woman, and child—about three thousand dollars worth of food per month for the band.

Pfeiffer returned to the fort August 22, and the next day Ka-ni-ache arrived, still determined upon revenge. He refused any consideration of a money settlement, but did agree to wait until after the court met at Mora. Carson hoped that if the man was guilty, he would be "promptly and legally punished, and . . . the Indians see that in our hands the scales of justice are evenly balanced and our obligations to them faithfully observed."[17] The case never reached the court at Mora. Ka-ni-ache returned to the Cimarron, and the case was transferred to Santa Fe, where Ka-ni-ache finally agreed to accept four hundred dollars as compensation.[18]

The building of Fort Stevens had made little progress before Alexander was interrupted by trouble at Doyle's ranch on the Huerfano at Undercliffe. Carson commended his promptness in quelling this trouble and sent a copy of a note from one of the settlers with a rumor of trouble and asked Alexander to send a detachment to the mouth of the Huerfano to investigate. If Alexander needed help, Carson with fifty men would be there in half a day. If any Utes were near the post, they would make the best spies he could get.

Meanwhile, Lieutenant General William Tecumseh Sherman was riding west on a tour of the forts. All along his route he found the Indians peaceful. When he came to Fort Stevens, the Alexanders entertained him pleasantly in the hospital tent. Finding no sign of hostilities in the area and being pressed by Congress to retrench expenditures, he ordered Alexander to terminate the project and go to Fort Garland to await orders.[19]

When Sherman arrived at Fort Garland, he wished to meet the Ute chiefs and try to reach an agreement about their future. Because he had decided to start his eastward journey September 22, runners were sent to ask the chiefs to come to the fort September 21. Ouray and Ancotash came as head chiefs of the Tabeguaches and the Mohuaches. Ka-ni-ache was not present, nor had he attended the last treaty-making session.

James F. Rusling, Brevet Brigadier General and Inspector of

United States Volunteers, left a detailed account of the visit and of Carson:

In age, he seemed to be about forty-five. His head was a remarkably good one. . . . His eye was mild and blue, the very type of good nature, while his voice was as soft and sympathetic as a woman's. . . . a man of rare kindliness and charity . . . simple as a child, but brave as a lion. . . . He talked and smoked far into the night each evening we spent together . . . he frequently hesitated for the right English word; but when speaking bastard Spanish (Mexican) or Indian, he was as fluent as a native. Both Mexican and Indian, however, are largely pantomime. . . . The Utes seemed to have the greatest possible confidence in him, and invariably called him simply "Kit." Said Sherman, while at Garland, "These Red Skins think Kit twice as big a man as me. Why his integrity is simply perfect. They know it, and they would believe him and trust him any day before me." And Kit returned this confidence, by being their most steadfast and unswerving friend. He declared all our Indian troubles were caused originally by bad white men. . . .

Said he, "To think of that dog Chivington, and his hounds, up thar at Sand Creek! . . . The pore Injuns had our flag flyin over 'em, that same old stars and stripes thar we all love and honor, and they'd been told down to Denver, that so long as they kept that flyin they'd be safe. . . . then . . . that durned Chivington and his cusses . . . literally massa-creed them . . . I don't like a hostile Red Skin. . . . I've fit 'em—fout 'em—as hard as any man. But I never yit drew a bead on a squaw or papoose, and I loathe and hate the man who would."[20]

The council convened in a large room behind Carson's quarters. On one side sat the Indians on buffalo robes. Facing them and puffing a cigar, sat Sherman, flanked by Governor Cummings and Carson. As Sherman explained that he was there to promote the happiness and welfare of the Indians, whose tribal existence could only be preserved by their going on a reservation, Kit translated into Mexican, "with profuse pantomime, after the Indian fashion," and one of the Indians translated into Ute. After conferring among themselves, the chiefs replied that they approved the suggestions of the Big Warrior, but as their young men opposed them, they feared the Utes would not see their wisdom unless the Cheyennes and Comanches first were persuaded to leave off fighting and settle on a reservation. Though the council continued more than an hour, and Sherman advanced all the arguments he could think of, Ouray and Ancotash imperturbably continued to reiterate their original stand. At last Sherman broke up the council in disgust, blurting as he strode back to his quarters, "They will have to freeze and starve a little more, I reckon, before they will listen to common sense!"[21]

But the Indians were talking sense, as Ouray explained two days later at another conference with Carson, Cummings, and Head on the bank of the Rio Grande. If they settled in one place, the Cheyennes and Comanches would know where they were and, one night when all were asleep, would kill many of them. At a promise that forts would be built near the reservation, with bluecoats to keep the Cheyennes and Comanches away, the Indians burst out laughing. The winter before, the Comanches had come right by the forts, found an encampment of Utes, and killed many. Why had the bluecoats let them pass? What would happen if a *paleface* came to the reservation and shot an Indian?

To the first question Carson had no answer, and he had to explain the court and jury system over and over before Ouray could accept the possibility of a white man's being hanged for killing an Indian. Ouray pursued the concept further and asked what would happen if a paleface stole a pony from an Indian. Told that the white man would have to return the pony, the Indians beamed with pleasure. When they broke into an excited discussion, the governor questioned Carson, who said that they were arguing over whether they would have to pay for stock they had stolen from the whites. They soon told Ouray to drop the question without further talk. The council ended without any firm agreement.[22]

Kit, Jr., related that the little Navajo boy, Juan, wandered away while Sherman was at the fort. Josefa found him in the conference room, sitting comfortably in the general's lap. Sherman was especially responsive to Carson's children,

A half dozen . . . boys and girls as wild and untrained as a brood of Mexican mustangs. One day the children ran through the room

*in which we were seated, half clad and boisterous, and I inquired,
"Kit, what are you doing about your children?"*

*He replied: "That is a source of great anxiety . . . I value edu-
cation as much as any man, but I never had the advantage of
schools, and now that I am getting old and infirm, I fear I have
not done right by my children."*

Sherman had been given a scholarship for twenty years at the
Catholic College at South Bend, Indiana,[23] and he offered to give
Carson half of it so that two of his sons could each have five years
at the college.

Sherman linked Carson with the great heroes of history and
legend. "Kit Carson was a good type of a class of men most useful
in their day, but now as antiquated as Jason of the Golden Fleece,
Ulysses of Troy, the Chevalier La Salle of the Lakes, Daniel Boone
of Kentucky, Irvin [Jim] Bridger and Jim Beckwith of the Rockies,
all belonging to the dead past."[24]

Even as Sherman was enjoying a few days with Carson and assuring himself that the Indians were peaceable, worse trouble was
brewing beyond the Sangre de Cristos. When Ka-ni-ache returned
from Santa Fe to the Cimarron, he found the new issue of rations
inadequate. His people were still hungry. They needed buffalo
meat. Taking most of the women and children and their belongings, the band started north, crossed Raton Pass, and camped temporarily on the Purgatoire.

The settlers there were already full of apprehension from Shavano's raid in June. Unaware of the explosive situation, Ka-ni-ache
and his band rode forward on October 3. As they passed the Gutierrez place on the right bank of the Purgatoire about five miles west
of Trinidad, the proprietor accused Ka-ni-ache of stealing corn. Denying this, the chief admitted that some of his people had stolen
to relieve their hunger. Suddenly a shot rang out. Gutierrez's son
had killed a Ute warrior. The others ran to their horses. At this
moment Colonel Alexander and his company of cavalry rode into
sight of what looked like the beginning of a fight, and the colonel
ordered a charge. The Utes retreated, then turned on the troopers
and killed one and wounded two as the band disappeared into the
foothills of the Sangre de Cristos.[25]

When Carson heard of the fight the next day, he was certain a general uprising had begun. He sent expresses to Conejos, Culebra, Costilla, and the settlers in the vicinity, as well as to Carleton. He sent troops to Francisco's to protect the cattle and to capture Ancotash's band of Utes camped nearby.

This flurry of preparation proved premature. On October 6 Ouray rode into Fort Garland to see Carson. He was not going to fight, he said. Any of his young men who wished to go to war would have to leave his camp. Carson told him to bring his band and camp near the fort. He then wrote to Governor Cummings and Major Head to bring the Indians' annuities to Fort Garland instead of the Huerfano, as formerly planned. He asked what funds they would have for feeding the ninety to a hundred lodges of Ouray's band, now increased by the band of Ancotash, who had joined him. Although he began to hope that events might occur that would make a peace with Ka-ni-ache possible, he again wrote to Carleton "earnestly soliciting" him to send troops, horses, pack mules, ammunition, and supplies.[26]

Closely pursued by Alexander, Ka-ni-ache was ranging the Huerfano. His band had killed several men and taken captive Mrs. McGure and four children. Carson did not think Alexander's sixty men and seventy-five citizen allies could catch the Utes, but he was afraid they might unite with Ouray's band and Alexander might attack them. He had sent Sergeant Moore with Ouray to prevent this from happening. Again he asked for reinforcements and supplies, as well as permission to feed the Indians if they camped near the post.[27]

Ouray had been as busy as Carson. While getting his band on the move to Fort Garland, he had sent messengers to warn the settlers on the upper Huerfano. A runner had gone to Ka-ni-ache, urging him to stop fighting and come in to the fort. When Ouray arrived with this news on the ninth, Carson sent a detachment of soldiers out to protect Ka-ni-ache's band, and all arrived at the fort October 10. Though some of the settlers had ignored Ouray's warning, the loss of life and property had been small. In the midst of the disturbances, Mrs. McGure and her children had been released unharmed.[28]

H. I. Farnsworth and Lucien Maxwell sent out circulars for the hostile Indians to come to Maxwell's for protection, but Carson responded that both peaceable and recently hostile Indians were with him—about a thousand in all—and he thought they should remain there. To promote future peace, Ka-ni-ache should not again go east of the mountains because of the enmity of the settlers on the Purgatoire.[29]

October 14 Ouray brought the hostile Indians to talk with Carson, who wrote Carleton that, lacking sufficient troops or means to carry on a war and at the same time protect the settlers, he had made a treaty of peace with Ka-ni-ache. Carson had been friends with Ka-ni-ache for over ten years, with obligations incurred on both sides, but he did not wish to be suspected of partiality. He was influenced, he wrote, not by personal feeling but "solely for the benefit of the public," and he relied on Carleton's support. He was issuing rations until further orders. The Indians had given up over forty head of stock taken in the raids. Carson had promised that one or two women left at Francisco's would be returned to the band. He asked that women and children left at Maxwell's be returned to the band at once, as well as ten horses and three mules the Indians had lost in the fight at Trinidad. Though he had made no promises about these, he felt that returning them would be a sign of good faith in the army's dealing with the Indians. He could not praise Ouray too much for his "straightforward conduct . . . he having acted in better faith than most white men during the recent troubles."[30]

It was reported that an officer had given the Indians whiskey, had got drunk himself, and had tried to kill Ka-ni-ache at the camp on the river before the fight of October 3. Carson thought this act should be severely punished "for the benefit of the service and the public good."[31]

While Carson was busy with Ka-ni-ache's rampage, he was summoned to Fort Union to be mustered out as colonel, U.S. Volunteers, and mustered in as lieutenant colonel, New Mexico Volunteers. This ceremony had to take place without him. He finally took the oath of allegiance as lieutenant colonel on November 10.[32]

By October 11, Alexander was ready to abandon Fort Stevens and bring his troops across the pass to report to Carson. He arrived

273

with a severe cold, and his wife had the pleasure of dining alone with "Old Kit Carson" on the following day.[33] She found him to be "a most interesting, original old fellow." He told her about the sacred fire kept going at Taos Pueblo and about Chief Ka-ni-ache, who dreamed of a future life for the Indians, where there were a few Mexicans but no other white people. The next morning she rode her spirited horse out into the valley with Carson, who introduced her to Ouray, who in turn introduced her to his wife. She considered them the finest looking people she had seen. In the Ute camp, when "Old Kit" appeared, the faces of the Indians "brightened into smiles, as they held out their hands." Carson shook hands with one old woman who, he told Mrs. Alexander, had accompanied fifty Ute scouts on his Navajo campaign. For twenty dollars and two red blankets the visitor obtained from Shavano a shield and headgear of white buckskin, highly ornamented with eagle feathers and scarlet cloth, that Carson told her were worth a good horse.

On October 22, Mrs. Alexander wrote, "General Carson left today for Maxwell's ranche with Keneatzie and his band, which have been ordered to go back there. He took his family down to Taos for the winter and has turned the house over to us." The Alexanders themselves left Fort Garland October 31 for a new assignment.

Alexander had been required to write a report of his movements and actions since the evening of October 2.[34] With this in hand, Carson, Maxwell, Ka-ni-ache, Ancotash, and Agent Henderson held council at Taos and agreed that the clash on the Purgatoire resulted from Colonel Alexander's impetuous charge, not from any aggressive action of the Mohuaches. Carson watched with regret as the band returned across the mountains to Cimarron to receive their annuities.[35] Agent Henderson rode with them and reported that they were happy with their goods, contented as they had not been for the past seven years.[36]

A period of peace followed at Fort Garland. The fort had been strengthened and was well armed and fully provisioned, and the Utes were convinced that Carson was their friend. Dr. Gwyther recalled that

it was a study to see him sitting, surrounded by them, talking as

*kindly and familiarly as to his own children . . . laughing, joking,
talking Spanish or the Ute tongue, with such abundant gesticula-
tions and hand-movements, that it seemed to me he talked more
with his hands and shoulders than with his tongue. I remember
more than one imminent peril averted . . . solely by Carson's
influence.*[37]

Keeping or restoring the peace during 1866 and 1867 was as
great an achievement for the ailing Carson as any of his campaigns
had been. A man less sensitive to danger, less alert, less well prepared, less courageous could not have done it. Carson probably
could not have done it without the help of Ouray, who not only
had visited the great cities in the east but also was aware of Carson's intensive preparations for whatever the Indians might do and
of his basic good will and desire to help them. Ouray also remembered the terrible days of 1854 and 1855, when the Apaches and
the Mohuaches had seen what punishment the bluecoats could
administer if they had to.

Chapter 21

Adios

Carson probably made up his mind to resign from the army during the winter of 1866–67. His command of Fort Garland made it possible for him to be with Josefa and the children only part of the year, for if the children were to get any schooling, they had to go back to Taos in the winter. The journey in October 1866 was not easy for Josefa, to whom another daughter, Estefana, was born December 23.

Carson was back at Fort Garland in January.[1] February 15 he wrote Carleton a long letter, still trying to obtain the best available conditions for the Indians. The Tabeguaches were still dissatisfied with the amended treaty, which arbitrarily included the Mohuaches, though no Mohuaches had signed it and Ka-ni-ache had so far repudiated it as to ignore a directive of the secretary of the interior of January 1864, assigning the Mohuaches to the Colorado agency.[2] Carson disapproved of the return of Ka-ni-ache's band to the Cimarron, but he declared that they would never peaceably share a reservation with the Tabeguaches because the chiefs and warriors of each tribe were jealous of the sagacity and prowess of their counterparts in the other tribe. The Mohuaches should have a separate treaty and a reservation of their own. If the Jicarillas were to be moved, they should go with the Tabeguaches, not the southern Apaches, who would only incite them to war.

Even though Carson had offered the paymaster every facility and assistance and had kept Sangre de Cristo Pass open during the winter, the men at Fort Garland had still not been paid since April 1866. On March 2 Carson wrote to Fort Leavenworth to complain about this neglect.

Carleton's transfer and the lessening of tension at the fort may have spurred Carson to tender his resignation in July 1867, but he gave ill health as the reason. Several other motives helped him to the decision. Josefa believed that she had some interest in a Spanish land grant through her Vigil connections, and Carson probably hoped to obtain enough land for a ranch near the mouth of the Purgatoire.[3] Tom Boggs was establishing a settlement there adjoining the ranch of William Bent, who was helping his old friend in seeking the superintendency of Indian Affairs of Colorado Territory. He may have had encouraging indications that Kit would be appointed.[4]

Carson was gravely ill. Riding horseback had become so painful that he was now doing most of his traveling by army ambulance, but his journeys in the line of duty were not finished. In August he was summoned by Brevet Major General Getty, Carleton's replacement, to report to Santa Fe. Congress had provided for the use of three companies of Ute and Apache scouts. Carson was ordered to Maxwell's Ranch to raise and organize this force, then to return to and resume command of Fort Garland.[5]

Pfeiffer had received appointment as a brevet lieutenant colonel of volunteers. Still waiting for a replacement, Carson wrote to him from Fort Garland on October 10, 1867, regretting that their professional association was ending.[6] By the first of November his replacement, Major H. B. Fleming, had arrived. After turning over the command of the post, Kit took Josefa, baby Stella, and little Rebecca in an army ambulance and, with the older children trotting alongside on their ponies, started for Taos. At Santa Fe on November 22, he was mustered out of the New Mexico Volunteers.[7]

During 1867 Kit testified for the Bent heirs in a suit against Maxwell for a share of the Maxwell estate. Maxwell lost, bought out the Bents' claim, and continued his friendship with Kit, including handling Kit's savings and his cattle. Carson had never been a businessman, nor had he been interested in acquiring wealth. He had let two great surges of gold fever boil around him without showing any interest. He had helped Ignacia Bent, had reared her daughter Teresina, had educated Nicanor Jaramillo, Josefa's brother's son, and had paid debts run up by his half brother, Moses. Various Indian children had grown up in his household. As long as he could work, he had a competence, but with his army pay ending and his health rapidly getting worse, the future looked bleak. Photographs of the time show a man weary beyond enduring, but he did not give up, and for the most part he remained cheerful. An officer, just meeting him, exclaimed, "So this is the great Kit Carson, who has made so many Indians run!" to which Carson replied, "Yes, sometimes I ran after them, but most times they war runnin' after *me*."[8]

Boggsville, the settlement on the Purgatoire, was established in 1867. In June of the same year Fort Lyon, replacing an older fort at Big Timbers, was established two or three miles below the mouth of the Purgatoire. H. R. Tilton, assistant surgeon for the fort, met Carson at the home of a mutual friend in the fall of 1867.[9] Hearing that Tilton was a successful amateur trapper, Carson greeted him warmly, declaring that the happiest days of his life had been spent in trapping, and offering the doctor the advice of an expert.

In January 1868, Carson's pressing need of income was alleviated when he was appointed superintendent of Indian Affairs of Colorado Territory. Some time during that spring he moved his family, with Pfeiffer's help, to Boggsville. They occupied three rooms in a six-room adobe house Tom Boggs had put up. John S. Hough, storekeeper for the little village, lived in the other end of the house with his family. Too ill to work, Carson spent most of the brief time that he lived there with Hough at the store. Dr. Tilton, who visited him often, diagnosed the illness as an aneurism of the aorta, so large that "the tumor pressing on the pneumo-gastric nerves and trachea, caused frequent spasms of the bronchial tubes which were exceedingly distressing."[10] The doctor could do little for him except to give him something to ease the pain, but both men enjoyed these visits.

In February he was requested to come to Washington with the

Ute chiefs to make a treaty with the commissioner of Indian Affairs. He hesitated about attempting the journey. He was so ill that he was not sure he would be able to hold up, and Josefa was soon to be confined with their seventh child. However, having been placed in a position of responsibility for the Indians, he felt an obligation to do his best. There was also the possibility that medical men in the East might be able to help him.

Travel had changed radically since his first journey to Washington twenty years before. From Fort Lyon he took the stage coach to Fort Hays, then the railway to St. Louis. There he was joined by Albert Gallatin Boone, grandson of Daniel and former trapper and Indian agent, for the trip to Washington. The other members of the delegation were bringing the Ute chiefs.

The treaty, completed in early March, restricted the Utes to 24,000 square miles on the Western Slope of Colorado and guaranteed that "no persons except those herein authorized to do so, and except . . . in discharge of duties enjoined by law, shall ever be permitted to pass over, settle upon, or reside in the territory."[11] If the game was not disturbed by outsiders, the area was large enough for the Utes to continue to live, as they had always done, by hunting.

Carson, obviously very ill, was now concerned only with getting home to Josefa. The crowds wearied him more than ever. Submitting to portraits in his weakened condition was very distressing. After having been photographed with General Carleton and other officers, he was asked to pose with the commission and the Indians. Some of these took offense when he replied, "Oh, I guess I won't be in it, this time," and strolled away. They felt that he was feeling self-important, when he was probably suffering severe pain from his illness. He had been closely associated with too many prominent men without becoming spoiled for his head to be turned by a simple thing like having his picture made with Carleton. The next morning he pleased the others by suggesting, "Boys, let's us four go out and have those pictures," but a residue of resentment remained.[12]

In the capital Carson also saw Frémont, who wrote to Jessie about him, "looking so ill and suffering he made him promise to see some good physician in New York, and . . . tried to make him promise also to go to me and let me take care of him at our country house on the Hudson."[13]

Carson had been delegated to take the chiefs on a tour of the great northern cities. Knowing how important it was to impress them with the size of the country as well as the multitudes of inhabitants, he agreed to go. A small hope remained, too, that the doctors of the great cities might have discovered some cure unknown to those in the capital.

After receiving her husband's letter, Jessie went at once to New York, determined to see Carson and to help him if she could. She sent her son to his room at the Metropolitan Hotel to tell him that she was coming to visit him. Carson was lying down, several Indians in the room with him. Unwilling to have Jessie come to his hotel room, he arranged to visit her at a friend's house on Madison Square. He had gone to see Dr. Sayre, he told her, who had informed him that he might die at any moment. After leaving the doctor, he had had a strange experience at the hotel, where he had lain down to rest.

Suddenly the bed seemed to rise with me—I felt my head swell and my breath leaving me. Then, I woke up at the window. It was open and my face and head all wet. I was on the floor and the chief was holding my head on his arm and putting water on me. He was crying. He said, "I thought you were dead. You called your Lord Jesus, then you shut your eyes and couldn't speak."

I did not know that I spoke . . . I do not know that I called on the Lord Jesus, but I might—it's only Him that can help me where I stand now.

I must take the chiefs to Boston. They depend on me. I told them I would. Then we go home, straight. My wife must see me. If I was to write about this, or died out here, it would kill her. I must get home, and I think I can do it.[14]

Captain Pettis almost saw his old colonel in the East, as Carson visited Philadelphia on his way to New York, but when Pettis stopped in New York, Carson had already left for Boston.[15]

The doctors in the big cities of the North could give him little hope. In Boston he sat for one last photograph. With his Ute friends he caught the train at Boston and returned by way of Chicago and Council Bluffs to Cheyenne. There he caught the stage, which stopped overnight at Nemaqua. Mariano Medina, Mexican trapper and Taos native, later related with pride that he had put the general up for the night.[16]

The stage brought Kit and the Ute chiefs to Denver about the end of March. Completely exhausted, he stayed at the Planter's House in Denver for several days. His chest and neck pained him. His legs ached, and he remembered that some veins had been enlarged many years before in a foot race to escape the Blackfeet. In the East he had caught a severe cold, adding to his misery. His Denver friends visited him at the hotel and did what they could for him. When he was ready to leave, D. C. Oakes, Ute agent who had returned to Denver before him, brought his team and carriage to the hotel and took him the rest of the way to LaJunta.[17] On April 11, Josefa met him there with a horse-drawn carriage.

Josefita was born two days later. In two weeks Josefa was dead.[18] This blow was almost more than Carson could bear. In the little community the people "were pretty close together," and there was no lack of someone to care for the children.[19] But Carson knew he had not long to live, and he needed to see Josefa's family. He aroused himself sufficiently on May 5 to send a remarkably cheerful and optimistic letter to Aloys Scheurich in Taos, giving his plans and asking that Ignacia Bent come to Boggsville. "Please tell the old lady there is nobody in the world who can take care of my children but her and she must know it would be the greatest of favors to me if she would come and stay until I am healthier and may make such arrangements as would suit her."[20] He sent the letter express, and eight days after its receipt Ignacia and Scheurichs were on their way to Boggsville.

On May 14 Dr. Tilton had Kit moved to Fort Lyon. With the snow melting, the water was rising. Crossing the river to the fort would become increasingly difficult, and Dr. Tilton wanted his patient where he could be treated often and quickly. Kit rested best on a buffalo robe and a blanket on the floor of the doctor's quarters, his head and shoulders propped up to aid his breathing. The day after his arrival, he made his will, appointing Tom Boggs administrator, the money realized from his estate to be used for the benefit of his children.[21] As soon as Scheurich arrived, he and

Tom Boggs went down to the fort. Carson wanted Scheurich, his children's godfather, to stay with him. He felt too weak to see Teresina and Ignacia, but he again sent word for them to take care of his children.

In the intervals between bouts of pain, he would talk about his life as a trapper. Or the doctor would read to him from Peters's book, and Kit would comment from time to time on the incidents related there. The doctor wrote later,

It was wonderful to read of the stirring scenes, thrilling deeds, and narrow escapes, and then look at the quiet, modest, retiring, but dignified little man who had done so much. . . . a true man in all that constitutes manhood—pure—honorable—truthful—sincere, of noble impulses, a true knighterrant ever ready to defend the weak . . . without reward other than his own conscience. Carson had great contempt for noisy braggarts and shams of every sort.

His disease progressed rapidly and he calmly contemplated his approaching death. Several times he repeated the remark, "If it was not for this," pointing to his chest, "I might live to be a hundred years old."

When Dr. Tilton explained that he might die from suffocation or a hemorrhage when the aneurism burst, he preferred the latter.

His attacks of dyspnoea were horrible. . . . I was compelled to give him chloroform to relieve him . . . he begged me not to let him suffer such tortures, insisting that death would be better by chloroform while attempting relief . . . than death by suffocation.

The night preceding death he spent more comfortably than he had for days before. . . . He coughed up a slight amount of blood during the night, and a very little in the forenoon.

He had been told that a grave symptom would be blood in the sputum, indicating that the aneurism was breaking through into the trachea.

In the afternoon, while I was lying down on his bed and he was listening to Mr. Sherrick [Aloys Scheurich], he suddenly called out, "Doctor, Compadre, Adios."

I sprang to him and seeing a gush of blood pouring from his

mouth, remarked, "This is the last of the general." I supported his
forehead on my hand, while death speedily closed the scene.[22]

At 4:25 p.m., the flag at Fort Lyon was lowered to half mast.
General Penrose, commander of the fort, quickly arranged a military funeral, ordering all men not on guard duty to form part of the
procession. On May 24, while the guns of the fort boomed at intervals of a minute and a slow march was played by three fifers and
three drummers, the cortege of visiting relatives, friends, army officers, and troops moved one mile west and across the Arkansas
toward Boggsville. There they halted. Three volleys were fired by
the cavalry and the infantry, taps was sounded, and the chaplain,
Rev. Gamaliel Collins, conducted the funeral service, accompanied by the continued booming of the cannon. The procession
then moved on to Boggsville, where Kit was buried beside Josefa
on high ground above the river. The rough board casket was lined
with material from the wedding gown of Mrs. Casey, wife of a
captain at the fort, and other women gave the flowers from their
bonnets to hide the bare wood of the coffin.[23]

In accordance with wishes expressed in a letter of May 5, 1866,
to Scheurich, both Kit and Josefa were disinterred in 1869 and
taken to Taos, where they were buried in the cemetery with the
rites of the Catholic Church.[24] Since 1854 Carson had been a
member of the Montezuma Lodge, AF and AM, of Santa Fe, to
which he presented his Hawken rifle. He had also belonged to the
lodge at Taos when it was established.[25] In 1908 the Masons of
Taos erected a simple headstone at his grave, and Kit, Jr., and
Charles provided a similar stone for Josefa. His home in Taos is
maintained as a museum by the Kit Carson Foundation.

Other localities with which his name is associated cherish me-
morials to Carson. In the plaza at Santa Fe stands a monument
erected by the New Mexico Grand Army. Atop the Mac Monnies
Pioneer Monument in Denver is a statue of Kit sitting a spirited
horse that prances against the sky. The Lukeman–Roth equestrian
statue stands in Kit Carson Park in Trinidad. A national forest in
New Mexico bears his name, as well as a county in Colorado, the
capital city of Nevada, and a river in that state. Fort Carson, the
large army training post near Colorado Springs, was named for

him during World War II, by popular vote of the men who trained there at the time. More familiar than any of these honors is the most important monument of all: the instant recognition with which every American reacts to the sound of his name.

Afterword

The term *frontiersman* is perhaps the most adequate descriptive word that can be applied to Kit Carson. Each of his successive careers—beaver trapper and mountain man, scout and guide for government expeditions, Indian agent, and army officer—was built to a considerable extent upon the careers that preceded it, and all were on the advancing edge of the American frontier. Beginning as an illiterate runaway, he ended as a brigadier general and achieved the status of national hero in the process. An analysis of his various careers shows how this was accomplished.

First of all, as a mountain man, contrary to popular belief, he was never a leader. Most of the leaders were good traders, but Kit was not much interested in, or very good at, that aspect of the fur business. To him trapping was a free and adventurous life, hard but enjoyable, and he looked back on it with nostalgia to the end of his days. In pursuing it, he became more knowledgeable about Indians, both peaceable and hostile, than most ordinary trappers. He was already a widely traveled veteran trapper before he came to the rendezvous country but, although he mastered the craft, the Fort Hall account books reveal that many trappers were more successful than he.

Kit was a fairly typical mountain man, although with a somewhat higher standard of conduct than many of the rank and file of which he was a member. He was content with his comfortable Indian marriage. Unlike his best friend, Dick Owens, he did not leave his children among the Indians when he left the mountains. Also, unlike Owens, he did not allow the hard times to force him into stealing horses from Indians and Mexicans. It is to be noted, however, that this difference did not break up their friendship. Kit was a tolerant, not a self-righteous man.

He was quiet and soft spoken, sociable and friendly with his fellow trappers. He was more independent than most of them, judging by the frequency with which he changed from one company to another. He disliked bullies and braggarts and was quick to let them know it. He was strong in his belief that he could trap wherever he pleased and was always ready to fight any who sought to prevent it. As a fighter he was fearless, but he was not reckless except in exposing himself to danger in order to help a comrade in need. He took it for granted that others would do the same for him.

His attitude toward Indians was typical of that of most of the mountain men and typical of that of the Indians toward each other. He resented their stealing of horses and furs and trade goods, and he was quick to retaliate by fighting to recover stolen property, just as they were themselves. But he never retaliated knowingly against the wrong party, as they often did. With peaceable Indians he associated on friendly terms, and his memoirs contain no expressions of prejudice against Indians as a race. His attitude toward the environment was also typical of trappers in general and similar to that of the Indians. He hunted for food but did not slaughter needlessly. He trapped for beaver and other furbearing animals to make a living and to buy his necessities. He gave little thought to the possibility of overtrapping any more than an individual farmer of those days gave thought to the possibility of overproduction.

When he could no longer make a living, he left the mountains, but he did so reluctantly and was among the last to leave. Carson acquired competence and confidence as a mountain man, but he did not acquire fame because he was not a leader. After he gained fame as a guide for Frémont, writers began to invent the fiction that Carson had had his own band of men, but these stories were all manufactured out of the whole cloth and have been thoroughly discredited.

Although Carson, by his own account, met Frémont accidentally, one cannot help wondering whether he did not, in fact, take passage on the river boat where they met because he had heard that Frémont was looking for a guide. At any rate, he put his best foot forward and convinced the young explorer that he would do the job as well as Captain Andrew Drips. He did it better than Drips would have done because Drips was a man of fifty-two and Carson was a man of thirty-two. Unlike Carson, Frémont never got along well with men of authority. It was a lucky thing for both Carson and Frémont that Carson was hired, and for Carson it was the great turning point in his life.

As a guide, scout, and hunter for Frémont's first three expeditions, Carson came to public attention through Frémont's reports, which were reprinted for years and widely read. Although Frémont did not write extensively about Carson, whenever he mentioned him, it was with obvious satisfaction and sometimes with lavish praise. Carson deserved all the credit that Frémont accorded him; he always worked harder for someone else than for himself. Throughout their association, he was always among those who volunteered for special assignments and he performed them so well that Frémont soon was dependent on him for anything "over and above the call of duty."

The imagination of the public of his time was also fired by Carson's encounters with hostile Indians and by his activities in the conquest of California during the Mexican War. Kit's chief rivals for fame were men of his own type who also worked for Frémont, notably Kit's good friends Lucien Maxwell and Dick Owens and his younger rival, Alexis Godey. Both Owens and Godey came to occupy a place in Frémont's esteem equal to that of Carson. Carson's advantage was only that he was first to reach this position. It may be worth noting that both Owens and Godey were selected to testify at Frémont's court-martial trial, whereas Carson was not. Perhaps Frémont judged Carson to be too forthright and partisan to make a good witness. As it turned out, Owens and Godey were not called to testify, nor would it have made any difference to the outcome had they been called.

Other mountain men whose fame rivals Carson's also became successful guides and scouts. Both Thomas Fitzpatrick and Joseph R. Walker were employed by Frémont himself, but they never received the praise he gave to Carson. John L. Hatcher worked for James W. Abert about the same time, but Abert did not range very far. Later, Jim Bridger served as guide for Grenville Dodge and others and added to his fame thereby, but Bridger was in his sixties and did not exert himself unduly.

Carson, of course, learned much from Frémont, but there is no denying that he was of tremendous value to the success of Frémont's explorations. Reporters were quick to recognize this and sought Carson out for interviews in which they succeeded in getting at least a summary account of his trapping period. The fact that Kit was left in California when Kearny and Frémont returned to Washington was another stroke of luck, for when he left with dispatches on his second transcontinental journey, he had Lieutenant George Brewerton along. Brewerton's account of their journey as far as New Mexico greatly enhanced Carson's fame. It gives eloquent evidence that although Carson never led a band of his own as a mountain man, he was perfectly capable of doing so and, on this trip, had ample opportunity to demonstrate all the skills he had learned in his earlier days in crossing deserts and swollen streams, and in dealing with threatening Indians.

Carson was involved in two controversial matters while with Frémont in California. The first was a preventive attack on an Indian village at the request of settlers near Lassen's ranch, who claimed the Indians were massing for an attack on them. Carson called the destruction of the village "a perfect butchery," but he apparently thought the large number of Indians was proof of the truth of the settlers' claim and expressed satisfaction that the Indians would not be able to attack the settlers for a long time. Even if this were true, it hardly justifies the "butchery" by present-day standards, but it was permitted by Frémont, joined in by nearly all of his men, and was not condemned by the standards of the time. Carson had no personal grievance against these Indians and allowed himself to be used by those who believed they had.

The second matter involved Carson's ordering the death of three captive Mexicans at Sonoma. Carson, we may judge, was not proud of this incident, for he did not mention it in his memoirs, though he did mention the death that preceded it of two American captives at the hands of some Mexicans. American friends of Carson in California questioned him about this later, and he explained that he checked with Frémont and followed his express order. Since Frémont placed the blame on his Delaware Indians in his memoirs and no one else mentions them in connection with it, Carson's explanation seems acceptable, and the blame is Frémont's, not Carson's.

At the beginning of Carson's third career—as Indian agent for the Plains Utes and the Jicarilla Apaches—these Indians were hostile, and for a while he served much of the time as a scout for various army detachments that were sent against them to end their depredations. Thus, Kit was able to continue his work as a scout, distinguish himself as a tracker, and employ his skills in getting the troops over rivers and mountains unfamiliar to them. When the Indians were finally pacified, his work involved supplying them with supplementary food, making annuity payments, and settling complaints and disputes that called for compensation either for whites or for Indians. It also brought him into close contact with both military and civil officers in the territory of New Mexico. The territorial governor was also the commissioner for Indian Affairs. Of Kit's clash with Governor David Meriwether we have only Meriwether's side of the story, written when he was eighty-six, forty years after the event. Lacking Carson's side of the story, we may still say that, although Kit may have been guilty of insubordination, he was certainly not guilty of cowardice as Meriwether charged.

As Indian agent, Kit had to keep accounts and make written reports and read instructions in order to comply with governmental policy. Since he was illiterate, this was difficult because the government provided no salary for a clerk. It did, however, provide funds for an interpreter, which most agents needed but Carson did not need. So he was able to hire a series of interpreters, who read and wrote for him and kept his accounts. He did learn to sign his name instead of making his mark as he had done heretofore. His signature always appears as C. Carson.

One of his clerks was John Mostin, who in 1856 wrote out Carson's memoirs for him at his dictation. These memoirs served as the basis for Dr. DeWitt Peters's biography of Carson. The original manuscript came to light in 1905 and was eventually acquired by the Newberry Library in Chicago. The identity of Mostin as the writer was not established until 1968.

This manuscript has proved to be an important historical document, in spite of some confusion in the chronology, especially between the years 1835 to 1841. In general, it is a clear, concise account, remarkably accurate in most respects because Carson seeks to tell a straightforward story and is not inclined to embroider his facts to make himself more important. Its accuracy is ascertained wherever it can be checked and compared with other accounts, and we may assume that portions that cannot be checked are also reasonably truthful and correct. This is important with reference to his service with Ewing Young, for Kit's account of Young's expedition to California and back is virtually the only knowledge we have concerning it. Since he was a participant in many important historical events, it is not too much to say that his memoirs make a valuable contribution to our knowledge of these events.

As an Indian agent, Carson ranks above the average because of his knowledge of the Indians' languages and customs, knowledge most agents lacked. He was also honest, whereas many agents were not. Some of them cheated both the government and the Indians. As agent, Carson developed a sympathy for the Indians which he had not felt earlier. Specifically, he recommended that the control of Indians be vested in the war department and that the dual civil and military control policy of the government be ended; that when placed on reservations, the commanding officer of the fort be made the Indian agent; that tribes of dissimilar cultures not be placed on the same reservation; and that sale of liquor to Indians be prohibited. He stated in 1865, "The rule for the government of Indians should be strong enough to inspire their respect and fear, yet protecting them from both internal dissension and external aggression." An Indian agent of the 1920s, Leo Crane, was so struck with this that he wrote, "Carson was right," and went on to observe that the Indian Service "has seldom been firm, it has been most confused and unjust; it has rarely been consistent; and it is always changing."

As agent, Carson had the respect of the Indians. He had it in part because they were aware of his reputation as an Indian fighter. More important was the fact that he understood and was willing to accept their principle of compensation for wrongs. When he would not accept their demands for compensation for white outrages, he would state a figure and they would bargain. They always went away satisfied that they had got as much as they could. This was the way they were accustomed to settling such matters among themselves.

❧ At the outbreak of the American Civil War, Carson resigned his agency and was chosen as Lieutenant Colonel of the First New Mexico Volunteers, serving under Ceran St. Vrain as colonel, for whom Carson had the greatest admiration and respect. St. Vrain soon found his health was not adequate for military service and Kit became colonel of the regiment, which was largely composed of Mexican–Americans. Under Carson, the regiment performed well at the battle of Valverde. When Carson was brevetted brigadier general of volunteers near the end of the war, his performance at Valverde was cited as the reason for his promotion. It is important to recognize that Kit made it, not on his reputation as an Indian fighter, but as the elected colonel of a volunteer regiment in a battle against Confederate troops. His soldiers were his wife's people and they were immensely proud of their general.

Nevertheless, it was as an Indian fighter that Carson was employed for the rest of the Civil War. His conduct of the Navajo campaign has made him the target of much unfair criticism, which appears to have grown rather than diminished in recent years. The source of this has been the undying hatred of the Navajo tribe, and their device has been to blame everything on Carson, just as Jefferson blamed everything on King George III in the American Revolution. It is not to be expected that Kit Carson will ever become popular on the Navajo Reservation any more than General W. T. Sherman will ever become popular in the state of Georgia. The reasons are the same in both cases. Both men waged a war of attrition that affected the civilian population as well as the military resistance. It is quite understandable that the Navajos should resent and condemn the destruction of their food supply and their forced removal from their homeland. This does not give them the right, however, to distort history by attributing policies and actions to Carson which were not his at all.

Any fair historical analysis must point out that: (1) both the removal policy and the "scorched earth" policy were ordered by Gen. James H. Carleton, not by Kit Carson; (2) the latter policy was made necessary by the fact the the Navajos had no central tribal authority and no organized, unified military resistance such as other tribes had; (3) the very fact that the Navajo name for Carson was "The Rope Thrower" indicates that he waged the war by taking captives, not by killing; (4) Carson repeatedly reported that the subsistence ration for captives was not adequate and urged that it be doubled at least; (5) Carson was not in charge of "the Long Walk" on which there were more deaths than in the whole military campaign that he waged; (6) Carson would not remain in charge at the Bosque Redondo Reservation and tendered his resignation rather than do so; (7) Carson had and felt a duty to the people of New Mexico to put an end to constant raids of the Navajos so costly in lives and property; (8) while the Navajos will never accept these facts, for obvious reasons of tribal pride, there is no reason why other people should not accept them.

As to the personal relations of General Carleton and Kit Carson, there can be no doubt that Carson recognized and was grateful for Carleton's efforts to teach him to be an efficient and capable military officer but that his natural independence and his previous experience caused him to chafe under the discipline. It is to his credit that he stuck with it. His conduct of the campaign against the Kiowas and Comanches demonstrated how well he learned his responsibilities. Carleton recognized his performance as one of great merit, but public opinion has been slow to recognize it.

As for his command at Fort Garland, it may be well to note that Carson practically put into effect his belief that the commanding officer of a fort in Indian country should also act as Indian agent. His declining health, however, forced him to a decision to end his army career, although financial considerations also provided an added reason.

Carson's inability to read or write continued to be a problem to him as an army officer. Those under him were able to take advantage of it in ways that were sometimes embarrassing, although many of his officers, especially those of his old regiment, were very helpful to him because of the pride they took in "their general." General Sherman stated that Josefa Carson signed her husband's name to reports for him and, since Sherman visited Fort Garland, he may actually have observed her doing so. She had not been with Kit on his active campaigns, however, so it is clear that he had learned to sign his name. Sherman's statement indicates that he found even writing his name a slow process and that he certainly never advanced far beyond making his signature.

Of all the mountain men, Carson was the first to achieve national acclaim. Latter-day historians have put forward the names of Jedediah Smith, Jim Bridger, and Thomas Fitzpatrick as Carson's rivals for the title of *primus inter pares*. Smith's career was a brilliant one, unfortunately cut short by his early death. He combined a successful business career with one of geographical exploration. In the latter field, he has an astonishing list of firsts to his credit. His meteoric rise was ended by death at the hands of Indians. He had previously lost large numbers of men to surprise attacks by Indians. His geographical discoveries entitle him to more historical importance as a mountain man than any other. His losses of men and of his own life raise some doubts about how well he mastered the art of survival in an environment fraught with danger. Carson's and Smith's paths never crossed. Kit's early visit to California came only shortly after Smith's, and his later service with Frémont took him over ground previously traversed by Smith. His exploratory travels were important but not so important or so spectacular as those of Smith. Kit was not a leader as Smith was, but he suffered no massacres and he survived as many dangers.

Jim Bridger was the antithesis of Smith in most respects. He rose from the ranks to be a leader among the mountain men, whereas Smith led from the outset. Bridger did this although more illiterate than Carson, since he could not sign his name. He fought the Blackfeet and was wounded, as was Carson. He married among the Indians, as did Carson, and he also took care of his children. He traveled less widely than Carson or Smith. He made less money than Smith, but he was shrewd enough as a trader to survive in the mountains for years after Carson had left. Like Carson, he had a later career as scout and guide, but it was confined to territory he already knew well. He did not have Carson's sense of duty. Early in his career he abandoned Hugh Glass, and all his life he loved to show up the ignorance of greenhorns. His career was one of adaptation to his environment and he survived longest in the mountains of any one.

Thomas Fitzpatrick was in partnership with Bridger and others in the Rocky Mountain Fur Company. He was nearly as ambitious as Smith and as shrewd as Bridger. He was unscrupulous in spreading the rumor of the bankruptcy of his rivals, Gantt and Blackwell. His path crossed Carson's several times. Carson was his employee for a short time but left him for Gantt, giving no reasons for his change. On the other hand, Carson served contentedly under Bridger on more than one occasion. Fitzpatrick survived a solitary escape from Indians and he adopted an Indian boy he called Friday and raised him among the whites. Like Carson, Fitzpatrick was employed by Frémont and acted as a sort of trusted camp manager, but Frémont did not praise him as he did Carson. Fitzpatrick also guided for General Kearny, but Kearny forced him to take over Carson's dispatches and forced Carson to guide him to California. Fitzpatrick was a distinguished Indian agent, noted for the Treaty of Fort Laramie. He married late in life and died of pneumonia in Washington, D.C.

Carson, with four careers, outlasted Fitzpatrick with three. Bridger had two, plus a few years of retirement. Smith had one brilliant career. Admirers of the mountain men are divided about the relative merits of these four. Only Carson, however, covered the entire scope of the expansion of the United States in the period up to 1865 and actively participated in every phase and aspect of it. Without settling the question of the premier mountain man, Carson unquestionably stands as the personification of the great westward surge known as Manifest Destiny, so ardently supported by a majority of the people of the time.

The best comparison with Kit Carson is Daniel Boone, who epitomizes the frontier expansion from the Appalachians to the prairies as Carson epitomizes the frontier expansion from the Great Plains to the Pacific Ocean. Both became legendary heroes, but in both the legend was solidly based upon fact. Their adventures have an epic quality like those of the Homeric heroes of the ancient Greeks. Both men were simple, modest, and genuine and remained unspoiled by the wide publicity and tremendous acclaim accorded them. Their reputations were not sought but were conferred upon them because they always did their best for the common or general good. They accepted the image the public created of them and tried to live up to it.

Boone's successor as an idol of the public was Davy Crockett; Carson's successor was "Buffalo Bill" Cody. No greater contrast could be found than that existing between Boone and Carson, on the one hand, and Crockett and Cody, on the other. The latter pair were simply two showmen, who cleverly sensed the appetite of the public for sensationalism and gave it what it craved. The small basis of real achievement possessed by Crockett was packaged in humorous exaggerated boastfulness by Crockett himself and it got him elected to Congress. The even smaller and less admirable accomplishments of Cody were presented to the public with the gaudy, meretricious allurements of his Wild West show with such success that the last frontier was prolonged in the public mind long after it was gone. Crockett and Cody were self-promoters, skilled at attracting attention and increasing their own popularity. They were the precursors of modern advertising.

Americans do well to remember Kit Carson as one of their heroes, for Fortune has seldom smiled upon a more deserving character. Given the increasingly complex society in which we live and the confused values of modern life, perhaps she never will do so again. When Kit died in 1868, soon after eating a buffalo steak cooked for him at his request by his friend Aloys Scheurich, he died at precisely the right time. The wanton slaughter of the buffalo began in the fall of that year and the completion of the transcontinental railroad the following year cut the great herd of buffalo into two distinct halves. It was the end of an era in the West. Carson's passing symbolized the changing of the old order of things of which he had been and would remain the truest representative.

Notes

Chapter 1

1. Harvey Lewis Carter, *'Dear Old Kit': The Historical Christopher Carson with a New Edition of the Carson Memoirs* (Norman: University of Oklahoma Press, 1968), 38; identified hereafter as Carson, *Memoirs*, when references are to pp. 37–150, and as Carter, *'Dear Old Kit'*, when references are to pp. 3–36, 151–238.

2. M. Morgan Estergreen, *Kit Carson: A Portrait in Courage* (Norman: University of Oklahoma Press, 1962), 5. Reference to William Carson was found in records of Cumberland County, formerly a part of Lancaster County, Pennsylvania.

3. Lawrence Elliott, *The Long Hunter: A New Life of Daniel Boone* (New York: Reader's Digest Press, 1976), 6, 7; Edwin Legrand Sabin, *Kit Carson Days (1809–1868)*, 2 vols. rev. ed. (New York: Press of the Pioneers, 1935), 1. Sabin's 1914 version, in one volume, was originally published by A. C. McClurg & Co. of Chicago. On December 1, 1761, William Carson acquired 692 acres on Third Creek, Loray District, Iredell County, North Carolina, from the grant of Lord Granville.

4. Scroggs family record on file at Kit Carson Home, Taos, New Mexico; Estergreen, *Kit Carson*, 9.

5. Estergreen, *Kit Carson*, 9, 11.

6. Now West Virginia.

7. Carson, *Memoirs*, 38; Bernice Blackwelder, *Great Westerner: The Story of Kit Carson* (Caldwell, Id.: Caxton Printers, 1962), 14.

8. Estergreen, *Kit Carson*, 14, 16. Both Blackwelder and Estergreen obtained information related many years after the event by members of the Carson family. Estergreen also used notes and memorabilia collected by Blanche Chloe Grant, containing direct quotations from Kit Carson's son Charles;

from Teresina Bent Scheurich; and from Rumalda Luna Boggs. The Grant papers are not at present available.

9. John Bakeless, *Daniel Boone, Master of the Wilderness* (New York: William Morrow, 1939), 340–82.
10. Lyn McDaniel, comp. and ed., *Bicentennial Boonslick History*, (Boonville, Mo.: Boonslick Historical Society, 1976), 47.
11. Ibid., 20. The Coopers came from Madison County, Kentucky, in 1807 and settled near Daniel Boone. Kit's sister Elizabeth married Robert Cooper.
12. Ibid., 14, 15.
13. Estergreen, *Kit Carson*, 20: "Lindsey owned a large-bore rifle. Most of its stock had been shot away, along with two of Lindsey's fingers on his left hand, in a skirmish with the Indians. Lindsey killed two, one with his rifle and the other with the Indian's own knife."
14. McDaniel, ed., *Bicentennial Boonslick History*, 9, 10.
15. Oversimplified as it is, this exposition ignores the displacement of Indian families who had settled on the land and were farming it, yet fell victim of the greed of their white neighbors, a facet of the Indian problem outside the scope of this book.
16. Estergreen, *Kit Carson*, 18, 19.
17. McDaniel, ed., *Bicentennial Boonslick History*, 24, 31.
18. William's marriage to the two Boone sisters was the only intermarriage between Lindsey's family and the Boones. Frederick Jackson Turner, *The Frontier in American History* (New York: Henry Holt & Co., 1935), p. 19, stated, "Kit Carson's mother was a Boone," citing as authority a pamphlet by a man named Hale. This is an error. Kit's mother was Rebecca Robinson.
19. Carter, *'Dear Old Kit'*, 188–90; Blackwelder, *Great Westerner*, 15.
20. During his service with Frémont, all government vouchers for his pay were signed with his mark. As an Indian agent and army officer, he learned to sign his name, always writing *C. Carson*. His inability to read embarrassed him, and he usually requested others to read to him by saying that they could do it much better than he. Many Carson biographers have been reluctant to admit Kit's illiteracy, but the evidence is indisputable. See Donald Jackson and Mary Lee Spence, eds., *The Expeditions of John Charles Frémont*, 2 vols. and supplement (Urbana: University of Illinois Press, 1970), 1:151.
21. McDaniel, ed., *Bicentennial Boonslick History*, 47.
22. D'Eglise was murdered by two Spaniards near Santa Fe. See David J. Weber, *The Taos Trappers* (Norman: University of Oklahoma Press, 1971), 38.
23. Ibid., 36–37.
24. Harvey L. Carter, *Zebulon Montgomery Pike, Pathfinder and Patriot* (Colorado Springs: Dentan Printing Co., 1956), 21, 23.
25. Weber, *The Taos Trappers*, 45–50.
26. Rex W. Strickland, "Robert McKnight," LeRoy R. Hafen, ed., *The Mountain Men and the Fur Trade of the Far West*, 10 vols. (Glendale: Arthur H.

Clark Co., 1972) 9:259–68. Guarasimas, about three hundred miles west of Chihuahua, was probably a mining town.

27. R. L. Duffus, *The Santa Fe Trail* (Albuquerque: University of New Mexico Press, 1975), 68–69.

28. John Bradbury, *Travels in the Interior of America* (1817; rev. ed., Ann Arbor: University of Michigan Microfilms, 1966), 17–21.

29. Bernard De Voto, ed., *The Journals of Lewis and Clark* (Boston: Houghton Mifflin Co., 1953), 434–39.

30. Charles L. Camp, ed., *James Clyman, Frontiersman* (Portland: Champoeg Press, 1960), 8–9; Richard M. Clokey, *William Ashley: Enterprise and Politics in the Trans-Mississippi West* (Norman: University of Oklahoma Press, 1980) is the best narrative and analysis of Ashley's enterprises.

31. Aubrey Haines, "Hugh Glass," in Hafen, ed., *Mountain Men*, 6:161–71; Warren Angus Ferris, *Life in the Rocky Mountains, 1830–1835* (Salt Lake City: Rocky Mountain Book Shop, 1940), 257–68. There is no evidence that Moses Carson told any of these stories to Kit, but the adventures of Colter and Glass were the two most frequently told tales of all and were still being told during the Mexican War. They are still appearing, sometimes as fiction, in modern magazines, but they are true.

32. LeRoy R. Hafen, "Etienne Provost," in Hafen, ed., *Mountain Men*, 6:373–375. Provost's name, spelled Provo, was left on a mountain, a city, and a river in the Wasatch Mountains.

33. Carson, *Memoirs*, 38.

34. David J. Weber, "William Workman," in Hafen, ed., *Mountain Men*, 7:381, 382.

Chapter 2

1. Carson, *Memoirs*, 38.

2. Louise Barry, *The Beginning of the West: Annals of the Kansas Gateway to the American West, 1540–1854* (Topeka: Kansas Historical Society, 1972), 135. The leader of this party could not have been Charles Bent. Having begun his career in the Missouri River trade, Bent did not take the southwestern trail before 1829.

3. Estergreen, *Kit Carson*, 23, 24.

4. Sabin, *Kit Carson Days* (1935), 1:10.

5. The *Missouri Intelligencer* was moved to Fayette that same year to escape the rampaging Missouri River. The town of Franklin had been laid out in 1816. Within ten years it became the busiest town west of St. Louis. During the floods of 1826, the river changed its course, and great slabs of land and trees crashed into the river. By 1828 little of the town was left. McDaniel, ed., *Bicentennial Boonslick History*, 22, 49–50.

6. David Workman returned to Missouri, where he reared José, William's son. Both later went to California, where David died at the La Puente ranch of William Workman in 1855. See Carter, *'Dear Old Kit,'* 39 fn.; Weber,

"William Workman," in Hafen, ed., *Mountain Men*, 7:385.

7. Among others, Lewis H. Garrard, *Wah-to-Yah and the Taos Trail* (Norman: University of Oklahoma Press, 1955); Josiah Gregg, *Commerce of the Prairies* (Lincoln: University of Nebraska Press, 1967); Duffus, *The Santa Fe Trail*.

8. Rufus B. Sage, *Letters and Scenes in the Rocky Mountains*, vol. 4 of the Far West and the Rockies Historical Series (Glendale: Arthur H. Clark Co., 1956), 160–61.

9. Gregg, *Commerce of the Prairies*, 75.

10. Ibid., 12–13.

11. Carson, *Memoirs*, 38, 42. The bracketed words were added by Carter.

12. Gregg, *Commerce of the Prairies*, 47–49.

13. In the treeless stretches of the prairie, the men scattered at camping time to gather blanket loads of dried droppings of the buffalo, or *bois de vache*, to make fires for cooking.

14. Garrard, *Wah-to-Yah*, 28–29.

15. Gregg, *Commerce of the Prairies*, 9.

16. Duffus, *The Santa Fe Trail*, 126.

17. "The Americans!"—"The Carts!"—"Another caravan!" The main caravan started from Missouri in April or May and arrived at Santa Fe in June or July. November was late for a caravan to arrive from Missouri.

Chapter 3

1. "Good day, Miss." Garrard's Spanish, apparently picked up on his journey, is often inaccurate. Spanish words that can be found in standard American-language dictionaries are not footnoted.

2. "How are you, gentlemen? Good! There will be a great fandango tonight. Many pretty girls."

3. Garrard, *Wah-to-Yah*, 166–67.

4. Janet Lecompte, "Mathew Kinkead," in Hafen, ed., *Mountain Men*, 2:189.

5. Ibid., 189–99; Weber, "William Workman," in Hafen, ed., *Mountain Men*, 7:382–83. Workman wrote to his brother David on February 13, 1826, that he had bought a large quantity of corn and wheat to make whiskey, and if David would buy him two 80-gallon stills and send them to Taos, he and Mathew Kinkead would pay half the cost, and Samuel Chambers would pay the other half.

6. Government census, 1827. Santa Cruz de la Cañada, population 6,508, was largest; Santa Fe, population 5,757, was next.

7. Lecompte, "Mathew Kinkead," in Hafen, ed., *Mountain Men*, 7:193. By 1830 Kinkead was a naturalized citizen of Mexico.

8. Weber, "William Workman," 383–84.

9. Mabel Dodge Luhan, *Winter in Taos*. (New York: Harcourt, Brace, 1935). *Sangre de Cristo* means "Blood of Christ."

10. David J. Weber, ed. and trans., *The Extranjeros: Selected Documents from*

the Mexican Side of the Santa Fe Trail, 1825–1828 (Santa Fe: Stagecoach Press, 1967), 144–45. For the Ezekiel Williams train, see Barry, *Beginning of the West,* 142.

11. Settlements along the Rio Grande north of Santa Fe were known as the Rio Arriba; those to the south, as the Rio Abajo.

12. George F. Ruxton, *Ruxton of the Rockies,* ed. LeRoy R. Hafen (Norman: University of Oklahoma Press, 1950), 174–75.

13. Ibid., 160–64.

14. Weber, *The Extranjeros,* 31. Guia (or Trade Permit) no. 50, issued December 14, 1827, for Chihuahua to Felipe Trammell.

15. Carson, *Memoirs,* 42.

16. Ruxton, *Ruxton of the Rockies,* 146–59.

17. Rex W. Strickland, "James Baird," in Hafen, ed., *Mountain Men,* 3:29; Strickland, "Robert McKnight," in Hafen, ed., *Mountain Men,* 9:259–68.

18. Carson, *Memoirs,* 42. Carson reported arriving in Taos in August 1828, but his activities since leaving for Missouri in the spring of 1828—about two months to go to the Arkansas and back to Santa Fe, three to five months in the employ of Trammell, and "a few months" at the copper mines—would extend well into 1829.

19. Harvey L. Carter, "Ewing Young," in Hafen, ed., *Mountain Men,* 2:385.

20. Robert Glass Cleland, *This Reckless Breed of Men* (New York: Alfred A. Knopf, 1950), 216.

21. Carter, "Ewing Young," in Hafen, ed., *Mountain Men,* 2:385 ff.; Kenneth L. Holmes, *Ewing Young: Master Trapper* (Portland: Binford & Mort, 1967), 21, 24; Iris Higbee Wilson, *William Wolfskill* (Glendale: Arthur H. Clark Co., 1965), 57–60. Young died in Oregon in 1841.

22. James Ohio Pattie, *Personal Narrative,* as quoted by LeRoy R. and Ann W. Hafen, in *The Old Spanish Trail* (Glendale: Arthur H. Clark Co., 1954), 123–126. Young's efforts to teach the Indians a lesson were not successful. In August 1827 the Mojaves traded with Jedediah Smith, allowed him to start rafting his supplies across the Colorado, then, as his horses swam across, fell upon his party of eighteen and killed ten of them.

23. Carter, "Ewing Young," in Hafen, ed. *Mountain Men,* 2:382–84; Cleland, *This Reckless Breed,* 212–24. The Young–Armijo controversy is narrated from the Mexican point of view in Weber, *The Taos Trappers,* 112–33.

Chapter 4

1. Saddle blankets made of dressed buffalo-calf skin. These were also used for other purposes, including making a bed. The equipment listed is what most trappers would carry. See Washington Irving, *The Adventures of Captain Bonneville* (New York: G. P. Putnam, 1861), 382; Osborne Russell, *Journal of a Trapper, 1834–1843,* ed. Aubrey L. Haines (Lincoln: University of Nebraska Press, 1965), 82.

2. Edwin Corle, *The Gila, River of the Southwest* (Lincoln: University of Ne-

braska Press, 1964), 66; Carson, *Memoirs*, 44.

3. The Verde was known in Carson's time as the San Francisco. The present San Francisco River, arising in the Mogollon Mountains of New Mexico, joins the Gila near Clifton, Arizona.

4. George Frederick Ruxton, *Life in the Far West*, ed. LeRoy R. Hafen (Norman: University of Oklahoma Press, 1951), 76.

5. Carson, *Memoirs*, 45; Cleland, *This Reckless Breed*, 229–30, quoting Sabin, *Kit Carson Days* (1914), 48.

6. Presumably Young's Spring near Truxton, Arizona. See C. L. Camp, "Kit Carson in California," *California Historical Society Quarterly* 1 (October 1922):117–18.

7. Alson J. Smith, *Men Against the Mountains: Jedediah Smith and the Great Southwest Expedition of 1826–29* (New York: John Day Co., 1965), 97.

8. At that time Padre Sanchez had the only orange orchard in California. See Hafen, *The Old Spanish Trail*, 196.

9. Harrison G. Rogers's *First Journal*, in Harrison Clifford Dale (ed.), *The Ashley-Smith Explorations and the Discovery of a Central Route to the Pacific* (Glendale: Arthur H. Clark Co., 1941), 194–221. Rogers continued his journal as Smith led his men up the Sacramento and into the Coast Range the following year. His last entry was Sunday, July 13, 1828. The next day the camp on the Umpqua River was overrun by Keliwatset and Umpqua Indians while Smith was away reconnoitering. Rogers was one of the fifteen men killed.

10. Carson, *Memoirs*, 46.

11. Peter Skene Ogden, *Journal, 1827–1828*, cited by Dale, ed., *The Ashley-Smith Explorations*, 289.

12. Ted J. Warner, "Peter Skene Ogden," in Hafen, ed., *Mountain Men*, 3:229.

13. Carson, *Memoirs*, 47.

14. Joseph J. Hill, "Ewing Young in the Fur Trade of the Southwest, 1822–1834," *Oregon Historical Society Quarterly* 24 (March 1923): 25; Smith, *Men Against the Mountains*, 171–72.

15. Carson, *Memoirs*, 47–48; Hill, "Ewing Young," 25.

16. Carson, *Memoirs*, 48 and fn.

17. Smith, *Men Against the Mountains*, 118.

18. Ships for California and Oregon usually stopped at the Hawaiian Islands for water and supplies. Natives were often hired as seamen or as laborers to work in California or Oregon. The Owyhee River and the Owyhee Mountains in Oregon and Idaho were named for these Kanakas.

19. Bars for selling pulque, a fermented drink made from the juice of the agave.

20. Smith, *Men Against the Mountains*, 118–21.

21. Carson, *Memoirs*, 48 and fn, 49.

22. Ibid., 49.

23. George Douglas Brewerton, *Overland with Kit Carson* (New York: Coward McCann, 1930), 140.

24. Carson, *Memoirs*, 49, 50.

25. Ibid., 50, 52. Carson recorded their return date as April 1830, forgetting that they had spent two winters on the expedition. Some of the trappers worked for wages, and the company got all the furs. Some got an outfit on credit and were obliged to work for the company until their debt was paid. A free trapper owned his outfit, trapped where he pleased, and sold his pelts where he pleased. Free trappers were welcomed because a brigade's assurance against Indian attack lay in its numerical strength.

Chapter 5

1. Expedition sent by John Jacob Astor in 1810 to establish a trading post at the mouth of the Columbia River.
2. Cornelius M. Ismert, "James Bridger," in Hafen, ed., *Mountain Men*, 6:87.
3. Dale, ed., *The Ashley-Smith Explorations*, 137–44. Bullboats were constructed by stretching new buffalo hides over green saplings, curved and tied into shape. Seams were patched with tallow or pitch.
4. Ibid., 242–76.
5. Frederic E. Voelker, "William Sherley (Old Bill) Williams," in Hafen, ed., *Mountain Men*, 8:365–94.
6. Ardis M. Walker, "Joseph Reddeford Walker," in Hafen, ed., *Mountain Men*, 5:361–80.
7. Zenas Leonard, *Narrative of the Adventures of Zenas Leonard* (Ann Arbor: University of Michigan Microfilms, 1966), 13.
8. Harvey L. Carter, "John Gantt," in Hafen, ed., *Mountain Men*, 5:105.
9. Harvey L. Carter, "Jedediah Smith," in Hafen, ed., *Mountain Men*, 8:347; Dale L. Morgan, *Jedediah Smith and the Opening of the West* (Indianapolis: Bobbs-Merrill, 1953), 323–30.
10. Carson, *Memoirs*, 52. A high mountain valley of moderate size was known as a hole to the trappers; an extensive one was called a park. Through Jackson's Hole runs the Snake River, which, after circling south around the Sawtooth Mountains, winds northward to meet the Columbia River as it flows south from Canada, halfway across the state of Washington.
11. Ferris, *Life*, 101. James Michener, in *Centennial* (New York: Random House, 1974), 292, wrote, "The rendezvous continued from 1825 to 1840. In 1831 it did not convene; the wagon train bringing the whiskey from Taos got lost and ended up 350 miles off course to the east, where the Laramie River enters the Platte. Name of the mixed up guide: Kit Carson." Michener is much admired for his historical fiction; unfortunately, his jibe at Carson is presented in an historical note as fact, which it definitely is not, as any reader of this chapter will realize.
12. Ferris, *Life*, 102–4.
13. Alexander Sinclair and his brother Prewitt were members of the Bean–Sinclair expedition of forty-five men that left Fort Smith on the lower Arkansas River on May 7, 1830.
14. Little Bear River is now called the Yampa River, so named by the Indians

because of a root found in plenty along its banks and much prized for food.

15. LeRoy R. Hafen, "A Brief History of the Fur Trade of the Far West," *Mountain Men*, 1:123–26.

16. *Fontaine Qui Bouille* has become Fountain Creek, which joins the Arkansas River at Pueblo, Colorado.

17. See Frances Fuller Victor, *The River of the West* (Hartford: R. W. Bliss & Co., 1870; reprint ed., Columbus, Ohio: Long's College Book Co., 1950), 83–84; Irving, *Bonneville*, 116–17; Sage, *Letters and Scenes*, 129; Russell, *Journal*, 51, 109.

18. Carson, *Memoirs*, 53–55.

19. Ibid. This incident occurred just south of the present city of Colorado Springs. Black Whiteman, one of the two Cheyenne Indians with Gantt's men, claimed that the white men shot only two of the Crows, the two Cheyennes accounting for the other deaths.

20. Ibid., 55–56.

21. Victor, *River*, 154–57.

22. Carson, *Memoirs*, 56. It has been questioned, with some reason, whether Meek went to California with Walker in 1834, as he claimed. If he did not, some other reconstruction of this incident may be possible. The truth of Meek's story of this Comanche fight has also been questioned. The association in his memory of the "mule fort" fight with the death of Guthrie makes it hard to discard the tale altogether.

23. This canyon is now known as the Royal Gorge.

24. Carson, *Memoirs*, 56–58.

25. Ibid., 58.

Chapter 6

1. Harold P. Dunham, "Ceran St. Vrain," in Hafen, ed., *Mountain Men*, 5:297–316.

2. Harold P. Dunham, "Charles Bent," in Hafen, ed., *Mountain Men*, 2:39–48; Samuel P. Arnold, "William W. Bent," in Hafen, ed., *Mountain Men*, 6:74.

3. Carter, *'Dear Old Kit'*, 58–59 fn.

4. Edgeley E. Todd, "Benjamin L. E. Bonneville," in Hafen, ed., *Mountain Men*, 5:53–56; Irving, *Bonneville*, 168.

5. The Spanish gave him the name Silvestre. See Hafen, *The Old Spanish Trail*, 111. George Stewart of Roosevelt, Utah, having heard the story of the original trail from elders of the tribe of Ute Indians at Ouray, followed the trail himself "league by league, mile by mile" and found that Silvestre was incomparable in his choice of a route for a poorly armed party.

6. Stewart grew up at Ouray on the Ute Reservation, where he heard this story from elders of the tribe, who remembered their elders speaking of Carson with great admiration.

7. Near Whiterocks, up the Uintah River near the mountains, Antoine

Robidoux built Fort Uintah during the early 1830s. His brother Louis was probably in charge while Carson was there with Captain R. B. Lee. See Weber, *The Taos Trappers*, 213–14. In Carson's time the Duchesne was considered a tributary of the Uintah. The Uintah is now designated as a tributary of the Duchesne, which joins the Green at Ouray.

8. At the mouth of the Duchesne of today stand the ruins of two log cabins that the Indians call Carson's Houses. Stewart believes that the houses were mended and repaired over the years until little if any of the original materials remains, but the ruins rest on the same spot as the houses built by Carson and his companions. Etienne Provost also wintered there in 1824–25 after the Bad Gocha massacre.

9. Carson, *Memoirs*, 59.

10. Ibid., 60.

11. Ismert, "James Bridger," in Hafen, ed., *Mountain Men*, 6:85–104.

12. Carson, *Memoirs*, 60–61. Teresina Bent said that Carson called this his "worst difficult experience."

13. Traders charged even higher prices to the Indians than to the trappers.

14. Often trappers did not know one another's names, used only nicknames. Some were averse to any publicity that might notify the outside world of their whereabouts. These conditions may have restrained Carson and Russell from naming other trappers, though Meek, quoted in *River of the West*, does so freely.

15. William P. Sampson, "Nathaniel Jervis Wyeth," in Hafen, ed., *Mountain Men*, 5:381–401.

16. Hafen, "A Brief History of the Fur Trade," *Mountain Men*, 1:138–55.

17. Carson, *Memoirs*, 61.

18. The trail of Thomas Biggs frequently intersected that of Carson as long as they remained in the mountains. We last hear of him buying a lot in Salt Lake City in 1855. See Janet Lecompte, "Thomas Biggs," in Hafen, ed., *Mountain Men*, 2:49–53. Mark Head was a Virginian of whom many tales of reckless daring were told. See Harvey L. Carter, "Mark Head," in Hafen, ed., *Mountain Men*, 1:287–93.

19. Victor, *River*, 141.

20. Janet Lecompte, "Abel Baker, Jr.," in Hafen, ed., *Mountain Men*, 1:200.

21. Russell, *Journal*, 7.

22. Ibid., 12. The Salt River mentioned here is a tributary of the Snake River, near the Wyoming–Idaho line.

23. Horse Creek on Green River got its name from the theft there of Smith's and Fitzpatrick's horses in 1823. See Irving, *Bonneville*, 193.

24. Carter, *'Dear Old Kit'*, 65 fn.

25. Carson, *Memoirs*, 63, 65.

26. Shunar's name was properly spelled Chouinard. Marc Simmons has recently located that name on a list of American Fur Company men.

27. Carter, *'Dear Old Kit'*, 65 fn.

28. Ibid., 64 fn.

29. The Arapaho name Waanibe is translated as "Singing Grass."
30. John Charles Frémont, *Memoirs of My Life* (Chicago and New York: Belford Clark & Co., 1887), 74.

Chapter 7

1. Russell, *Journal*, 30; Carson, *Memoirs*, 65, 75. Because the chronology of the *Memoirs* seems somewhat confused at this point, the events are rearranged in this narrative in correct sequence. Transposition of sections of the *Memoirs* can be traced by page number given in the footnotes.
2. Harvey L. Carter, "The Divergent Paths of Frémont's 'Three Marshalls'," *New Mexico Historical Review* 48, no. 1 (January 1973):11–12; Russell, *Journal*, 13.
3. Carter, "The Divergent Paths of Frémont's 'Three Marshalls'," 68:12; Russell, *Journal*, 15–17. Indians generally fought naked because they had learned that wounds through the bare skin healed better than those in which the missile had gone through their clothing first.
4. Presently called the Shoshone River, tributary of the Bighorn.
5. Russell, *Journal*, 30–31.
6. Carson, *Memoirs*, 75, 77.
7. Russell, *Journal*, 32.
8. Stinking Creek is now Ruby River. It flows into the Jefferson River from the east.
9. Russell, *Journal*, 33; Carson, *Memoirs*, 77.
10. A stream that rises in the mountains but sinks into the desert without reaching an outlet.
11. Russell, *Journal*, 34–38. Russell had studied the Shoshone or Snake language intensively while serving as storekeeper at Fort Hall during the autumn of 1834. The activities of Russell are given at some length because he gives a fairly detailed account of the life of a mountain man, paralleling in several events that of Carson.
12. David Lavender, "Thomas McKay," in Hafen, ed., *Mountain Men*, 6:259–77.
13. Dennis Ottoson, in a letter to Harvey L. Carter in 1973, first made the suggestion that Antoine Godey, mentioned at this point in the *Memoirs*, was not Alexis (or Alexander) Godey, the hero of Frémont's Fourth Expedition, but Antoine Godin. Frequently spelled "Goda" in the Fort Hall Account Books, the name was undoubtedly misunderstood by John Mostin, Carson's amanuensis. There are no entries for Alexis Godey in the Fort Hall ledgers, and none for Carson or Goda in the spring of 1836, during the hunt on the Humboldt.
    Godin, the half-Iroquois who had precipitated the Battle of Pierre's Hole in 1832, was himself treacherously killed in May 1836 on the bank of the Snake opposite Fort Hall. The half-Blackfoot, James Bird, called for him to cross over and trade for furs. When Godin complied, the Blackfeet invited him to smoke. As the pipe came around to him, he was shot. See Aubrey L.

Haines, "Antoine Godin," in Hafen, ed., *Mountain Men*, 2:178; John E. Wickman, "James Bird, Jr.," in Hafen, ed., *Mountain Men*, 5:41–42.

14. Carson, *Memoirs*, 65.
15. Mary's River was renamed the Humboldt River by John Charles Frémont.
16. Fort Walla Walla, originally Fort Nez Perce, was a Hudson's Bay Company post at the junction of the Walla Walla River with the Columbia. The Whitman Mission was about fifteen miles east of it.
17. Carson, *Memoirs*, 65, 67.
18. Ibid.
19. Victor, *River*, 199–202; Nard Jones, *The Great Command: The Story of Marcus and Narcissa Whitman and the Oregon County Pioneers* (Boston: Little, Brown & Co., 1959), 111–13.
20. Jones, *The Great Command*, 112–13. The Whitmans were destined for martyrdom by the Cayuse Indians at Waiilatpu in 1847.
21. On modern maps, this river is usually named the Big Wood.
22. Fort Hall Account Books, Oregon Historical Society Library, Portland, Oregon. Donald McLean bought Carson a pipe on October 12.
23. Russell, *Journal*, 52. Rose later returned to Pennsylvania, entered school, and learned enough in six months to take charge of the school. Investing his fur money in real estate, he became a prosperous businessman. James B. Marsh, *Four Years in the Rockies, or, The Adventures of Isaac P. Rose* (New Castle, Pa.: W. B. Thomas, 1884; rpt. ed., Columbus: Long's College Book Co., 1960), 236.
24. Carson, *Memoirs*, 73.
25. Ibid., 74; Victor, *River*, 196.
26. Russell, *Journal*, 53.
27. Ibid., 54–55.
28. Carson, *Memoirs*, 74.
29. Fort Hall Account Books, ledger no. 2, pp. 120–21, and Russell, *Journal*, 1837.
30. Marvin C. Ross, ed., *The West of Alfred Jacob Miller* (Norman: University of Oklahoma Press, 1951). These paintings preserved probably the best visual impressions to be found of the trappers and their mountains.
31. J. Cecil Alter, *Jim Bridger* (Norman: University of Oklahoma Press, 1962), 167–68.
32. Joe Meek said that Bridger's Negro servant, Jim, shot him. See Victor, *River*, 197; Alter said that the shot came from Bridger's own gun. See Alter, *Bridger*, 167–68.
33. The name Umentucken, not of Indian origin, was probably a creation of Joe Meek. For the romance of Umentucken, see Alter, *Bridger*, 158–59, 168; Victor, *River*, 104–7, 178, 179, 197.
34. Russell, *Journal*, 59–60.

Chapter 8

1. Alan C. Trottman, "Lucien Fontenelle," in Hafen, ed., *Mountain Men*, 5:94.

2. Carson, *Memoirs*, 67, 69.

3. Site of present-day Casper, Wyoming. See Struthers Burt, *Powder River: Let 'er Buck* (New York and Toronto: Farrar & Rinehart, 1938), 10–13.

4. Carson, *Memoirs*, 69; Robert Newell, *Memoranda*, ed. Dorothy O. Johansen (Portland: Champoeg Press, 1959), 36.

5. Victor, *River*, 249–50; Carson, *Memoirs*, 54.

6. Twenty-Five Yard River is present-day Shield's River, which joins the Yellowstone about five miles below Livingston, Montana. Carson remembered that the brigade ascended the North Fork of the Missouri. Both Russell and Newell recorded trapping up the Gallatin, crossing the divide to the Madison, and ascending the Madison until they caught up with the Blackfeet. See Carson, *Memoirs*, 69; Russell, *Journal*, 86; Newell, *Memoranda*, 36.

7. Russell, *Journal*, 83–86.

8. Victor, *River*, 230. Mansfield was a crony of Bridger, who as a stripling was given the name "Old Gabe" by Jedediah Smith for his soberly effective way of relaying messages from Ashley and Henry to the other men. See also Carson, *Memoirs*, 70.

9. Carson, *Memoirs*, 69–71. The trapper who rescued Kit was probably David White, who stole a horse and went over to the Hudson's Bay Company a few days later. See Newell, *Memoranda*, 37.

10. Russell, *Journal*, 88.

11. This crossing was later named Raynolds Pass. Henry's Lake was named for Andrew Henry, partner of William Ashley.

12. Russell, *Journal*, 89; Newell reports meeting one more Blackfoot family—man, wife, and child—whom they spared. Hafen, "Robert Newell," *Mountain Men*, 8:266; Newell, *Memoranda*, 37.

13. Edwin G. Gudde, ed., *Sutter's Own Story* (New York: G. P. Putnam's Sons, 1936), 17.

14. Carson, *Memoirs*, 70 and fn.

15. Russell, *Journal*, 90–91.

16. This sheltered valley is now Brown's Park National Wildlife Refuge. The force and volume of the Green are greatly reduced by the impounding of water in Flaming Gorge Reservoir.

17. Merrill J. Mattes, "Seth E. Ward," in Hafen, ed., *Mountain Men*, 3:361.

18. The Laramie Mountains, not the Black Hills of South Dakota.

19. Carson, *Memoirs*, 71, 73.

20. Alter, *Bridger*, 184–88.

21. This child died in Taos, about 1843, after falling into a kettle of boiling soap. See F. W. Cragin Papers, Pioneer's Museum, Colorado Springs, Colo., notebook 12: 21.

22. Hafen, "Robert Newell," *Mountain Men*, 8:270–71; Newell, *Memoranda*, 38. Fort Vasquez, built by Andrew Sublette and Louis Vasquez, was one of four fur-trading posts located on the Platte River below present-day Denver.

23. E. Willard Smith, "Journal," from *To the Rockies and Oregon*, vol. 3 of the Far West and the Rockies, 173–80.

24. Newell, *Memoranda*, 39, said, "The Shyanes stole 100 horses." See also Victor, *River*, 257–59; Janet Lecompte, "Levin Mitchell," in Hafen, ed., *Mountain Men* 5:241–42.

25. Newell identified Philip Thompson, Dick Owens, Elwin Michel (Levin Mitchell), William New, Kelly Belcour, and Exevia (Xavier) Malona among the thieves. He stated that they took fourteen animals at Fort Hall and thirty from the Snake Indians. See Newell, *Memoranda*, 39; Hafen, "Robert Newell," *Mountain Men*, 8:271.

26. George Stewart of Roosevelt, Utah, saw the ruins of this fort as a child and heard the story of the horse thieves from elders of the Ute tribe at Ouray.

27. Victor, *River*, 260.

28. Hafen, "Robert Newell," *Mountain Men*, 8:271–72; Newell, *Memoranda*, 39.

29. Carson, *Memoirs*, 78.

30. Elizabeth Arnold Stone, *Uintah County: Its Place in History* (Laramie: Laramie Printing Co., 1924), 41–46; Matthew C. Field, *Prairie and Mountain Sketches*, collected by Clyde and Mae Reed Porter, ed. Kate L. Gregg and John Francis McDermott (Norman; University of Oklahoma Press, 1957), 142–56; Albert B. Reagan, "Forts Robidoux and Kit Carson in Northeastern Utah," *New Mexico Historical Review* 10 (April 1935): 121–32; Joseph Williams, *Narrative of a Tour from the State of Indiana to the Oregon Territory in the Years 1841–1842* (Cincinnati: J. B. Wilson, 1843), 38–39.

31. Carson, *Memoirs*, 71.

32. James F. Meline, *Two Thousand Miles on Horseback. Santa Fe and Back. A Summer Tour Through Kansas, Nebraska, Colorado, and New Mexico in the Year 1866* (Albuquerque: Horn & Wallace, 1966), 248.

33. Carter, *'Dear Old Kit,'* 72 fn.

34. The Colorado and the Gunnison were both called Grand River by the trappers. The Colorado was nearer to Brown's Hole. Since, from Carson's reference, the Utah country referred to seems to be near New Park, it was probably the Colorado River and its tributaries, the country of the Bunkara Utes, also known as Grand River Utes. Carson, *Memoirs*, 78–79 and 119 fn. Dick Owens was not a fellow traveler of Carson when he left the mountains in 1841. Whether he preceded or followed Carson to the region of Bent's Fort is unknown, but he was living at Greenhorn, with an Indian wife and at least two children, about 1843, where he and John Burroughs had a memorable encounter with a grizzly bear. John Brown, *Mediumistic Experiences* (San Francisco: N. p. 1897), 66.

35. David Lavender, *Bent's Fort* (Lincoln: University of Nebraska Press, 1972), 164.

36. Carson, *Memoirs*, 79.

37. Ibid.

38. Teresina Bent Scheurich, source of some material on Carson's later life, denied this Cheyenne marriage, but Jesse Nelson, husband of Susan Carson, Kit's niece, was closely associated with Kit during the years of 1848 to 1856, and he affirmed the marriage. There was no reason that Carson should not marry, and a marriage would have seemed a practical solution to his problems as a parent.

Chapter 9

1. Blackwelder, *Great Westerner*, 99. Adaline also stayed with Kit's sister Elizabeth—Mrs. Leander Amick—for several years. Elizabeth's daughter, Mrs. L. P. Slaughter, told Sabin that Adaline was with her family until she was about eleven years old. Kit's sister would take no money for caring for the child, and Kit rewarded her to some degree by bringing presents when he came to visit, among these a prized mahogany rocking chair. Sabin, *Kit Carson Days* (1914), 202–3.
2. Carson, *Memoirs*, 81.
3. Jackson and Spence, eds., *Expeditions*, 1:xxvi.
4. Ibid., 96.
5. Ibid., 103. The Bentons were Episcopalians. Senator Benton was too formidable to be lightly defied by his own clergyman.
6. Ibid., 121–22.
7. Carson, *Memoirs*, 81.
8. Jackson and Spence, eds., *Expeditions*, 1:146–58.
9. Charles Preuss, *Exploring with Frémont*, trans. and ed. Erwin G. and Elizabeth I. Gudde (Norman: University of Oklahoma Press, 1958), xxi–xxix, 3, 18. Preuss was extremely neurotic. He committed suicide in 1854.
10. The Creoles were native-born descendants of French settlers, unmixed with any other European element of the population, or with Indian or Negro strains.
11. Jackson and Spence, eds., *Expeditions*, 1:xxii–xxvi.
12. Frémont, *Memoirs*, 70.
13. Ibid., 74.
14. Ibid., 585.
15. Jackson and Spence, eds., *Expeditions*, 1:180.
16. Ibid., 179–88.
17. Ibid., 186–88.
18. Preuss, *Exploring*, 21.
19. Alter, *Bridger*, 197–200.
20. Preuss, *Exploring*, 23. Literally, the voyageurs were saying, "There will be no life for us!"
21. Jackson and Spence, eds., *Expeditions*, 1:197–203.
22. Ann W. Hafen, "Jean Baptiste Charbonneau," in Hafen, ed., *Mountain Men*, 1:205–24. After having been educated by William Clark and having traveled for years in Europe and Africa with Prince Paul of Wurtemburg,

Charbonneau had returned to live as a mountain man and friend of the Indians.

23. Jackson and Spence, eds., *Expeditions*, 1:213–23. In the draft of Frémont's manuscript, Carson was reported to have said, "All of us shall never see that fort again," meaning that some were certain to be killed.
24. Carson, *Memoirs*, 81–84.
25. Jackson and Spence, eds., *Expeditions*, 1:230.
26. Ibid., 1:230–55. The lake at the base camp is now Boulder Lake.
27. Preuss, *Exploring*, 38.
28. Jackson and Spence, eds., *Expeditions*, 1:258–62.
29. Preuss, *Exploring*, 40.
30. Jackson and Spence, eds., *Expeditions*, 1:269.
31. Later named Titcomb Lakes.
32. Jackson and Spence, eds., *Expeditions*, 1:270 fn. Modern explorers have determined that the summit reached was not Frémont Peak but Woodrow Wilson Peak. Just north of there is Gannet Peak, the highest point in Wyoming, but not in the Rockies.
33. Preuss, *Exploring*, 45–46.
34. Frémont's boat was a forerunner of the pleasure craft now plying the rough gorges of the Rockies.
35. Carson, *Memoirs*, 84. The spelling "Jaramilla" in the manuscript of Carson's memoirs is to be attributed to John Mostin, his amanuensis. Josefa's mother was Apolonia Vigil.
36. Nina Otero, *Old Spain in Our Southwest* (New York: Harcourt, Brace, 1936), 43. At the Kit Carson Home in Taos is displayed a dress Carson gave Josefa as a bride.
37. Garrard, *Wah-to-Yah*, 181.

Chapter 10

1. Otis E. Young, *The West of Philip St. George Cooke* (Glendale: Arthur H. Clark Co., 1955), 109–36.
2. R. C. Crump, *The Snively Expedition* (New York: Edward Eberstadt & Sons, 1949), entire pamphlet; William Campbell Brinkley, *The Expansionist Movement in Texas* (Berkeley: University of California Press, 1925) 107–17.
3. Carson, *Memoirs*, 84–85. Carson's sarcasm was perhaps not merited by Governor Armijo, who was a businessman, not a military man. He also had to avoid setting foot on American, as distinguished from Texan, soil.
4. Ibid., 87.
5. Ibid., 87–88; Jackson and Spence, eds., *Expeditions*, 1:445, 382, 387; Lavender, *Bent's Fort*, 240; Harvey L. Carter, "Lucien Maxwell," in Hafen, ed., *Mountain Men*, 5:301. Beaubien's store had been looted by angry "anti-Texians." The Beaubien family had fled, and Maxwell did not return to the expedition.

6. Built in 1837, the fort was in the charge of Marcellin St. Vrain in 1843.
7. Jackson and Spence, eds., *Expeditions*, 1:426–50.
8. See Carter, "The Divergent Paths of Frémont's 'Three Marshalls'," 5–25. Godey signed his name either Alexis or Alexander.
9. The springs were later named Manitou Springs. Ute Pass led from these springs to the Bayou Salade.
10. One of the fifteen was Jacob Dodson, of a family of free Negro servants of St. Louis. Dodson was listed as a voyageur but worked mainly as a body servant for Frémont.
11. The Laramie Plains would not be visible from the main branch of the Poudre, which curves west and south to its source near the head of the Laramie. See Gertrude Barnes, "Following Frémont's Trail Through Northern Colorado," *Colorado Magazine* 19, no. 5 (September 1942): 185–89. The easy way into the mountains from the east is by way of Kenosha Pass, but it leads southwest, and Frémont was instructed to go to Oregon. He closely paralleled the route and experience of William H. Ashley in 1825, whose diary, covering the period March 25 to June 27 of that year, is reproduced and annotated by Dale L. Morgan in *The West of William H. Ashley* (Denver: Old West Publishing Co., 1964), 104–17.
12. Jackson and Spence, eds., *Expeditions*, 1:452–64. This arid region is the Great Divide Basin in Southern Wyoming.
13. James W. Nesmith, "Diary of the Emigration of 1843," *Oregon Historical Quarterly*, quoted in Jackson and Spence, eds., *Expeditions*, 1:476.
14. Jackson and Spence, eds., *Expeditions* 1:465–83. Soda Springs was usually called Beer Springs by the mountain men, who fancied that the effervescent water tasted like beer.
15. Ibid., 483–501.
16. These men were expected to obtain provisions from Fitzpatrick, but they got lost. Some were discovered far west of the fort, walking down the Snake toward Oregon.
17. Howard Stansbury, who surveyed the lake in 1849 and 1850, named the place Frémont Island, "in honor of him who first set foot upon its shore."
18. Jackson and Spence, eds., *Expeditions*, 1:501–11.
19. Carson, *Memoirs*, 88–89.
20. Jackson and Spence, eds., *Expeditions*, 1:512–22. This was the desolate plain over which Osborne Russell wandered in 1835.
21. Ibid., 523–32.
22. Ibid., 532–51. A month later, Mr. Perkins, a missionary at the Dalles, guided Frémont and Preuss to a high point from which they could observe Mount Rainier and Mount St. Helens, both of them active. In November 1841, Perkins reported, ashes from Mount St. Helens had fallen at the Dalles.
23. Preuss, *Exploring*, 94–95.
24. Jackson and Spence, eds., *Expeditions*, 1:553–61. For Abert's complete orders, see *Expeditions*, 1:160–61.

25. Ibid., 573–87. Frémont had reached Klamath Marsh, about thirty miles above the lake.

26. Now called Humboldt Lake. Frémont's persistence in searching for the Buenaventura River is puzzling. He should have known that Walker and Chiles had crossed the Sierra Nevada without finding any indication of such a river. He should also have known that Captain Charles Wilkes of the U. S. Navy had found in 1841 that the source of the Sacramento was west of the Sierra Nevada.

27. Jackson and Spence, eds., *Expeditions*, 1:588–93.

28. This lake has not been identified, but in comparing modern maps with the one prepared for Frémont's *Memoirs of My Life*, one finds its position very near that of Hart Lake in southcentral Oregon.

29. Jackson and Spence, eds., *Expeditions*, 1:593–600.

30. Ibid., 1:600–602. This ridge has been identified as the Granite Range.

31. Ibid., 1:602–5.

32. Ibid., 1:605–10. This stream was later named the Truckee River in honor of the Paiute Indian chief who told the Townsend-Stephens-Murphy party at Mary's Sink about the river coming out of the mountains and about the pass leading to another river flowing to a plain with many cattle and horses. See Dale L. Morgan, ed., *Overland in 1846: Diaries and Letters of the California-Oregon Trail*, 2 vols. (Georgetown, Calif.: Talisman Press, 1963), 1:19, 20.

33. Jackson and Spence, eds., *Expeditions*, 1:610–11. The Carson River.

Chapter 11

1. Jackson and Spence, eds., *Expeditions*, 1:613–19. Probably they crossed the East Walker River twice and the West Walker once. The howitzer has never been found. See Ernest Allen Lewis, *The Frémont Cannon: High Up and Far Back* (Glendale: Arthur H. Clark Co., 1981), for everything known about the howitzer.

2. Jackson and Spence, eds., *Expeditions*, 1:613–23.

3. Ibid., 1:624–26.

4. The map prepared for Frémonts *Memoirs* places the entrance to the high Sierra on the Carson River. See Jackson and Spence, eds., *Expeditions*, 1:624–25 fn., for the opinion of Vincent P. Gianella, "Where Frémont Crossed the Sierra Nevada in 1844," *Sierra Club Bulletin* 44, no. 7 (1959).

5. Jackson and Spence, eds., *Expeditions*, 1:624–28. This camp was at Grover's Springs. See Gianella, "Where Frémont Crossed," 56.

6. Jackson and Spence, eds., *Expeditions*, 1:628–29. This basin was Faith Valley. The principal peaks opposite the camp were Elephant's Back and Red Lake Peak; along the base of the latter is a canyon leading to Carson Pass. See Jackson and Spence, eds., *Expeditions*, 1:635, quoting Gianella, 60.

7. Preuss, *Exploring*, 106–12.

8. Jackson and Spence, eds., *Expeditions*, 1:630.

9. Ibid., 629–31.
10. Ibid., 629–33.
11. Preuss, *Exploring*, 108–10.
12. The lake, named Mountain Lake, and later Lake Bonpland, by Frémont, was given its Indian name, Tahoe, by the citizens of California.
13. The height was computed by the temperature at which water boiled. The barometer had been broken. For uncertainty about point of crossing, see Jackson and Spence, eds., *Expeditions* 1:638, and Preuss, *Exploring*, 111. Lorraine Dyson, who lived nearby and studied the terrain for years, states that all clues indicate Carson Pass. But Larry Cenotto, who is well acquainted with the topography of Amador County, believes that the route followed by Frémont had little in common with the Carson Pass traversed by many gold rush emigrant trains.
14. Jackson and Spence, eds., *Expeditions*, 1:633–41.
15. Ibid., 1:641–51.
16. Ibid., 1:651–54.
17. Ibid., 1:657 fn.; Carson, *Memoirs*, 91.
18. Jackson and Spence, eds., *Expeditions*, 1:657.
19. Ibid., 1:677–79.
20. Carson, *Memoirs*, 92–93.
21. Preuss, *Exploring*, 127–28, 130.
22. Jackson and Spence, eds., *Expeditions*, 1:680–81, 683–84.
23. Carson, *Memoirs*, 93. Pablo and Fuentes went east with the expedition. Pablo was cared for in the Benton home and received some education. Fuentes accompanied Frémont on his third expedition. See Frémont, *Memoirs*, 409.
24. Jackson and Spence, eds., *Expeditions*, 1:686–88.
25. Ibid., 683–91.
26. Preuss, *Exploring*, 130.
27. Jackson and Spence, eds., *Expeditions*, 1:692–93.
28. Ibid., 1:697; Preuss, *Exploring*, 133.
29. Preuss, *Exploring*, 134.
30. Jackson and Spence, eds., *Expeditions*, 1:706. Fort Uintah was destroyed by the Utes after the expedition passed. Robidoux, who was absent, escaped being killed with the rest of the men. The women, mostly Utes, were carried away.
31. Ibid., 1:697–708; Preuss, *Exploring*, 133–35.
32. Carson, *Memoirs*, 95.
33. Now Savery Creek, a corruption of St. Vrain.
34. The main fork of the Colorado, often called the Grand by the trappers.
35. Jackson and Spence, eds., *Expeditions*, 1:708–17. They crossed the Continental Divide at Hoosier Pass and descended the Middle Fork of the South Platte. See p. 715 fn.
36. Ibid., 1:717–20; Carson, *Memoirs*, 95.

Chapter 12

1. J. J. Webb, *Adventures in the Santa Fe Trade, 1844–1847*, ed. Ralph P. Bieber (Glendale: Arthur H. Clark Co., 1931), 63–65.
2. Carson, *Memoirs*, 95–96.
3. Ibid.
4. Frémont, *Memoirs*, 427; see Carter, "The Divergent Paths of Frémont's 'Three Marshalls.'"
5. Carson, *Memoirs*, 96. Carson's Piney River is the Eagle River of today. The party probably crossed the Continental Divide east of Homestake Peak at Little Homestake Lake, rather than at Frémont Pass farther east.
6. On the site of present-day Salt Lake City. Carson reports having gone up the Uintah to its source, but the Uintah is not near the Provo. Perhaps the confusion over which was the tributary of the other had already arisen, and Carson called the more imposing of the two rivers the Uintah. Provo River was named for Etienne Provost.
7. Frémont, *Memoirs*, 431; Carson, *Memoirs*, 96.
8. Carson, *Memoirs*, 99; Frémont, *Memoirs*, 432–33; A. J. Smith, *Men Against the Mountains*, 147–54.
9. Pilot Peak rises between U. S. 40 and Nevada 30 near the Utah–Nevada border. The Hastings Cutoff contributed to the Donner tragedy.
10. Named Crane's Branch for one of the Delawares later killed by the Klamath Indians.
11. Frémont, *Memoirs*, 3, 439. For instructions for the third expedition, see Jackson and Spence, eds., *Expeditions*, 1:396. The *Memoirs* give a different version from that given in *Expeditions*; Abert had directed Frémont to apply his efforts "to the geography of localities within reasonable distance of Bent's Fort, and of the streams that run east from the Rocky Mountains, and he will so time his operations, that his party will come in during the present year." Abert to Frémont, February 2, 1845, quoted in Jackson and Spence, eds., *Expeditions*, 1:396.
12. Frémont, *Memoirs*, 423.
13. See account of quarrel with Mason in Jackson and Spence, eds., *Expeditions*, 2:348.
14. Frémont, *Memoirs*, 440, quoted from John Milton, "Il Penseroso."
15. Mariposa is Spanish for butterfly. The river was named for the many mariposa poppies, on whose slender stems the blossoms flutter like butterflies. This area was part of the Mariposa Grant that Frémont later acquired. See Frémont, *Memoirs*, 444–47.
16. Ibid., 462. On March 9, Larkin wrote to the secretary of the navy that Castro had received orders from Mexico not to allow Frémont to enter California.
17. Carson, *Memoirs*, 101.
18. From a letter to his wife, Frémont, *Memoirs*, 460.

19. Ibid., 478; Carson, *Memoirs*, 103.
20. Stepperfeldt was called Stepp by his companions and usually by Frémont in the *Memoirs*.
21. Frémont, *Memoirs*, 489. The secretary of the navy was George Bancroft, the noted historian.
22. Frémont, *Memoirs*, 488, 489, 490.
23. Ibid.
24. Ibid., 491.
25. Carson, *Memoirs*, 104.
26. Frémont, *Memoirs*, 492.
27. Ibid., 494.
28. Ibid., 495; Carson, *Memoirs*, 106.
29. Frémont, *Memoirs*, 496–97; Carson, *Memoirs*, 107.

Chapter 13

1. Jackson and Spence, eds., *Expeditions*, 2:192.
2. Used here to indicate Californians of Mexican or Spanish birth who were opposed to annexation by the U. S.
3. Frémont, *Memoirs*, 500–520.
4. Frémont, *Memoirs*, 530; Jackson and Spence, eds., *Expeditions*, 2:166–68.
5. Ibid., 535.
6. Carson, *Memoirs*, 101, 102 fn.
7. T. S. Martin, "Narrative of John C. Frémont's Expedition to California in 1845–46," dictated in 1878, Bancroft Library, Berkeley, Calif.
8. Frémont, *Memoirs*, 516–17. In *Expeditions*, 2:124–25, Jackson and Spence review all the evidence and conclude that the attack took place during the April stay at Lassen's Ranch, and that there is little support for Frémont's statement in his *Memoirs* that there was a second attack in June.
9. Jacob Leese was a member of the Bean–Sinclair party of trappers from Arkansas. With several others, Leese had migrated to California, where he had married Rosalia Vallejo, sister of the general. Leese and the Vallejos were pro-American, but Frémont did not trust them.
10. Frémont, *Memoirs*, 516–26. Congress later voted to recompense Vallejo and to pay Sutter for the use of his fort.
11. Carson, *Memoirs*, 107–10.
12. Douglas S. Watson, *West Wind: The Life Story of Joseph Reddeford Walker* (Los Angeles: Percy H. Booth, 1934), 96–98.
13. Frémont, *Memoirs*, 520.
14. Ibid., 525.
15. LeRoy R. Hafen, ed., "The W. M. Boggs Manuscript about Bent's Fort, Kit Carson, the Far West and Life Among the Indians," *Colorado Magazine* 7 (March 1930): 62–63. Jasper O'Farell, an eyewitness, gave the same account in the *Los Angeles Star*, September 27, 1856, as quoted in H. H. Bancroft, *History of California*, 7 vols. (San Francisco: History Co., 1888),

5:171–72. Alexis Godey, who was nearby at the time, in defending Frémont during his presidential campaign, claimed that Carson had the men
shot when they resisted arrest and that they were carrying letters to De la
Torre. See the *New York Evening Post*, October 30, 1856. The responsibility, however, clearly rests with Frémont.

16. Frémont, *Memoirs*, 533. Quoting from Lieutenant the Hon. Fred. Walpole,
    R. N., *Four Years in the Pacific in Her Majesty's Ship Collingwood, from
    1844 to 1848.* "The Duke" was the Duke of Wellington, conqueror of
    Napoleon at Waterloo.
17. Theodore Talbot to his sister, July 25, 1846, Jackson and Spence, eds., *Expe-
    ditions*, 2:489 fn. 3.
18. Frémont, *Memoirs*, 567.
19. Carson, *Memoirs*, 111–12. Kearny sent most of his force back to Santa Fe
    and marched to California with only about a hundred dragoons.
20. Frémont, *Memoirs*, 585–86. From a statement given to Senator Benton by
    Carson on a later visit to Washington. Using this statement in a speech in
    the Senate, Benton said, "The truth of this, as of everything else he says, I
    underwrite."
21. Frémont, *Memoirs*, 585–86; Carson had no chance to testify at the court-
    martial, which occurred during the winter of 1847–48, while he was in
    California.
22. Sabin, *Kit Carson Days* (1935), 518–24.
23. Carson, *Memoirs*, 114. The Battle of San Pascual, a costly defeat for the
    Americans, occurred near present-day Escondido.
24. Before his capture, Godey had cached Stockton's reply in a hollow tree,
    where it was found later. It is now in the Gaffey Manuscripts, Huntington
    Library, San Marino, Calif.
25. "The wolf will escape." This description of the escape was given in a
    speech by Senator Benton, quoted in Frémont, *Memoirs*, 588–89. See also
    Carson, *Memoirs*, 114–15.
26. Frémont, *Memoirs*, 589.
27. Carson, *Memoirs*, 115; Frémont, *Memoirs*, 588–589; Sabin, *Kit Carson
    Days* (1914), 288–94.
28. Frémont, *Memoirs*, 579–80.
29. Ibid., 597–99.
30. Carson, *Memoirs*, 116.
31. Jackson and Spence, eds., *Expeditions*, 2:251, 254.
32. Ibid., 269.
33. Sabin, *Kit Carson Days* (1935), 554.

Chapter 14

1. Carson, *Memoirs*, 116.
2. From an article by Beale, 1871, quoted in Stephen Bonsal, *Edward
   Fitzgerald Beale: A Pioneer in the Path of Empire, 1822–1903* (New York

and London: G. P. Putnam, 1912), 286–87; see also Sabin, *Kit Carson Days* (1935), 557.

3. Carson, *Memoirs*, 117.

4. Ibid.

5. Bonsal, *Beale*, 287.

6. Ibid.

7. Garrard, *Wah-to-Yah*, 176; see also manuscript account by Teresina Bent Scheurich at Charles Bent House, Taos, New Mexico; H. H. Bancroft, *History of Arizona and New Mexico* (Albuquerque: Horn & Wallace, 1962), 432; Lavender, *Bent's Fort*, 300–303; Leroy R. Hafen and Carl Coke Rister, *Western America* (New York: Prentice Hall, 1941), 329.

8. Sabin, *Kit Carson Days* (1935), 562.

9. Garrard, *Wah-to-Yah*, 177, 185–86. In *Ruxton of the Rockies*, 191, Ruxton reported that it was rumored that Big Nigger escaped. See also C. A. Weslager, *The Delaware Indians* (New York: Rutgers University Press, 1972), 408–9; Janet Lecompte, *Pueblo-Hardscrabble-Greenhorn* (Norman: University of Oklahoma Press, 1978), 195; these accounts give evidence in support of Ruxton.

10. Garrard, *Wah-to-Yah*, 171–73; Lavender, *Bent's Fort*, 314–18.

11. Garrard, *Wah-to-Yah*, 240.

12. Ibid., 250.

13. Carson, *Memoirs*, 117.

14. Bonsal, *Beale*, 30–31, cited by Sabin, *Kit Carson Days* (1935), 569.

15. Frémont, *Memoirs*, 74.

16. Jessie Benton Frémont, *The Will and the Way Stories* (Boston: D. Lathrop Co., 1891), 40–42. Somewhat later, Scott's *Lady of the Lake* struck Carson "as the finest expression of outdoor life that he had ever heard." Upon hearing Captain A. W. Archibald of Trinidad quote the opening lines, he asked for the entire poem. After hearing it read every night for three weeks, Carson often quoted stanzas from it with great approval and pleasure. See Sabin, *Kit Carson Days* (1914), 508.

17. Frémont, *Memoirs*, 562.

18. James K. Polk, *Polk, The Diary of a President: 1845–1849*, ed. Allan Nevins (New York: Longmans, Green & Co., 1929), 241–42.

19. Ibid.

20. Secretary of War's dispatch of June 11, 1847, cited by Sabin, *Kit Carson Days* (1935), 569, 570. After the court-martial, Polk reduced Frémont's punishment to a reprimand, and Benton thought he should remain in the service, but Frémont resigned.

21. House Exec. Doc. no. 17, 31st Cong., 1st sess., p. 247, cited by Sabin, *Kit Carson Days* (1935), 572; Jackson and Spence, eds., *Expeditions*, 2: 362.

22. This interview, reprinted as Appendix B in Carter, *'Dear Old Kit'*, is very similar to part of the memoirs dictated by Carson in 1856.

23. Sabin, *Kit Carson Days* (1935), 573.

24. George H. Carson of Fayette, Missouri, cited in Sabin, *Kit Carson Days* (1935), 575.
25. Carson, *Memoirs*, 118.
26. Sabin, *Kit Carson Days* (1935), 575.
27. Carson, *Memoirs*, 118.
28. William T. Sherman, *Memoirs of General William T. Sherman*, 2 vols. (New York: D. Appleton & Co., 1886), 1:46–47.
29. "Kit Carson, famous in Mountain annals, has arrived in Monterey, via Santa Fe and Los Angeles. He left Washington about the 20th of June with the mail." *San Francisco Californian*, December 1, 1847. See Sabin, *Kit Carson Days* (1935), 578; J. A. Hussey, "Kit Carson at Cajón—Not Tejón," *California Historical Society Quarterly* 29 (March 1950): 31–34.
30. George D. Brewerton, *Overland with Kit Carson: A Narrative of the Old Spanish Trail in 1848*, ed. Stallo Vinton (New York: Coward McCann, 1930).
31. Ibid., 38.
32. Ibid., 65–66.
33. Ibid., 68.
34. Ibid., 69.
35. Ibid., 75.
36. "Friend! Friend!"
37. Brewerton, *Overland with Kit Carson*, 83–85.
38. Ibid., 96.
39. Ibid., 100–104.
40. Ibid., 114–20.
41. Ibid., 139.
42. Ibid., 140.
43. Ibid., 141. See also Carson, *Memoirs*, 119.
44. Brewerton, *Overland with Kit Carson*, 143.
45. Bancroft, *History of Arizona and New Mexico*, 416, 441.
46. Carson, *Memoirs*, 121.
47. William Brandon, *The Men and the Mountain: Frémont's Fourth Expedition* (New York: William Morrow & Co., 1955), 71–73; Janet Lecompte, "A Letter from Jessie to Kit," *Bulletin of the Missouri Historical Society* 29, no. 4 (July 1972): 263.
48. Carson, *Memoirs*, 121–22.
49. Victor, *River*, 458.
50. Sabin, *Kit Carson Days* (1914), 203.

Chapter 15

1. Details of Frémont's disaster are taken mostly from LeRoy R. Hafen, ed., *Frémont's Fourth Expedition: A Documentary Account of the Disaster of 1848–1849, with Diaries, Letters, and Reports by Participants in the Tragedy*, vol. 11 of the Far West and the Rockies Historical series (Glendale: Arthur H. Clark Co., 1960).

2. In his memoirs Carson did not mention his relationship with Frémont at this time, perhaps because of his disagreement with his friend and the latter's disastrous failure. The laudatory valedictory quoted in the preceding chapter is his last mention of his former leader.

3. James F. Rusling, *Across America; or, The Great West and the Pacific Coast* (New York: Sheldon & Co., 1874), 136. If Carson, as Rusling stated, "confirmed . . . that Frémont . . . was somewhat of a charlatan," it was because Carson was unfamiliar with the word, for he never elsewhere stated or implied that Frémont was insincere, dishonest, or pretentious.

4. A belt of majestic cottonwoods along the Arkansas about twenty-five miles below the mouth of the Purgatory River.

5. Lavender, *Bent's Fort*, 264, 331–32.

6. Ibid.

7. Carson, *Memoirs*, 122; DeWitt C. Peters, *The Life and Adventures of Kit Carson, the Nestor of the Rocky Mountains* (New York: W. R. C. Clark & Meeker, 1859, 1874), 327–28.

8. Hafen, *Frémont's Fourth Expedition*, 298.

9. Ibid., 44.

10. Aubry had won distinction by riding the 780 miles from Santa Fe to Independence in five days and sixteen hours. For a dramative narrative of his feats, see J. Frank Dobie, *I'll Tall You a Tale* (Boston: Little Brown, 1931), 103–9.

11. Hafen, *Frémont's Fourth Expedition*, 206–9.

12. Ibid., 34. Patricia Richmond to Harvey L. Carter, April 4, 1983. We are indebted to Patricia Richmond, Crestone, Colorado, for a brief report of her conclusions, after much investigation, concerning the site of Frémont's disaster and the route followed, which differs from previously accepted information, but which appears to us extremely plausible. She writes, "Following Carnero Creek they left it at Hell's Gate, the gap of the Carnero, and ascended Cave Creek to the summit of Boot Mountain. Dropping into the valley at the head of La Garita Creek, they proceeded across the table land and ridges of Mesa Mountain. Stumps, an inscription, and mules' skeletons mark the route to Camp Dismal at the head of Wanamaker Creek. By Christmas Day they had moved to Camp Hope at the head of Rincon Creek. From this point the rescue party descended the Embargo Creek drainage to the Rio Grande. The main party moved the baggage toward the San Luis Valley by crossing ridges separating headwaters of Embargo and Ground Hog creeks. The expedition descended La Garita Creek and emerged from the mountains about five miles from where the ascent had begun. The surviving members were rescued by Alexis Godey near Alamosa, Colorado."

13. Sabin, *Kit Carson Days* (1935), 615, citing Frémont's manuscript memoirs, Bancroft Library, Berkeley; see also Brandon, *The Men and the Mountain*, 238–56.

14. Hafen, *Frémont's Fourth Expedition*, 171; see also Carter, "The Divergent

Paths of Frémont's 'Three Marshalls.'" Carter gives details of Owens's later life. Circleville, Kansas, became his final resting place.

15. Jim Berry Pearson, *The Maxwell Land Grant* (Norman: University of Oklahoma Press, 1961), 3–11; Lawrence R. Murphy, "Charles H. Beaubien," in Hafen, ed., *Mountain Men*, 6:23–35.

16. Pearson, *The Maxwell Land Grant*, 11.

17. Carson, *Memoirs*, 122–23; Peters, *Life and Adventures of Kit Carson*, 328–30.

18. Carter, "Lucien Maxwell," in Hafen, ed., *Mountain Men*, 6:303.

19. Quantrille D. McClung, *Carson-Bent-Boggs Genealogy* (Denver: Denver Public Library, 1962), 71; Blackwelder, *Great Westerner*, 243; Sabin, *Kit Carson Days* (1914), 217.

20. Carson, *Memoirs*, 124–26; see also Sabin, *Kit Carson Days* (1935), 618–21; Colonel Henry Inman, *The Old Santa Fe Trail* (New York: MacMillan Co., 1897), 165; Forbes Parkhill, *The Blazed Trail of Antoine Leroux* (Los Angeles: Westernlore Press, 1965), 139.

21. Alexander Barclay Papers, November 23 and November 25, Barclay Diary, Bancroft Library, Berkeley.

22. Carson, *Memoirs*, 126–27; Sabin, *Kit Carson Days* (1935), 623; Peters, *Life and Adventures of Kit Carson*, 349–50.

23. Harvey L. Carter, "Tim Goodale," in Hafen, ed., *Mountain Men*, 7:148–53. In 1864, Goodale moved to the Bitterroot Valley and became active in the early history of Idaho.

24. LeRoy R. Hafen and Francis M. Young, *Fort Laramie and the Pageant of the West, 1834–1890* (Glendale: Arthur M. Clark Co., 1938), 159–66.

25. Peters, *Life and Adventures of Kit Carson*, 350–52.

26. Carson, *Memoirs*, 127–28. The settlement at Red River was renamed Questa in 1884 when a post office was established there.

27. Carson, *Memoirs*, 128–29, fn. 129. The dragoons took Fox to Taos. He was jailed, but his accuser had recovered sufficiently to leave town before the return of Fox, and he was released.

28. Later Kansas City.

29. Maurine Nelson Bradshaw, Jesse's great-granddaughter, states in *Pioneer Parade* (New York: Vantage Press, 1966), 13, that Jesse and Susan were married at Boonville, Missouri, in 1851. The adventure related is from Carson, *Memoirs*, 129–32. Jesse Nelson added details of the journey in an interview with F. W. Cragin; see Cragin Papers, notebook 8, pp. 61, 65. See also Peters, *Life and Adventures of Kit Carson*, 377–78.

30. According to Josiah Gregg, *Commerce of the Prairies*, 15 fn., the island was named for an adventure of Auguste Pierre Chouteau, who, about the year 1816, battled 150 to 200 Pawnees to victory from the island.

31. Cragin Papers, notebook 8, pp. 61, 65.

32. Ibid., 49.

33. These adventures, based on an interview with Teresina Bent Scheurich many years later, are recounted by Sabin, *Kit Carson Days* (1935), 632–33.

34. Nolie Mumey, *The Life of Jim Baker, 1818–1898* (Denver: World Press, 1931), 81.
35. Now Cañon City, Colorado. Carson, *Memoirs*, 132.
36. LeRoy R. Hafen, "Louy Simmons," in Hafen, ed., *Mountain Men*, 5:320. Simmons, who died of "senile dementia" in 1894, told several versions of his life with Adaline.
37. Carson, *Memoirs*, 133.
38. Cragin Papers, notebook 27, p. 57. Interview with William Shortredge, one of the ferrymen.
39. *Daily Alta California*, August 9, 1853. Cited by Sabin, *Kit Carson Days* (1935), 634.
40. *San Francisco Herald*, September 5, 1853. Cited by Sabin, *Kit Carson Days* (1935), 634.
41. *Sacramento Union*, September 11, 1853. Cited by Sabin, *Kit Carson Days* (1935), 634.
42. Carson, *Memoirs*, 133.
43. Peters, *Life and Adventures of Kit Carson*, 408.
44. *Napa County Reporter*, March 13, 1875. Cited by Sabin, *Kit Carson Days* (1935), 635–36.
45. LeRoy R. Hafen, ed., "W. M. Boggs Manuscript," *Colorado Magazine*, no. 2 (March 1930): 63–64.
46. Lindsey to Kit, Russian River, August 1, 1854, quoted in Sabin, *Kit Carson Days* (1935), 777–78.
47. Cragin Papers, notebook 8, p. 75.
48. Captain James Hobbs, *Wild Life in the Far West* (Hartford: Wiley, Waterman, & Eaton, 1872), 447–48, cited by Sabin, in *Kit Carson Days* (1935), 954–55.
49. Charles M. Harvey, "Kit Carson, Last of the Trailmakers, 1809–1868," *Century Magazine* 80 (October 1910): 874–75.
50. Carson, *Memoirs*, 133.

Chapter 16

1. Sabin, *Kit Carson Days* (1935), 776. This later became part of Brewerton's book, *Overland with Kit Carson*.
2. Marshall D. Moody, "Kit Carson, Agent to the Indians in New Mexico, 1853–1861," *New Mexico Historical Review* 28, no. 1 (January 1953): 1–20.
3. The agent received around $1,500 a year. Allowance for an interpreter was $500 a year; for gifts and provisions for the Indians, $3,600 a year. See Letters received from or relating to Kit Carson, 1854–1860, National Archives microfiche, Washington, D.C., FMT 21, Roll 1.
4. Sabin, *Kit Carson Days* (1935), 775–76.
5. Bureau of Indian Affairs, Annual Reports of Governor Meriwether, 1853, 1854, 1856, North Texas State University, Denton, Texas, Microfiche, Roll 4,158.

6. Bureau of Indian Affairs, Meriwether Annual Report, 1854, Microfiche, Roll 4,158.

7. Young, *The West of Philip St. George Cooke*, 254.

8. Bureau of Indian Affairs, Meriwether Annual Report, 1854, Microfiche, Roll 4,158.

9. Sabin, *Kit Carson Days* (1914), 379.

10. Ibid.; Carson, *Memoirs*, 134–35; Moody, "Kit Carson, Agent," 4.

11. Moody, "Kit Carson, Agent," 5.

12. Hamilton Gardner, "Philip St. George Cooke and the Apache, 1854," *New Mexico Historical Review* 28 (April 1953): 115–32.

13. Carson, *Memoirs*, 137; Gardner, "Philip St. George Cooke," 122. Sykes was commended by both Carson and Cooke. He had served in the Mexican War and later served in the Civil War. See Francis B. Heitman, *Historical Register and Dictionary of the United States Army from Its Organization September 29, 1789, to March 2, 1903*, 2 vols. (Washington, D.C.: United States Government Printing Office, 1903), 1:941.

14. Gardner, "Philip S. George Cooke," 122.

15. Ibid., 123.

16. Ibid.; Sabin, *Kit Carson Days* (1914), 382.

17. Cooke's report, quoted by Sabin in *Kit Carson Days* (1914), 382.

18. Gardner, "Philip St. George Cooke," 122–25.

19. Moody, "Kit Carson, Agent," 4.

20. Carson, *Memoirs*, 138–39.

21. Ibid.; Young, *The West of Philip St. George Cooke*, 262.

22. Lieutenant Robert Johnson, who had come to Carson's aid on the Santa Fe Trail in 1851.

23. Gardner, "Philip St. George Cooke," 126–30, says Cooke commanded this campaign and does not mention Carleton. Though Cooke was in command, Carleton had charge of the active campaign, and Carson praised him for his handling of it. Carson, *Memoirs*, 141–42.

24. Gardner, "Philip St. George Cooke," 130. The "spies" are now known as "scouts."

25. Sabin, *Kit Carson Days* (1914), 384.

26. Territory of New Mexico, Executive Department, "Journal of Proceedings," 1854, Mic. T–17. Meriwether, who was on leave from March through June 1854, returned to Santa Fe July 22.

27. Carson to Meriwether, cited by Moody, in "Kit Carson, Agent," 7.

28. Carson, *Memoirs*, 143.

29. Ibid.

30. Sometimes called Blanco, this chief was described by Meriwether as "one of the most forbidding looking beings I ever saw. . . . Had but one eye, and his face scarred by smallpox in a most terrible manner." See David Meriwether, *My Life in the Mountains and on the Plains*, ed. Robert A. Griffen (Norman: University of Oklahoma Press, 1965), 227.

31. LeRoy R. Hafen, "The Fort Pueblo Massacre and the Punitive Expedition

Against the Utes," *Colorado Magazine* 4, no. 2 (March 1927): 49–58. A more recent and very able account is Lecompte, *Pueblo-Hardscrabble-Greenhorn*, 246–53, 270–74.

32. Carson, *Memoirs*, 144–45.
33. Hafen, "Fort Pueblo Massacre," 49–58; Morris F. Taylor, "Action at Fort Massachusetts: The Indian Campaign of 1855," *Colorado Magazine* 42 (Fall 1965): 292–310.
34. Sabin, *Kit Carson Days* (1914), 389.
35. McClung, *Carson-Bent-Boggs*, 71.
36. Bureau of Indian Affairs, Carson report, September 1855.
37. Hafen, "Fort Pueblo Massacre," 57–58.
38. Carson, *Memoirs*, 147.
39. Sabin, *Kit Carson Days* (1914), 392.
40. Meriwether, *My Life*, 226–32.
41. Carson, *Memoirs*, 147. Griffen (226 fn.) stated, "It is apparent that the Governor's memory tricked him into connecting two unrelated events." He pointed out other details on which Meriwether's memory was in error (fns. 226, 227, 229).
42. Moody, "Kit Carson, Agent," 9–10.
43. Ibid., 8.
44. Carson, *Memoirs*, 147, 149. Page 150 gives a concise exposition of the writing of the *Memoirs*.
45. Ibid. Turley, brother of Simeon Turley, the distiller of Taos Lightnin', killed at Arroyo Hondo in 1847, probably had been the first to suggest the writing of the memoirs. See *Liberty Weekly Tribune*, December 19, 1856; Sabin, *Kit Carson Days* (1935), 779–82; Irving to Turley, November 9, 1857, Turley Papers, State Historical Society of Missouri, St. Louis; Lester F. Turley, El Monte, Calif., to Bernice Blackwelder, July 8, 1962, Turley Papers. The original manuscript, found among the effects of Peters's son, who died in Paris in 1905, was acquired by Edward E. Ayers and eventually passed to the Newberry Library in Chicago.
46. Smith H. Simpson, quoted in Sabin, *Kit Carson Days* (1914), 506.
47. New Mexico report, Bureau of Indian Affairs, 1853.
48. Morris F. Taylor, "Ka-ni-ache," *Colorado Magazine* 43, no. 4 (Fall 1966): 284.
49. About 102 bushels. The Conejos rises in the San Juans and joins the Rio Grande south of Alamosa, Colorado, about eighty miles northwest of Taos.
50. Carson report, Bureau of Indian Affairs, 1858.
51. Moody, "Kit Carson, Agent," 17.
52. Ibid., 16.
53. Carson report, Bureau of Indian Affairs, September 1859.
54. Ibid., Aug. 1860.
55. McClung, *Carson-Bent-Boggs*, 79–81.
56. Letter quoted in Sabin, *Kit Carson Days* (1935), 782.

57. A. B. Sanford, "Reminiscences of Kit Carson, Jr.," *Colorado Magazine* 6, no. 5 (September 1929): 179–84; Charles Carson, quoted by Sabin, *Kit Carson Days* (1935), 783.
58. Smith H. Simpson, letter to Sabin, 1911. See Sabin, *Kit Carson Days* (1935), 649, 651.
59. Ibid.; William S. Bridgeman, "Kit Carson, the Famous American Frontiersman," *Munsey's* 42 (December 1909): 336.
60. See also Meline, *Two Thousand Miles on Horseback*, 246–51.
61. Albert D. Richardson, *Beyond the Mississippi* (Hartford: American Publishing Co., 1867), 261.
62. Mrs. Hal Russell, "Memoirs of Marian Russell," *Colorado Magazine* 20, no. 5 (September 1943): 181–96. Carson usually called Josefa "Chepita."
63. Pearson, *The Maxwell Land Grant*, 11. In 1862 Maxwell built a many-roomed mansion on the little Cimarron. In 1870, having realized successful gold mining developments, he sold his huge land grant, except for his house and a thousand acres, to a syndicate; he then invested in the Texas Pacific Railroad and lost money; next he established a bank in Santa Fe and lost money on that. He then bought the old Fort Sumner tract on the Pecos and stocked it with cattle and sheep. When he died on July 25, 1875, he was still considered a moderately wealthy man. See also Ralph Emerson Twitchell, ed., *The Spanish Archives of New Mexico*, 2 vols. (Cedar Rapids: Torch Press, 1914), 1:60.
64. Kit Carson's Will, typed copy in Historical Museum of New Mexico, Santa Fe. Original in Pueblo County Court House, Pueblo, Colo.
65. Cragin Papers, notebook 8, p. 67. Carson believed that the injuries from this fall damaged his heart and caused the aneurism that eventually killed him, but that is unlikely.
66. Sabin, *Kit Carson Days* (1935), 783, 784.
67. *Rocky Mountain News*, June 13, 1860; Charles M. Clark, M. D., *A Trip to Pike's Peak and Notes by the Way* (Chicago: S. P. Rounds, 1861), 75. Dr. Clark reported seeing Carson in Denver in 1859. In *John D. Young & The Colorado Gold Rush*, ed. Dwight L. Smith (Chicago: R. R. Donnelly, 1969), 138–39, Young reported seeing Carson in Denver in June 1860, as did the *Rocky Mountain Herald* of June 16.
68. Named for Cuerno Verde, a Comanche chief killed there in 1779 in a battle with Governor Anza of New Mexico, this creek flows into the St. Charles River a few miles before that stream joins the Arkansas.
69. Luther Perry Wilmot, "A Pleasant Winter for Lew Wilmot," *Colorado Magazine* 47, no. 1 (Winter 1970): 10–19.

Chapter 17

1. Sabin, *Kit Carson Days* (1914), 394. In fifteen other places, the unofficial, but long-continued, practice is to keep the flag flying twenty-fours a day. In four places, but not at Taos, this is done by official sanction. Whitney

Smith, *The Flag Book of the United States* (N. p., 1970), 82.

2. Executive Department, *Journal of Proceedings*, Territory of New Mexico, mic. T–17, North Texas State University, Denton, Texas. (Hereafter identified as Territory of New Mexico, Exec. Dept., *Journal*.)

3. Sabin, *Kit Carson Days* (1914), 396.

4. Carson to Cutler, September 22, 1862, National Archives and Records Division, Washington, D.C., Military Service Record, Christopher Carson. (Hereafter identified as Carson, Service Record); see also Territory of New Mexico, Exec. Dept., *Journal*, Connelly statements, especially letter of November 17, 1861.

5. McClung, *Carson-Bent-Boggs*, 8, 71, 74.

6. Sabin, *Kit Carson Days* (1914), 398.

7. Territory of New Mexico, Exec. Dept., *Journal*.

8. Edward W. Wynkoop, Manuscript 2 in Colorado State Historical Society Library, Denver, Colo., pp. 20–22. Wynkoop, a Colorado Volunteer who played a prominent part in repelling Sibley's invasion, was a long-time friend of Carson. He was the source of many of these stories.

9. Connelly to Seward, December 28, 1961, Territory of New Mexico, Exec. Dept., *Journal*.

10. Carson's report to Canby, February 26, 1862, *The War of the Rebellion: Official Records of the Union and Confederate Armies*, prepared by Brev. Lt. Col. Robert N. Scott, ser. 1, vol. 9 (Washington, D.C.: GPO), pp. 502–3.

11. LeRoy Boyd, "Thunder on the Rio Grande, the Great Adventure of Sibley's Confederates for the Conquest of New Mexico and Colorado," *Colorado Magazine* 24, no. 4 (July 1947): 131–40.

12. Canby's report, *War of the Rebellion*, ser. 1, vol. 9, pp. 487–93.

13. Sabin, *Kit Carson Days* (1914), 394–408; Max L. Heyman, *Prudent Soldier: A Biography of Maj. Gen. E. R. S. Canby, 1817–1873* (Glendale: Arthur H. Clark Co., 1959), 162–70, map, 171.

14. Canby report, *War of the Rebellion*, ser. 1, vol. 9, p. 659.

15. Boyd, "Thunder on the Rio Grande," 139–40.

16. Sanford, "Reminiscences," 179–84. These events may have occurred over a longer period of time than is implied.

17. Letter, Carson to Canby, September 21, 1862, in Lawrence C. Kelly, *Navajo Roundup*, (Boulder: Pruett Publishing Co., 1970), 4. Kelly stresses Carson's reluctance to continue in the service during the Navajo Campaign in this fine collection of documents, upon which he has made many useful observations. We have relied upon it heavily in this account, since it contains all the relevant documents.

18. Frank McNitt, *Navajo Wars: Military Campaigns, Slave Raids and Reprisals* (Albuquerque: University of New Mexico Press, 1972), 10–101. McNitt has furnished most of the background material upon which we have relied in narrating the Navajo Campaign.

19. Territory of New Mexico, Exec. Dept., *Journal*, 1861–63.

20. Kelly, *Navajo Roundup*, 2.

21. Ibid., 2–3.

22. Aurora Hunt, *Major General James H. Carleton, 1814–1873: Western Frontier Dragoon* (Glendale: Arthur H. Clark Co., 1958), 211–52; Clarence G. Clendenen, "General James Henry Carleton," *New Mexico Historical Review* 30 (January 1955): 23–40.

23. It may be that part of Carleton's training of Carson consisted of reading military history to him. An anecdote tells of Carson's fascination with William the Conqueror and his unique manner of swearing. When visiting a military hospital, Carson saw a sergeant threatening a patient with a knife. Instantly drawing and cocking his pistol, he commanded, "Drop that thar knife, or by the splendor of God, I'll let daylight through you." Wynkoop, manuscript 2.

24. Kelly, *Navajo Roundup*, 9.

25. Carson letters, Bancroft Library, quoted by Sabin, *Kit Carson Days* (1935), 773–74.

26. Kelly, *Navajo Roundup*, 9 fn.

27. Ibid., 11–12.

28. Hunt, *Carleton*, 114–17; 247–52.

29. Ibid., 42, 112, 113, 117. As a second lieutenant, Carleton had trained under Sumner at Carlisle, Pa. He served under him at Fort Leavenworth and accompanied him to New Mexico in 1851. Carleton's second wife was Sophie Garland Wolfe, niece of General John Garland. Two of their children were born in New Mexico. Carleton helped build Fort Union and was commandant there in 1852.

30. Carleton to Adjutant General Thomas, March 19, 1863, in Kelly, *Navajo Roundup*, 16–17.

31. Kelly, *Navajo Roundup*, 13–14.

32. Ibid., 15.

33. Ibid., 35, 43, 45–50.

34. Carson to Cutler, December 20, 1863, in Kelly, *Navajo Roundup*, 84.

35. Carleton to Carson, September 19, 1863, in Kelly, *Navajo Roundup*, 52.

36. Kelly, *Navajo Roundup*, 50.

37. Sabin, *Kit Carson Days* (1914), 425–26.

38. Ibid.

39. Kelly, *Navajo Roundup*, 15–16.

40. For an excellent analysis and summary of the Navajo problem at this time, see Max L. Heyman, Jr., "On the Navajo Trail: The Campaign of 1860–1861," *New Mexico Historical Review* 26 (January 1951): 44–63. See also Richard C. Hopkins, "Kit Carson and the Navajo Expedition," *Montana Magazine of Western History* 18, no. 2 (April 1968): 52–61.

41. Kelly, *Navajo Roundup*, 17–20.

42. This board was composed of Colonel Christopher Carson, First New Mexico Volunteers; Maj. Henry D. Wallen, U.S. Army, Acting Inspector General; Surgeon James M. McNulty, U.S. Volunteers, Medical Inspector; Brev. Capt. Allen L. Anderson, U.S. Army, Acting Engineering Officer; and Capt.

Benjamin C. Cutler, Assistant Adjutant General, U.S. Volunteers. See Kelly, *Navajo Roundup*, 23.

43. Laura C. M. White, "Albert H. Pfeiffer," *Colorado Magazine* 10, no. 6 (1935): 217–22.

44. Carson Letters, Bancroft Library, quoted in Sabin, *Kit Carson Days* (1935), 786.

45. Kelly, *Navajo Roundup*, 26 fn.

Chapter 18

1. The Navajos, who had a religious fear of the dead and all their possessions, did not touch the body, on which was found a purse containing $5,301. See Ruth M. Underhill, *The Navajos* (Norman: University of Oklahoma Press, 1956), 10; Kelly, *Navajo Roundup*, 35, 36. This unauthorized scout may have been to look for signs of gold, in which interest ran high. The Navajos' fear of contact with the dead helps to explain why these Indians did not scalp their prisoners, as stated by Raymond E. Lindgren, ed., "A Diary of Kit Carson's Navaho Campaign, 1863–1864," *New Mexico Historical Review* 21 (July 1946): 243. Although few Navajos were killed, those slain were commonly scalped. Lindgren's opinion that "the barbarous practice should not have been commenced by us" was held by many of the soldiers of the campaign. Unfortunately, Carson could not, or did not, prevent the practice.

2. Carson to Carleton, July 24, 1863, in Kelly, *Navajo Roundup*, 30.

3. Carleton to Carson, August 18, 1863, in Kelly, *Navajo Roundup*, 31–32.

4. Carson report, August 19, 1863, in Kelly, *Navajo Roundup*, 40 fn., 38–41.

5. Bear Springs, site of former Fort Fauntleroy, later Fort Lyon. Rebuilt in 1868 as the second Fort Wingate. See Kelly, *Navajo Roundup*, 27 fn.

6. Now Ganado, Arizona. Probably to avoid confusion with Pueblo, Colorado, as well as to honor Ganados Muchos (Many Cattle), an important Navajo chief, the name was changed in 1870.

7. Kelly, *Navajo Roundup*, 28–33.

8. Ibid., 31.

9. Ibid., 37–51.

10. Letters, August 7 and 19, 1863, in Kelly, *Navajo Roundup*, 35, 36.

11. The Little Colorado.

12. Kelly, *Navajo Roundup*, 37–51, 78.

13. Carey letters to Carleton, in Kelly, *Navajo Roundup*, 65, 66, 78–79.

14. Kelly, *Navajo Roundup*, 53.

15. Ibid., 61.

16. Carey reports, in Kelly, *Navajo Roundup*, 65, 66.

17. Kelly, *Navajo Roundup*, 56, 70–71.

18. Black Lake.

19. Kelly, *Navajo Roundup*, 68–69.

20. Ibid., 75–77: Carson report of third scout, December 6, 1863.

21. Not to be confused with the Mescalero named Manuelito.

22. Kelly, *Navajo Roundup*, 69–70.

23. Carson report, December 20, 1863, in Kelly, *Navajo Roundup*, 84.

24. Carleton to Carson, December 31, 1863, in Kelly, *Navajo Roundup*, 87.

25. Lecompte, "A Letter from Jessie to Kit," 260–63.

26. McCormick to Carson, in Sabin, *Kit Carson Days* (1935), 787. For an account of Frémont at this period, see Allan Nevins, *Frémont, the West's Greatest Adventurer* 2 vols. (New York: Harper & Brothers, 1928), vol. 2.

27. McNitt, *Navajo Wars*, 42, 43, 367–71, 341, 236, respectively.

28. Ibid., 149, 196.

29. Ibid., 341.

30. Kelly, *Navajo Roundup*, 88–90, 93.

31. Carson's report, January 24, 1864, in Kelly, *Navajo Roundup*, 100.

32. Ibid., 37 fn. See notes 27 to 30 above.

33. Pfeiffer's report, January 20, 1864, in Kelly, *Navajo Roundup*, 102–5.

34. Carey's report, January 21, 1864, in Kelly, *Navajo Roundup*, 105–7. Carey had followed the main canyon. Park rangers believe that he exited through Bat Trail at the mouth of Monument Cañon, though he may have traversed the Cañon de Chelly to its eastern end.

35. Carson to Carleton, January 1864, in Kelly, *Navajo Roundup*, 109.

36. Report of Capt. Joseph Berney, April 7, 1864, in Kelly, *Navajo Roundup*, 115–16.

37. Report of Capt. Francis McCabe, May 12, 1864, in Kelly, *Navajo Roundup*, 134–36.

38. Report of Capt. John Thompson, April 15, 1864, in Kelly, *Navajo Roundup*, 125.

39. Report of Capt. A. B. Carey, March 20, 1864, in Kelly, *Navajo Roundup*, 132–33.

40. Kelly, *Navajo Roundup*, 144.

41. Ibid., 148, 116.

42. Ibid., 112, 119.

43. Ibid., 150–51.

44. Ibid., 141.

45. Ibid., 146–47.

46. Ibid., 143.

47. Ibid., 125–26. Gerald Thompson, *The Army and the Navajo* (Tucson, University of Arizona Press, 1976), 18–133, gives a full, well-documented account of the problems and conflicts at the Bosque.

48. Underhill, *The Navajos*, 46, 129; Lynn Robison Bailey, *Bosque Redondo: An American Concentration Camp* (Pasadena: Socio-Technical Books, 1970), 102.

49. Kelly, *Navajo Roundup*, 126–28.

50. Thompson, *The Army and the Navajo*, 49–50.

51. Kelly, *Navajo Roundup*, 168; Underhill, *The Navajos*, 129–31.

52. Underhill, *The Navajos*, 141–42, 145–47; Charles Amsden, "The Navaho

Exile at Bosque Redondo," *New Mexico Historical Review* 8 (January 1933): 48. This article, pages 31–50, is a good critical analysis of the Navajo problem and the metamorphosis of the tribe.

53. Underhill, *The Navajos*, 136.
54. Ibid., 20, 38, 39.
55. Unfortunately, hatred of Carson remains strong among the Navajos and the Apaches. The Kit Carson Cave near Church Rock, New Mexico, had been vandalized and was closed to the public in 1979. When Thelma Guild asked the Indians about this at the trading post at Red Rock State Park, one replied angrily, "No one here will talk about Kit Carson. He was a butcher!"
56. In "The Curious Case of the Slandered Scout, the Aggressive Anthropologist, the Delinquent Dean, and the Acquiescent Army," *Denver Westerner's Brand Book* 28 (Boulder, 1973): 93–112, Harvey L. Carter presents a defense of Carson's reputation against a recent attack in academic circles.
57. Rusling, *Across America*, 137, 139.
58. Thompson, *The Army and the Navajo*, 158–65.

Chapter 19

1. Kelly, *Navajo Roundup*, 169; Carson to Carleton, September 1, 1864, Carson, Service Record.
2. Carleton to Carson, September 5, 1864, Carson, Service Record.
3. The account of the Battle of Adobe Walls is based on Carson's reports dated December 4, 1864, and December 16, 1864, *War of the Rebellion*, 41:939–43, and on Captain George H. Pettis, "Kit Carson's Fight with the Comanche and Kiowa Indians," *Weekly New Mexican*, March 22, March 29, and April 5, 1879. (Also found in the University of New Mexico Library, Albuquerque, Anderson Room, New Mexico Historical Society Publication no. 12). See also Sabin, *Kit Carson Days* (1914), 440–66.
4. "Come here! Come here!"
5. In his 1874 edition of the Carson biography, Peters classed it as a defeat. Thus, in his dramatic overstatement of the Cañon de Chelly expedition during the Navajo Campaign and in his failure to appreciate Carson's masterful handling of the Adobe Walls Campaign, Peters perpetuated two interpretations of historic events that were diametrically opposed to the truth. The persistence of these views in popular thought has done untold damage to Carson's reputation.
6. Carleton to Carson, December 15, 1864, *War of the Rebellion*, 41:944.
7. Carleton to Adjutant General U.S. Army, Washington, D.C., *War of the Rebellion*, 48: 1,245. Carson's commission and his letter of acceptance are filed in the National Archives, Washington, D.C., under Letters received from and relating to Kit Carson, 1854–60, his years as Indian agent.
8. *War of the Rebellion*, 48: 317, 338, 344, 360.

9. Mrs. Hal Russell, "Memoirs of Marian Russell," *Colorado Magazine* 21, no. 1 (January 1944): 29–37; Albert Thompson, "Kit Carson's Camp Nichols in No Man's Land," *Colorado Magazine* 11, no. 5 (September 1934) 179–86. The site of the post was in the present Oklahoma Panhandle, known at that time as No Man's Land.
10. J. P. Dunn, Jr., *Massacres of the Mountains* (New York: Archer House, 1958), 343–62; Lavender, *Bent's Fort*, 383–85.
11. *War of the Rebellion*, vol. 5, series 3, p. 443.
12. Carson, Service Record.
13. Carson, Service Record, Spec. Ord. no. 22, August 5, 1865.
14. Ibid.
15. *War of the Rebellion*, vol. 48, ser. 1, pt. 2, p. 1,089.
16. Wynkoop, Manuscript 2, 23.
17. At what is now Wichita, Kansas.
18. Charles C. Royce, *Indian Land Treaties in the United States*, 18th Annual Report of the Bureau of American Ethnology (1900), 838–39, plate 57, Special Map of Texas and Adjoining States; Sabin, *Kit Carson Days* (1914), 475–76.
19. Carson, Service Record, Spec. Ord. no 11, October 11, 1865.
20. Carson, Service Record, Spec. Ord. no. 81, October 30, 1865.
21. Carson to Carleton, November 29, 1865, Carson, Service Record.
22. Letters Received from and Relating to Kit Carson, 1854–60, National Archives, Washington, D.C.
23. Carson, Service Record, Spec. Ord. no. 13, December 8, 1865.
24. Carson to Carleton, June 17, 1866, James Rood Doolittle Papers, no. 210, Stephen H. Hart Library, Colorado Historical Society, Denver; Gene M. Gressley, ed., "Report on Fort Garland Made by Christopher (Kit) Carson to Major Roger James [*sic*], June 10, 1866," *Colorado Magazine* 32, no. 3 (July 1955): 215–24.
25. Carson, Service Record.

Chapter 20

1. Carson to Carleton, June 17, 1866, Doolittle Papers, Colorado Historical Society, Denver.
2. Carson to Major Jones, June 10, 1866, National Archives, Washington, D.C., Records of Fort Garland, correspondence of Brevet Brigadier General Christopher Carson, Microcopy, Pioneer's Museum, Colorado Springs, Colorado. Unless otherwise stated, all facts of this period are from this source and will appear under Records of Fort Garland, Carson File. Though signed by Carson, that part of the Jones report using specialized knowledge and special terms of geology was doubtless prepared by some officer of the Topographical Corps.
3. Carson to Carleton, June 14, 1866, Records of Fort Garland, Carson File.
4. Carson to Carleton, June 17, 1866, Doolittle Papers.

5. Taylor, "Ka-ni-ache," 289–90.
6. Carson to Captain W. G. Mitchell, A. A. A., Fort Leavenworth, March 2, 1867, Records of Fort Garland, Carson file.
7. Carson to Fort Marcy and to De Forrest, July 1, 1866, Records of Fort Garland, Carson file.
8. "The Autobiography of Worthington Whittredge," ed. John I. H. Baur (New York: *Brooklyn Museum Journal*, 1942), 47–49.
9. Duane Vandenbusche, "Life at a Frontier Post: Fort Garland," *Colorado Magazine* 43, no. 2 (Spring 1966): 141; Sabin, *Kit Carson Days* (1935), 761.
10. "Fort Stevens," *Colorado Magazine* 43 (Fall 1966), 303–7.
11. Whittredge, "Autobiography," 47–49.
12. Meline, *Two Thousand Miles on Horseback*, 246–51.
13. Ibid., 127.
14. Sanford, "Reminiscences of Kit Carson, Jr." See also Carson to Carleton, August 9, 1866, Records of Fort Garland, Carson file.
15. Carson to Carleton, August 19, 1866, Records of Fort Garland, Carson file.
16. Taylor, "Ka-ni-ache," 293–96.
17. Carson to Carleton, August 24, 1866, Records of Fort Garland, Carson file.
18. Taylor, "Ka-ni-ache," 296.
19. Ibid., 295.
20. Rusling, *Across America*, 136–38.
21. Ibid., 113–15.
22. Ibid., 125–30.
23. Later Notre Dame University.
24. Sherman letter, cited in Edward S. Ellis, *The Life of Kit Carson* (New York: Grosset & Dunlap, 1889), 249–52.
25. Taylor, "Ka-ni-ache," 296–99.
26. Carson to Carleton, October 8, 1866, Records of Fort Garland, Carson file.
27. Carson to Carleton, letter no. 2, October 8, 1866, Records of Fort Garland, Carson file.
28. Carson to Carleton, October 15, 1866, Records of Fort Garland, Carson file.
29. Carson to Farnsworth and Maxwell, October 14, 1866, Records of Fort Garland, Carson file.
30. Carson to Carleton, October 15, 1866; Carson to De Forrest, undated, Records of Fort Garland, Carson file.
31. Ibid.
32. State Records Center and Archives, Santa Fe, New Mexico.
33. Diary of Evelina B. Alexander, April 10, 1866, to January 17, 1867. Bancroft Library, Berkeley, Calif.; James H. Wilson, *The Life and Services of Brevet Brigadier General Andrew Jonathan Alexander, United States Army* (New York: N. p. 1887), 95–101. Alexander was later commended by the War Department for his prompt action against the Indians, and Carson was commended for having made peace without orders to do so. Alexander's orders to report to New Orleans were cancelled, and he returned to Fort Garland and later was assigned to service in Arizona.

34. Carson to Alexander, October 16, 1866, Records of Fort Garland, Carson file.
35. Carson to Farnsworth and Maxwell, October 14, 1866; Carson to Carleton, February 15, 1867, Records of Fort Garland, Carson file.
36. Taylor, "Ka-ni-ache," 302–3.
37. Major John H. Nankivell, Infantry, U. S. Army, "Fort Garland, Colorado," *Colorado Magazine* 16, no. 1 (January 1939): 13–28.

Chapter 21

1. Letter and tri-monthly reports, January 20, 1867, Records of Fort Garland, Carson file.
2. Taylor, "Ka-ni'ache," 289–90.
3. Sanford, "Reminiscences of Kit Carson, Jr.," 179–84.
4. Carson, Service Record; Sabin, *Kit Carson Days* (1914), 654, 214 fn.
5. Carson, Service Record: Spec. Ord. no. 55 and 67, Aug. 2 and 18, 1867.
6. Sabin, *Kit Carson Days* (1935), 791.
7. Carson, Service Record.
8. Sabin, *Kit Carson Days* (1914), 504–5.
9. Tilton to John S. C. Abbott, January 7, 1874, printed in John S. C. Abbott, *Christopher Carson, Known as Kit Carson* (New York: Dodd, Mead and Co., 1901), 343–48.
10. Ibid.
11. Royce, *Indian Land Treaties*, plate 9, Colorado, nos. 566, 616, 617. This was substantially the same as the treaty of 1863.
12. Sabin, *Kit Carson Days* (1914), 489–90.
13. Frémont, *The Will and the Way Stories*, 43.
14. Ibid., 44–48.
15. Sabin, *Kit Carson Days* (1914), 491.
16. Cragin Papers, notebook 27: 93.
17. Marita Hayes, "D. C. Oakes, Early Colorado Booster," *Colorado Magazine* 31, no. 3 (July 1954), 216–26.
18. Tilton gave the date of her death as April 27. The date on the tombstone at Taos is April 23, 1868, but this stone was not erected until many years later. A letter of Robert H. Whatley, dated Boggs Ranch, C. T., April 28, 1868, to Colonel Albert H. Pfeiffer, Fort Garland, C. T., says, "It has become my painful task to announce to you the sudden death of Mrs. Carson; she died last night at 8 o'clock P.M. and will be interred tomorrow afternoon." A copy of this letter was kindly furnished by Mrs. Raymond Settle, Monte Vista, Colorado.
19. Sabin, *Kit Carson Days* (1914), 487.
20. Estergreen, *Kit Carson*, 274–75, reproduced this letter in full.
21. Carson's estate amounted to $11,045.65.
22. Tilton letter to Abbott, Abbott, *Christopher Carson*, 343–48.
23. Albert W. Thompson, "The Death and Last Will of Kit Carson," *Colorado*

Magazine 5 (October 1928): 183–91.

24. Brother Claudius Antony, "Kit Carson, Catholic," *New Mexico Historical Review* 10 (October 1935): 324–25.

25. Sabin, *Kit Carson Days* (1914), 508; Carter, *'Dear Old Kit'*, 178 fn. A. F. and A. M. stands for Ancient Free and Accepted Masons.

Bibliography

Unpublished Sources

Bancroft Library, Berkeley, California.
    Alexander, Evalina B. Diary.
    Barclay, Alexander. Papers.
    Martin, T. S. "Narrative of John C. Fremont's Expedition to California in
    1845–46." Dictated in 1878.
Carson, Kit. House and Museum, Taos, New Mexico.
Colorado State Historical Society Library, Denver, Colorado.
    Wynkoop, Edward W. Manuscript 2.
National Archives and Records Service, Washington, D.C.
    Letters Received from and Relating to Kit Carson, 1854–60. Mic. FMT21.
    Roll 1.
    Military Service Records.
    Records of Fort Garland, Correspondence of Brev. Brig. Gen. Christopher
    Carson.
New Mexico Historical Museum, Santa Fe, New Mexico.
    Carson, Christopher. Will. Typed copy.
    Museum of New Mexico Manuscript Collection and Christoper Carson
    file.
New Mexico State Records Center and Archives, Santa Fe, New Mexico.
    Carson, Christopher. Papers.
North Texas State University Library, Denton, Texas.
    Bureau of Indian Affairs, Annual Reports 1853–63, microfiche. Roll 4158.
    Territory of New Mexico, Executive Department, "Journal of Proceedings,
    1851–72," microfilm, T–17.
Oregon Historical Society Library, Portland, Oregon.
    Fort Hall Account Books.
Pioneer's Museum, Colorado Springs, Colorado.

Cragin, F. W. Papers. Collection of notes from interviews.
Stephen H. Hart Library, Colorado Historical Society, Denver, Colorado. Christopher Carson Collection no. 109.
Doolittle, James Rood. Papers, no. 210
State Historical Society of Missouri, St. Louis, Missouri. Turley Papers.
Stewart, George E. Personal interview, July 3, 1979. Letter, February 1980. Roosevelt, Utah.
University of New Mexico Library, Archives Division, microfilm, Albuquerque, New Mexico. Bent, Charles. Papers.
Whatley, Robert H. Letter to Albert H. Pfeiffer, April 28, 1868. Courtesy of Mrs. Raymond Settle, Monte Vista, Colorado.

Published Sources

Abbott, John S. C. *Christopher Carson, Known as Kit Carson.* New York: Dodd, Mead and Company, 1901.

Alter, J. Cecil. *Jim Bridger.* Norman: University of Oklahoma Press, 1962.

Amsden, Charles. "The Navaho Exile at Bosque Redondo," *New Mexico Historical Review* 8 (January 1933).

Antony, Brother Claudius. "Kit Carson, Catholic," *New Mexico Historical Review* 10 (October 1935).

Athearn, Robert G. "The Education of Kit Carson's Son," *New Mexico Historical Review* 31 (April 1956).

———. *William Tecumseh Sherman and the Settlement of the West.* Norman: University of Oklahoma Press, 1956.

Bailey, Lynn Robison. *Bosque Redondo: An American Concentration Camp.* Pasadena: Socio-Technical Books, 1970.

———. *The Long Walk: A History of the Navajo Wars 1846–68.* Los Angeles: Westernlore Press, 1964.

Bakeless, John. *Daniel Boone, Master of the Wilderness.* New York: William Morrow, 1939.

Bancroft, Hubert Howe. *History of Arizona and New Mexico.* Albuquerque: Horn & Wallace, 1962.

———. *History of California,* 7 vols. San Francisco: History Co., 1888.

Barnes, Gertrude. "Following Frémont's Trail Through Northern Colorado," *Colorado Magazine* 19, no. 5 (September 1942).

Barry, Louise. *The Beginning of the West: Annals of the Kansas Gateway to the American West, 1540–1854.* Topeka: Kansas Historical Society, 1972.

Bell, John R. *Journal of the S. H. Long Expedition.* Vol. 6 of The Far West and the Rockies, edited by LeRoy R. and Ann W. Hafen. Glendale, California: Arthur H. Clark Co., 1957.

Bennett, James A. *A Dragoon in New Mexico, 1850–58.* Albuquerque: University of New Mexico Press, 1948.

Binkley, William Campbell. *The Expansionist Movement in Texas.* Berkeley: University of California Press, 1925.

Blackwelder, Bernice. *Great Westerner: The Story of Kit Carson.* Caldwell, Idaho: Caxton Printers, 1962.

Bonsal, Stephen. *Edward Fitzgerald Beale: A Pioneer in the Path of Empire, 1822–1903.* New York and London: G. P. Putnam's Sons, 1912.

Boyd, LeRoy. "Thunder on the Rio Grande, the Great Adventure of Sibley's Confederates for the Conquest of New Mexico and Colorado," *Colorado Magazine* 24, no. 4 (July 1947).

Bradbury, John. *Travels in the Interior of America.* 1817; rev. ed., Ann Arbor: University of Michigan Microfilms, 1966.

Bradshaw, Maureen Nelson. *Pioneer Parade.* New York: Vantage Press, 1966.

Brandon, William. *The Men and the Mountain: Frémont's Fourth Expedition.* New York: William Morrow & Company, 1955.

Brandt, Lucas. "Pioneer Days on the Big Thompson," *Colorado Magazine* 7, no. 5 (September 1930).

Brewerton, George Douglas. *Overland with Kit Carson: A Narrative of the Old Spanish Trail in 1848.* Edited by Stallo Vinton. New York: Coward McCann, 1930.

Bridgeman, William S. "Kit Carson, the Famous American Frontiersman," *Munsey's* 62 (December 1909).

Brown, David L. *Three Years in the Rocky Mountains,* from *Cincinnati Daily Morning Atlas,* September 8, 11, 12, 13, 1845. Microcard, North Texas State University Library, Denton, Texas.

Brown, John. *Mediumistic Experiences.* San Francisco: N. p. 1897.

Brown, John Henry. *Reminiscences and Incidents of Early Days of San Francisco (1845–50).* San Francisco: Grabhorn Press, 1933.

Burt, Struthers. *Powder River: Let 'er Buck.* New York: Farrar & Rinehart, 1938.

Camp, Charles L., ed. *James Clyman, Frontiersman.* Portland, Oregon: Champoeg Press, 1960.

———. "Kit Carson in California," *California Historical Society Quarterly* 1 (October 1922).

Carley, Maurine. "Oregon Trail Trek No. One," *Annals of Wyoming* 27, no. 2 (October 1955).

Carter, Harvey L. "The Curious Case of the Slandered Scout, the Aggressive Anthropologist, the Delinquent Dean, and the Acquiescent Army," *Denver Westerner's Brand Book* 28 (Boulder, 1973).

———. *'Dear Old Kit': The Historical Christopher Carson.* Norman: University of Oklahoma Press, 1968.

———. "The Divergent Paths of Frémont's 'Three Marshalls,'" *New Mexico Historical Review* 68, no. 1 (January 1973).

———. *Zebulon Montgomery Pike, Pathfinder and Patriot.* Colorado Springs: Dentan Printing Company, 1956.

Chacon, Rafael. "Campaign Against Utes and Apaches in Southern Colorado,

1855; From the Memoirs of Major Rafael Chacon." Translated by his son, Eusebio Chacon. *Colorado Magazine* 11, no. 3 (May 1934).

Chittenden, Hiram Martin. *History of the American Fur Trade of the Far West.* 2 vols. Stanford, California: Academic Reprints, 1954.

Clark, Charles M., M. D. *A Trip to Pike's Peak and Notes by the Way.* Chicago: S. P. Rounds' Steam Book and Job Printing, 1861. Microcard, North Texas State University Library, Denton, Texas.

Cleland, Robert Glass. *This Reckless Breed of Men.* New York: Alfred A. Knopf, 1950.

Clendenen, Clarence G. "General James Henry Carleton." *New Mexico Historical Review* 30 (January 1955).

Clokey, Richard M. *William H. Ashley: Enterprise and Politics in the Trans-Mississippi West.* Norman: University of Oklahoma Press, 1980.

Conard, Howard Louis. *"Uncle Dick" Wootton.* Chicago: W. E. Dibble & Co, 1890.

Cooke, Philip St. George. *Exploring Southwestern Trails, Journal of _____.* Edited by Ralph P. Bieber and Averam B. Bender, vol. 7 of the Southwestern Historical Series. Glendale: Arthur H. Clark Co., 1938.

_____. *Scenes and Adventures in the Army.* Philadelphia: Lindsay and Blakiston, 1857.

Corle, Edwin. *The Gila, River of the Southwest.* Lincoln: University of Nebraska Press, 1964.

Covington, James Warren, "Federal Relations with the Colorado Utes, 1861–65," *Colorado Magazine* 28, no. 4 (October 1951).

Crump, R. C. *The Snively Expedition.* New York: Edward Eberstadt & Sons, 1949.

Dale, Harrison Clifford, ed. *The Ashley-Smith Explorations and the Discovery of a Central Route to the Pacific.* Glendale: Arthur H. Clark Co., 1941.

Davidson, Levette Jay. "Colorado Folklore." *Colorado Magazine* 18, no. 1 (January 1941).

DeVoto, Bernard. *Across the Wide Missouri.* Boston: Houghton Mifflin Co., 1947.

_____, ed. *The Journals of Lewis and Clark.* Boston: Houghton Mifflin Co., 1953.

Dobie, J. Frank. *I'll Tell You a Tale.* Boston: Little Brown & Co., 1931.

Duffus, R. L. *The Santa Fe Trail.* Albuquerque: University of New Mexico Press, 1975.

Dunn, Jacob Piatt, Jr. *Massacres of the Mountains.* New York: Archer House, 1958.

Dye, Job Francis. *Recollections of a Pioneer, 1830–1852.* Los Angeles: Glen Dawson, 1951.

Elliott, Lawrence. *The Long Hunter: A New Life of Daniel Boone.* New York: Reader's Digest Press, 1976.

Emory, W. H. *Lieutenant Emory Reports,* with introduction and notes by Ross Calvin. Albuquerque: University of New Mexico Press, 1951. (Reprint of

338

Notes of a Military Reconnaissance by Lieut. W. H. Emory, printed as Senate Executive Document no. 7, 30th Cong., 1st sess.)

Estergreen, M. Morgan. *Kit Carson: A Portrait in Courage.* Norman: University of Oklahoma Press, 1962.

Farnham, Thomas J. *Travels in the Great Western Prairies, the Anahuac and Rocky Mountains, and in Oregon Territory.* Edited by Reuben Gold Thwaites. New York: AMS Press, 1966.

Ferguson, Philip Gooch. "Diary." From *Marching with the Army of the West, 1846–1848.* Edited by Ralph P. Bieber. Glendale: Arthur H. Clark Co., 1936.

Ferris, Robert G., ed. *Prospector, Cowhand, and Sodbuster.* Vol. 11 in the National Survey of Historic Sites and Buildings. Washington: National Park Service, 1967.

Ferris, Warren Angus. *Life in the Rocky Mountains, 1830–1835.* Arranged by Herbert S. Auerbach; annotated by J. Cecil Alter. Salt Lake City: Rocky Mountain Book Shop, 1940.

Field, Matthew C. *Prairie and Mountain Sketches.* Collected by Clyde and Mae Reed Porter. Edited by Kate L. Gregg and John Francis McDermott. Norman: University of Oklahoma Press, 1957.

"Fort Stevens," *Colorado Magazine* 63, no. 4 (Fall 1966).

Frémont, Jessie Benton. *The Will and the Way Stories.* Boston: D. Lathrop Co., 1891.

Frémont, John Charles. *Memoirs of My Life.* Chicago and New York: Belford Clarke & Co., 1887.

Gardner, Hamilton. "Philip St. George Cooke and the Apache, 1854." *New Mexico Historical Review* 28 (April 1953).

Garrard, Lewis H. *Wah-to-Yah and the Taos Trail.* Norman: University of Oklahoma Press, 1955.

Gibson, George Rutledge. *Journal of a Soldier Under Kearny and Doniphan, 1846–47.* Edited by Ralph P. Bieber. Glendale: Arthur H. Clark Co., 1935.

Goodwin, Cardinal. *John Charles Frémont: An Explanation of His Career.* Stanford, California: Stanford University Press, 1930.

Gregg, Josiah. *Commerce of the Prairies.* Lincoln: University of Nebraska Press, 1967.

Gregg, Kate L. *The Road to Santa Fe.* Albuquerque: University of New Mexico Press, 1952.

Gudde, Erwin G., ed. *Sutter's Own Story.* New York: C. P. Putnam's Sons, 1936.

Hafen, LeRoy R. *Broken Hand: The Life of Thomas Fitzpatrick.* Denver: Old West Publishing Co., 1973.

———. "Etienné Provost, Mountain Man and Utah Pioneer." *Utah Historical Quarterly* 36, no. 2 (Spring 1968).

———. "Fort Davy Crockett, Its Fur Men and Visitors." *Colorado Magazine* 29, no. 1 (January 1952).

———. "The Fort Pueblo Massacre and the Punitive Expedition Against the Utes." *Colorado Magazine* 4, no. 2 (March 1927).

————. "When Was Bent's Fort Built?" *Colorado Magazine* 31, no. 2 (Spring 1954).

————, ed. *Colorado Gold Rush: Contemporary Letters and Reports, 1858–1859.* Vol. 10 of Southwest Historical Series. Glendale: Arthur H. Clark Co., 1941.

————, ed. *Frémont's Fourth Expedition. A Documentary Account of the Disaster of 1848–1849, with Diaries, Letters, and Reports by Participants in the Tragedy.* Vol. 11 of The Far West and the Rockies, edited by LeRoy R. and Ann W. Hafen. Glendale: Arthur H. Clark Co., 1960.

————, ed. *The Mountain Men and the Fur Trade of the Far West.* 10 vols. Glendale: Arthur H. Clark Co., 1965 to 1972.

————, ed. *Relations with the Plains Indians.* Vol. 9 of the Far West and the Rockies Historical Series, ed. LeRoy R. and Ann W. Hafen. Glendale: Arthur H. Clark Co., 1959.

————, ed. *To the Rockies and Oregon.* Vol. 3 of the Far West and the Rockies Historical Series, ed. LeRoy R. and Ann W. Hafen. Glendale: Arthur H. Clark Co., 1955.

————, ed. "The W. M. Boggs Manuscript about Bent's Fort, Kit Carson, the Far West and Life among the Indians." *Colorado Magazine* 7, no. 2 (March 1930).

Hafen, LeRoy R. and Ann W. *The Old Spanish Trail.* Vol. 1 of the Far West and the Rockies Historical Series, edited by LeRoy R. and Ann W. Hafen. Glendale: Arthur H. Clark Co., 1954.

Hafen, LeRoy R. and Carl Coke Rister. *Western America.* New York: Prentice-Hall, 1941.

Hafen, LeRoy R. and Francis Marion Young. *Fort Laramie and the Pageant of the West, 1834–1890.* Glendale: Arthur H. Clark Co., 1938.

Harvey, Charles M. "Kit Carson, Last of the Trailmakers, 1809–1868." *Century Magazine* 80 (October 1910).

Hayes, Martha. "D. C. Oakes, Early Colorado Booster." *Colorado Magazine* 31, no. 3 (July 1954).

Heap, Gwinn Harris. *The Central Route to the Pacific.* Vol. 7 of The Far West and the Rockies, edited by LeRoy R. and Ann W. Hafen. Glendale: Arthur H. Clark Co., 1957.

Heitman, Francis B. *Historical Register and Dictionary of the United States Army, from Its Organization September 29, 1789, to March 2, 1903.* 2 vols. Washington, D.C.: United States Government Printing Office, 1903.

Hewett, Edgar L. *Kit Carson: "He Led the Way."* Taos. Kit Carson Memorial Foundation, 1955.

————. "Tom Tobin." *Colorado Magazine* 23, no. 5 (September 1946).

Heyman, Max L., Jr. *Prudent Soldier: A Biography of Major General E. R. S. Canby, 1817–1873.* Glendale: Arthur H. Clark Co., 1959.

————. "On the Navajo Trail: The Campaign of 1860–61." *New Mexico Historical Review* 26 (January 1951).

Hill, Joseph J. "Ewing Young in the Fur Trade of the Far Southwest, 1822–

1834." *Oregon Historical Society Quarterly* 24 (March 1923).

Hobbs, Captain James. *Wild Life in the Far West*. Hartford: Wiley, Waterman, and Eaton, 1872.

Holmes, Kenneth L. *Ewing Young: Master Trapper*. Portland: Binford & Mort, 1967.

Hopkins, Richard C. "Kit Carson and the Navajo Expedition." *Montana Magazine of Western History* 18 (April 1968).

Hough, Emerson. *The Way to the West, and the Lives of Three Early Americans: Boone, Crockett, Carson*. Indianapolis: Bobbs-Merrill Co., 1903.

Hulbert, Archer Butler, ed. *Southwest on the Turquoise Trail*. Stewart Commission of Colorado College and the Denver Public Library, 1933.

Hunt, Aurora. *Major General James Henry Carleton, 1814–1873: Western Frontier Dragoon*. Glendale: Arthur H. Clark Co., 1958.

Hussey, John Adam. "Kit Carson at Cajón—not Tejón." *California Historical Society Quarterly* 29 (March 1950).

Inman, Colonel Henry. *The Old Santa Fe Trail*. New York: MacMillan Co., 1897.

Irving, Washington. *The Adventures of Captain Bonneville*. New York: G. P. Putnam, 1861.

———. *Astoria*. Philadelphia: Carey Lea & Blanchard, 1836.

Jackson, Donald and Mary Lee Spence, eds. *The Expeditions of John Charles Frémont*. 2 vols. and supplement. Urbana: University of Illinois Press, 1970.

Jones, Nard. *The Great Command: The Story of Marcus and Narcissa Whitman and the Oregon County Pioneers*. Boston: Little Brown and Co., 1959.

Kelly, Lawrence C. *Navajo Roundup*. Boulder: Pruett Publishing, 1970.

Lavender, David. *Bent's Fort*. Lincoln: University of Nebraska Press, 1972.

Lecompte, Janet. "Gantt's Fort and Bent's Picket Post," *Colorado Magazine* 61, no. 2 (Spring 1964).

———. "A Letter from Jessie to Kit." *Bulletin of the Missouri Historical Society* 29, no. 4 (July 1973).

———. *Pueblo-Hardscrabble-Greenhorn*. Norman: University of Oklahoma Press, 1978.

Narrative of the Adventures of Zenas Leonard. Ann Arbor: University of Michigan Microfilms. Zerox. 1966.

Lewis, Ernest Allen. *The Frémont Cannon: High Up and Far Back*. Glendale: Arthur H. Clark Co., 1981.

Liberty Weekly Tribune, Sec. 19. 1856. State Historical Society of Missouri, Columbia.

Lindgren, Raymond E., ed. "A Diary of Kit Carson's Navajo Campaign, 1863–1864." *New Mexico Historical Review* 21 (July 1946).

Luhan, Mabel Dodge, *Winter in Taos*. New York: Harcourt Brace, 1935.

McClung, Quantrille D. *Carson-Bent-Boggs Genealogy*. Denver: Denver Public Library, 1962.

McDaniel, Lyn, ed. *Bicentennial Boonslick History*. Boonville, Missouri: Boonslick Historical Society, 1976.

McNitt, Frank. *Navajo Wars: Military Campaigns, Slave Raids, and Reprisals*. Albuquerque: University of New Mexico Press, 1972.

Magoffin, Susan. *Down the Santa Fe Trail and Into Mexico*. New Haven: Yale University Press, 1926.

Marsh, James B. *Four Years in the Rockies, or, The Adventures of Isaac P. Rose*. New Castle, Pa.: W. B. Thomas, 1884; Reprint ed., Columbus, Long's College Book Co., 1960.

Meline, James F. *Two Thousand Miles on Horseback. Santa Fe and Back. A Summer Tour Through Kansas, Nebraska, Colorado, and New Mexico, in the Year 1866*. Albuquerque: Horn & Wallace, 1966.

Meriwether, David. *My Life in the Mountains and on the Plains*. Ed. Robert A. Griffen. Norman: University of Oklahoma Press, 1965.

Moody, Marshall D. "Kit Carson, Agent to the Indians in New Mexico, 1853–1861." *New Mexico Historical Review* 28, no. 1 (January 1953).

Morgan, Dale L. *The Humboldt, Highroad of the West*. New York: Farrar & Rinehart, 1943.

———. *Jedediah Smith and the Opening of the West*. Indianapolis: Bobbs-Merrill, 1953.

———, ed. *Overland in 1846: Diaries and Letters of the California–Oregon Trail*. 2 vols. Georgetown, California: Talisman Press, 1963.

———. *The West of William H. Ashley*. Denver: Old West Publishing Co., 1964.

Morgan, Dale L. and Eleanor Towles Harris, eds. *The Rocky Mountain Journals of William Marshall Anderson: The West in 1834*. San Marino, California: Huntington Library, 1967.

Mumey, Nolie. *The Life of Jim Baker, 1818–1898*. Denver: World Press, 1931.

Nankivell, Major John H. "Fort Garland, Colorado," *Colorado Magazine* 16, no. 1 (January 1939).

Nevins, Allan. *Frémont, Pathmarker of the West*. New York: D. Appleton-Century Co., 1939.

———. *Frémont, the West's Greatest Adventurer*. 2 vols. New York: Harper & Brothers, 1928.

———. "Kit Carson, 'Bayard of the Plains.'" *American Scholar* 8, no. 3 (Summer 1939).

Newell, Robert. *Memoranda*. Edited by Dorothy O. Johansen. Portland: Champoeg Press, 1959.

New York Evening Post, October 30, 1856.

Otero, Nina. *Old Spain in Our Southwest*. New York: Harcourt Brace & Co., 1936.

Parkhill, Forbes. *The Blazed Trail of Antoine Leroux*. Los Angeles: Westernlore Press, 1965.

Pattie, James Ohio. *Personal Narrative*. Ann Arbor: University of Michigan Microcopy, 1966.

342

Pearson, Jim Berry. *The Maxwell Land Grant.* Norman: University of Oklahoma Press, 1961.

Peters, DeWitt C. *The Life and Adventures of Kit Carson, the Nestor of the Rocky Mountains.* New York: W. R. C. Clark & Meeker, 1859, 1874.

Pettis, Captain George H. *Kit Carson's Fight with the Comanche and Kiowa Indians, November 1864.* Albuquerque: New Mexico Historical Society Publication no. 12. University of New Mexico Library. First appeared in the Santa Fe *Weekly New Mexican.*

Polk, James K. *Polk, The Diary of a President, 1845–1849.* Edited by Allan Nevins. New York: Longmans, Green & Co., 1929.

Pratt, William Chauncey. *Lone Elk: The Life Story of Bill Williams, Trapper and Guide of the Far West.* Denver: John Van Male, 1935.

Preuss, Charles. *Exploring with Frémont.* Translated and edited by Erwin G. and Elizabeth Gudde. Norman: University of Oklahoma Press, 1958.

Reagan, Albert B. "Forts Robidoux and Kit Carson in Northeastern Utah." *New Mexico Historical Review* 10 (April 1935).

Richardson, Albert D. *Beyond the Mississippi.* Hartford: American Publishing Co., 1867.

Rocky Mountain Herald, June 1, 1860.

Rocky Mountain News, June 13, 1860.

Ross, Marvin C., ed. *The West of Alfred Jacob Miller (1837).* Norman: University of Oklahoma Press, 1951.

Royce, Charles C. *Indian Land Treaties in the United States.* 18th Annual Report of the Bureau of American Ethnology, 1900.

Rusling, James Fowler. *Across America, or, The Great West and the Pacific Coast.* New York: Sheldon & Co., 1874.

Russell, Osborne. *Journal of a Trapper: 1834–1843.* Edited by Aubrey L. Haines. Lincoln: University of Nebraska Press, 1965.

Russell, Mrs. Hal. "Memoirs of Marian Russell." *Colorado Magazine* 20, no. 5 (September 1943); 21, no. 1 (January 1944); 21, no. 4 (July 1944).

Ruxton, George F. *Life in the Far West.* Norman: University of Oklahoma Press, 1951.

————. *Ruxton of the Rockies.* Edited by LeRoy R. Hafen. Collected by Clyde and Mae Reed Porter. Norman: University of Oklahoma Press, 1950.

Sabin, Edwin Legrand. *Kit Carson Days (1809–1868).* Chicago: A. C. McClurg & Co., 1914; revised edition, 2 vols, New York: Press of the Pioneers, 1935.

Sage, Rufus B. *Letters and Scenes in the Rocky Mountains.* Vols. 4 and 5 of The Far West and the Rockies, edited by LeRoy R. and Ann W. Hafen. Glendale: Arthur H. Clark Co., 1956.

Sanford, A. S. "Reminiscences of Kit Carson, Jr." *Colorado Magazine* 6, no. 5 (September 1929).

Scott, P. G. "Pioneer Experiences in Southern Colorado." *Colorado Magazine* 9, no. 1 (January 1932).

Sherman, William T. *Memoirs of General William T. Sherman.* 2 vols. New York: D. Appleton and Co., 1886.

Simpson, Lieutenant James H. *Navajo Expedition: Journal of a Military Reconnaissance from Santa Fe, New Mexico, to the Navajo Country Made in 1849.* Edited and annotated by Frank McNitt. Norman: University of Oklahoma Press, 1964.

Smith, Alson J. *Men Against the Mountains: Jedediah Smith and the Great Southwest Expedition of 1826–29.* New York: John Day Co., 1965.

Smith, Dwight L., ed. *John D. Young and the Colorado Gold Rush.* Chicago: R. R. Donnelly, 1969.

Smith, Whitney. *The Flag Book of the United States.* N. p. 1970.

Stone, Elizabeth Arnold. *Uinta County: Its Place in History.* Laramie: Laramie Printing Co., 1924.

Taylor, Morris F. "Action at Fort Massachusetts: The Indian Campaign of 1855." *Colorado Magazine* 62 (Fall 1965).

———. "Ka-ni-ache." *Colorado Magazine* 63, no. 4 (Fall 1966).

Thompson, Albert W. "The Death and Last Will of Kit Carson." *Colorado Magazine* 5, no. 5 (October 1928).

———. "Kit Carson's Camp Nichols in No Man's Land." *Colorado Magazine* 11, no. 5 (September 1934).

Thompson, Gerald. *The Army and the Navajo.* Tucson: University of Arizona Press, 1976.

Turner, Frederick Jackson. *The Frontier in American History.* New York: Henry Holt & Co., 1935.

Turner, Henry Smith. *The Original Journals of Henry Smith Turner: With Stephen Watts Kearny to New Mexico and California, 1846–1847.* Edited by Dwight L. Clarke. Norman: University of Oklahoma Press, 1966.

Twitchell, Ralph Emerson, ed. *The Spanish Archives of New Mexico.* 2 vols. Cedar Rapids: Torch Press, 1914.

Underhill, Ruth M. *The Navajos.* Norman: University of Oklahoma Press, 1956.

Vandenbusche, Duane. "Life at a Frontier Post: Fort Garland." *Colorado Magazine* 63, no. 2 (Spring 1966).

Victor, Frances Fuller. *The River of the West.* Hartford, Connecticut: R. W. Bliss & Co., 1870; reprint, Columbus, Ohio: Long's College Book Co., 1950.

The War of the Rebellion: Official Records of the Union and Confederate Armies. Prepared by Brevt. Lt. Col. Robert N. Scott. Washington: Government Printing Office, 1883.

Watson, Douglas S. *West Wind: The Life Story of Joseph Reddeford Walker.* Los Angeles: Percy H. Booth. 1934.

Webb, James Josiah. *Adventures in the Santa Fe Trade, 1844–1847.* Edited by Ralph P. Bieber. Glendale: Arthur H. Clark Co., 1931.

Weber, David J., ed. and trans. *The Extranjeros: Selected Documents from the Mexican Side of the Santa Fe Trail, 1825–1828.* Santa Fe: Stagecoach Press, 1967.

———. *The Taos Trappers: The Fur Trade in the Southwest, 1540–1846.* Norman: University of Oklahoma Press, 1971.

Weekly New Mexican. March 22, March 29, April 5, 1879.

Weslager, C. A. *The Delaware Indians.* New York: Rutgers University Press, 1972.

White, Laura C. Manson. "Albert H. Pfeiffer." *Colorado Magazine* 10, no. 6 (1935).

Whittredge, Worthington. "The Autobiography of Worthington Whittredge." Edited by I. H. Baur. *Brooklyn Museum Journal,* 1942.

Williams, Joseph. *Narrative of a Tour from the State of Indiana to the Oregon Territory in the Years 1841–2.* Cincinnati: J. B. Wilson, 1843.

Wilmot, Luther Perry. "A Pleasant Winter for Lew Wilmot." *Colorado Magazine* 67 (Winter 1970).

Wilson, Iris Higbee. *William Wolfskill.* Glendale: Arthur H. Clark Co., 1965.

Wilson, James H. *The Life and Services of Brevet Brigadier General Jonathan Alexander, United States Army.* New York: N. p. 1887.

Young, Otis E. *The West of Philip St. George Cooke.* Glendale: Arthur H. Clark Co., 1955.

345

Index

348

366